1806

EDWARD ROWE SNOW
DISASTER AT SEA

EDWARD ROWE SNOW
DISASTER AT SEA

Three Volumes in One

**MARINE MYSTERIES AND DRAMATIC
DISASTERS OF NEW ENGLAND**

**SEA DISASTERS AND INLAND
CATASTROPHIES**

**PIRATES, SHIPWRECKS AND HISTORIC
CHRONICLES**

AVENEL BOOKS
NEW YORK

Originally published in separate volumes under the titles:
Marine Mysteries and Dramatic Disasters of New England
copyright © 1976 by Edward Rowe Snow
Sea Disasters and Inland Catastrophies
copyright © 1980 by Edward Rowe Snow
Pirates, Shipwrecks and Historic Chronicles
copyright © 1981 by Edward Rowe Snow
All rights reserved.

Compilation © 1990 by Outlet Book Company, Inc.

This 1990 edition is published by Avenel Books, distributed by
Crown Publishers, Inc., 225 Park Avenue South, New York, New
York, 10003, by arrangement with Dodd, Mead & Company.

Printed and bound in the United States of America

Library of Congress Cataloging-in-Publication Data

Snow, Edward Rowe.
    [Disaster at sea]
    Edward Rowe Snow : Disaster at sea : 3 volumes in 1 / by Edward
Rowe Snow.
       p. cm.
    Reprint (1st work) Originally published: Pirates, shipwrecks, and
historic chronicles. New York : Dodd, Mead, c1981.
    Reprint (2nd work) Originally published: Sea disaster and inland
catastrophes. New York : Dodd, Mead, c1980.
    Reprint (3rd work) Originally published: Marine mysteries and
dramatic disasters of New England. New York : Dodd, Mead, c1976.
    ISBN 0-517-69511-1
    1. New England—History, Local. 2. Shipwrecks—New England-
-History. 3. Pirates—New England—History. 4. Treasure-trove—New
England—History. 5. Tales—New England. 6. Disasters—New
England—History. 7. Shipwrecks—History. I. Title
F4.5.S664   1990
974—dc20   89-18438
                                               CIP

8 7 6 3 4 3 2 1

CONTENTS

EDWARD ROWE SNOW
DISASTER AT SEA

MARINE MYSTERIES AND DRAMATIC DISASTERS OF NEW ENGLAND

To Victoria Zehringer Snow

ACKNOWLEDGMENTS

Various institutions aided me in my research including the Boston Atheneum, the Boston Public Library, the Bostonian Society, and the Massachusetts Archives.

Many individuals gave me freely of their ability and time. Some have asked for and have been given anonymity. Others whom I wish to mention are:

Dorothy Snow Bicknell, Laura Ann Bicknell, Richard Carlisle, Frederick G. S. Clow, Arthur Cunningham, James Douglas, Walter Spahr Ehrenfeld, Jean Foley, Suzanne Flandreau, Robert Grunin, Marie Hanson, Melina Herron, Dorothy Haegg Jacobson, Trevor Johnson, Joseph Kolb, Larry Molignano, Richard Nakashian, Joel O'Brien, William Pyne, Elva Ruiz, Helen Salkowski, Frederick Sanford, Chester Shea, Alfred Schroeder, William Smits, Donald B. Snow, Barbara Urbanowitz, Ann Wadsworth, Susan Williams.

John R. Herbert, prominent Quincy newsman and banker, assisted me in several difficult stories. As he has done for more than a quarter century, he helped solve many of the problems that the writing of the book involved.

Anna-Myrle Snow, my faithful wife and fellow researcher,

gave me many hours of assistance in the preparation of this book in spite of her deep involvement in tennis.

EDWARD ROWE SNOW
Marshfield, Massachusetts

CONTENTS

PART THREE: At Sea

PART ONE

~~~~~~

Along the Waterfront

CHAPTER 1

THE BRINK'S HOLDUP

On the evening of January 17, 1950, shortly after seven o'clock, masked bandits stole more than $2,000,000 in checks, bonds, and currency from the North End headquarters of Brink's Incorporated on Prince Street in Boston, Massachusetts. Delivering cash for payrolls and returning the day's receipts to Brink's were the most important tasks of the company.

The Prince Street building, located close to the waterfront and harbor across from the frigate *Constitution*, was considered an impenetrable stronghold. From the front entrance a series of locked doors led to a cement vault where the money was kept.

At the time, the Brink's robbery was the greatest holdup in American history and excited the imagination of people all over the world.

The very first thought concerning the Brink's holdup was born in the mind of Tony Pino, a middle-aged ruffian of Boston's North End. One day he was watching the regularity with which scores of armored trucks with armed guards daily entered and left the Brink's garage at 165 Prince Street, at the corner of Prince and Commercial Streets. Then Pino began

9

visiting various locations in which the Brink's trucks were often seen. He watched the ease with which the guards handled thousands of dollars in cash, almost always acting with the relative nonchalance that people accustomed to handling money show to those of us who never have and never will be able to assume that matter-of-fact attitude.

Later Pino took to acquainting himself with residents of apartments or tenements overlooking the Brink's building. Occasionally he would be invited to the roofs on hot nights or at other times. These visits gave him an excuse to observe what was going on at Brink's while remaining inconspicuous. When surveying the Brink's garage entrance and the other doors that led into the building, he observed carefully the time those employed there entered and the time they left.

Then came the day he believed himself ready for the first physical move of his plan. It would be a continuous operation that was actually never to end until the great theft was carried out. Pino organized a criminal band of Boston area crooks second to none. The men he interviewed would maim, kill, and act relentlessly toward other humans whenever the occasion required. Those in the group were to be held together by strong underworld agreements and forged into a single unit that had but a single objective—to steal more than a million dollars!

People in the North End have told me that Pino began his crooked life as a child by stealing coal. Later he renewed his close friendship with the boyhood chums who thought as he did. He eventually concentrated on two men, Stan Gusciora and Specs O'Keefe, who had been brought up in similar fashion in the tenement districts of Boston.

Gusciora, or Gus, as he was known, was quicker in action and had a tougher manner, while Specs was acknowledged to be the smartest of the three.

Taking the two men to the scene of their future crime, Pino

showed them details of the building that housed Brink's Incorporated, and his crude charts of the coming and going of the many employees. Specs later admitted that the very audacious brashness of Pino's plan staggered him, but after careful consideration, he decided that he would accept the general scheme Pino outlined. Nevertheless, Specs O'Keefe believed that certain changes would have to be made, and he planned the robbery in a substantially different manner from Pino.

Pino had suggested two possible methods of operation. The first had the planners hiding at night in the building itself, where they could overcome the employees who would enter the edifice the next morning. The other possibility that Pino considered was to grab the Brink's head cashier and use his knowledge to open the vault.

O'Keefe was not too fond of either method. To investigate further, he and his friend Gus began roaming around outside the building at times when they were not apt to get caught. They gradually accumulated knowledge of astonishing importance. Finally they were able to enter this modern treasure citadel in the North End with no more bother than burglars have getting into a house in the suburbs! Not only could they enter the sprawling establishment with the greatest of ease, but they discovered that when they were ready to leave they were able to vanish in the same inconspicuous manner.

One night they experimented and found they could get into the garage adjoining the treasure house simply by manipulating the lock with an ice pick. Once inside, by inserting a piece of celluloid in a second lock, they successfully opened the door into the main building. After stepping inside, tense and alert, they expected to hear alarm bells ringing and other security measures thwarting their further attempts at entrance. They waited as the minutes passed. Absolutely nothing occurred.

Then quietly, for they had donned rubbers to reduce the

sound of their footsteps, they walked along the corridor. Soon the criminals reached the vault room itself, where the two most interesting items they noticed were a tally board and a burglar alarm system. In reconnoitering in this way, they discovered that they would need to solve the problem of the alarm system before there was any chance of their being able to accomplish their purpose.

Night after night, according to Specs O'Keefe, the gang visited the interior of the Brink's building until they became thoroughly familiar with the layout and the problems they might encounter. They learned that a few minutes after seven each night the cashiers in the vault room set the switch of the automatic alarm. Soon the crooks in their nocturnal visits began the habit of carefully studying the tally board, which recorded each day's receipts, and realized that it often registered more than a million dollars!

Wondering how they might nullify the effects of the alarm, the prospective thieves figured that if they could remove even for a few hours the lock cylinders from each successive door all the distance from the front of the building to the vault room itself, have keys made, and replace the locks without detection, there would be no trouble with the alarm. One night they took away the cylinders, visited a locksmith who cut keys for them, and returned the cylinders before the morning workers arrived. The thieves were able to solve the problem of the final lock in the series, but they never revealed how.

Finally, with all in readiness, the crooks decided that January 17 would be the date for the burglary. According to their plan, seven men would enter together. Breaking through to the vault, they would tie up the cashiers and take the money. Two others would wait outside in a truck to transport the actual robbers away from the scene of the theft. Another man would be on top of a nearby roof ready to warn if danger came. The eleventh crook, Joe McGinnis, would meet the others at a hideout and take over all the money.

A stolen, green three-quarter-ton Ford truck, chauffeurs' uniforms, navy jackets, Halloween masks, and special rope for tying up the cashiers comprised the equipment they had ready for that evening.

On Tuesday night, January 17, 1950, a drizzle was falling, which was ideal for the gangsters. The operation began when the seven men arrived at the Brink's building. Their outfits were such that they would have been taken for ordinary employees. Specs O'Keefe stood briefly at the front door of the building at 165 Prince Street. Casually he opened the door with his recently-made key, and the seven crooks filed inside. Then every man paused to don his Halloween mask, each ready for whatever lay ahead.

Shortly after seven o'clock that evening, cashier Thomas Lloyd was working as usual checking the money at the vault. Four other colleagues were with him: James Allen, a veteran bank worker with more than twenty-two years of experience, Sherman Smith, Herman Pfaff, and Charles Grell. Then came that moment of incredible drama at about ten minutes after seven. Seven bandits appeared before the five employees.

"Five of us were in the vault and the outer cage near the vault," Allen later explained in an interview with me. "Seven men, all of medium size and armed, wearing masks, walked into the back of the vault and right up to the cage. One of them spoke to us.

" 'We'll let you have it if you move.' I heard the others talking but their voices were far too low to understand.

"The vault door, leading out into the cage, was filled with cash, checks, negotiable securities, and coin. The inner door was open, and there was a substantial amount on the cage floor. They made us open the cage door itself and then roughed us up a little. One of them ripped off my glasses. They pushed us down on the floor and not too gently snatched our pistols away. They then tied us up, plastering adhesive tape across our mouths."

Within a short time the seven bandits put more than a million dollars into two giant Federal Reserve Bank bags, cursing because the actual weight of the currency prevented their carrying the coins along also. The coins, in fact, were worth another million dollars.

Eighteen minutes later the seven bandits quietly left the building. There still is controversy as to whether or not they were hurried by the sounding of a buzzer immediately before they fled the Brink's establishment, but in any case, they stepped into two cars and sped away into oblivion.

A few minutes later the Brink's guards untied themselves and notified the police authorities of the gigantic robbery. Pandemonium broke loose, and as soon as it was physically possible Boston Police Superintendent Edward W. Fallon took over. Ordering 150 policemen—captains, lieutenants, sergeants, and detectives—to assemble at headquarters, Fallon explained that this Brink's crime was actually a climax to a series of 1949 and 1950 robberies.

Superintendent Fallon told the others in detail what had taken place and emphasized the vital necessity for solving this gigantic, overwhelming robbery, the largest haul in the history of America.* He stated that the money had been taken from payrolls and receipts of many substantial firms, and that in their haste the thieves had overlooked $880,000 consigned to

---

* The previous record for armed robbery was held by bandits who on August 21, 1934, took $427,000 from an armored bank truck while the guards were picking up $25,000 from the Rubel Ice Corporation plant in Brooklyn, New York. Boston's only comparable holdup was at the B. F. Sturtevant plant in Hyde Park, where a payroll valued at $115,000 was taken. The second greatest Boston loss had been $29,000 at the American Sugar Refinery in South Boston.

the General Electric Company and $120,000 belonging to Filene's department store.

Evidently the timing under which the crooks operated was accurate to the closest degree. They had chosen a moment when all Brink's drivers had reported in, parked their cars in the huge gloomy cavern of the first floor garage, made their financial adjustments with the cashiers, and then left for the night.

Upstairs where the gigantic cement vault, impregnable if closed and locked, was located, the five workers had been counting funds and transferring them into envelopes. The physical arrangement of the building was believed to provide maximum security, but, of course, the robbery itself nullified this theory.

Two days later a telephone call coming from New Jersey from a never-identified man who claimed to be a driver of one of the get-away cars asserted that all the money had been hidden "within a minute's drive of the holdup scene." This message sent squads of policemen to the North End within a few hours, and many areas were searched, but in vain.

Boston banks were quick to assure the public that in spite of this greatest theft in the nation's history, the robbery took away only one dollar for every $2700 normally in circulation in the Boston Reserve District in 1950, a total of $2,700,000,000.

The first phase of the Brink's affair was rapidly drawing to a close. Soon, except for an occasional mention, the robbery disappeared from the front page of the Boston papers, and the public turned to other matters of interest.

For several years clues to the solution of the crime were few and far between. Even the fact that more than $98,000 of the loot was in bills whose serial numbers were known did little to solve the robbery.*

* There were ten $1000 bills, a hundred $100 bills, forty fifties, and 400 twenties, as well as 3400 tens, 3400 fives, 1200 twos, and 15,000 ones that

But unfortunately for the criminals, as has been the case since time immemorial, the robbers who had been so successful in planning the robbery were not to be so lucky after the burglary had taken place. Individual greed seems to have been the major factor in the gradual loosening of the ties that up to the night of the robbery were so definite and binding.

As it happened, every one of the eleven men involved in the robbery was among those picked up for the customary questioning, but all eleven were released. By this time the loot had been divided. Each member of the gang received $100,000, the exact amount of the reward offered for their detection.

Specs O'Keefe stored his $100,000 overnight with a "friend." Returning in less than twenty-four hours, he counted the money again only to discover that it had shrunk to $98,000 in one day! He took what was left away with him, putting $5,000 aside for his own expenses and hiding $93,000 at the home of Adolph Maffie. As matters turned out, Specs never saw any of the $93,000 again. With Stanley Gusciora he fled to Pennsylvania, where the two stole pistols, bullets, and clothes. Arrested for those thefts, they were convicted and imprisoned for several years.

Back in Boston, $380,000 of the loot had been stored in a covered basket. When opened after an interval of time it contained exactly $345,000! The person who had guarded the basket barely saved himself from being shot to death at once at the order of Specs O'Keefe by claiming that when the police put him under surveillance he stored the cash with a friend and thus could not be held responsible.

The police searched diligently for the slightest clue to the

---

made up the known bills. The stolen money included silver certificates of the 1935–C issues, and the exact numbers of 50 of the one dollar bills from L–39152501 E to L–39153000 E.

Including the $98,000, the exact amount of money stolen was $1,218,211.29 in cash and $1,557,183.83 in checks and negotiable securities, for a total of $2,775,395.12.

robbery. Finally their efforts were rewarded. Fragments of the green Ford truck were discovered in a nearby dump, with the evidence indicating that a blowtorch and sledgehammer had been used in an attempt to destroy the car. It appeared that the criminals had tried to bury the truck remains, but hard frozen ground had thwarted their efforts. Week after week police detectives worked tracing down each major clue, until finally they had assembled enough disjointed facts to implicate eight of the eleven robbers.

Nevertheless, there was insufficient evidence to convict, and as the months passed, the FBI realized they needed more facts. They were especially frustrated because they knew that the Federal three-year statute of limitations would take effect in the first month of the following year.

During the waning weeks of 1952, the eight suspected holdup men were brought to one central location. Nevertheless, the year 1953 arrived, and the FBI did not have sufficient evidence to hold the criminals. On January 16, 1953, with one day remaining of the three-year statute of limitations that is Federal Law, the Grand Jury stated there simply wasn't enough evidence for a trial, and the eight men were not indicted. And so it was that at midnight the FBI transferred their efforts to aiding the state of Massachusetts, whose legal representatives could act for three years more under its six-year statute of limitations. J. Edgar Hoover made it clear that his organization would "never quit the Brink's Case." If the FBI cracked the mystery, Hoover emphasized, all the evidence would be turned over to Massachusetts.

After completing his Pennsylvania jail sentence in February 1954, Specs O'Keefe returned to Boston. To his consternation, he discovered that Adolph Maffie had spent practically every dollar of the $93,000 Specs had entrusted to him. It is a miracle that O'Keefe did not kill Maffie on the spot, but the latter promised substantial restitution.

Nevertheless, O'Keefe held Maffie prisoner, locked and tied up, while he decided what his next move might be. Maffie told him to see Pino. Keeping Maffie bound, O'Keefe went to Pino to ask Pino to advance him $25,000.

Specs waited several weeks for money and, as Pino did not provide him with any funds, Specs threatened Pino. Since the threats produced no results in the way of money, Specs kidnapped Vincent Costa, another gang member who was also Pino's brother-in-law. Pino now gave Specs $2500 and O'Keefe released Costa.

Retaliation against Specs by others in the gang was soon to follow, and the fact that O'Keefe stayed alive during the next few weeks says much for his sagacity, alertness, and agility. One day, while getting into his Oldsmobile, he noticed another car parked nearby. Then as he turned into a relatively narrow street, the strange car pulled up alongside and an occupant in the back seat began to spray Specs' car with bullets from a sub-machine gun. The moment the other car approached O'Keefe dropped down on the floor boards so that every bullet missed him.

A few weeks later his luck did not hold out. While parking his car, he was shot twice, sustaining a wound in the wrist and another in the chest. A physician who took care of gangland injuries kept him alive with penicillin. Specs recovered to begin serving a sentence of more than two years because of conviction for an earlier crime.

Officials in the FBI, who had never really lost track of O'Keefe's activities, decided to make a proposal to him. Two days after Christmas, two agents of the FBI visited O'Keefe in Hampton County Jail at Springfield, Massachusetts, where he had been incarcerated. They were still interested in the Brink's case, the FBI men explained, and they knew Specs was also interested. He might like to know that his old comrades were cashing in on their good fortune. His close friend Anthony

Pino had acquired a brand new residence, while his late associate Vincent Costa had invested in an automobile agency and was beginning to prosper. The FBI men then left to allow the message to penetrate O'Keefe's mental defenses, and a day or so later they made a return visit.

On January 6, 1956, almost six years after the Brink's robbery—but only ten days after their first visit—the two members of the FBI made a third call on Specs. The persuasive triple visits affected Specs in such fashion that his defenses collapsed and his surrender soon became complete. Deciding to tell everything he knew about his part in the robbery, Specs first revealed the entire list of those involved in the holdup of January 17, 1950. They were Henry Baker, Joseph S. Banfield, Vincent J. Costa, James I. Flaherty, Michael Geagan, Stanley Gusciora, Adolph Maffie, Joseph F. McGinnis, Joseph James O'Keefe, Anthony Pino, and Thomas F. Richardson.

Later, under the most dramatic security measures in Massachusetts history, Specs was removed from jail and escorted secretly under heavy guard to the office of District Attorney Garrett Byrne. There under merciless questioning, O'Keefe not only reiterated his complete account but also remembered a few extra details for good measure.

Just six days after O'Keefe's confession the blow fell for the surviving members of the Brink's gang. Two had died, but six members of the original eleven were arrested by the FBI. Stanley Gusciora was already in jail at the time. When he heard that Specs had "betrayed" him, he broke down and cried like a baby. Later that year he suddenly collapsed, and he died of a tumor a short time afterward.

It was not long after Stanley Gusciora's death that all members of the Brink's gang still alive were brought together for trial in Boston. On a warm September day in 1956 the trial began, and forty-five days later O'Keefe's comrades were sentenced to jail for life. District Attorney Byrne pleaded for clemency in the case of Specs, stating that O'Keefe should not get a life sentence. He emphasized the fact that both Massachusetts and the FBI would have been eternally embarrassed if it had not been for Spec's confession, and four years later, in November 1960, Specs O'Keefe was paroled. He was given a new identity. In the spring of 1976 he died of natural causes.

Did this crime pay? Everyone vitally concerned with its history is emphatic in stating that the Brink's robbery did not pay those who perpetrated it, but it did have certain fringe benefits for many of their immediate associates who profited substantially at the time.

Money from the robbery has been discovered in relatively miniscule amounts from time to time, but the bulk of the illegal treasure still eludes the authorities. On several occasions I have toured the North End of Boston in a vain attempt to discover what many others have failed to find, some of the more than $1,000,000 still missing from the famed Brink's holdup.

Often with my older brother, the late Winthrop James Snow, I would climb down around old musty brick walls, passageways, and arches, including the Captain James Gruchy tunnel * at 455 Commercial Street, later taken over by the Coast Guard. Win was an expert in the brick and tile industry and gave me many pointers on where and how the thieves might have secreted the major part of the cash, which so far has never been found.

* See my *True Tales of Buried Treasure* and C. L. Reeves' book *Captain Gruchy's Gambols.*

CHAPTER 2

THE MOLASSES DISASTER

While studying at Harvard University more than forty years ago I had drilled into my rather reluctant mind the importance of the economic triangle represented by molasses from the West Indies, slaves from Africa, and rum from Medford and Boston.

Molasses has always been a vital import into the port of Boston. Millions upon millions of gallons of the sticky, sweet liquid have been turned into candy and a spread for bread. Molasses has also been an ingredient in New England gingerbread and cookies. Moreover, the United States Industrial Alcohol Company, which ran the Purity Distilling Company in the North End of Boston, changed molasses into distilled alcohol.

The gigantic tank, 52 feet high and 91 feet in diameter, in which the United States Alcohol Company stored molasses in crude form was a prominent landmark of the North End waterfront area. This commercial neighborhood was dominated in the year 1919, as it is in 1976, by Copp's Hill Cemetery. In 1919, from the vantage point of the graveyard high on the hill, a person would have an outstanding view of the surrounding area to the north. He would see Bunker Hill Monument, the battleship *Constitution*, Commercial Street, the Public

Works Department of the City of Boston, the paving division of Boston, the Fire Station with Fireboat Engine 31, the warehouses of the Boston and Worcester Railway, the Eastern Massachusetts Railway, and in the immediate foreground, the trestle of the Boston Elevated tracks high in the air.

It is often said that half a century and more ago winters were colder than they are today, but in January 1919 the streets of Boston were nearly free of snow. Although there were a few days of chilly weather, several unexpectedly warm days arrived during the middle of that month. As Alton Hall Blackington expressed it in his book *Yankee Yarns*, it was so warm that the children of the North End "played marbles and danced on the sidewalk to the tunes of a hurdy-gurdy."

With noon approaching on January 15, it seemed like a real spring day. Men walked around without overcoats, and girls strolled bareheaded, enjoying the warmth of the unexpected weather.

At the Worcester freight terminal on the waterfront, Percy Smerage was checking leather bales, beer barrels, and potatoes. Four freight cars on which he had completed tallies, or counts, were fully loaded.

Suddenly there was a terrific noise "like a thousand machine guns" followed by an unbelievable roar as the enormous tank, containing 2,300,000 gallons of molasses, split into several sections. A veritable geyser of the yellowish brown liquid shot up into the air, and a river of molasses three times as high as a man billowed forth in all directions.

The heavy, sluggish, overwhelming torrent pushed its bulky way out from the tank, engulfing everything in its path. The loaded freight cars were picked up like fragments of wood in a tidal wave. A fifth freight car, only half filled, was pushed right through the wall of the railroad terminal. It was an awesome, unbelievable sight. The weight of the molasses dropped three workers and several horses down into the basement of the freight terminal, men and horses perishing together.

When the molasses hit the Boston Fire Station, the building was lifted from its foundation and battered against the harbor wharf pilings, killing three fire fighters of Fireboat 31. One of them, Engineer William Leahy, was crushed to death by a billiard table that literally flew through the air and smashed into him. The surviving fire fighters on duty labored long and heroically in spite of injuries, pulling victims from collapsed buildings and other scattered debris in the area.

An unidentified cadet from the training ship *Nantucket* rescued a woman from the third floor of a tenement. Alton Hall Blackington, photographing the rescue, slipped and fell into the molasses, but was successful in taking his pictures.

As witnesses described it later, the disaster began with a muffled roar and a "clangor of steel against steel and the crash of rending wood." However, the roar and the din were momentary. After the explosion great ribbons of thick, brownish fluid pushed everywhere, moving at the approximate rate of speed of heavy liquid cement. The huge tossing geyser simply overwhelmed any object which lay in its path, becoming what one expert later called an "adhesive flood." It inundated everyone and everything.

In a single stroke the force of the explosion tore the great tank apart, plate by plate. The outward shock was followed by a tremendous vacuum that actually pulled or sucked into rubble any nearby structure that was not damaged by the initial blast.

The steel plates, half an inch thick, were catapulted in every direction by the unleashed energy of the explosion. Crashing into the elevated trestle, the plates knifed through the steel girders that supported the tracks and the trains, missing one of several moving elevated cars by less than a hundred yards.

The outward force of the explosion forced a team of horses and a wagon from the pavements of the freight yards through a board fence, pushing them to the corner of Commercial and Charter Streets. Late that afternoon the carcasses of the horses were taken from the molasses ooze and removed from the area.

One example of individual suffering was that of Martin J. Clougherty. A prominent Boston sportsman, boxing referee, and manager of the Pen and Pencil Club, Clougherty lived at 6 Copp's Hill Terrace, the family home since 1872. The blast picked up his 69-year-old mother, Mrs. Bridget Clougherty, and blew her right through a window, killing her almost at once. The house itself was lifted in one piece from its underpinnings.

Mrs. Clougherty's son later told of his experience. "I could not sleep this morning before the explosion," stated Martin. "I wanted to get up and go out, and I don't know why. I wouldn't say it was a premonition. Anyway I'm glad I didn't go out. My dear old mother told me to sleep longer as I had put in three or four sleepless nights after refereeing bouts. I distinctly heard the rumbling which preceded the explosion.

"First I thought it was an elevated train on fire. Anyway, in less time than it takes to tell it I dreamed that I had found myself in the river and heavy weights were pressing on my chest.

"I must have had my mother's prayers with me for by some means I managed to extricate myself before I smothered to death. Indeed I thought that I had been thrown into the Charles River. I found my sister and dragged her out of the rubble, but I could not find my mother or my brother."

A huge powerful man, Martin Clougherty was seriously injured and suffered for several hours from shock. Mrs. Clougherty, who was in the kitchen when the blast shattered the house, died almost at once, although Clougherty's brother, who was also there, was only slightly injured when he was rescued.

The entire area was simply plastered with molasses—rooftops, trees, overhead wires, and grass plots were all covered with the sticky substance. Commercial Street was a river of molasses at least four feet deep.

Harry F. Dolan, attorney for the United States Industrial Alcohol Company, stated that the actual explosion may have come from an outside source. He was reasonably sure that the blast did not originate in either the tank or its contents. The tank, Dolan explained, was of the most modern construction, the maker more than reliable.

"The damage," said the attorney, "will be enormous. There were more than 2,300,000 gallons in the container when it burst, and I am certain that $500,000 would fall far short of reimbursement to the company alone.

"The disaster concerns us vitally and every effort is being made to determine exactly the cause, and who is concerned in it. The fluid was to be used in filling government contracts for alcohol for the manufacture of munitions. The firm has been filling war contracts almost since the war started, and before accepting contracts for the United States, it completed a number for the French and British governments.

W. L. Wedger, the state explosives expert, believed the explosion came from within the tank itself. He explained that the interior of the huge tank was lined with pipes for the purpose of heating the molasses so that it would flow freely into the tank cars in which it was transported to the plant in Cambridge. He stated that a mixture of gas and air "found vent in the blast."

The pier on which the tank was erected in 1916 was originally known as the Great White Spirit Wharf. Just before the disaster the huge structure had received several shipments of molasses, the last being a cargo from the American steamship *Milero*, which completed unloading 600,000 gallons from Matanzas on January 14.

When the *Milero* arrived, the weather was relatively cold, and there was minor difficulty when the colder molasses was discharged into the warmer supply already there.

A pumping station stood between the dock from which the ships discharged and the tank itself. Built as a subcellar with concrete walls and floor, the pumping station had machinery designed to suck the molasses through a 14-inch pipe from the ship through the room into the tank. As occasion demanded, the contents of the tank was transferred to freight cars especially built to carry the molasses along the street tracks of the Boston Elevated Railway to the distillery in Cambridge.

Before the tank was built in the vicinity of Copp's Hill, molasses had been unloaded at the wharf of the Boston Molasses Company in South Boston. Because of the long haul to Cambridge, it was decided to construct a tank on what by then had come to be known as Gas House Wharf. Rebuilt, the pier had served adequately until the disaster.

The United States Industrial Alcohol Company maintained only one employee at the tank wharf, William H. White of Sharon. He was in charge of the pumping station between the dock and the tank and was away at dinner when the disaster occurred.

Five of those killed worked in the city yards. Eating in a flimsy structure at lunchtime, they were engulfed when the explosion occurred and succumbed at once.

The devastated area presented such a fantastic spectacle that it drew enormous crowds. Onlookers gathered at many vantage points, including Copp's Hill Park, Commercial Street, and the lower part of Charter Street, and stared in awe at the scenes of utter ruin.

Thirty-three enlisted men from the U.S.S. *Pawnee*, which was lying close by the scene of the disaster, assisted in vital rescue work. Under the command of Ensign C. J. Campbell, they dug out several dead bodies from the molasses ooze near the elevated structure and managed to rescue five other persons still alive.

Directly under the overhanging girders of the elevated tracks they discovered the body of a woman of about seventy, so heavily smeared with molasses that she was believed dead until she spoke, asking for a priest. A priest soon came and called for an ambulance, and the woman was taken to the Relief Hospital. The sailors never discovered her name or whether she survived the ordeal.

A girl appealed to the sailor cadets from the training ship *Nantucket* for help. She told them she and a friend had been standing on Commercial Street in front of North End Park at the time of the blast. Her companion had been drawn toward the tank in a suction-like wind, while she found herself shot through the air away from the tank to land twenty feet from where she had been standing. Although the cadets dug in the debris where she thought the boy had been lost, he could not be found nor was his body ever discovered.

The work of the Women's Volunteer Relief Corps was praised by both the firemen and the police. Every available ambulance of the American Red Cross was sent to the scene, with Mary Converse in command of the ambulances at the disaster.

Firemen from Fireboat Engine 31 soon turned strong streams of water on the brown molasses fluid. The force proved fairly effective. Unfortunately, in places the molasses was so deep and clung in such a tenacious manner to the ground and the debris that an unbelievably long time was needed to wash the substance into the harbor.

Superintendent E. M. Byington of the Boston Fire Department Construction and Supplies Department was placed in charge of the almost impossible task of pumping out the cellars and basements in the area. Even after a week of work, several locations in the area were still deep in molasses. The

worst hazard was a deep pool at the northern side of the Bay
State freight house, a pool that stretched all the distance from
Commercial Street to the cap-logs at the edge of the water-
front.

Even with a number of Fire Department pumps working
twenty-four hours every day, the drop in the level of the molasses was almost imperceptible. After days of pumping, the
cellars of the freight house and other buildings in the area were
still filled with molasses almost to the level of the first floor.
The cellars of every store in the long brick block stretching
from Copp's Hill Terrace to Charter Street on Commercial
Street were still filled to the brim with molasses five days after
the disaster.

Those who watched as the ruins were being cleared noticed
with horror the number of horses that had been caught, still
hitched to their wagons, when the explosion took place. Five
of the unfortunate beasts of burden were pulled from the molasses in front of the remains of the freight shed of the Boston
and Worcester Railway. As the debris was moved away, the
five horses were discovered in a single heap. They had died
rearing and struggling to free themselves from the awesome
combination of wreckage and molasses.

It was just beyond the pile of horse carcasses that the remains of Henry Laird were found. He had been missing for
several days. The body was on its side, the face turned outward. It was necessary to turn a stream from a fire hose on the
body to clear away the congealed syrup for identification purposes. The dead man either had sought safety under the truck
where he was discovered, or the flood of molasses had carried
him there. His remains were still jammed under the truck when
his head was uncovered, and powerful jacks were needed to
lift the tons of debris from his body.

A total of thirteen persons were known to have lost their
lives in the tank disaster.

After everything had been done for the living, the officials began asking each other why the tank had collapsed. Few of those engaged in supervising the clearing of debris agreed with the theory that the mere collapse of the tank could cause such havoc. It was the accepted decision of most of those examining the ruins that an explosion in the tank itself ripped the sides apart and gave the "avalanche of molasses the impetus which it manifested."

By Friday morning, January 17, the belief that an explosion had been responsible for the disaster had gained considerable strength. United States Inspector of Explosives Daniel F. O'Connell expressed the opinion that there was some evidence of fermentation, and stated that in many instances the holes in the tank were much larger than the rivets. The theory that the structure collapsed because of the fullness of the tank was not supported by O'Connell, although the huge molasses container was filled to capacity. Inspector O'Connell's report, which was forwarded to the Bureau of Mines in Washington, included an estimate that there had been 70 gallons of alcohol for every 100 gallons of molasses, presenting a condition of hazardous volatility.

Another factor considered was the beating upon the metal tank of the strong rays of the sun, which heated the structure. This, according to some, caused the liquid inside the tank to ferment and give off gas. The roof of the tank had four vent holes, but it was never made clear whether these vents allowed the escape of gas that might form inside. It was believed by those who worked at the tank that all four vents were either screwed down tight or had been jammed or gummed by molasses, thus preventing the escape of gas.

The evident force that crumpled the strong steel supports of the Elevated roadway was mentioned as reason to believe that an explosion of some sort must "have been the propulsion." Sections of the steel sides of the tank flew through the air to drop into Commercial Street itself.

Former Building Commissioner Patrick O'Hara stated positively that the disaster was the result of an explosion. He was familiar with the construction of the tank, and remarked that four years before he had inspected it carefully. He added that explosions of molasses were not unknown, and in this statement he had the backing of several chemists on the scene.

Chief John H. Plunkett of the Boston Fire Department stated that "the molasses in the tank had to be heated in order to keep it at a temperature which would allow it to be drawn easily from the tank. The heating was done by means of steam pipes run into the tank.

"In heating such tanks, great care must be used to prevent overheating. Molasses when fermenting, or when heated, throws off an alcoholic gas which has a tremendous pressure. Railroad authorities are always particular about providing vent for this gas when moving molasses.

"There is no regulation over the construction and use of such tanks. In my opinion there should be," the chief concluded.*

The task of delving through the wreckage took the full time of more than three hundred men from the Public Works Department, aided by a force from the Elevated railway and employees of the Hugh Nawn Contracting Company, for more than five weeks. There were thirty-five men cutting the fragments of the tank into movable pieces with acetylene torches, while the elimination of the molasses was a slow, painful job that kept the firemen constantly at their high pressure hoses.

It is said that never before in the history of the country did

* Because the tank was considered a receptacle and not a building, the municipal building department had absolutely no authority to supervise the construction of the tank. Commissioner Herbert A. Wilson introduced a new bill to give the municipal building authorities the power to regulate the construction of such structures in the future.

so many people file lawsuits for such a disaster. One scientist testified for three weeks, at times well into the night. It was not until 1926, six years after the disaster, that the molasses hearings came to a close.

Not only was it found that the tank itself had not been built strongly enough, but it came out in court that no real examination or inspection of the structure had ever been made! It was the conclusion of the experts that as the molasses weighed eleven pounds to the gallon, making a pressure of more than two tons per square foot on the sides and bottom of the container, the comparatively weak tank, never properly inspected, simply collapsed. Blame for the disaster was charged to the United States Industrial Alcohol Company, and the bill they eventually had to pay came to more than a million dollars.

As a result of the molasses disaster of 1919, more stringent regulations regarding the approval and inspection of similar tanks were enacted.

CHAPTER 3

THE PICKWICK CLUB COLLAPSE

Shortly before three o'clock in the morning of the Fourth of July 1925, an ominous cracking sound was heard by dancers at the Pickwick Club, located in the Old Dreyfus Hotel at 12 Beach Street in downtown Boston, a relatively short distance from the Atlantic Avenue waterfront and actually on the edge of Chinatown. Then the lights went out. For many of the more than one hundred and fifty merrymakers in the third-floor club it was a moment of terror that would end in death.

Band leader Billy Glennon and his trio of musicians were preparing for the "Good Night" number that would terminate the night's activities, but it was never played.

Sand and dust began to seep down from the ceiling, and then the entire floor collapsed. The ceiling of the club fell in, followed by both the fourth and fifth stories of the old hotel. Gigantic sections of the upper floors hung down, held together only by huge squares of tarpaper that still adhered to flooring and shattered walls.

In moments all available police and fire apparatus started for the scene of the disaster. Slowly, through the morning, order emerged from the chaos. A few hours after the collapse, under the glare of floodlights and flares, a systematic search through the ruins was in progress. By dawn thirteen bodies had been recovered. The total count would eventually reach forty-four victims.

Rescue Company One of the Boston Fire Department was an early arrival on the scene. Using an acetylene torch the fire fighters cut through the steel supports of the elevator cage. Then three trucks hooked onto the long elevator cables, and as a united effort was made, the cables began to stretch all the way across the street. Finally the cables and the cable drum toppled away from the top of the shaft. As they fell, a great cloud of dust, dirt, and even flames was seen. Hoses from the fire department soon extinguished the flames.

All day long screams were heard coming from several areas in the debris. At about ten in the evening the last cry was heard. Shortly before midnight a huge derrick lifted a section of the dance floor, revealing the remains of three more men and two women.

The legs and body of Mrs. Edith Jordan, a bride of a few weeks, were caught in the collapse, but she could talk to rescuers and did so for no less than eight and a half hours of effort. Finally liberated, she was rushed to the hospital but died before she could be removed from the ambulance.

The driver's license of Frank Jones of Beach Street in Wollaston, Massachusetts, was discovered in the ruins. His home was called and Frank Jones himself answered. Jones explained that he had lost his license in some manner two months before. He had no idea how the card turned up at the club, which he had not visited for several weeks.

As soon as the news of the Pickwick Club disaster became known, police lines were set on Washington Street and Harrison Avenue, just beyond the Beach Street debris. A bystander watching the grim spectacle described the crowds of onlookers.

"At the most, only a few hundred of them could see anything of the debris and the dust-covered, weary firemen and laborers engaged in digging for bodies. Except when the front wall crumbled to a pull from the fire department cables, there was nothing spectacular, nothing thrilling to see.

"Nonetheless, neither showers nor darkness routed them.

"If today had not been a holiday, the work of the police assigned to handling the crowds would have been more difficult. As it was, they had an opportunity to establish lines during the early morning hours when the district was almost deserted.

"Well before noon, however, the streets in the vicinity were crowded. Men and women appeared in windows and on roofs of buildings gazing on the sight. Eagerly snatching at rumors of faint cries heard down under the debris or of bodies being brought to the surface, the spectators waited, individuals changing now and then but the mass remaining the same tense, high-strung unit.

"Police officers commented on the fact that so many persons who took up their vigil at the ropes early in the day were still there when darkness fell.

" 'Some of them haven't eaten all day,' said one officer. 'They stand there, asking civilian officials and newspapermen who pass through the lines for information but never approaching an officer. Some of them must have friends or relatives who they think may have been in the place and yet they are too timid to go to the police.'

"Occasionally there would appear on the fringe of the crowd a man or more often, a girl, whose mission, it was obvious, was not to gratify morbid curiosity. Shyly, as if fearful of hearing the worst, as if preferring no news to definite information, she would accost officials or newspapermen leaving the scene.

" 'Do you know, mister, have they heard anything of so-and-so?' 'Have they taken out a girl in a blue dress, about twenty-two?' 'Maybe my chum is in there. Did you hear anything about—?'

"These questioners were probably not relatives of the persons of whom they sought word. More likely they were chums and pals, members of 'the gang,' who knew that their partners-in-play at times made merry at the nightclub.

"It never required long for rumors of such cries from the debris to reach the crowd. Invariably, as the word spread, there would issue from the watchers a mighty 'Hello-o-o, hello-o-o' that not even shouted calls for silence could suppress. It may have been a belief that their answer would be heard down in the depths of the debris that actuated the spectators; more likely, it was pent-up emotion bursting free. Crowds are ever hungry for a chance to cheer or yell—they had mighty little opportunity for either yesterday."

About two o'clock on that July Fourth afternoon jazz music could be heard playing in various Chinese restaurants in the vicinity. To the watchers below, the shadows of couples dancing made a strangely contrasting background for the gigantic piles of rubbish and debris from which the police were still taking dead bodies.

Rain began to fall shortly before sunset, and it was hoped that the dense crowds would thin out. Twenty minutes later a blanket-covered bundle on a stretcher was carried over to an ambulance, and those who were watching realized that bodies were still being found.

Half an hour after sunset myriads of lights that had been gathered together by the Edison Company were placed in position to give the most illumination possible. Fifty lights were put up along the distant side of the disaster, while twenty-five more were set up in buildings along Beach Street.

As darkness wore on, the watchers realized that their part in the grisly spectacle was similar to sitting in a gallery at a show—a terrible show, of course. They observed firefighters, police, officials, and laborers carrying out their duties in the midst of the giant lights, similar to actors on a spotlit stage.

The famous Gordon's Washington Street Olympia Theatre was temporarily closed. Two hundred early patrons were about to watch the show when the authorities decided to clear the theatre, for it was realized that one side wall of the theater ran along the ruins of the club. An actor announced that as rescuers were still searching for bodies a few feet away, it had been decided to stop the performance. There was no disorder as the patrons filed out, and it was explained to them that the measure was purely precautionary.

One story that aroused indignation was told by Harold Shaw, a waiter at the club. He declared that the side door of the premises was barred with a trick lock to prevent outsiders getting in. Shaw explained that the lock could be manipulated only by a member of the club who was familiar with the complicated mechanism.

At the time of the disaster Timothy Barry was president of the Pickwick Club and his brother was floor manager.

Almost every department of city and state was blamed for the disaster by those who lost loved ones in the collapse.

Investigations soon revealed that the Pickwick Club's walls actually had been weakened weeks before. Hugh Urquhart, an engineer who made a careful examination at the scene, revealed that on the Friday before the collapse he had been checking an elevator he had installed. Visiting 6 Beach Street, Urquhart had occasion to look at the exposed underpinnings of the Pickwick Club building, where he found seven four-foot piers with six-foot spaces between them. The clay under the piers had been removed, leaving them hanging alone with nothing to support them in any way!

District Attorney Thomas C. O'Brien was told that in excavating for a garage next door to the old hotel building, a steam shovel had been used. At the time an agreement had been made to protect and strengthen the hotel building. Actually, the lateral support had been removed, leaving the

Pickwick Club in a very dangerous state. However, even after half a century, there still are many opinions as to what type of structural weakness brought the building down.

Both Mayor James Michael Curley and Governor Alvin T. Fuller acted at once in representing the city and the commonwealth respectively. Mayor Curley made at least seven visits to the site in the next few days, while Governor Fuller appointed Attorney General Jay R. Benton to write a daily personal report to him on the investigation's progress.

At a grand jury assembled because of the disaster, testifying witnesses were called for visit after visit to the court so that the members of the jury could be crystal clear in their understanding of certain controversial points. Apparently determination of where to assign blame rested on interpretation of the General Laws. Although the Commonwealth of Massachusetts covers the situation in Chapter 143 of the General Laws, Boston is excepted from the general laws of the Commonwealth.

In the building laws for Boston, paragraph one, section three, the Boston Commissioner for Buildings is ordered to examine any edifice that has recently had a fire. On April 13 the building did have a fire, but although structural weakness was noted after the blaze, it was never repaired.

Many city residents and some officials claimed that the commonwealth was responsible for the collapse because a commonwealth-chartered group controlled the building. Secretary of the Commonwealth Frederick W. Cook emphatically and correctly stated that exclusive of the commonwealth, Boston had its own laws regarding buildings. "Any attempt to divert to the office of the secretary of state the responsibility for continued occupancy of an unsafe building, because it was supposed to be occupied by a chartered corporation is not only ridiculous but dastardly," concluded Cook.

Civil suits totaling more than a million dollars eventually were filed. Many of those interested in the political aspect of the situation wondered if the "higher-ups" would be made to answer for anything that contributed to the tragedy of July 4, 1925. There was a persistent rumor that some "higher-up" official had given the go-ahead for unrestricted revelry and dancing that July 4 eve in the weakened structure.

Those in the corridors outside the grand jury rooms were actually divided in their purposes. One group included lawyers interested in prospective clients, another those who desired to emphasize the civil liability aspect. It was also reported that one lawyer was bemoaning the fact that three of his clients, "all good pay," had died in the collapse.

Who was blamed after all the evidence was studied?

Governor Fuller's report included the statement that, without question, the premises would have been ordered vacated if a careful city inspection after the April 13 fire had been made. He also emphasized as a contributory factor the excavations made for the construction of a garage next door to the old hotel building, after which suitable and proper shoring had not been carried out.

General George Washington Goethals, who built the Panama Canal, made an inspection of the premises. He declared that the underlying cause of the building's collapse was the rotten condition of the concrete pilings.

The grand jury eventually indicted twelve men, including contractors, foremen, two city department officials, and several officials directly connected with the property or the Pickwick Club itself. The cause of the collapse was officially determined to be the failure of concrete piers under the building and the lack of lateral bracing. Nevertheless, all charges against those indicted were dropped.

Never before in Boston history had such a building disaster occurred. The panorama of the Pickwick Club collapse could not be forgotten by those who saw it.

PART TWO

From Massachusetts to Maine

CHAPTER 1

~~~~~~~~~~

THE LAWRENCE MILL
DISASTER

Sailing up the Merrimack River from the Massachusetts coast, the adventuresome mariner eventually sights the buildings, steeples, and chimneys of Lawrence, which many have called Massachusetts' only "made city," as it was actually planned as a textile center.

When the clipper ship business of Boston was first affected by the progress of steamers, several shrewd capitalists and bankers of Massachusetts decided to seek other fields in which to make their investments. For the first time in the history of the state these industrial leaders planned to build and operate a city actually made to their own order. In 1845 they formed the Essex Company to utilize the power created by Bodwell's Falls in the Merrimack River near the area soon to be called Lawrence, Massachusetts, after Amos Lawrence, a prominent member of the group. Built almost overnight, Lawrence was incorporated as a town in 1847, and became a city six years later. As the years went by, other Bostonians became interested in the growing textile industry in this new city. Immigrants from Italy, Poland, Syria, Armenia, and Canada popu-

41

lated the area. The first mayor, elected in 1853, was Charles Storrow.

Four giant mills were soon completed, one of which—the Pemberton Mills—some said, was put up in much too rapid a fashion. It was asserted that it had been erected in a relatively flimsy manner. For example, in one case the wrong size horizontal beams for the upper stories had been furnished. The beams were too short and could not cross the vertical girders. Jury-rigged beams were substituted. In addition, several architects indicated that the walls of the mills were too thin, and they pointed out that unsatisfactory cast-iron pillars had been used in certain instances.

Nevertheless, all warnings and adverse comments were ignored. When it was announced that the great Pemberton Mills complex was finished, spindles and looms were moved in, and men, women, and children workers arrived. All went well for several years, and the objections were forgotten as month after month went by without incident or trouble.

Then came January 1860. On January 10, late in the afternoon, all the workers were busily engaged at their various occupations, keeping the spindles and looms functioning. The three turbine wheels, each yielding two hundred horsepower, were smoothly operating, and the boiler that heated the huge edifice, but housed in a separate building for safety, was operating perfectly. A line of hose ran from the pumps to every room in the mill.

Suddenly, at ten minutes before five, this vast, towering structure, 284 feet long and 84 feet wide, with most of the 650 looms and 29,000 spindles in operation, started to disintegrate.

One survivor, whose name does not come down to us, told his story later. He had been standing in the second-story carding room, where it was his task to light the burners. With no previous warning there was a fearful noise. As he stared spellbound the shafting ripped down from the ceiling, accompanied by a terrific noise from overhead.

He remained "nailed to the spot" in terror at such an unaccountable spectacle. He then heard the overseer shout for him to jump clear, but as he did so he was struck and knocked unconscious by the debris that hit him.

An instant later he recovered consciousness, finding himself buried in rubbish and debris so effectively that he nearly gave up hope of ever getting out alive. Nevertheless, dripping with blood, he shoved and pushed, forcing his way to the top of the rubble. As he did so, he climbed across the lifeless remains of a young girl. He pulled himself free and fought along a passageway that revealed two more mangled bodies. Finally he escaped from the ruins and the rubble.

A twenty-year-old girl also extricated herself from the ruins. She told how she had been working on the second floor at the time of the collapse. Suddenly, less than twenty feet away, she sighted portions of the building bulging inward. She began to run in the opposite direction but was caught by other crumbling walls in her path. She started for a side door, but it shattered into fragments as she approached it. Finally she fought her way to a window and was able to leap to the ground and flee from the collapsing structure.

Another woman survivor explained how she had been working on the third floor. Suddenly the entire ceiling above seemed to fall on her, and then she realized that her own floor was collapsing as well. As the building continued to disintegrate, she was caught by fragments of machinery. A heavy beam struck her head. She was held by the wreckage and was unable to move. Then pressure began to force her arms and legs away from her body in opposite directions, but a moment later another wall collapsed, and she felt herself freed. Squirming and wriggling, she fought her way out of the rubble and escaped.

An exploring party discovered a little girl. She lay apparently crushed beneath a gigantic iron block, her back pressed against a heavy timber and her left arm thrust to the elbow in a circular piece of metal. She was hopelessly wedged in the midst of heavy machinery. Four men tried to lift the iron girder but failed to budge it. A giant of a man who was unusually strong then attempted the task. Straining and groaning, he finally forced his body against the block and succeeded in lifting it a fraction of an inch. The others pulled the girl out. To their joy, the men found that the iron girder had been braced against another powerful obstruction in such a way that the girl, although tightly wedged, had been inside a protective metal shield around her body and actually was not seriously injured at all!

At one point in the rescue attempts a volunteer called for help in pulling on a rope attached to a projecting timber from under which cries had been heard. No one would help, for they feared the timber would come down on them. A woman then stepped out of the group. Standing by the single volunteer, she appealed to the others. Ashamed, several of the men also grabbed the rope. They pulled with a concerted effort and the timber slid out, revealing two victims still alive. They were rushed to the hospital.

Among the sufferers in the debris was an overseer who had been a favorite of the workers. As the search for victims went on, his voice was suddenly heard from the very depths of the ruins. Fighting down through the debris, the workers were almost to him when a fire broke out and pushed them back.

"Hurry," he cried, "I'll kill myself rather than burn to death!" Several minutes later they reached him, but he had cut his throat. Rushed to the hospital, he died of his self-inflicted injury on the way.

A large number of workers who had been in the weaving room on the lower floor had been able to crawl up on the debris of the second floor by going through a window that was still open. The heavy stone floor of the second story had not collapsed, and thus became a haven of safety, allowing many workers to save themselves there.

One forty-year-old woman had a miraculous escape. Working on the top floor, she had been precipitated headlong into the debris along with timbers, roofing, bricks, and machinery but managed to land on the bottom unharmed.

Walking along outside the building, a man heard the cry of a girl asking if Lizzie Hunt were still alive. The reply came from another section of the ruins that Lizzie was still unhurt. Both were later rescued and united.

In one section of the ruins the dead bodies of three girls were found, locked in each others arms. As the fire was then approaching, attempts were made to pull the remains out together, but this could not be done, and the bodies of all three were consumed by the fire.

In another section of the ruins a woman was dragged out, still alive. Her left arm had been torn from its socket, and her body and legs were terribly mangled. In spite of her injuries, she survived.

The dead body of a girl was discovered jammed between two giant girders, pressed in such a manner that the head was actually squeezed to the thickness of a hand. A woman nearby was rescued naked. Her clothing had been ripped completely off by the friction of debris and timbers.

Many heroic deeds were witnessed that terrible afternoon and evening. Little Mary Flint had shouted out for rescuers to save her friend Nash, who lay severely wounded near her. Mary's cry did help the rescuers to discover Nash's dead body. Nash's brother, caught alongside of him, died the moment he was uncovered. Poor Mary later succumbed to her own injuries.

Just before the flames started, a young girl was pulled to

safety. When questioned as to her condition, she replied that she was indeed all right, and "nothing is hurt." Actually, her right arm had been broken near the wrist. The excitement of her deliverance was so strong that she was totally unaware of her injury.

When the flames began, conditions soon became unbearable. The waterworks pipes connected to the mills had been broken when the building collapsed, and the presence of cotton waste saturated with oil made it almost impossible to put out the flames.

During the hours immediately following the building's collapse, the fire fighters of Lawrence and surrounding towns worked without relief. When the men were so exhausted that they could do no more, women volunteers spelled them, working the fire engines and doing their tasks well. Finally, at one o'clock the next morning, fire fighters won their battle and the conflagration was put out. Survivors and others saw nothing except a broad area of black smouldering ruins where 525 workers had been laboring the day before.

All New England, on hearing of the disaster, sent aid. The overwhelming need was to help children whose parents had perished. Brothers, sisters, and tiny babies had to be helped. Aged, infirm parents who had depended on their dead children were also in desperate need.

The city hall was converted into a hospital to shelter and bed the survivors. A desperate need for blankets, sheets, bandages, and medicine was announced, and eventually these arrived in Lawrence from many locations. Doctors and nurses worked throughout the night to aid the stricken. Many women who had never before attempted such tasks served as nurses in the emergency.

One man later stated that the spectacle he had witnessed had been "awesome, horrible, sickening, loathsome and shocking, all in one."

Sympathizing and curious thousands came to Lawrence from every part of New England. Each arriving train brought scores of visitors. Groups walked over to what was left of the Pemberton Mills and gazed at the rubble in wonder. It seemed an unbelievable disaster. Each day the bridge, the ice-bound canal, and the street that overlooked the debris of what had once been a six-story mill were thronged with living masses of humanity pressing as close to the ruins as the smoking remains would allow.

As the piles of debris gradually cooled, workers searched for additional bodies, applying themselves relentlessly to the gruesome task. On the morning after the disaster a cold, drizzling rain set in, which soon changed to snow.

Derricks were moved in to help in searching the ruins, and as the hours went by, more human remains were uncovered and transported to a so-called dead room nearby. Some bodies were found in almost perfect condition, similar to many remains found after the holocaust at the Cocoanut Grove in Boston more than eighty-two years later. Other bodies were so mutilated and disfigured that they could only be identified by the clothing they wore.

According to the jury brought together to assess blame, the disastrous calamity was caused by the imperfect and insufficient material used and the improper arrangement of that material in the construction of the building. The master mason in charge of the construction told the jury that "the walls were altogether too weak for such a structure." He testified that he had warned the mill owners, but his statements had been entirely disregarded. His warning went unheeded. The building eventually collapsed, bringing death to eighty-eight victims and misery to their relatives. Scores more suffered disfigurement and painful injury.

~~~~~~~~

CHAPTER 2

AMERICA'S FIRST REVOLUTION

The Seal of the town of Ipswich, Massachusetts, declares that village to be "The Birthplace of American Independence." The story behind the inscription is interesting and important but relatively unknown beyond the Ipswich area. Dating the struggle for independence from 1775–76 is to ignore the first American revolution.

In the year 1686, the people of New England were enjoying virtual freedom from British control. The charter granted by King Charles I in 1630 was their only connection with England. They elected their own legislatures and chose their own officials. Later King Charles II felt that the New Englanders were getting out of hand and sent Edward Randolph to Boston as his special investigator. Randolph reported to the king that the colonists would not obey his commands, whereupon he was instructed to appoint commissioners with real power. Randolph's efforts were practically ignored. This so angered Charles that he ordered a *Quo Warranto* in the court of King's Bench, whereby the Massachusetts Bay Charter was rendered legally void. As of May 20, 1686, Massachusetts was without a charter.

During this so-called Inter-Charter period, Joseph Dudley

became president of the Massachusetts Provisional Government. Commissioned by the new monarch, King James II, Dudley governed from May 24, 1686, to the following December 20. He was succeeded by Sir Edmund Andros, a close friend of James II.

Andros arrived in Boston aboard the *Kingfisher*, Sunday, December 19, 1686, to take over the governorship of the disfranchised colonies. A staunch loyalist, the new governor was a gentleman of high connections and came from an important family. There are many who believe with historian John G. Palfrey that Andros had "a personal grudge against Massachusetts, on account of old affronts" and would be "as oppressive and offensive as the King desired." However, any governor sent to New England just after the people had lost their charter would be hated as the agent of a king they neither knew nor understood.

Sir Edmund Andros set up his government during the first half of 1687, appointing twenty-five councilors. In March he announced a repressive plan of taxation without representation and ordered every town in his domain to choose a local tax commissioner. The tax to be collected was twenty pence a head plus a penny a pound on the total valuation of each man's property.

Then he took another step that alienated him from many Bostonians. Belonging to the Church of England, he had no place to worship in Boston, that hotbed of Dissenters, and so demanded that the South Church be made available for him. Protests from church members merely brought a company of redcoats to protect the governor as he worshipped alone. The Bostonians, who were thus forced to wait in the streets for Andros' services to finish, were quite naturally resentful. This enforced triumph of the Church of England over the Dissenters was perhaps the first important step Andros took on his road to imprisonment.

A meeting of great importance to New Englanders took place in the town of Ipswich, Massachusetts, on August 23, 1687—a protest against Andros' action in ordering the appointment of a local commissioner to prepare tax lists.

The citizens of Ipswich went on record as being ready to rebel against the representative of the King of England in his demand for the appointment of a tax commissioner. They refused to appoint the commissioner, claiming that "the sd act doth infringe their Liberty as Free Borne English subjects of his Majesties by interfering with ye statutory Laws of the Land."

Needless to say, Governor Andros did not agree with this statement by the Ipswich town meeting and sent his soldiers to arrest the six most active members: John Andrews, chairman of the selectmen and moderator of the meeting; John Appleton, town clerk; William Goodhue; Robert Kinsman; Thomas French; and the Reverend John Wise. They were brought back to Boston and imprisoned.

On October 3, 1687, after twenty-one days in jail, the six defendants were brought to trial in Boston. The entire colony seethed with excitement and expectation. Judge Joseph Dudley announced what he believed was the brutal truth, that "the people in New England were all slaves . . . and that they must not think the privileges of Englishmen would follow them to the end of the world." The prisoners were convicted and fined from fifteen to fifty pounds each; in addition they were to share costs amounting to four hundred pounds. The Reverend Mr. Wise was forbidden to preach and the others were not allowed to hold office.

Andros had gained a temporary victory. Every town in Massachusetts now fell in line and appointed tax commissioners. But it became known that Judge Dudley had called the New Englanders slaves, and his statement rankled deep in the hearts of the liberty-loving people of Massachusetts. The citizens of Boston and the surrounding countryside held secret meetings and discussions that were to lead to important developments within the next few weeks. When Sir Edmund Andros returned to Boston in March 1689 after a campaign to what is now Maine, he noticed a change in the people's attitude that approached open hostility. Andros' soldiers began deserting by the score, forming small independent bands.

It became noised about that Governor Andros "intended nothing but RUINE TO THEM," and the town of Boston was soon in great turmoil. Local leaders met and agreed that unless they acted quickly, the discharged soldiers and others would start "a great stir and produce a bloody Revolution," as Cotton Mather's son admitted later. They appointed a delegate, probably Cotton Mather, to prepare a Declaration of Independence, indicating that they expected the worst and, secretly, may have hoped for it.

On April 16, 1689, Andros mentioned in a letter that a "general buzzing among the people" was quite noticeable. But it was not until April 18, at eight in the morning, that "it was reported . . . that at the north end they were all in arms." Captain John George of the British frigate *Rose* was seized and at nine o'clock drums were beaten throughout the town as if by prearranged signal. The insurrectionists descended upon the leading lieutenants of Governor Andros. They captured William Sherlock, Ravenscroft, White, George Foxcroft, Edward Randolph, Broadbent, and Crafford and hurried them off to prison. When the keeper objected, he, too, was thrust into prison, and Scates, a bricklayer, became the new jailer.

There was a mighty demand for the aged Simon Bradstreet, governor at the time the charter was withdrawn and now nearly ninety years old, to take over the reins of government. The insurrectionists escorted Bradstreet and several others to the Town House. As they looked down upon the milling crowd gathered in the street, Bradstreet and his friends heard themselves acclaimed as the only persons qualified to establish the new government. The new executives then gathered at the Town House and nervously read over their previously prepared Declaration.

This first American Declaration of Independence is indeed a notable document, surprisingly similar in spirit to the Declaration of 1776. I quote from the more interesting and important parts of the lengthy text:

THE DECLARATION OF THE Gentlemen, Merchants, and Inhabitants of *Boston*, and the Country Adjacent, April 18, 1689.

We have seen more than a decade of Years rolled away, since the *English* World had the Discovery of an horrid . . . Plot . . . to Crush and break a Country . . . entirely.

To get us within the reach of the desolation desired for us . . . we . . . first have our Charter Vacated . . . before it was possible for us to appear at Westminster. . . .

We were put under a *President and Council* without any liberty for an Assembly . . . by a Commission from his *Majesty*. . . . The Commission was as *Illegal* for the form of it, as the way of obtaining it was *Malicious* and *unreasonable*. . . . Yet we made no Resistance thereunto . . . because we took pains to make ourselves believe as much as ever we could of the Whedle then offer'd unto us. . . .

In little more than half a year we saw this Commission superseded by another, yet more Absolute and Arbitrary, with which Sir *Edmund Andros* arrived as our Governor: who . . . planned to make Laws and raise Taxes as he pleased. . . . We were chiefly *squeez'd* by a crew of abject Persons, fetched from *New York* . . . by these were extraordinary and intollerable Fees extorted from everyone upon all occasions. . . .

It was now plainly affirmed . . . that the people in *New England* were all *Slaves*. . . . Accordingly we have been treated with multiplied contradictions to *Magna Charta*, the rights of which we laid claim to.

Persons who did but peacefully object against the raising of Taxes without an Assembly, have been for it fined, some twenty, some thirty, and others fifty Pounds. . . . Packt and pickt Juries have been very common things. . . . Without a *verdict*, yea, without a Jury sometimes have People been fined most unrighteously, and some . . . have been kept in long and close Imprisonment without . . . *Habeas Corpus* allowed unto them. . . .

Writs of Intrusion began everywhere to be served on People. . . . We do therefore seize upon the Persons of those few *Ill men* which have been (next to our Sins) the grand Authors of our Miseries. . . . In the meantime . . . we commit our Enterprise unto Him *who hears the cry of the Oppressed.*

The contributors to this Declaration of Independence then composed a letter to Sir Edmund Andros, telling him that the people had taken arms and seized the town. They said that for the purpose of "quieting and securing . . . the People from . . . emminent Dangers . . . We judge it necessary you forthwith surrender and deliver up the Government and Fortification. . . . Otherwise we are assured they will endeavor the taking of the Fortification by Storm, if any Opposition be made." The letter was signed by the fifteen leaders in the Town House, including Simon Bradstreet, John Nelson, William Stoughton, and Waite Winthrop.

Sir Edmund Andros was barricaded in at the defenses on

Fort Hill when the letter from the revolutionists reached him. Andros was sooned joined by Joseph Dudley and Colonel (Charles) Lidget. The governor asked Dudley if he would go out to the homes of the ministers of Boston and request them to appear at the fort, where possibly they could quiet the people. But Dudley told Andros that he would be captured the moment he left the fort, and the plan was abandoned.

At the Town House when the venerable Simon Bradstreet went out on the balcony to accept the cheers of the multitudes, as I mentioned above, his act probably prevented bloodshed, as historian Samuel G. Drake wrote in 1856. Colors were run up on Beacon Hill as a signal to the thousands on the Charlestown side that the moment for action was at hand. In the harbor the British frigate *Rose* opened her gunports and hoisted her battle flags. However, Captain Winthrop sent a note out to the lieutenant in command of the frigate saying that if the *Rose* fired a single shot into the town, her master, Captain John George, who had been captured by the revolutionists, would be executed. This bold note accomplished its purpose. Though the lieutenant commanding the *Rose* pretended he would soon fire, he never did, and finally accepted defeat and sent in his sails as a token of surrender.

But the excitement was not yet ended. Watching his chances, Governor Andros signaled for a boat to approach from the frigate and went down on the Battery Wharf with ten of his associates. The unruly mob outguessed the group, however, and captured the boat as it landed at the wharf. In the boat were hand grenades, small arms, and "a quantity of match!" Governor Andros and his party hurried back to the fort when they saw their scheme had miscarried.

A battalion of soldiers led by John Nelson of Long Island, Boston Harbor, then appeared at the fort and ordered Governor Andros to surrender. For a moment it looked as though the guns of the fort would be fired into the unruly crowd of soldiers and civilians, but after due consideration Sir Edmund decided that surrender was his best move. It had been a bloodless revolution.

After his acknowledgment of defeat, Andros was taken to the Town House, where Mr. Bradstreet waited to receive him. William Stoughton was the first to speak. He told the governor in no uncertain terms that he had only himself to blame for "the disaster" that had befallen him. Andros was confined for the night in Mr. John Usher's house and the next day taken to Fort Hill and imprisoned. Later he was incarcerated at Castle Island, from which he made two unsuccessful attempts to escape. His first escape attempt was foiled when an alert guard noticed military boots showing under the woman's clothing Andros was wearing as disguise. The second time he got as far as Rhode Island before being apprehended.

Happily for the people of New England, affairs in England were also reaching a state of crisis. A new king, William of Orange, was brought over from the Continent to take the throne away from James II. Increase Mather, who had fled from Boston to England, obtained audience with the new king and interceded as best he could on behalf of the New Englanders. On July 4, 1689, exactly eighty-seven years before the Declaration of Independence was drawn up in Philadelphia, King William told Increase Mather that he would approve the results of the American Revolution of 1689, without, however, renewing the old charter. The following month the king sent a Royal Letter ratifying the government of New England, but actually the colonists did not receive all the liberties for which they asked.

Stuart opposition to William of Orange was still strong in England and did not collapse until the Battle of the Boyne on July 1, 1690. But with the defeat of the Stuart supporters, there was no more danger to the New Englanders from across the sea. They would not be punished for their revolution in

New England, for in England the same thing had happened, and they would be allowed many of the things for which they had rebelled.

It was not until the 1760's that England and New England were once again in conflict, and then the difficulties could not be resolved without a great war. Whether or not the accession to the English throne by William of Orange prevented this country from realizing her independence in 1689 rather than 1775 is a question that offers an interesting subject for debate.

CHAPTER 3

~~~~~~

MOLL PITCHER

Thirty years ago, when Alton Hall Blackington took me to the site of the famed Moll Pitcher's home on the North Shore of Massachusetts, I was impressed by the atmosphere that seemed to pervade the area, even though Moll Pitcher had been dead for generations. Blackington, who was always meticulous in his research and writings, explained to me the deep hold this seer of a former century had everywhere in New England.

Samuel Adams Drake was the first writer of the modern era to tell us of the accomplishments of Moll Pitcher. In his book on New England legends, Drake explains that

[the city of Lynn] is likely to be celebrated throughout all time as having been the residence of the most successful fortune-teller of her day and generation—we might also say of whom we have any account in mystical lore, ancient or modern. While she lived she was without a rival in her peculiar art, and the prophetic words that she let fall were capable of being transmuted into gold.

It was once said of Napoleon that he left a family, but no successor. Moll Pitcher left no one her wonderful gift of foretelling the future by practising palmistry, or by

57

simply gazing into the bottom of a teacup. . . . Yet even the most incredulous were compelled to admit her predictions to be wholly unaccountable; while those who came to laugh went away vanquished, if not fully convinced.

What is singular is that her reputation has rather increased than diminished with time. We have no account of her dupes, nor is there any "Exposure" extant.*

Moll Pitcher dwelt at the foot of High Rock, a remarkable cliff of dull red porphyry, which stands high over Lynn as the Citadel does over Quebec. During the fifty years that she pursued her trade of fortune-telling she was known all over New England for her successful predictions, some of which occurred ten and even twenty years after she had foretold them. She was a woman of shrewdness, penetration, and wit, and the residents of Lynn accepted her claim to foreknowledge because of the unequivocal testimony of the many hundreds who could attest to the accuracy of her predictions.

According to reports of the period, Moll was not the decrepit, withered, and toothless crone of Spenser, or Otways' "wrinkled hag, with age grown double,/Picking dry sticks and mumbling to herself." In the prime of her life Moll was a woman of medium stature, with an unusually large head, dark brown hair, and a thin, pale, and rather intellectual face. Her countenance was clouded with habitual sadness, indicating a mind burdened with the confidences, even the crimes, of the hundreds of individuals who sought her advice. She had a full forehead, arched eyebrows, eyes that seemed to read the secret thoughts of those who approached her, a nose "inclined to be long," and thin lips, but her visage had none of the wildness of the traditional witch of legend and lore.

* Samuel Adams Drake, *New England Legends*, pages 137–148.

During her active years, when she lived in a lonely and little frequented section of Lynn, Moll was consulted not only by the poor and ignorant, but by the rich and educated as well. Her most valued clients came from the wealthy seaports of the area. Common sailors and sea captains, cabin boys and the owners of ships, all visited her humble abode to learn the luck of coming voyages. It is even claimed that vessels were deserted on the eve of sailing because of Moll's predictions of doom.

Her advice was also much sought by treasure seekers, a rather numerous class in her day. To them Moll would reply, "Fools! If I knew where money was buried, do you think I would part with the secret?"

Moll Pitcher, born in 1738, was originally from Marblehead and is said to have inherited the gift of prophecy from her grandfather, John Dimond, who had the reputation there of being a wizard. Whenever a violent gale at sea arose, Dimond would go to the old burying ground on the hill, and there in the midst of the darkness and the storm, he would direct vessels then at sea, instructing them on how to weather the gale. Pacing up and down among the gravestones, in a voice that could be heard even above the howling of the tempest, he would shout his orders to the helmsman or the crew, just as if he were actually on the quarter-deck of the craft. Although astounded and terrified by his behavior, very few of the simple fisherfolk of Marblehead doubted his ability to bring ships safely into port.

Moll Pitcher's father was master of a small vessel and was not noted for wizardry of any type. In 1760 Moll, whose proper name was Mary Dimond, married Robert Pitcher, a shoemaker. She lived until 1813 when she was seventy-five. According to Lynn historian Alonzo Lewis, who remembered her, Moll was related to some of the best families in Essex.

He states that, except for her fortune-telling pretension, there was nothing disreputable in her life, and that her descendants were living and respected when he wrote.

Such is the picture of the celebrated fortune teller that has come down to us from her contemporaries. However, American literature presents quite a different portrait, drawn in verse.

In the year 1832 John Greenleaf Whittier published, anonymously, a poem in which Moll Pitcher is presented less than favorably. In an unusual opening statement to the poem, Whittier says:

> I have not enough of the poetical mania in my disposition to dream of converting, by an alchemy more potent than that of the old philosophers, a limping couplet into a brace of doubloons, or a rickety stanza into a note of hand. Moll Pitcher (there's music in the name) is the offspring of a few weeks of such leisure as is afforded by indisposition, and is given to the world in all its original negligence—the thoughts fresh as when first originated.

Whittier's poem is the story of a maiden, fond and fair, whose sailor lover has gone on a long voyage to sea, where "He sought for gold—for yellow gold," in order to return a rich man and marry the girl waiting at home for him. While he is away, the maiden's mind becomes filled with gloomy forebodings concerning her lover. Obeying an uncontrollable impulse, she seeks the well-trodden path leading to Moll Pitcher's abode, in order to learn her destiny. While on her way to the house, she encounters Moll, who is thus described:

> She stood upon a bare tall crag
> Which overlooked her rugged cot—
> A wasted, gray, and meagre hag,
> In features evil as her lot.

She had the crooked nose of a witch,
  And a crooked back and chin;
And in her gait she had a hitch,
And in her hand she carried a switch,
  To aid her work of sin,—
A twig of wizard hazel, which
Had grown beside a haunted ditch,
Where a mother her nameless babe had thrown
To the running water and merciless stone.

  The fortune teller has a secret enmity towards her trembling
visitor and wickedly determines to bring evil on the girl. Moll
leading the way,

The twain passed in—a low dark room,
  With here and there a crazy chair,
A broken glass—a dusty loom—
A spinning-wheel—a birchen broom,
  The witch's courier of the air,
As potent as that steed of wings
  On which the Meccan prophet rode
Above the wreck of meaner things
  Unto the Houris' bright abode.
A low dull fire by flashes shone
Across the gray and cold hearthstone,
Flinging at times a trembling glare
On the low roof and timbers bare.

  In these mysterious surroundings, the weird woman proceeds
to try her art by looking into the sorceress's cup. Presently she
speaks.

Out spoke the witch,—'I know full well
  Why thou hast sought my humble cot!

Come, sit thee down,—the tale I tell
  May not be soon forgot.'
She threw her pale blue cloak aside,
  And stirred the whitening embers up,
And long and curiously she eyed
  The figures of her mystic cup;
And low she muttered while the light
Gave to her lips a ghastlier white,
And her sunk eyes' unearthly glaring
Seemed like the taper's latest flaring:
'Dark hair—eyes black—a goodly form—
  A maiden weeping—wild dark sea—
A tall ship tossing in the storm—
  A black wreck floating—*where is he?*
Give me thy hand—how soft, and warm,
  And fair its tapering fingers seem!—
And who that sees it now would dream
That winter's snow would seem less chill
Ere long than these soft fingers will?
A lovely palm!—how delicate
  Its veined and wandering lines are drawn!
Yet each are prophets of thy fate—
  Ha!—this is sure a fearful one!
That sudden cross—that blank beneath—
  What may these evil signs betoken?
Passion and sorrow, fear and death—
  A human spirit crushed and broken!
Oh, thine hath been a pleasant dream,
But darker shall its waking seem!'

Overcome by the terrible prophecy, to which her own fears
give ready belief, the poor girl loses her senses. She is always
watching for the sail in the offing, but it does not come. Wandering up and down the rocky shores of Nahant, she gazes

vacantly out to sea. Then one day, in spite of Moll's fatal prediction, the lover's ship sails into the bay, and with it the one thing capable of restoring the maiden's reason again.

The witch, however, does not escape the consequences of her malevolence. She dies miserably in her wretched hovel, cared for in her last moments by a little child of the woman she has so cruelly wronged.

I prefer the real story of Moll Pitcher to that of the poet Whittier.

~~~~~~~~

CHAPTER 4

FANNY CAMPBELL,
WHO LOVED AND WON

No less than twenty female pirates have been mentioned in the various books I have written. Among them were Madame Ching and Mrs. Lo, who operated pirate fleets after their husbands' deaths, and Madame Wong, who began her career without help from the other sex. The Pennsylvania-born pirate Rachel Wall, who married the man of her choice at Long Wharf in Boston, was mentioned in a broadside, but we do not know why she became a pirate. Ann Bonney and Mary Read became pirates for the sheer adventure of it. Mrs. Edward Jordan became a renegade in 1809 when she and her husband stole a ship. The Danish woman outlaw Alwida became a pirate to avoid marriage but eventually married the very person whose attentions made her take up piracy in the first place. Maria Cobham was a female fiend who relished her murderous avocation.

Fanny Campbell, the subject of this chapter, turned pirate for one single, unselfish motive.

In 1917 John Austin Belden of Wareham, Massachusetts,

was suffering from the grippe. Visited by Dr. Charles Edward Lovell, a relative of his, he began talking about ancestors in general. Growing more and more personal, Belden finally reached a point in the discussion where the doctor held up his hand.

"Now, John," he began, "this is all well and good, but I advise you to be careful about asking me to tell you too many things concerning our ancestors. You know, I am in possession of knowledge which you might not wish to discover."

"What do you mean by that?"

"Well, it's this way, John. If I tell you what I know, you may always be sorry I spoke up; and if I don't tell you, then everything will be as it was before. Would you like to know all about your ancestors? If not, the knowledge will die with me. Which way do you want it?"

"I'd like to know, Charles, especially now that you've got my curiosity aroused. You might as well tell me what you're hinting at and get it over with. Come on, Charles; let's have it."

And so it was that Dr. Lovell revealed to his astonished relative that one of his ancestors had turned pirate more than a hundred years earlier and had never been apprehended. Dr. Lovell explained that the entire carefully written story was in his possession, and if John Belden wished it, Dr. Lovell would will the material to him.

In October 1930 Dr. Lovell died, and Mr. Belden came to possess the precious document with its startling revelation. The day he acquired the information Belden took it upstairs into his room. There he opened the sealed envelope, which contained the strange history of his own great-great-grand-mother, together with a drawing of her in color. He stayed in his room that night until he had learned all the remarkable facts of his ancestor's life. Her story follows:

In the year 1773, two fishermen, Henry Campbell and

Richard Lovell, lived side by side at the base of High Rock, Lynn, Massachusetts. Campbell's daughter, Fanny, and Lovell's son, William, had grown up with each other and fallen in love. William was then nineteen and Fanny a year younger.

William Lovell, who had sailed and fished in Boston Bay from the time he could walk, was anxious to become a deep-sea sailor and received permission from his parents to take a voyage from Boston. Six months later he returned, tanned and mature, and Fanny was very pleased with the change in her young friend. William told her about the foreign lands he had visited, and she in turn expressed a desire to make an ocean voyage herself.

Then came the eve of his second sailing, and the two climbed to the top of High Rock, where they talked of the future. Fanny was an active girl. She rowed a boat, shot panthers in the nearby Lynn Woods, rode a horse, and could handle a sailboat with the best of men. William confided to her that he would leave the sea if she so desired, but she told him to go ahead and work his way up until he was captain of his own vessel. At the conclusion of their talk they returned home.

William Lovell arose early the next morning and sailed away aboard the ship *Royal Kent*.

Meanwhile, at the Campbell residence, Fanny had another caller, a young man William had never met. His name was Captain Robert Burnet, and he was an officer in the British navy. Captain Burnet at first was but casually interested in Fanny, however later his attentions turned to love.

While at sea, William thought frequently of the girl back in Lynn and determined to ask her hand in marriage on his return. But before this could be, a day's sail from Port au Plate, a suspicious-looking schooner appeared on the horizon and gave chase.

As the stranger closed the distance between the two vessels, she displayed a skull and crossbones from her forepeak. The captain of the *Royal Kent* ordered all hands to prepare the cannons for defense, and soon the ship was firing at the pirate craft. The six-pounders caused devastating damage to the sea ruffians, but still they came nearer and nearer. Finally the pirates overtook the *Royal Kent*, threw grapnels across to the ship, and boarded her. Fighting their way along the deck, the marine bandits soon overwhelmed the American sailors, whom they outnumbered four to one. In the skirmish the *Royal Kent's* captain killed the pirate chieftain and in turn was run through by the sword of another pirate. In all, the American sailors killed more than twice the number they lost, but this worked against them afterward. With their numbers diminished, the pirates forced the Americans to join their ranks. The *Royal Kent* was then scuttled.

The pirates went ashore at Tortuga, each man burying his own share of the treasure taken from the *Royal Kent*. No one knew where his fellow pirate had buried his loot; and if a man happened to be killed, it was only by chance that this treasure was ever recovered.

The pirates soon went to sea again. Seriously wounded in the engagement, Lovell was allowed to recover before he was ordered to take an active part in sailing the pirate craft. One night the ship was practically becalmed close to the shores of Cuba. Lovell and two companions, Jack Herbert and Henry Breed, were chosen for the same watch. Together they decided to make an attempt for freedom before morning. The three New Englanders were in full charge of the vessel during the graveyard watch. A light wind had sprung up, and when the moment for action came, they headed the schooner into it, lashed the wheel amidships, and silently let a small boat over the side. With great caution they put a few provisions aboard the boat and then scrambled down the rope ladder. Keeping an eye on the schooner, they rowed desperately for the shore half a mile away, and when the breeze freshened they hoisted sail and set a course for Havana.

After many hardships they reached the Cuban capital, elated at their success in escaping the pirates. Before they could find friends, however, the three Americans were arrested on suspicion of being pirates themselves. Technically they had been pirates ever since they were put aboard the outlaw schooner, and they had no proof that they had been forced to join the buccaneers.* Thrown into jail before they could get help, they waited week after week for their trial. Six months went by before they were brought to the advocate for their appearance in court. When no evidence was brought forward against them, the judge ordered them returned to their cells. Their despair was complete.

Back in Massachusetts, Fanny Campbell waited anxiously with no word from her lover. Months went by. Captain Burnet's visits to her home became more and more frequent, but Fanny remained true to her sailor sweetheart.

In Havana, the three Americans watched the months pass, but no one came to release them. Finally, two years after they had been imprisoned, William's friend, Jack Herbert, escaped from the jail. After making his way to an American ship then at the pier in Havana, he told his story and received permission to hide aboard until the vessel was due to sail. Then he was allowed to travel back to Boston on the ship. Bearing a letter to Fanny from William, he visited the girl shortly after landing. His unexpected call made her very happy. She questioned him about the great bastille in which William and young Breed were still incarcerated, and he explained how the guards

---

* Under similar conditions, to escape the possible charge of piracy, other suspected pirates brought the infamous John Phillip's head to Boston in a pickle barrel as evidence. See my *Pirates and Buccaneers of the Atlantic Coast*, p. 123.

were placed around the prison in such numbers that it was practically hopeless to attempt an escape.

When it was time for Herbert to return home, Fanny obtained his address—the foot of Copp's Hill in Boston. As he left, she mysteriously told him to make himself ready at a moment's notice for a strange adventure she was planning, an event that might take place at any time, day or night, in the near future. Although he was bewildered by her secretive manner, Jack Herbert agreed, and as he traveled by stagecoach from Lynn to Boston his mind dwelt on Fanny Campbell and her plans.

Captain Burnet called on Fanny the following evening and learned that William was still alive. Burnet had never considered William a real obstacle to his intentions, believing the lad merely a childhood sweetheart who would soon be forgotten. Fanny, however, convinced Burnet that night that she loved William alone, and in his disappointment the captain left her home earlier than he had planned, chagrined at the turn events had taken.

At Copp's Hill in Boston, Jack Herbert awaited developments. A week after his visit to Fanny's home, a man dressed as a common sailor knocked at his door and reminded him of his promise to be ready for a strange adventure. The visitor explained the situation carefully and got Herbert's agreement to sail on the brig *Constance*, a new sailing vessel soon to start a voyage to Cuba.

The following night Herbert went aboard the brig to find her well armed. The captain, Brownless by name, was a tyrant; the first mate, Banning, an imbecile; but the second officer, an unusual character named Channing, was a good sailor and well liked by the Americans in the crew.

As it happened, the captain was planning to proceed to England by way of Cuba. Once in England the entire crew would be pressed into the British navy for a term of three years. Channing already knew of the captain's scheme and had decided to use it to his own advantage.

Early one day when the *Constance* had reached the warmer waters of the West Indies and the brig was less than two days' sail from Cuba, Channing went down into the captain's cabin and found the master just getting up. Stepping to the captain's table, he seized a brace of pistols there and took a cutlass down from the bulkhead. Then Channing confronted the master.

"Captain Brownless, you are my prisoner!"

"Sir?"

"You are my prisoner!"

"Mutiny?"

"If you wish, but resistance is futile. If you attempt to leave the cabin you are a dead man."

Realizing his weapons were gone, Captain Brownless agreed to surrender. Channing tied up the captain and locked him in his cabin. Going to the quarters of the first mate, he explained what had happened.

"Why, that's piracy!" shouted Banning.

"Yes," answered Channing, "you are right."

Banning looked up at the young man and noticed his determined countenance. "How about me? Will you spare my life?"

"There's no danger at present if you remain quiet."

Channing then tied Banning up and locked him in his quarters, after which he went to Jack Herbert, who had the helm.

"Call the crew aft, Jack," he ordered. Ten minutes later, with the crew assembled on the deck, Channing explained that he had taken over the ship. Although there was some grumbling, shouts of delight came from every American present when it was learned that Captain Brownless had planned to impress them into the British navy as soon as they reached England. They agreed to accept Channing as their new captain.

The cook, a British subject, had other ideas and decided to

kill Channing and take the ship back as soon as he had the opportunity. Strangely enough, Captain Brownless had worked
out a similar plan, having made arrangements with the brig's
jailer to escape. The following night, independent of each
other, the two men started for Channing's quarters. Meeting in
the darkness outside the second mate's door, they fought and
fatally wounded each other, each thinking he had engaged in
combat with Channing.

A crew member came across the bodies and aroused Channing at once. The pirate captain was horrified at what had
occurred. At noon the following day he gathered the sailors
together for a burial service at sea. After Channing read a
portion of the Bible, the remains of the two men were slid
overboard into the sea and the voyage continued.

Several days later the *Constance* sighted a British bark, the
George out of Bristol. Confident of the firepower of his six
carronades, the *George*'s captain decided to engage in battle
with what he suspected was a pirate craft, but after a short
exchange with cannon, the Britishers realized they were losing
the engagement and surrendered. They were soon secured below deck on the bark, command of which was given to Jack
Herbert.

The two vessels sailed along side by side for a few days,
when suddenly mutiny broke out aboard the *George*. Channing
watched from the other craft as Herbert was roped and thrown
to the deck. He crossed over to the *George* at once in a small
boat. Going aboard with drawn pistols, he put down the mutiny, but was forced to kill one of the mutineers.

Finally the ships reached the desired point off the Cuban
shore near where William Lovell was a prisoner. Channing
ordered Jack Herbert to pick eight loyal members of his crew
and tell them all about the fort where his two former comrades
were imprisoned. Late that night the nine conspirators left the
vessel in a small boat and rowed for the fort. When they

reached land, the sailors put one man on the beach to guard their boat. The others crept silently toward the nearest sentry. Jumping on the unfortunate Spaniard, they quickly overcame him. They took care of the next guard in a similar way. Two more soldiers, representing the entire complement of sentries then remaining on duty, were surrounded and tied up, after which the four victims, still relatively unharmed, were carried into the guardhouse and locked away for the night.

Armed with the keys, Herbert stealthily walked with his associates into the subterranean passageway that led to the cell. Quietly unlocking the door, he found Breed and Lovell, awakened them, and led them out of the prison. An hour later all eleven Americans were in the boat, rowing desperately for the brig. Their luck had been good, but it couldn't possibly last much longer. Sure enough, just as they pulled up to the side of the *George,* they all heard the distant, unmistakable roll of the fort drums. The citadel was being aroused, for their daring feat had been discovered.

The anchors were weighed and the sails set. The two vessels were soon a substantial distance offshore and, as it turned out, all danger from the Spaniards was over.

Captain Channing, whose greeting to William Lovell was reserved but friendly, appointed him first mate of the *Constance.* Several days later the captain called Lovell down into the cabin and there revealed to the startled mate that he, Captain Channing, was in reality Fanny Campbell. She had dyed her face brown, cut her hair short, and donned a marine officer's uniform to complete the disguise. Needless to say, the pair had a happy reunion, but Fanny cautioned William against letting the others know.

For the next few days the *Constance* and the *George* continued their voyage uneventfully, but then they fought and captured a British merchantman. From this ship they learned that the British and Americans were engaged in a formal war, the Revolution. Realizing that her two craft could become privateers and escape the stigma of piracy, Fanny called the crews together and explained the situation. All but four men who were British agreed to become privateers. Of course it was not in order, but Fanny declared that formal application for privateer status would be made the moment they reached Massachusetts.

The next day a British armed sloop appeared and was quickly overcome by the two American craft. The discovery that Captain Burnet, who had sought Fanny's hand, was an officer aboard the sloop was quite a shock to both Fanny and William, but Burnet was shackled below with the other prisoners. Although Captain Burnet recognized Fanny, he did not tell the Americans that their captain was a woman, and they never did find out.

Fanny heard from the prisoners that Boston was occupied by the British, so she set course for Marblehead. It was in that harbor a week later that her two craft were made legal privateers of the new nation.

The next day Fanny and William reached High Rock, Lynn, and made their presence known to their happy families. The two lovers announced that their marriage would take place the very next week. After their wedding, William reluctantly went back to sea as captain of one of the privateers. His friend, Jack Herbert, was master of the other.

William served his country until the war came to an end, after which he made several long trips to China and then retired from the sea. By that time the family of William and Fanny Lovell was a large one. When their sons and daughters grew up and were married, the fact that Fanny had been a pirate at one time was kept secret. Their descendants are many and, as I have already mentioned, include John Austin Belden of Wareham.

CHAPTER 5

NANCY'S BROOK

Dino Valz was the first person to take me around the White Mountains. Dr. Robert Moody of Boston University introduced the two of us in 1934 when I was struggling with my first book. Dino had climbed the famed Matterhorn, and when he suggested doing the Presidential Range, Mrs. Snow and I accepted the challenge and went with him. I'll always remember his motto—"just one more hill." After what seemed like a hike of a hundred miles we all spent the night in the Lake of the Clouds hut, actually a substantial building. There was an overflow of visitors, and at least two dozen couples slept on the tables, arranged side by side in one long row.

Dino was the first person to tell me about Nancy and Nancy's Brook. Since then I've done a tremendous amount of research. The beginnings of the story were written more than a century ago by Anna C. Swasey, said to have been the great-granddaughter of Nancy's father, who was killed in the battle of Bunker Hill. Her account is the chief source of information of the early part of the story.

The tale of Nancy's tragedy begins in the year 1778, when a tired, bedraggled traveler of slight but erect build entered the tiny village of Dartmouth. His appearance was that of a poor man, but an "indescribable air of good-breeding" set him aside from the usual run of tramps who from time to time visited the area.

Approaching a farm house, he decided to knock at the door and offer his services if a job could be found for him. A middle-aged woman answered his knock, and he bowed deeply.

"I am looking for honest work," he explained.

"Come inside," was the woman's answer. "My husband has just returned from the field and might be able to help you."

The husband stepped into the room, and when he learned that the slenderly built traveler needed work, he explained that the man should apply at the farmhouse of Colonel Joseph Whipple, who lived half a mile away.

"I heard that two of his hands enlisted today, and he might be able to hire you."

The farmer told the visitor, Henry Lorrimer, that he should follow the path outside the house until he came to a deeply-rutted road. There he should turn to the right. Colonel Whipple's residence was the first frame house he would reach, and the colonel was the richest man in the countryside.

Henry thanked the farmer and was given a mug of cool water and a piece of brown bread. After finishing his repast, he started out for Colonel Whipple's residence.

It was nearly sunset when he reached the Whipple farmhouse, and Henry was very tired. He had observed the Crystal Hills in the southeast as he hiked, while off to the southwest the blue Franconia Mountains were visible. Slowly rising smoke from a dozen widely scattered chimneys enhanced the countryside vista.

Henry knocked at the door, and a pretty girl dressed in blue homespun answered.

"Colonel Whipple's daughter, I presume?"

"No, I am Nancy, one of the help."

He explained why he was at the door and asked if he could

talk with Colonel Whipple. Nancy went to fetch her employer, who soon appeared.

"Good evening," said the colonel. "How may I help you?"

"I wish work and have walked all the distance from Boston to obtain it," explained Henry.

The two men engaged in conversation, during which Colonel Whipple discovered Henry's name and that, although Henry was willing, he knew nothing of farm life. However, the colonel accepted him on trial and told him to be on hand for the prayer service at eight. Henry was then sent to the kitchen to have supper, which consisted of boiled ham, venison, brown bread, and milk. As he finished, the clock struck eight and the occupants of the house filed into the room. Besides the colonel, there were Mrs. Miller, the housekeeper; two farm hands; and Nancy.

Colonel Whipple opened the Bible and read the Fifty-first Psalm by the illumination of Mrs. Miller's candle. After a simple prayer he gave the benediction, and then the two farm hands left for bed.

Nancy also retired for the night, after which Mrs. Miller showed Henry to his room. Five minutes later he was asleep on a feather bed.

The next morning Henry was given both indoor and outdoor tasks. His body was as frail as a woman's, and his accomplishments soon showed the housekeeper that he was more help in the kitchen than in the yard. Thus Henry often worked alongside Nancy indoors, and they enjoyed "each other's society."

One day a thunderstorm approached just as the farmers were gathering hay. The help of everyone on the farm was needed to get the hay into the barn before the rain began. Henry's hands were soon blistered by his unaccustomed use of the scythe.

The very next day Mrs. Miller faced a minor emergency. The raspberry patch was threatened by a windstorm that would "shake 'em all off," and she sent Nancy and Henry to pick the fruit. They were successful in getting several quarts of berries, but finally Henry's blistered hands bothered him so much that he sat down to rest.

"I wonder why your hands blister while the other men's hands are not affected," mused Nancy, as she sat down beside him.

Henry explained that he was not used to farming and that he originally came from Devonshire, England. Surprised, Nancy told him that she, too, had crossed the ocean from Devonshire to settle with her family in Charlestown. Her father had been killed at Bunker Hill, and their house had been burned. Nancy's mother had died of grief several weeks later. Colonel Whipple, her father's friend, was willing to adopt Nancy, but she was independent and preferred to join his household as a servant.

Henry then confessed that he had a very dark past, involving card playing and fighting. His father was French, of "brilliant exterior but thoroughly selfish," and had married his mother for her money. She died of consumption when Henry was seven, and by the time he was ten his father had squandered all her wealth and left the country.

His mother's brother adopted Henry, sent him to Eton, and for a time all went well. Then his father's "untamed blood" showed in Henry's veins, and he neglected his studies.

When his next quarterly allowance came, he ran away to Dover, signed on an American ship, landed in New York, and there he left the vessel. Henry then wrote to his uncle, who responded with a farewell sum of three hundred pounds and a note stating that "the vile French blood of your father will probably be your ruin."

Henry took up card playing and soon was desperately in danger of financial disgrace. He wagered everything on one throw of the dice, and when he lost attempted to stab his opponent with a stiletto. Henry was forcibly restrained until he calmed down, and the next morning he decided to leave New York. He hiked north until he reached Massachusetts, from where he decided to head for the mountains of New Hampshire. He had ended his lengthy walk at Colonel Joseph Whipple's farmhouse.

By the time his long tale was concluded, both Henry and Nancy realized that they should get back to the housekeeper with their raspberries, for Mrs. Miller would begin to wonder. Before they left the berry patch, however, they decided that they were more than just interested in each other.

The weeks went by and what the farmers called Royal October "stained the vast forests with a thousand shades and tints. Mount Agiochook was already snow-capped."

One day a load of apples arrived at Mrs. Miller's kitchen, and had to be "festooned," that is, cut up and strung to dry for the winter. Of course, Nancy and Henry were chosen for the task, and all day long and into the evening they cut and strung the fruit. Mrs. Miller visited them long after darkness had fallen, and they were still cutting and stringing.

"I'd help you, but two's company and three is not," she said, and left them.

Prompted by Mrs. Miller's comments, Henry and Nancy agreed that they were very fond of each other, and before the night was over they had made plans to marry. The entire farm was informed of their decision, and soon a definite date for the marriage was arranged.

Of course, the countryside reacted to the engagement. One of the most outspoken was old Dame Wentworth, relative by marriage to Governor Benning Wentworth of Portsmouth, who at sixty-three had married twenty-year-old Martha Hilton.

"There's my son John at six feet two," she complained. "She could have had him last year and been Mistress Wentworth. She has thrown herself away on this slim boy. Well, she won't live to see the day when she'll wish she had married my boy instead," she finished with far more truth than she realized.

Nancy's plans now involved a trousseau, and she thought at once of the Indian friend whom she had nursed through typhoid fever. The Indian lived in Lancaster, nine miles away. She was an excellent seamstress and had promised that she would make Nancy's wedding dress when the time came. Nancy decided to go to Portsmouth, purchase the cloth for her gown, and take it to Lancaster for the fitting. She had saved a substantial sum while working for Colonel Whipple, and she took a modest portion of it when she left Dartmouth.

Nancy journeyed to Portsmouth by horseback on October 27, obtained the cloth for her wedding dress, and was back in Dartmouth two days later. She was now ready for the ride to Lancaster. As Henry was needed on the farm, a hired man was to go with her. It was just two weeks before the wedding when they galloped away from the farmhouse. The couple's new home was finished and furnished, and except for her wedding gown, Nancy's sewing was complete. It was now the middle of November and the trees were bare, but the day was warm and bright. A squirrel ran across their path, and every so often a deer would be seen. As they neared Lancaster the distant ring of a woodcutter's axe was heard and then faded away in the distance.

Meanwhile, matters were taking a turn that eventually would spell disaster.

Colonel Whipple had an important business transaction in Portsmouth which he had to attend to in person within ten days. As the weather was so favorable, he decided to leave within a few hours and asked Henry if he would like to accompany him. Henry answered in the negative and returned to his room, where he had put Nancy's relatively small fortune in gold and currency. But his restless mind suddenly became overwrought; he wondered if the colonel had already started out.

Going to the barn, he found his employer about to saddle his horse and finished the task for him.

"Sure you'll not change your mind?" questioned the colonel. Henry hesitated. He thought of the glamour of the relatively large community of Portsmouth and of the money with which Nancy had entrusted him.

The colonel climbed into his saddle. He looked at Henry and asked, "Are you sure you don't want to come along?"

"I'll go!" cried Henry. "Just give me a minute." He rushed up to his room, then flooded with sunlight, and placed all Nancy's wealth into a money belt, which he secured around his waist. Ten minutes later the two men galloped away from the Whipple farm, just as Nancy had done several hours earlier.

Meeting Deacon Hiram Piper on the horsepath, they asked him if they could get him anything in Portsmouth, but the deacon told them there was nothing he needed as he was on his way to Lancaster.

Hours later Henry found himself wondering whether the Devil had made him go to Portsmouth with the money, but by the time the two men entered the outskirts of the town he had convinced himself that he had taken the money to prove that the Devil and his father's bad blood would not win out this time. He would return with the money to his beloved Nancy, confess that he had for a few hours given in to the Devil, and all would be well again.

But it was not to be.

The colonel and Henry stopped for the night and camped. They would continue to Portsmouth early the next morning. Meanwhile Deacon Piper reached Lancaster and saw Nancy on the street as she was leaving the seamstress's home. He asked her how long Henry was staying in Portsmouth.

"That's the first I've heard he was there," Nancy replied, and she began to feel afraid. Bidding good-bye to the deacon, she hurried over to the seamstress, told her to put the finishing touches to the wedding dress, donned her bonnet and cloak, and with a few almost frantic farewells, started out for home. She could not go by horseback, for the farm hand had ridden to Northumberland and was not due back until after dark.

Nancy had often hiked the distance of nine miles to Dartmouth and decided to walk. She started out at once, reaching Colonel Whipple's residence in less than three and a half hours. Of course Mrs. Miller was flabbergasted to see her.

"What message did Henry leave for me?" were Nancy's first words, and Mrs. Miller explained that the colonel needed him and Henry had finally decided to go.

Nancy, strangely suspicious, went to her room and found no note from her lover. Then she opened Henry's door and went to the hiding place where he had secreted her gold and certificates. The hiding place was empty!

Running down to the housekeeper, Nancy explained that she must find Henry. Mrs. Miller warned her that not only had he been gone for ten hours but that the weather was likely to change.

Nancy was firm and said that her entire future might depend on what would happen in the next few hours. Bundling herself up for another hike, for every horse was out of the stables, she explained that she knew where the colonel always stopped as a halfway mark for the night, and she said she could easily reach that campsite before the men started for Portsmouth.

Mrs. Miller tried to prevent Nancy from leaving, but the girl, desperate in her knowledge that the money was missing, believed that the only way she could solve the problem was to reach her lover at the campsite. Taking a few slices of bread, she started off on her perilous errand.

Dartmouth was soon miles behind her. If it had not been for the mission she was on, Nancy would have enjoyed her trip through the forest. An hour went by, the sun set, and it grew colder. Nancy didn't notice that the stars were not out until a stray snowflake chilled her cheek.

For half an hour more she made good progress, but then the storm hit in earnest. Stumbling and slipping as the snow beat down on her, she was soon barely able to walk. Suddenly the snow stopped and the waning moon broke through the clouds.

Nancy's heart gladdened, but then the moon vanished and the snow started again. The storm soon became more violent than before. As the girl trudged along she thought she could hear the cry of wild beasts even above the gale. A huge branch fell across her path, and she climbed over it. The whistle and roaring of the wind through the trees began to frighten her. The cold grew more intense against her snow-covered body, and she longed to rest briefly in the partial shelter of a towering rock; she knew that if she did she would never get up.

Finally Nancy reached the gateway to Crawford Notch itself. The first part of her journey was finished. Praying aloud for renewed strength, she picked up a sturdy tree branch and used it for a staff. Even with this aid she slipped from time to time on the snow-covered rocks. The trees were obscured from view by the driving snow, but she heard the increasing roar of the Saco River and was able to use it for her guide. She kept on, walking close to the river bank. Suddenly she slid down on her hands and knees into the stream. Trembling and crying, Nancy fought her way back up to the bank, crawling painfully over the boulders to safety.

The storm continued and drifts started to pile up. Nancy's teeth began to chatter and her hands became numb. Her wet clothes slowly froze, but she fought on, hoping to reach the campfire at any moment.

Then, in spite of the drifts and the wind, she finally recognized her surroundings as the clearing she was seeking. Surely enough, there ahead was a dark spot from the campfire on the snowy ground, but Henry and Colonel Whipple were no longer there. Nancy scrambled forward and reached the spot, where a few embers still glowed in the ashes. Perhaps she could kindle a warming blaze. The falling snow prevented this, however, and soon all was blackness.

It was then that hope died for Nancy. Nevertheless she plunged ahead into the storm. A mile beyond the campsite she stumbled and sank to her knees. Her head dropped to her breast, and numbness overwhelmed her.

Realizing that she would freeze to death unless she kept moving, the girl tottered to her feet again to continue the hopeless journey in pursuit of her loved one. Her brain grew confused as she staggered through the woods, but she was able to notice that she was approaching a brook. She sank down, grasping a small tree at the brook's edge, and then she leaned her head against the tree. There Nancy succumbed to the fatal drowsiness and died at the edge of the brook that now bears her name.

The snowstorm ended before dawn, and a group of Dartmouth farmers discovered the frozen body of the girl who had followed her faithless lover even at the cost of her life.

The news of Nancy's death eventually reached Henry and Colonel Whipple in Portsmouth. Henry had found a gambling location in that town and had been ready to win untold riches with Nancy's money, but the Devil was not with him and he had lost everything again. This time, however, he did not attack those who gambled with him, and the next morning he sadly started back for Dartmouth with Colonel Whipple, who was unaware of Henry's activities of the night before. Returning home, the two men made arrangements for Nancy's funeral. The Indian seamstress, on hearing of the death of her good friend, journeyed to Dartmouth and was allowed to garb Nancy in the beautiful wedding dress she was never to wear in life. Then Nancy was buried in the village graveyard.

Henry, whose real surname was St. Dennis, soon became dissatisfied with his job and with himself. He took his meager savings and hiked to Boston. He signed on as a sailor on a merchant ship and was lost overboard at sea in a gale several months later.

CHAPTER 6

~~~~~~~~

A CLAMBAKE

In the 1930s, before World War II threatened, for a period of four years I organized and ran real old-fashioned clambakes on various islands in Boston Harbor. Calf Island, named for Robert Calef, a principal in the Cotton Mather witch controversy,* was my favorite location, and during that period we enjoyed at least forty delightful clambakes there.

Early in the morning on the day of the scheduled event a group of us would dig about 2000 clams, clean them thoroughly, and then store them in a cool cellar. A few hours later I would send two trusted youths out to Calf Island in my canoe, with nothing but their own lunches and a few matches.

On the island, the boys would gather enormous piles of driftwood of all sizes down on the beach at the site of the bake, and then start collecting rockweed from the low-tide ledges until they had more than we would need. Next they would scoop a depression in the gravel at least twelve feet across and start lining it with smooth-surfaced beach stones and rocks. Once the stones were firmly set into the depression, tiny branches and hay from the island were loosely packed on top of them, followed by faggots and small sticks. Then driftwood

* See my *Supernatural Mysteries*, pages 48–57.

about the size of relatively tiny timbers was added, on top of which coconut-sized stones and rocks were carefully piled. Finally came a special layer of quickly combustible wood.

After all this, the boys applied the matches, and within a period of from half an hour to forty minutes the entire mass would usually have burned and settled down to resemble a miniature volcanic crater, with the stones deep in the midst of the glowing embers.

If all went well, our boat would just have docked at Calf Island Pier, and we would hurry our supplies down over the bank and onto the shore at the site of the bonfire. The clams were brought over in buckets, along with sweet potatoes and corn, and a canvas tarpaulin was made ready.

At this point two rakes were used to pull over and remove the last embers, and the pile of rockweed, which had been kept in the shade, was hurried forward and spread on top of the white-hot rocks. Then the sweet potatoes were spread out over the steaming rockweed, followed by the corn. Next the buckets containing the glistening white clams were placed around the edge of the pit. At a given signal everyone grabbed a bucket and poured the clams right into the waiting steam. These were raked into an even pile; the canvas tarpaulin was raised over and then lowered onto the entire affair; more seaweed was added; and another set of rocks was used to weigh down the sizzling entirety, so that the sweet potatoes, the corn, and the clams all would get full benefit of the steam rising from the scalding-hot rocks below.

That done, a critical decision lay just ahead. The bake was steaming away and the clams eventually would begin to show signs of almost being ready, but what about the corn and potatoes? How long before they would be cooked thoroughly?

There was only one way to find out. (Actually, I have attended clambakes—I'll not reveal where—that were not properly managed. After the tarpaulin was removed and everything

was handed out, it was discovered that the potatoes were not
ready, the corn only half cooked, and, although the clams were
edible, they didn't have that delightful ability to slip down your
gullet that properly steamed clams have.) We would always
wait a full hour before the first approach to moving the tarpaulin. At that exact end of the hour, every member of our
group was alert. About three minutes after the full hour had
elapsed, the clambake master would order a corner of the tarpaulin slightly raised and shove his gloved hand into the steaming mass, withdrawing as fast as possible a clam, a potato, and
an ear of corn. Only then would he make his decision. Usually
all was well, and everyone would be served within a few minutes. However, if the sweet potatoes needed another few minutes, we would wait ten minutes more. But then everything
came off and dinner was served!

As the clambake enthusiasts were eating, watermelons were
brought down and cut for dessert at the end of the feast.

Of course all has changed since those days. It is practically
impossible to conduct a clambake today as in the 1930s, and
more than thirty years ago I reverted to Colonel Ezekial Cushing's method of serving clams, called Clam Boil. Now, as in the
days of Colonel Cushing, a leading personality of Casco Bay
two hundred years ago, everyone drinks clam broth from a cup
or large shell. The happy human slips the clam's leatherlike
skin cap from its neck and then tips his or her own head at an
angle of about 17¼ degrees, drops the previously resisting
clam down the throat, and experiences pure ecstasy in the
process.

It is said that at one Casco Bay picnic held at Long Island
in 1883 by the Maine Commercial Travelers' group, the combined length of the tables if placed end to end would have
totaled a mile. Of course, apart from the enormous number of
clams such a feast would have required, I have figured out that
there might not have been enough craft in all Casco Bay to

bring the passengers necessary to fill the seats at a table of such length. But it is a good story and I'll not challenge it further.

The greatest number at any of my clambakes was 273, and those of us who did the work were utterly exhausted at the close of that glorious feast.

CHAPTER 7

JAMEISON, THE GOOD PIRATE

In addition to a fascinating history colored with tales of piracy, mutiny, and buried treasure, Hingham, Massachusetts, offers much of interest to the historian concerned with the period immediately following the War of 1812.

Every time I visit this delightful South Shore area, I think of the autumn of the year 1951, when Torrey Little and I were exploring in the attic of his great auction barn at Marshfield Hills. We came across a large sea chest he had obtained some months before. On the inside of the cover was a painting of a sailing vessel, the *Molo,* and in one of the drawers a long dirk and an old pair of handcuffs. The sea chest and its contents were all that remained of the possessions of one Nickola, or Nicholas Jameison, whom I call the Good Pirate.

Jameison was a remarkable man, an expert navigator who left his mark on the Massachusetts South Shore for many years. Born in Grennock, Scotland, he was the youngest of thirteen children. His father, a rich clothing merchant, wished him to take up the same trade, but at an early age the boy became interested in the sea. After a liberal education, the youth visited Europe. He was detained in France by the Napoleonic Wars, but his father was able to send him money from time to time.

89

Following a trip to Waterloo, young Jameison went to sea, and a short time later his father died.

The young man was shipwrecked near New Orleans in 1820 and found himself in dire straits. All that he had been able to save from the disaster were his sea chest, his nautical instruments, and about twenty dollars. Once in New Orleans, he attempted to ship out again.

On July 11, 1820, Captain August Orgamar arrived in New Orleans aboard the so-called privateer *Mexican,* a small schooner mounting several cannon. Captain Orgamar allegedly represented the famous General Prascelascus of Mexico, but several American sailors told Jameison that they wouldn't ship with Orgamar because he was actually a pirate. Nevertheless, the Scot was hungry, worried, and desperate for work. When Orgamar told him the position of navigator was open and assured him that the *Mexican* was strictly a privateer, Jameison accepted the job.

However, once at sea, Captain Orgamar threw off all pretense. After a small Spanish brig was captured, he murdered the crew, took off all the cargo and money, and scuttled the craft. When Jameison protested, the grinning captain informed him that war was war. The young Scot knew then what he was in for and cursed himself for being a fool.

A week later, when another craft was seized, the members of the captured crew were given their choice of joining up or being killed. They all joined, after which the captain set sail for a secluded harbor where a division of booty was made. After the spoils were allotted, fifteen ugly-looking individuals, who evidently had been awaiting the craft, appeared from out of the forest. They signed on as crew members.

Jameison had noticed that the crew was getting hard to manage. Apparently Orgamar, brutal enough himself, was in danger of losing control of his vessel to a band of outlaws who practiced even less restraint. Jameison felt that a showdown between Orgamar and his ruffian crew was imminent, and indeed the Scot did not have long to wait. Two nights later, under a full tropical moon, five crewmen went below, grabbed Captain Orgamar from his bunk, and hauled him up on deck.

"Sorry, Orgamar, but I am taking over as the new captain," said their leader, a cutthroat named Jonnia. "You must decide either to join the crew with me as your commander, or to be set adrift in an open boat."

"I choose the open boat," said the captain, acting as dignified as he could under the humiliating circumstances. His sea chest and a few provisions were then put in a boat, and he was set adrift.

Jameison begged to be allowed to go along with Orgamar, but the pirates all laughed at him.

"We need you as navigator, as you well know," was all that Jonnia would say.

Now began a period of terrorism at sea. Whereas Orgamar had seized only Spanish ships, the mutineers declared vessels of all nations subject to capture and sinking. The savagery of the pirates increased with each new encounter.

Finally Jameison had all he could stomach. During one particularly vicious assault, he objected openly to Captain Jonnia's acts and, for his insubordination, was struck and beaten with a cutlass, receiving terrible wounds about his head and shoulders. He was then tied to the mast along with many victims from the captured craft.

"Which do you choose, obedience or death?" Jonnia asked him. Jameison, knowing his worth to the pirates as navigator, gambled on defiance.

"Captain Jonnia, I want to live, of course, and you need me as navigator. I'll stay on, change my name, grow a beard, and keep quiet in front of others you may capture. But, I warn you now, I'll jump ship if I get the chance."

Impressed by the frankness of Jameison's speech, Captain

Jonnia thought it over for a moment and then decided to go along, at least until he got a new navigator. Jameison now became Nickola Monacre.

The weeks went by and, as vessel after vessel was captured and scuttled, the captain forgot both the episode and his intention to find a new navigator.

On December 21, 1821, the pirates were off Cape Cruz, Cuba, when they sighted an American schooner bearing down on them from northern waters. It was the 107-ton *Exertion,* owned by Joseph Ballister and Henry Farnam, which had left her home port of Boston on November 13, 1821, bound for Trinidad, Cuba, with a heavy cargo of foodstuffs, furniture, and other commodities aboard. Total value of the cargo was eight thousand dollars. The master was Captain Barnabas Lincoln of Hingham, Massachusetts; the mate, Joseph Brackett of Bristol, Maine; the cook, David Warren of Saco, Maine; and there were four seamen: Thomas Goodall of Baltimore, Thomas Young of Orangetown, George Reed of Scotland, and Carl Francis de Suze of Saint John's, Newfoundland.

From the deck of the *Exertion,* Captain Lincoln studied the *Mexican* with his spyglass and realized that he was outgunned and outmanned. He had six men in his crew against forty on the *Mexican.* He decided to surrender without a fight. The two schooners hove to side by side. The pirates ordered Captain Lincoln to report aboard the *Mexican,* but when the *Exertion*'s boat was "hove out" it filled with water and sank at once.

The buccaneers sent over their own boat and Captain Lincoln was taken aboard the *Mexican.* There he shook hands with Captain Jonnia, who told him he had been detained by a Mexican government privateer. Jonnia said there would be a few formalities and then he would be freed. Of course, Jonnia had not the slightest intention of keeping his word. The pirates took over the *Exertion* and the Americans were made prisoners.

Captain Lincoln stood by helplessly and watched as his trim schooner was looted and the members of his crew were shackled in irons. When the pirates attempted to sail the schooner in over a sandbar, they ran her aground. Captain Lincoln was then ordered into a small boat and rowed a long distance to an island where he was left together with the members of his crew and four Spanish prisoners from a previously captured schooner.

The next day Jameison rowed ashore and introduced himself to Captain Lincoln, revealing his true identity. The two men held several long conversations during which Lincoln learned Jameison's strange history. The *Mexican*'s navigator asserted that he would never be captured alive as a pirate, for he carried a bottle of laudanum with him at all times. After making a vain effort to take the poison away from the pirate, Captain Lincoln promised that he would do what he could for Jameison if he himself got away.

The following day Jonnia informed Lincoln that he needed an extra man aboard his craft and that Carl de Suze,* who he claimed was a fellow Spaniard, suited him. But when de Suze heard about Captain Jonnia's plan, he strenuously objected, rushing to Captain Lincoln with tears in his eyes.

"Captain, I'll do nothing but what I am obliged to do, and am very sorry to leave you. You know I am helpless." The Newfoundlander left the group immediately, and Lincoln never saw or heard from him again.

On January 5 more prisoners were landed on the island, bringing the group to twelve in number. The pirates brought supplies to the captives and announced that they were sailing away but would be back in a day or two. Jameison had a brief chance to confer with the American sea captain. As he secretly

* It is believed that de Suze was a collateral ancestor of Carl de Suze, a leading Boston radio personality.

handed him a letter, the pirate advised Lincoln to place no faith at all in Jonnia's promise.

As the outlaws rowed away, Jameison shouted across in English to the American sailors, "Mark my words, I'll come back if I'm alive. Do not forget what I tell you now."

As soon as he could, the captain opened and read the letter which Jameison had left with him.

January 4, 1822

Sir—

We arrived here this morning, and before we came to anchor had five canoes alongside ready to take your cargo . . . You may depend on this account of Jameison . . . The villain who bought your cargo is from the town of Principe, his name is Dominico, as to that it is all I can learn; they have taken your charts aboard the *Mexican* . . . Your clothes are here on board, but do not let me flatter you that you will get them back; it may be so and it may not. Perhaps in your old age, when you recline with ease in a corner of your cottage, you will have the goodness to drop a tear of pleasure to the memory of him whose highest ambition should have been to subscribe himself, though devoted to the gallows, your friend,

NICKOLA MONACRE

Excuse haste.

The supplies left by the pirates consisted of bread, flour, fish, lard, a little coffee and molasses, two kegs of water, and a cooking pot. The days passed rapidly and the food supply diminished daily. Although the marooned men all agreed to ration the supplies, each morning showed that at least one of their number had been guilty of cheating during the night.

The island where they had been marooned was a wretched

one. Centipedes, scorpions, lizards, flies, gnats, and mosquitoes made life miserable all hours of the day and night. To
add to their discomfort and apprehension their water supply
grew smaller and smaller.

Three miles away was another low island connected by a
long sandbar to the place where they were marooned. As there
were mangrove trees on the second island, Mr. Brackett and
George Reed attempted to cross over in waist-deep water, but
were chased back by a large shark.

On Tuesday, January 22, Captain Lincoln discovered a
hatchet. The next day one of the Spaniards armed himself with
a sharp pole and successfully crossed over the bar in water
three feet deep. Luckily, he was not bothered by sharks. A few
days later they all waded across to explore the new island.
Wreckage, which included two lashing planks, several old
spars and part of the bow, was discovered where it had drifted
from the remains of the *Exertion*. That afternoon the survivors
caught an iguana that weighed a pound and a half when
skinned, a very small meal for so many hungry men.

The following Friday a vessel hove in sight but, although
all the marooned men waved frantically, the craft sailed away
without noticing them.

The next day the castaways decided to build a boat from
the salvaged lumber. Work had hardly started when David
Warren began to sicken. On the following Monday Captain
Lincoln noticed that the lad's eyes were shining like glass, and
the others realized that the boy was very ill. Late that afternoon Warren motioned to the others that he wished to make
a statement.

"I have a mother in Saco where I belong," he said. "She is
a second-time widow, and tomorrow, if you can spare a scrap
of paper and a pencil, I will write something."

But when morning came, David Warren of Saco was dead.
The others carried his body to a suitable spot and buried him

there. Captain Lincoln read a funeral service, and a Spaniard named Manuel placed a cross at the head of the grave.

Supplies grew desperately short, but the men discovered some herbs, which the Spaniards called Spanish tea. They resembled pennyroyal in look and taste, although not so pungent, and proved a poor excuse for a full meal.

On Thursday, January 31, 1822, the boat was finished and placed in the water. It was a disappointment, leaking badly. After considerable discussion, it was agreed that only six could go in her, with Mr. Brackett in command. At sunset the dangerous voyage began. Captain Lincoln stood on the shore and watched with the others as the six men vanished into the setting sun. Four of them were rowing. Mr. Brackett stood at the helm, and the sixth man was bailing steadily.

On February 5, the marooned sailors on shore discovered a boat drifting by on the southeast side of the island. Captain Lincoln urged sailors Goodall and Reed to go out on an improvised raft constructed of debris from the *Exertion* wreckage and make an attempt to salvage the craft. Five hours later the pair returned with the news that the boat was the same one they had built on the island, and the castaways thought with horror of the fate of their six companions in those shark-infested waters.

By February 6 the spirits of the five men were completely broken. The provisions were nearly gone. Then, around noon, a sail was seen in the distance and an hour later a gun was fired. The craft anchored close to shore and three men began rowing in toward the marooned sailors. Captain Lincoln walked down to meet the visitors and recognized no one. The leader, a clean-shaven individual, jumped out into the shallow water and raced up to Lincoln.

"Do you now believe Nickola is your friend?" the man cried out.

And indeed it was Nickola. Nicholas Jameison was clean-shaven and happy and he had with him in the boat one of Captain Lincoln's former sailors, Thomas Young of Baltimore. But there was no news of Carl de Suze, who had gone aboard another prize. When the greetings were over, Jameison noticed the cross on Warren's grave and asked if all the others were dead. When it was explained how six men had rowed away for help, Jameison agreed with Captain Lincoln that it looked bad indeed for the missing men.

Captain Lincoln was given the choice of sailing to either the port of Trinidad on Cuba or Jamaica. He chose Trinidad, asking Jameison for the loan of a boat if it was too far out of the way. But Jameison insisted that Lincoln and the others journey with him to Cuba. They agreed to go over to the bar where the *Exertion* had been beached to see if they could find signs of Brackett and the other five men. As they sailed along Jameison explained how he had escaped the other pirates. He had been put aboard a captured vessel as a prize master, was allowed to choose his own crew, and had been able to escape the other pirates.

When the castaways and their rescuers reached the schooner, they found a sail and a paddle they recognized as coming from the boat they had launched and knew then that Brackett had reached the *Exertion*. But there was no sign of the six missing men. The schooner had been stripped clean, for there were no masts, spars, rigging, furniture, food or anything else left except the bowsprit and a few barrels of salt provisions. With a deep feeling of sadness Captain Lincoln finally left his old command and returned to Jameison's sloop. The journey for Cuba began.

On Monday, February 11, they were still sailing toward Cuba when a vessel that seemed to be a pirate craft approached and sent a shot whizzing through their mainsail.

"It's the men from the *Mexican* again," cried one of the Spaniards, "and God help us."

But Captain Lincoln didn't share their apprehension, believing that the craft was a Spanish man-of-war. He asked Jameison to stop and accept whatever the future might bring. But the others decided to fight.

After a brief skirmish Jameison surrendered. Two small, armed boats were sent over from the brig, which proved to be the eighteen-gun Spanish man-of-war *Prudentee*. Captain Lincoln and the others were taken aboard and questioned by Captain Caudama.

"Why did you fire on a Spanish man-of-war?" he asked in English.

"We feared that you were pirates and did not wish to be captured by them again," Captain Lincoln explained, at the same time removing his ship's papers from his money belt and giving them to the Spanish commander. When the documents were examined, the Spanish captain smiled broadly.

"Captain Americana, your troubles are over. Never mind what has happened now. Go below and we shall enjoy dinner. Which are your own men?" Lincoln pointed them out, and they were given the freedom of the deck, but when Jameison was discussed it was a different matter. The Spanish captain decided that the Scot and his three sailors should be placed in irons.

As soon as possible, Captain Lincoln interceded for Jameison. The Spanish captain promised to do what he could for Jameison and requested that Lincoln give him a written statement to the effect that he had been politely treated while aboard the brig. Lincoln gladly complied.

At Trinidad, the American skipper was released and given the cabin of a sea captain to live in while awaiting help. Two days later he met Captain Carnes of the schooner *Hannah*, who offered passage home, which was gladly accepted. The *Hannah* arrived in Boston, March 25, 1822, after an uneventful voyage.

Later Captain Lincoln learned that Mr. Brackett and his party had also reached safety, but Carl de Suze was never heard from again. He also learned that the pirates from the *Mexican* were chased by an English government vessel and eleven were hanged after capture. The others escaped into a mangrove swamp, where it is said they perished. Perhaps one of these unfortunates was the luckless de Suze.

A happier ending was in store for Nicholas Jameison. Over two years after his farewell to the Scot, Captain Lincoln received a letter from Jameison saying that he was residing at Montego Bay, Jamaica. Lincoln immediately wrote and asked him to journey to Boston.

Upon receipt of the letter Jameison packed his sea chest and engaged passage with Captain Wilson of Cohasset, arriving in Boston in August 1824. Captain Lincoln was at the wharf to greet him and took him at once to his Hingham home. At the time the captain was "sailing in trade" between Boston and Philadelphia, and he signed on the former pirate as mate.

Later Jameison became established at Hingham, sailing out of the harbor during the summer months in the mackerel fishing industry. When fall came, he set up a fine navigation school, teaching the difficult problems of navigation to the young men of the South Shore. Many sea captains from Hingham, Cohasset, Scituate, Duxbury, Marshfield, Kingston, and Plymouth owed their early training to the former pirate.

One day a pupil of Jameison's was given a mate's berth aboard a ship sailing into European waters, and Jameison allowed him to borrow his sea chest. When the youth returned in the spring of 1829, he found that Jameison had gone out mackerel fishing again. Toward the end of April, Jameison started out again on a trip to sea but was seized with a fatal illness and carried into Provincetown. He died May 1, 1829, and was buried on Cape Cod.

The boy kept the chest. In 1835 he became an officer aboard the new ship *Molo*, built at Medford, Massachusetts. While sailing back from Europe the following year, the *Molo* encountered a blinding snowstorm and was wrecked at the lonely Faeroe Islands, halfway between Norway and Iceland. The sea chest was miraculously saved and brought back to the United States, where it remained in the owner's family until 1931.

Somewhere in a Provincetown graveyard lie the remains of Nicholas Jameison, the Good Pirate, who did everything he could to help an American sea captain out of his distress over a century and a half ago. Mary Lee Lincoln, a resident of Hingham and the grandniece of Captain Barnabas Lincoln, died on November 12, 1954, at the age of 99 years, 9 months, 13 days. She had often heard this story told by her family, and as a child was deeply interested in the pirate account. On many occasions she related this tale to her relatives, one of whom, Howard Leavitt Horton of Abington, Massachusetts, assisted me in several of the details of this chapter.

CHAPTER 8

THE HAUNTED SCHOOLHOUSE

The "haunted schoolhouse" of Newburyport, rebuilt many years ago, still stands on Charles Street in that colonial town. The structure, a private residence now, was originally a primary school for boys whose ages ranged from five to fourteen. The pupils came from the humbler Newburyport families, the sons of fishermen, tradesmen, and mill-workers, and their clothes were tattered and patched.

When first erected, the schoolhouse was an ordinary one-story structure raised upon a three-foot foundation. It had a pitched roof with four windows on each of the two longer sides and an attic above. At the time the ghost appeared, the schoolhouse was in a state of neglect. The faded green blinds and the peeling gray paint of the building gave it an air of shabbiness, and, all in all, there was something about the school and its surroundings that oppressed the beholder and strengthened a willingness to believe the strange story of the schoolboy ghost.

To enter the school, one climbed the six steps in front and opened the battered door before stepping into a small hallway with two large windows at each end. Close and stuffy, the entry gave off an odor eternally connected with schools. Directly opposite the front door was a multi-paned partition window that looked in upon the schoolroom. To the right of the entrance were two sets of stairs, one going up to the attic, the other to the cellar, where the coal was stored. Both stairways had doors that were usually fastened with a latch.

The schoolroom itself was a large one and held seats for sixty pupils, with a teacher's desk at the right of the room. On the walls were several maps, torn and soiled. Otherwise the walls were perfectly bare; there was not even a closet in the room. It was perhaps the last place where one would expect to find a ghost.

Many have repeated the story that in the year 1858 the incumbent teacher beat a thirteen-year-old boy until he was black and blue, then, after school, threw him down into the cellar, where he died during the night. Whether or not there is any truth to this legend is uncertain, but the subsequent story that the boy's ghost had been seen in the schoolhouse caused considerable excitement throughout Massachusetts.

In 1871 it became generally known that strange disturbances were taking place in the Charles Street School. Peculiar phenomena had occurred from time to time within the building, but no one had paid too much attention because the teachers and the school committee were not anxious to start trouble.

But the two teachers who ran the school in 1870 and 1871 were forced to give up their positions after their lives had been made miserable by the constant intrusion of a strange power they could neither see nor feel. It was not a being they could scold or whip, and it did not appear at stated intervals. It could not be hunted down and destroyed; it was something intangible and malevolent.

Miss Lucy A. Perkins was appointed teacher in the fall of 1871. She was twenty-one, strong and willing to do her duty in the classroom. Shortly after her arrival, the knocks and pounding, said to be manifestations of spirits, began. On one occasion, the sound was so loud that Miss Perkins could not carry on her spelling lesson; the banging came so rapidly and powerfully that all voices were drowned out. The noises issued from the attic stairs and the entry. At times they faded until they resembled the tap of fingers, and again they increased in volume until they might have come from the batterings of a mighty sledge hammer.

In an attempt to quiet the fears of her pupils, the teacher suggested that the sounds were probably made by rats and the wind, but eventually she was forced to give up this subterfuge and admit that she really didn't know what was causing the noises.

One afternoon during the month of January 1873, a series of raps came upon the outer door. Miss Perkins went to admit the visitor, but no one was there. In the schoolroom in front of the pupils' desk was a stove with a cover that was raised by a wire handle. That day the handle was seized by invisible fingers and raised several inches, then restored to its place.

The teacher's bell was often moved about the room. One day before school began, the pupils outside in the yard suddenly heard the bell ringing, though there was no one in the building. When the teacher came down the street, the pupils told her what had happened. They were more frightened at the bell incident than at any of the knockings or the cover-raising episode.

The schoolroom proper was ventilated by a shutter in the ceiling that could be opened or closed by pulling a cord hanging down into the room. The alleged demon often opened and closed the vent for mischief. And any door in the building might slam without warning, although no one could be seen nearby.

One day Miss Perkins heard the door leading to the attic

swing open, and as she went out to close it, two more doors swung open. She tried in vain for ten minutes to catch up with the opening doors. The door leading to the cellar had a bolt; Miss Perkins closed that door and bolted it. Instantly the lock slipped back and the door swung open so hard that it crashed into a clothes hook and received a deep dent.

A weird light began to appear during storms when the sky was heavily overcast. Light seemed to creep in and hover over the frightened faces of the awed pupils.

At various times a strange current of air appeared to circulate above the pupils with unusual speed, creating a noise like that of a great flight of birds. A black ball twelve inches in diameter often appeared in the ventilator, dropping just below the opening and then quickly disappearing. This phenomenon was often accompanied by a terrific rushing of wind around the building itself. Gusts of cold air shot into all the crevices, the entire building shook, and the chimney gave off sounds that resembled the playing of a pipe organ. On these occasions the unhappy teacher and her frightened pupils would sing at the top of their voices, trying to drown out the noises by song.

One afternoon a boy named Abraham Lydston, thirteen years old, suddenly noticed a child's hand pressed against the partition window. He shouted out, "Teacher! Teacher! The murdered boy's hand!" Soon everyone could see the hand pressed against the window pane. Miss Perkins rushed into the vestibule, but in the two or three seconds she took to reach the hall, the apparition had vanished.

Late in October 1872, the murdered boy's face appeared at the same pane of glass. The teacher ran out again, but there was nothing in sight.

On November 1, 1872, the ghost appeared during a geography class and stood at right angles to the partition window opposite the teacher's desk. One of the boys, whose desk was

near the open door, shouted out, "There's a boy out there!"
Miss Perkins hurried out and saw the form of a young boy
standing in the vestibule.

"What are you doing out here?" she demanded of the ghost-
like figure.

The apparition receded from her toward the attic stairs. It
was the image of a young boy with blue eyes and yellow hair.
He was wearing a brown coat, black trousers, and a wide band
around his neck of the type used by undertakers to prevent the
lower jaw of a dead person from dropping open. The most
extraordinary thing about the apparition was that Miss Perkins
could look right through it and see the sash and wainscotting
on the wall. The ghost was perfectly transparent, but easily
visible.

Miss Perkins began to tremble and thought that she was
going to faint. As she steadied herself against the wall, the
door leading to the attic opened of its own accord, and the
figure slowly ascended the attic stairs.

Regaining her strength, the teacher followed the apparition
up the stairs and finally trapped it in a corner. But when she
thrust out her hands to grasp the boy, they met in the middle
of his transparent chest, and all she had touched was air. The
ghost began to disintegrate and soon disappeared.

On the following Friday the apparition appeared again and
went through the same maneuvers, but this time it also introduced certain innovations. It brought two ghostly friends and
spent most of the afternoon hammering away on the attic
floor. Once there was the cry "Damn it, where's my hammer?"
Evidently the ghost found his hammer, for soon he could be
heard adjusting the cover of a box and nailing it shut.

A week later the ghost began to laugh softly in a disagree-
able manner most disconcerting to teacher and pupils alike.
The teacher asked for volunteers to investigate, and a student
agreed to accompany her to the attic, which seemed to be the

source of the laughter. But when they reached the attic, the disembodied laugh jumped around them here and there, and they retreated to the schoolroom in great confusion.

By this time there was tremendous excitement in Newburyport over these strange occurrences. A special meeting of the school committee was held on February 19, 1873. Two of the committeemen stated that nothing was wrong at all, though the chairman, who also served as postmaster, decided that there was much to explain. But there was little action to be taken. When the newspapers began publishing accounts of the affair, mediums and spiritualists descended on the town to view with their own eyes the schoolroom where the apparition of the murdered boy had appeared.

At another meeting held on February 24th, it was agreed that Miss Perkins should be given a well-deserved vacation. The school was placed in charge of Nathan A. Mounton, and the visitations allegedly stopped. When Miss Perkins married and moved away, the incident was almost completely forgotten.

When I first learned of the schoolhouse ghost, I went to the Newburyport Public Library and talked with Miss Grace Bixby. She told me that her mother had often told her the story, and suggested that I go to see ninety-year-old George Leeds Whitmore, who had been in Newburyport at the time of the sensational events. After two interviews with Mr. Whitmore I had what I needed for my story.

When I first visited Mr. Whitmore's Merrimac Street residence, he admitted that he knew something about the affair that he had never told before. I was impatient to learn what it was, but he answered, "Don't hurry me, son, don't hurry me. It'll all come to me if you just give me time."

I waited quietly.

"Now, I think that I learned the truth about the Charles Street Schoolhouse and Miss Perkins from Tot Currier, who worked in the shop with me years ago. He's dead, and so is everyone else that I knew then, and I guess it won't do anyone any harm to tell the true story at this late day. Why, that happened over three-quarters of a century ago, didn't it?

"The boys who carried out the hoax, for hoax it was, were four in number. They were Tot Currier, whose real name was William, Abe Lydston, Edgar Pearson, and Ed De Lancy— all dead now. They got the idea for the ghost when De Lancy received an object glass which could catch reflections from the sun and throw pictures on any flat surface.

"It took De Lancy several months to master the thing, but when he did he could shine pictures from within the glass forty or fifty feet away. He really became pretty good at it. The figure he used came out clear and distinct, and when it flashed inside a building, well, it would fool anyone not in on the secret.

"When Ed heard about the noises coming from the schoolhouse he decided to have some fun, so he pulled Tot, Abe, and Edgar into the scheme. Tot didn't attend school, but Abe and Edgar did, and they helped matters from inside the classroom while Tot ran around the attic and the entryway.

"Miss Perkins, poor woman, is dead and gone now, but they sure had fun with her, and it was partly her fault, because she was pretty superstitious. The day she went up into the attic, she actually fainted.

"Tot told me all about it one day in the shop, and he explained how he ran out before she came to. Tot never grew very large, but he really was a little devil. Yes, I suppose the boys were mean to have teased the poor soul that way."

After talking another half hour with the old man, I said good-bye to him, and as I pondered what he had told me, I wondered how many of the ghost stories of the world might have similar explanations. Of course, Mr. Whitmore's tale does not account for the other happenings, such as the stove lid, the black ball, the strange wind and other noises mentioned earlier in this chapter. Can you explain them?

CHAPTER 9

~~~~~

TWO UNBELIEVABLE
DISCOVERIES AT SEA

Tales of babies and young folk who are either discovered at sea or who survive and wash ashore under spectacular circumstances have always appealed to me. In other books I have told stories of such events. In *Famous New England Lighthouses* I wrote of the rescue of a baby off the shores of Mount Desert Rock. In the same book I told of another baby who was put into a box at sea. The box was tied between two feather mattresses and set adrift. It washed ashore in a great storm and was pulled up by the keeper of Hendricks Head Light. When he cut it open, the bundle revealed the baby, still alive, with a note attached to its clothing. The child grew up, and the note that told its story was preserved through the years.

The following tale is not in any volume now in print. It begins at Provincetown on Cape Cod.

The seaport of Provincetown, Massachusetts, located far out on the end of Cape Cod, has witnessed tens of thousands of arrivals and departures of almost every type of vessel. Equally at home in the spacious Cape End Harbor, as it was once known, were mighty men-of-war of the eighteenth-century British fleet and the present giant warships of our American navy.

In the year 1803, a trim, eighty-ton fishing schooner named *Polly* sailed from Provincetown Harbor. Bound for Bay Chaleur, an inlet between Quebec and New Brunswick, she carried ten sailors. Among the crew was a ten-year-old cabin boy, Ned Rider, the nephew of Peter Rider, the *Polly*'s captain.

The voyage was Ned's first trip, and long before the tall church at Provincetown faded into the distance he began to wish he had stayed at home, where he could put his two feet on a surface that did not roll. As the *Polly* continued her journey up the coast, passing Thatcher's Island and the Isles of Shoals, Ned became more and more seasick. But as the days went by, he slowly recovered and began to lose the feeling of giddiness. By the time the schooner reached Mount Desert Rock, young Ned had fully regained his enthusiasm for the sea.

The fishermen passed Sable Island and before long reached Bay Chaleur. The fishing there proved highly successful, surpassing the most optimistic hopes. Within a few days the last basketful of salt had been wet and the long fishing lines were back on the reels; the *Polly* had a full hold. Captain Peter Rider ordered the hatches battened down and set his course for the journey back to Provincetown Harbor.

Two days later, early on a Sunday morning, the *Polly* lay becalmed off Saint Paul's Island, some ten miles to the northeast of Cape Breton. As the boat drifted with the current, Ned came up on deck and stood by the rail. He watched the gulls wheeling back and forth over the stern and he listened to their almost plaintive cries. Then he heard a new sound in the distance. It resembled for all the world the lusty yell of a young child, but where could a child be calling from out on the broad Atlantic?

Offshore from the main body of Saint Paul's Island was a

large rock, shaped like a pinnacle, and Ned wondered if the voice could be coming from there. Rushing below, he aroused Captain Rider and told the veteran mariner what he had heard. The captain decided to humor his nephew and agreed to come up on deck and listen to the noise the boy had heard. As soon as he reached the rail Captain Rider paused, but he heard only the cry of the seagulls as they twisted and turned above the stern. He was inclined to dismiss the incident from his mind.

"That's what you heard, lad. It was a seagull, make no mistake. Some of those gulls have a different sound from the others and that is what alarmed you."

But just as the captain was preparing to go below, there was another pitiful cry. This time it apparently did come from the distant rock, and even the captain was impressed with the human quality of the sound. He decided to have two of his men row over to the rock and investigate.

Ned jumped in with the two sailors who had been chosen, and soon the men were rowing toward the pinnacle. Still becalmed, the *Polly* scarcely moved on the glasslike surface of the sea as the men neared the rock.

Five minutes later the rowboat reached its destination, and Ned clambered out. There was nothing in sight at first, and so he climbed around to the other side of the boulder. Then he heard the cry again, this time from a distance of just a few feet. In less than a minute he had reached the spot from where the sound came. It was a small niche in the giant ledge, which was rapidly being engulfed by the oncoming tide. There, just about to start crying again, was a frightened little girl. The tide was coming in. She was in water up to the waist, and it was not long before she would have been swept away by the rising sea.

Climbing down from the pinnacle into the niche, Ned took the little girl by the hand. Carefully he pulled and led her up over the sharp points to the top of the rock. Then, holding tightly to each other, they descended the other side. The men in the boat gasped in astonishment when they saw what Ned had found.

The girl and her rescuer got into the boat, and the sailors rowed away from the rock. Nearing the *Polly*, they attracted the attention of the crew. Captain Rider stood by the rail to receive the dripping child, who was now crying steadily from fear, excitement, and relief.

"Well, now," exclaimed the captain, "how did such a little girl as you get off on that rocky ledge so far from shore?"

The child's only answer was another series of sobs. The cook brought some warm chocolate, and the captain's bunk was prepared for the girl so that she could take a nap. Her wet clothes were removed, and one of Ned's heavy shirts given her for a nightdress. Ten minutes later she was asleep.

The men gathered to discuss this remarkable occurrence. How could such a thing happen? Who would maroon a tiny child on a niche in a lonely rock out in the Atlantic where the tide would soon drown her?

"I'd give anything to catch the man who did this thing," said Mate Ben Smith with a vengeance, "for either he or I would go overboard!"

"In any case," said Captain Rider calmly, as if he had already appraised the situation, "it is true that we don't know how the girl got on the rock, or where she came from, but I for one am not going to try too hard to find out. While we're not exactly fixed for a nursery aboard, at least we are far more human than the critters who left that child out on the rock to die."

So it was decided that the *Polly* would keep the little girl aboard for the remainder of the trip. Shortly after midnight a breeeze sprang up, and by dawn the fishing schooner was speeding along at seven knots, bound for Provincetown Harbor with as strange a cargo as ever a Cape Cod fisherman had taken from the sea.

By the time the *Polly* was abeam of Thatcher's Island, the crew had voted to name the child Ruth, in memory of Ruth Adams, whose father, one of the crew, still mourned her death three years before. When they sailed into Provincetown Harbor and rowed ashore, the astonishment on the faces of the women of Cape End Harbor was considerable, to see a tiny girl step out of one of the boats.

Captain Rider, whose wife had died, lived with his mother and his nephew Ned, whose own parents were dead. It had been agreed that Ruth would live with them, and the child proved a welcome addition to the family. As time passed, she came to look upon Ned, who was seven years older, as her brother.

In the summers Ned went fishing, and in the fall, winter, and spring he attended school. Finally his formal education came to an end, and he took command of the *Polly* from his aging uncle, who told friends that he was happy to retire from the sea and "stay home for a spell."

His interest in Ruth grew, and Ned became determined to discover what he could concerning who the girl was and where she came from. After several years of sailing, he was in the vicinity of Saint Paul's Island once more. He went ashore, but he found to his disappointment that no one lived on the island at all, and so his questions remained unanswered. He did, however, discover evidence of several shipwrecks and later learned that the island had been the scene of many terrible disasters in its early history. Nevertheless, from all he could gather, he decided that the child must have been left on the rock during calm weather, as there had been no evidence of a shipwreck nearby at the time she was found.

Back at Provincetown, when Ned returned from the trip

that had taken him ashore at Saint Paul's, he went at once
to his home. Ruth met him at the door and threw her arms
around him. Then, shyly blushing, she drew back and looked
at him with a new awareness as she realized that she no longer
thought of him as a brother. Now about sixteen years old (for
of course her exact age was never known), she appeared to
be a grown woman.

Thus it was that Ruth and Ned recognized their true affection for one another. Ned explained what he had been doing
at Saint Paul's Island and ended by telling her of his failure
to find out anything about her.

Having known for years that she had been found at sea on
a fishing trip, Ruth sensed what Ned was leading up to when
he talked about her background. After a long discussion he
suddenly proposed that they get married. She accepted him at
once. The entire town turned out for the wedding, and Captain
Peter Rider built the pair a new house, one of the finest on
Cape Cod. They lived happily ever after, unconcerned by the
fact that Ruth's mystery was never solved.

Thirty years ago I visited Saint Paul's Island and learned
that some years after Ruth had been found, a lighthouse had
been erected on the rock. Located across a natural channel
of water from the main part of the island, it is now connected
by a cable car to Saint Paul's Island.

Several generations of the descendants of Ruth and Ned
now populate Cape Cod, and many others have migrated off-
Cape. For those grandchildren and great-grandchildren this
will always be an intriguing story.

Another account of finding a child at sea involves one of
the most unusual events in the history of the Gloucester fishing
fleet. It occurred while the schooner *Belvidere* was crossing
George's Bank.

Captain Samuel Elwell, whose ancestor had a phenomenal

escape from death in the great storm of 1786, had indulged in a large Saturday evening meal. When he followed it with the usual early Sunday breakfast, he became so sick that he went below and turned in.

Falling asleep almost at once, he dreamed of seeing a small coffin-shaped box tossing back and forth on the waves. In his dream he attempted to steer the schooner so that the box could be drawn up on board. Time and again he thought he was on a course that would allow him to reach the box, and on one attempt he was so close he could see inside the box. It contained the body of a small girl surrounded by seaweed packed in such a manner that the child was held securely in the center of the container. He made a desperate attempt to get the box but failed utterly. The dream ended with the box containing the girl passing under the counter at the stern of the *Belvidere*.

A short time later, Captain Elwell awakened and came out on deck, but he appeared so disturbed that when the members of the crew saw him they asked for an explanation.

"I saw a child's dead body in my dream, and although I attempted to rescue the box the child was in, I failed, after which I awakened suddenly."

The crewmen advised the captain to forget the incident, saying that odd dreams were often the result of eating rich food. The first mate told him that after eating the wrong thing, he often had similar fancies of imagination in his dreams, and vainly attempted to have the captain dismiss the entire dream from his mind.

Less than half an hour later the captain sat down on a fish box to look out over the ocean. An interval of time passed. Then, quite a distance away, he noticed an object that might have been a box. Passing his hands before his eyes to make sure he was not in another dream, he half rose and gave a shout.

"Look! Isn't that a box?"

The crew joined him, and the captain ordered the man at the wheel to set a course for the box. Minutes later the schooner *Belvidere* came up on it, and several boat hooks pulled the wooden object alongside the fishing vessel. The captain looked down and saw that the box was nailed securely shut. Whatever might be inside could only be guessed at until they brought it aboard.

Five minutes later they had pulled it over the gunnel, and hatchets soon pryed the lid off. As fragment after fragment of the lid was pryed away from the box, the men discovered that closely-packed seaweed prevented them from seeing what was inside. They loosened the seaweed and a short time later the body of a little girl was revealed. She was about four years of age and evidently had been dead a week or ten days.

The remains were lifted from the box and temporarily placed on the deck. The men examined the box carefully and discovered that there were holes bored in the sides of the container. The box, made of coarse hard wood and nailed securely, evidently had been built for the purpose of containing the child's body, with the holes bored to make certain the box would go to the sea bottom.

All agreed that, considering the partial decomposition of the child's remains, the body should be replaced in the box and the box weighted down, nailed shut, and sent to the bottom, since the vessel was not to return to port for at least a week. Thus the child was buried at sea for the second time. Captain Elwell never learned the story of the tragedy that was revealed to him in a dream.

CHAPTER 10

NUNGESSER AND COLI

The story of Nungesser and Coli combines a tale of the ocean, what is under the ocean, and an airplane that flew over the ocean.

Charles Nungesser was a famous World War I French ace who had the remarkable record of shooting down forty-five enemy planes. Early in 1927 he became interested in the $25,-000 prize offered by French-born Raymond B. Ortieg, a New York hotel man, for an airplane flight between France and New York. Nungesser went to his good friend François Coli, an older man who had also become an experienced aviator during the war and had some long distance flights to his credit. They decided they would use a Levasseur biplane already built, and by adding extra gas tanks and making several structural changes fit it for crossing the Atlantic. They painted their plane white and called her *L'Oiseau Blanc*, or *The White Bird*.

Finally the day came when *L'Oiseau Blanc* would have her tryout. The two fliers went down to Villa Coublay, climbed into the cockpit, and took off. The plane reached a top speed of 105 miles an hour and apparently responded well to all the controls, as both men were pleased with the results.

Definite plans for the Atlantic flight were then made. Provisions, including tins of tuna and sardines, biscuits, bananas, and chocolate, were put aboard. Two giant thermos jugs of hot coffee and three quarts of brandy were also stored on board the airplane.

The morning of May 8, 1927, was chosen for the attempt. The mechanics wheeled out the Levasseur biplane from the hangar at Le Bourget Field a few seconds after 4:30 A.M. Even at that early hour a large crowd of enthusiastic Frenchmen was there to say farewell. Handshakes were exchanged and then Nungesser raised his hand for silence.

"You know what this thing means, and we both do. We are taking a risk, I know, but we are taking it willingly and with all our hearts." Nungesser then turned to General Leon Girod, who had given him his first plane in World War I. "General, if we shouldn't make it, then I am relying on you to bear witness to the fact that we took no unnecessary risks and that we prepared our flight as carefully as it could have been prepared."

"Yes, I know, I know," answered the general, "but you are going to make it."

Nungesser shook hands again with a few intimate friends and hugged his brother. Another brother awaited his arrival at New York.

Just then an orderly hurried up with a message, the latest weather forecast. Coli read it. Nungesser spoke to his companion. "What does it say, anything vital?"

"No. A minor disturbance is beginning to form. We'll have to alter course a little farther northward to avoid it. That's all, if you concur at this time. Do you?"

Nungesser nodded and the two of them took their places in the plane. Off to the west a fire was burning, and from time to time flashes of lightning illuminated the horizon.

At 5:18 in the morning, the engine was started. Nungesser let it run for several minutes before he signaled that he was ready. The mechanics scrambled to pull the chocks away from the wheels, and the beautiful *White Bird* began to roll slowly down the runway. *L'Oiseau Blanc* was carrying an unusually heavy load. More than five tons of weight had to be lifted from the ground off a runway barely 2,500 feet long. Nungesser proceeded to the extreme end of the runway, then turned the aircraft to face the wind. He fought to get every ounce of power from the engine before he released the brakes. The crucial moment arrived. The plane started down the runway, gathering speed by the second.

Halfway down the runway she cleared the ground—but fell back to earth. Then for a second time she rose into the air. She bounced back again, her speed still increasing. Now she was 600 feet from the end of the runway, with possible disaster ahead—500 feet, 400, and then 300—still *L'Oiseau Blanc* held to the ground.

With less than twenty yards of the take-off space remaining, the plane rose slowly until she was ten feet in the air. Still in a slow climb, the plane headed straight for the line of trees a quarter mile from the end of the runway, cleared them, was seen by the crowd for a few fleeting seconds, and then vanished into the unknown. Five minutes later there was a vivid flash of lightning and the thunderstorm began in earnest. The watching hundreds ran for shelter.

On the evening of May 9, 1927, the night after *L'Oiseau Blanc* had left Paris, a special edition of the French newspaper *La Presse* was published. It announced the wonderful news that Nungesser and Coli had accomplished their objective and landed successfully in New York. *La Presse* described the details of the epic flight. It told how all the ships in New York Harbor had blown their whistles and sirens. It stated that Nungesser had landed safely on the surface of the water in New York Harbor without the slightest difficulty and under very favorable conditions. The two men, according to the newspaper, had remained spellbound in the cockpit for several minutes, temporarily paralyzed by the fact of victory. Then they had stood up and waved to the little group of tugs and motorboats that gathered. After this they had embraced each other in sheer happiness. A motorboat came alongside. The two fliers were transferred from *L'Oiseau Blanc* to a motorboat, which took the transatlantic fliers ashore in New York. There they were smothered with ticker tape as hundreds of thousands of New Yorkers cheered them in their auto cavalcade along Broadway.

Understandably, every Frenchman who read the news was excited by the reported triumph of his fellow countrymen.

Unfortunately, the entire story was false.

It is true that a plane was sighted bobbing up and down in the waters of New York Harbor. It is also true that two men were seen in the plane. It is true that Robert Nungesser, the flier's brother, was standing on a New York pier with an American flier, studying the lines of the airplane through binoculars. But that is all.

It was soon discovered that the plane in New York Harbor was an American hydroplane. A French newsman in New York, with a Paris deadline to make, had sighted the plane. Realizing what would happen if the plane were the Nungesser-Coli craft, he took the chance of getting a report out ahead of everyone else. He wired to Paris what *would have happened* had the airplane been that of the French fliers—and then the bubble burst!

What did happen to Nungesser and Coli?

After they left Le Bourget Field that May morning they were joined by four French fliers, who escorted them to the English Channel. Then one by one the French fliers left, each giving a final salute as he returned to the mainland of Europe. The last French soil over which the two men flew was at Étretat, where a memorial was later erected to them.

Shortly after ten o'clock a plane believed to be *L'Oiseau*

Blanc was heard between Cherbourg and Southampton, but the thick morning haze prevented an actual sighting. Twenty hours then elapsed with no report of the French fliers.

At ten o'clock the following morning, a plane believed to be the French craft was sighted in the air over Newfoundland. Another report reached New York from St. Pierre, a tiny island south of Newfoundland, that *L'Oiseau Blanc* had flown over at eight o'clock that morning.

Unfortunately, as the hours went by, fog set in—thick, heavy fog that obscured everything. Rockland, Maine, then reported that a plane had been heard in the general vicinity flying down the coast. The lighthouse keeper at Seguin, Maine, is said to have confirmed the news a short time later, stating that he heard the noise of an engine overhead at about the time *L'Oiseau Blanc* might have been passing above that island. Several other reports came from islands in Casco Bay. Then there was nothing but complete, overwhelming silence, a silence that has continued ever since that May day almost half a century ago.

In Paris the cheering crowds were confronted with a bulletin stating that earlier reports of success were wrong. Mobs formed. Angry, disappointed Frenchmen broke into the newspaper office, carried out hundreds of copies of the erroneous papers, and publicly burned them in a nearby park.

Nothing further was heard of the fliers. The hours lengthened into days, the days became weeks, then months, and finally years.

One day in 1947—the exact date is unknown—Robert MacVane, a lobsterman from Cliff Island, Maine, was fishing in comparatively deep water when something caught on his trap line. He pulled to the surface a piece of wreckage from an airplane. He was then fishing at a point directly off the southwesterly tip of Jewel Island, the next island to the south of Cliff Island.

The water in the region is 96 to 146 feet deep, and bringing the fragment to the surface had been hard work. Later a large mass of the plane was hooked and lifted, but in the attempt to retrieve it, the wreckage broke away and sank again. At one point MacVane had six feet of the plane above the surface.

I was given several fragments of this aircraft and took them to the South Weymouth Naval Air Station in Massachusetts. Commander Lawrence E. Oliver had them examined, and the conclusion arrived at at the Naval Air Station was that the plane fragment was from an aircraft of the World War II period.

From time to time I journeyed with different groups of scuba divers to the scene of the find off Jewel Island, and in the following months much additional material was brought to the surface. (The efforts of divers Hans Krone of Richmond, Virginia, and Howard White of Kensington, Connecticut, a member of the Harvard class of 1959, deserve special mention.)

Miss Johanna von Tiling, of Cliff Island, who has a deep interest in things nautical, was a great help in our efforts to solve the mystery of the airplane fragments. Late in November 1959 Miss von Tiling wrote to me that David H. MacVane, Jr., of Cliff Island, brought up airplane wreckage from the same general area on November 24, while hauling traps off Jewel Island. An airplane section, in one piece when raised to the surface, separated into several fragments at points of corrosion and sank.

On September 25, 1960, Robert MacVane "again tangled" with the wreckage and pulled to the surface some twisted fragments of metal described by Miss von Tiling as "grayish except where chaffed, where it looks greenish." The location was in eighteen to twenty fathoms of water about 700 yards southwest of a buoy that had been placed for me the year before.

A visitor to Cliff Island, who wishes to remain anonymous, brought the entire mystery into sharp relief some time later. Tremendous publicity all over America and Europe developed. The visitor, a former member of the French World War II resistance forces, was of the opinion that the fragments, which were on exhibition at Cliff Island, could easily have been from the Nungesser-Coli plane. I went out to Cliff Island and brought a piece of the latest find back to Boston.

Major Marc Palabaud of the French air force and Charles D. Pampelonne, the French consul in Boston, visited the offices of the Quincy, Massachusetts, *Patriot Ledger* to examine the fragment. After several hours of inspection, Major Palabaud asked for and received the fragment, which was sent across the ocean to France for an exhaustive examination.

On February 11, 1961, *Paris Match* published a lengthy article with many pictures about the Nungesser-Coli flight and the subsequent discovery of airplane fragments off Jewel Island, Maine. *"ILS AVAIENT BATTU LINDBERGH"* was the banner headline. The theme that "they had beaten Lindbergh" was stressed, for if the fragments found in United States territorial waters were definitely from the Nungesser plane, then the two Frenchmen had crossed the Atlantic from Paris before Lindbergh's flight, only to crash off the rugged coast of Maine. The *Match* article was buoyant and hopeful that the mystery might soon be cleared up.

A short time later word came from D. Foster Taylor of the J. H. Taylor Foundry Company in Quincy, Massachusetts, that he and his son, David Taylor, had tested fragments from the plane and were of the opinion that it could not be the Nungesser plane. When they fractured a piece of the metal, it did not appear to have crystallized sufficiently for the time that had passed. They stated definitely that the material was not corroded enough to have been under water for thirty-four years. Later they sent a fragment to the Charles Batchelder Company of Botsford, Connecticut, and received a letter from John Dougherty of that company.

Mr. Dougherty stated, on February 6, 1961, that a "spectographic analysis reveals the sample to be 2024 (24 S) Ross Aluminum Alloy of the following composition:

Copper	4.80	Manganese	.71	Tin	.00
Iron	.25	Magnesium	1.58	Chromium	.00
Silicon	.13	Nickel	.00	Lead	.00
Zinc	.01	Titanium	.01		

"This alloy has been used extensively in aircraft for many years," stated Mr. Dougherty. "Its high copper content gives it relatively low corrosion resistance, which fact would seemingly rule out any marine application and tend to bolster the wrecked airplane theory." The material was definitely from an airplane of the general World War II period.

Several days after the airplane fragment arrived in Paris, the French aeronautical engineers came to the same conclusion. The twisted piece of wreckage sent across the ocean was not from *L'Oiseau Blanc*.

They agreed with Mr. Dougherty that the metal was from an airplane, but not of 1927 vintage. Chemical tests made on their fragment showed the metal was Duralumin, an alloy of aluminum and copper commonly used in aircraft construction.

The French metallurgists did, however, make an important discovery. Under a thick layer of corrosion and barnacles, the engineers found a row of red letters about an inch high, and were able to make out A, C, and O, possibly part of the acronym ALCOA. The fragment of plane was definitely not of French construction.

It was suggested by the French government, however, that dragging operations be carried out so that the remainder of the wreckage could be brought to the surface. It was remotely possible that the Nungesser-Coli plane, believed to have been heard by the keeper at Seguin, a relatively short distance from Jewel Island, did crash in the vicinity, and a search of the bottom area might still solve a world mystery. The French suggestion was never carried out, however.

Of course, the news that the fragments were not from the French plane brought great disappointment to aviation enthusiasts all over the world who had hoped that the enigma of Nungesser and Coli would be solved.

If the objects now on the sea bottom off Jewel Island do not have any connection with the Nungesser-Coli mystery, what are they? After investigating the matter, I am of the opinion that it is possible the fragments are from one of the two other planes known to have crashed in the area.

The deck log of the U.S.S. *Tuscaloosa*, a heavy cruiser, for April 5, 1944, reveals that while the cruiser was in Casco Bay waters a few miles from Jewel Island, one of the four biplanes aboard was catapulted into the air. On its return journey to a point alongside the ship, the plane spun in at too low an altitude and crashed into the sea. Aboard were the pilot, Ensign K. W. Baker, USNR, and the enlisted radioman, C. E. Duiguid, USN.

The plane capsized immediately after crashing, and although the crash boat proceeded at once to the scene, the boat's personnel did not have time to recover the occupants of the aircraft, which sank at once.

Bryon M. Tripp, who was serving aboard the heavy cruiser at the time, recalled later that the ship was then very close to land and relatively near Jewel Island. Tripp said that he remembered the memorial service aboard the *Tuscaloosa* a few days later, after all efforts to locate the plane on the bottom had failed.

Residents of Casco Bay for many years had also spoken of the wreck of a training plane from the Brunswick, Maine, Naval Air Station. They maintained that the plane roared in over Cliff Island and then disappeared off Jewel Island with a crash which could be heard for miles.

My letter to the Brunswick Naval Air Station did not produce any affirmative statement that such a plane had come from that station, but it seems reasonable there was a basis for the belief in this story on the part of many people. For example, Phyllis MacVane saw the plane as it flew over Cliff Island and headed out toward Jewel Island in a snow squall. She heard a crash a few minutes later off the southwest end of Jewel Island.

On two occasions we went scuba diving where we thought we might find the plane. On the second occasion we went down to 134 feet and did identify a plane that the Brunswick Air Base eventually decided was a B-12 trainer that had crashed during World War II.

It was a great disappointment that we had not found *The White Bird*. Of course, I realize the chances that the French plane *L'Oiseau Blanc* crashed in Casco Bay after having been heard passing over Seguin Light are relatively small. But the plane must have gone down in the sea somewhere, as it was never heard from again. Jewel Island is in a direct line west from Seguin Light, and the plane may be in the area roughly bounded by Jewel Island, Peak's Island, Cape Elizabeth, and Halfway Rock Light, located about two and one half miles southeast from Jewel Island. According to the lighthouse keeper's calculation, he heard the sound of the engine fade away to the west, and it was apparent the craft was headed for the mainland in the general direction of Massachusetts.

There is no record of this engine being heard again, so the plane may have gone down somewhere in Casco Bay in the general area I have outlined. But years and years of search have not revealed its location, and I am afraid that unless some lucky scuba diver visits it on the ocean bottom, or a lobsterman catches the plane in his lines, *L'Oiseau Blanc* will never be found.

CHAPTER 11

SHARKS

I

Shark scares along the New England coast occur almost yearly. When a shark is sighted at the height of a summer season, it brings into sharp relief the long history of these dangerous, unpredictable inhabitants of the ocean.

My first encounter with a shark occurred in Massachusetts Bay while canoeing with my wife across to Nahant from Winthrop more than a third of a century ago. As we approached the Nahant shore, Mrs. Snow and I suddenly sighted a giant shark, which frightened both of us. When we first saw the triangular fin, we mistook it for a lobster buoy. But when the shark rolled over on its back, presenting a white belly as its hideous jaws yawned wide, I recognized what it was. As soon as the shark had passed under the bow of the canoe, I smacked my paddle with great force flat against the surface of the water, which made a sound like a rifle shot. This ruse must have worked, for the shark swam away rapidly, making us very happy. We were even more elated when a shark was captured the next day and brought in to Merryman's Wharf, Winthrop. We viewed the remains and both agreed it could have been the same shark.

On another occasion, when Minot's Light off Cohasset, Massachusetts, was still a manned lighthouse station, I was about to dive from the tower into the sea, but the keeper warned me that there was a sizable shark lurking below, perhaps awaiting scraps from the keepers' dinner, which were occasionally thrown into the water from the quarters eighty-eight feet above.

The thought of being the prey of sharks did not fill me with joyous anticipation, but I took the dive anyway, as those who were to photograph the incident were ready for action. On the other hand, I was anxious to disappoint the shark, and when I hit the water I swam so fast that I probably approached my best record for speed as I raced to the waiting boat.

Another encounter with sharks occurred when Jerry Thomas of Weymouth and I were scuba diving, attempting to find several grindstones lost overboard from a wreck of more than a century ago off Fourth Cliff, Scituate. On this occasion the sharks visited us in pairs, simply overwhelming us and causing us to abandon our diving activities. I remember that we failed to find a single grindstone, although the following year Donald Hourihan discovered one at the same wreck and brought it ashore.*

II

We now go back through the pages of time to the year 1826. The location is a considerable distance from the mainland of New England.

On the night of August 27, 1826, Lieutenant Edward Smith was commander of the schooner *Magpie* with a crew of twenty-four. The schooner's fore-topsail was set, with the yard braced for the starboard tack and the foresail in the brails.**

The mate noticed a small black cloud and decided to warn

* See my *Fantastic Folklore and Fact*, p. 229 and illustration.
** A brail is a rope, fastened to the leech or corner of a sail and leading through a block, by which the sail can be hauled up or in as in furling.

Lieutenant Smith. He looked down the hatchway into the cabin.

"Mr. Smith," he called, "I think the land breeze will be coming off rather strong, sir. The clouds now look black."

"Very well," answered his superior officer. "I'll be up on deck in a moment."

The cloud, swelling to tremendous proportions, moved toward the schooner. Suddenly, without further warning, a terrific squall hit the *Magpie*. The storm came so fast that the mate was unable to call the watch, and the schooner began to capsize! Just at that moment Lieutenant Smith was putting his foot down on the last step of the ladder. As the *Magpie* heeled over, he was thrown into the water and the schooner sank beneath him.

Two of the sailors, caught below, went to the bottom with the vessel. The survivors found themselves in the water, swimming around in the darkness without anything to cling to. They were amazed a short time later to see the schooner's longboat come to the surface nearby. It must have broken loose from its position on the bows, but there it was—swamped, of course.

Thinking only of themselves, all the survivors scrambled into the boat, causing it to capsize at once. Then they attempted to climb onto the keel, but since only a few could huddle there, the others clung to the gunwales.

Lieutenant Smith realized that unless the men turned the boat over and bailed her out, many of them would drown. Under his direction they righted the craft, and two men slid over the gunwales and began bailing the water out with their hats.

Suddenly there was a disturbance in the water, and the triangular fin of a shark was seen gliding along less than fifty feet away. In the excitement that followed, the boat went over again, and the men began to fight for places on the keel. As the shark drew near, one sailor after another would gain temporary possession of the keel and then be dislodged by a frantic companion.

Smith urged the men to kick in the water with their feet, for he believed that sharks would not attack under such conditions. Splashing the water with their feet all the time, the men righted the boat.

Four men climbed in. All began bailing steadily until they had cleared the longboat of water down to the thwarts, or seats. Twenty minutes more would have been enough time to allow all hands to get in, but a great noise was heard a short distance away, and the horrified men in the water saw no less than fifteen sharks approaching them. Over went the longboat again.

At first the sharks appeared to be harmless, swimming among their potential victims and only rubbing against the legs of the men. At times they would leap about, apparently playing in the water. Then came the terrifying moment when one man felt sharp teeth bite into his leg. An agonizing scream came from his mouth as he felt his leg completely severed from his body.

No sooner had blood been tasted by the sharks than the dreaded mass attack took place. The air filled with shrieks as one and then another unfortunate sailor lost a leg or an arm. Some of the crew were torn from the boat to which they tried to cling, while others sank to their death from fear alone.

Lieutenant Smith, treading water as he clung to the gunwales, continued giving orders with clearness and coolness, and his men still obeyed. Again the boat was righted, and again two men slid over the gunwales to bail her out. The survivors, as before, clung to the sides and kept the boat upright. Lieutenant Smith himself held on to the stern and cheered and applauded his men.

But the sharks had tasted blood and were not to be driven from their feast. In one brief moment, while Smith was resting from his splashing, a giant shark moved toward him, seized his legs, and bit off both of them just above the knees. With a deep groan and shudder the lieutenant released his hold and started to sink. The crew, who had long respected their gallant commander and knew his worth and courage, grasped their dying leader and lifted him onto the stern of the longboat. Even now, in his agony, Smith spoke only of rescuing the remaining few. As he was giving instructions, one of the men in the water tried to get into the boat, causing it to heel to one side, and Smith rolled off the stern. His last bubbling cry was lost amid the shrieks of his former companions. He sank into the ocean and was seen no more.

Every hope died with him. All but two of the crew gave in to despair, with loud cries of grief and cursing. The boat overturned again. Some who had not been too seriously injured by the monsters of the deep endeavored to climb upon the keel. By now, however, they were exhausted from their struggles and soon gave up the unequal fight, not caring when or how they met death. They either were eaten immediately by the sharks or, courting death, threw themselves from the boat and drowned. One of the last to perish was a sailor named Wilson.

Only two survivors remained, Jack Maclean and gunner Tom Meldrum. The sharks seemed sated for the time being. Jack and Tom, who had been clutching the keel, finally managed to right the boat. Maclean climbed in over the bow and Meldrum over the stern. Still uninjured and in comparative security, they began to bail again. After twenty minutes they had lightened the boat and both sat down to rest, exhausted.

A short time later the sharks returned. The creatures endeavored to upset the boat, swimming along and bumping it time and time again. But after circling the craft for a while, they vanished.

The two men, tired as they were, resumed bailing and continued until the boat was nearly dry, then fell into a sound sleep, their minds relieved by their relative security. Day dawned before they awoke to horrible reality. Heat, hunger, thirst, and fatigue settled on the unfortunate pair. They looked out over the water as far as they could see, but only an endless ocean, a cloudless sky, and a fiercely burning sun greeted them. They had no oar, no mast, no sail, no food or drinking water— nothing but the bare planks of the boat.

The sea was as smooth as glass. The hopelessness of their situation struck them. Hunger, the burning rays of the sun, the sharks, and after a time fear of each other almost overcame them.

Then later that morning Meldrum, scanning the sea, saw a white sail on the horizon.

"By God, there is a brig!" he called out.

The two men jumped into each other's arms and were soon laughing and crying together. Waving and shouting, they watched the brig, forgetting everything—their sunburn, their hunger, and even their thirst.

Suddenly the vessel swung around three points* and started on a tack that would take her on a parallel course to their boat, probably too far away to notice them.

In vain they hailed; in vain they threw their jackets in the air. They were not seen, and the brig continued on her new course. The shipwrecked sailors watched a man going aloft on the vessel. They could see him distinctly, but the man paid them no attention in spite of their frantic waving and shouting.

Time was slipping away. Once they got abaft the beam of the brig, every second would lessen the chance of their being seen. Then it was that Meldrum looked first at the brig, then at his companion.

"By heaven, I'll do it, or we are lost!"

* A point is 7½ degrees of the compass, originally spoken of as ¹⁄₁₂ of a quadrant.

"Do what?"

"I'll tell you, Jack, I'll swim to her; if I get safely to her, you are safe."

"What! Jump overboard and leave me all alone?" replied Maclean. "Look at that shark which has followed us all night. Why it is only waiting for you to get into the water to swallow you. No, no—wait, wait, perhaps another vessel will come!"

Both men watched the fin of the shark move through the water about twenty yards from the boat. Now and then others could be seen. Still, death surely awaited them in the boat, too.

"Well," said Tom finally, "if we wait we must die, and if I get to the brig, we will be saved. If the sharks come, God will protect me! Goodbye. Now if you see those devils in chase of me, splash or make some noise to frighten them, but don't tell me you see them coming. God bless you, Jack. Keep your eye upon me, and keep making signals to the brig."

Meldrum let himself overboard with as much calmness as if he were merely taking a recreational swim. Maclean cheered his companion, looked across at the oncoming brig, and wildly waved his jacket. Then he turned to watch the sharks. Seeing three monsters swim past the boat in the direction of his companion, he splashed his jacket in the water to scare them away, but they lazily pursued their course toward his companion.

Meldrum was swimming strongly. There was no doubt that he would pass within hail of the brig provided the sharks did not get him first. He kicked the water and splashed as he swam. Then came the chilling moment when he saw one of the horrible creatures at his side. Frightened, he swam and kicked so that he made a big splash constantly, but he entertained little hope of success.

With a freshening wind, the brig was running faster through the water, but Meldrum was now close enough for those on the brig to hear him. He hailed and shouted at the top of his lungs. Not a soul was to be seen on deck except the man at the wheel, and he was too intent upon his course to notice the call. The brig passed close to the swimmer, and then every second increased the distance between them. Hope was gone, and the swim had exhausted him. The sharks now waited for the moment to dispose of their victim.

Meldrum knew a return to the boat was impossible. He realized that in his exhausted condition he never could reach her. Then, just as he began to offer up his last prayer to God, he saw a man look over the quarter of the brig. Raising both his hands at once to attract the man's attention, he began to tread water. Then to his joy he saw the flash of a telescope as the man on the quarter-deck first aimed the glass at him and then gave a shout of acknowledgment. A moment later the brig hove to and the crew let a boat down. Five minutes afterward gunner Tom Meldrum was pulled to safety out of the sea. The sharks swam away. Within ten minutes Jack Maclean was rescued, and both survivors were aboard the brig. They had won their awesome fight with death.

III

Few New Englanders have heard what in my opinion is one of the strangest shark stories of all times. With the help of author George H. Toole, I am able to tell the tale. Fully documented and sworn to, the account involves the brig *Nancy,* the schooner *Ferret,* and Lieutenant Michael Fitton, an officer aboard the *Ferret.*

Fitton had heard of walking sticks made from the backbone of a shark and wanted one for himself. On August 13, 1799, he was standing at the rail of the schooner *Ferret* watching several sharks tear at the remains of a dead bullock floating in the water. He decided it was a good chance to get his shark backbone. After failing several times, finally he caught a shark on a hook baited with a choice piece of pork. Soon the monster was on deck with Fitton watching as it was cut open.

To the amazement of everyone, when the sailors opened the stomach of the shark, a substantial bundle of papers tied with a string was revealed! When dried and examined, the bundle was found to contain the papers of the brig *Nancy,* which had been captured in the quasi-war with France and England, and was even then awaiting a final court decision on her disposition.

Fraudulent papers, prepared so that the *Nancy* would be declared ineligible for capture, had already been presented at court. When the new evidence was presented, the court stated officially that these papers were forged, and the papers found in the stomach of the shark were certified as the actual papers of the brig *Nancy.* Thus the shark had nullified the *Nancy* captain's scheme.

The jaws of the shark were preserved through the years, and are still on exhibition although the creature was caught 177 years ago!

IV

When in 1946 I visited Keeper Charles Ellis of Highland Light down on Cape Cod, he told me a weird tale of being in a boat attacked by a maddened shark on November 13, 1920. He recorded the tale and I include his unusual story here.

"I always liked the lightboat *Hedge Fence No. 9.* I had about the narrowest escape ever at that time, too. One day a schooner ran into us and loosened our plates. She was a three-sticker and misstayed at the wrong time to crash us.

"It was a head wind and a head tide, and we were out of luck. After sheering off, she dropped anchor nearby, and our old man, Captain James Frizell, told me to row over with him and investigate. We launched a small fourteen-foot dory, and he had the stroke oar. We started rowing for the schooner, and then it happened.

"I saw a big fin coming for us, and all I could think of was that it was too late for sharks to be in the sound—November 13. I yelled at the captain.

" 'I see it,' he cried. Then the shark came up right in front of us, rolled over, and tried to nudge us so that we'd go over.

" 'Hit him with your oar,' I yelled, and the old man brought his oar down on the shark's head. It must have hurt, for the shark then gave up and swam off. But not for long, for after he got about fifty feet away, he turned and I could see his big fin cutting through the water like a knife as he came after us again.

"Then there was a soft thump and we were actually lifted out of water. But the old man was ready this time, and whanged his oar time after time on the shark. Finally the shark decided to call it a day, and sank out of sight. We were both scared stiff, and rowed as fast as we could to the other vessel. But the fish didn't show up when we rowed back an hour later, and we were very thankful. It isn't any fun swapping punches with a fifteen-foot shark at any time. I'll never forget that November 13th."

~~~~~~~~~~

DARK DAYS
IN NEW ENGLAND

Boston, the rest of New England, and New York have had many dark days noted in the pages of recorded history, but the most remembered years are 1682, 1716, 1780, and 1881. By dark days I mean those when the sky is almost as dark during the daytime as at night.

The first of these dark days in New England was described by no less a personality than Boston's Cotton Mather (1663–1728). A remarkable clergyman and author, Mather seemed at his best when preaching to pirates soon to be swung off into eternity on the gallows. His manuscript "Angel of Bethesda" covers many subjects.* Mather evidently enjoyed writing about piracy, hurricanes, dark days, and unexplained phenomena, and in the manuscript he mentions the unusual cloud effects of 1682, when atmospheric refraction produced strange appearances.

One evening in 1682 at Lynn, Massachusetts, after the sun had set, a man named Handford went out of doors to ascertain if the new moon had risen. His attention was taken

* See Gordon W. Jones, *Angel of Bethesda*, 1972.

by a black cloud of strange appearance. After looking at it a short time he discovered that it contained the figure of a man completely armed, standing with his legs apart, holding a pike in his hands. Handford called to his wife, who came out and also noticed the huge blackness of the apparition. Neighbors soon joined in observing the spectacle. After a while the figure radically changed, and the black cloud became a large ship, fully rigged, with all sails set. It was identifiable as plainly as if the ship were seen in the harbor. To the settlers of Lynn it seemed the handsomest craft they had ever observed, with its high, majestic bow and black hull.

Finally, though the image still remained in the cloud, one by one, the people went back into their houses. Around midnight, the cloud vanished and the sky was clear. Many reliable people in the town saw the apparition and all agreed that it had happened. What it was and how it can be accounted for is still unknown.

Mather also saw New England's next dark day. On Sunday, October 21, 1716, people were gathered in the various houses of worship when one hour before noon, the greatest dark day known up to that time descended on the northeast. It became so dark, according to historian Sidney Perley, that church members could not recognize others seated just across the aisle of the meeting house. They were unable to locate friends unless these happened to be outlined against a window.

A writer of the period says that "one could not recognize another four seats away, nor read a word in a psalm book." Some ministers sent to neighboring houses for candles, not wanting anything to interrupt the services. Others, believing it would soon pass away, simply sat and waited. Still others were ready to believe that the darkness of the last days was settling like a "pall over nature before its dissolution."

A half hour later it grew light enough for the clergy to finish the services. Gathering at the close of the meetings, the congregations talked about the probable cause of what was almost a supernatural event.

For several days the sky had been more or less overcast. A writer of the period stated that the atmosphere was "full of smoke." It descended near the earth when the wind was from the southwest. On this particular Sunday dark clouds of smoke had passed over, and it was thought that the wind, changing to the eastward, brought the smoke back and darkened the land. That was the explanation accepted at the time by many people. Cotton Mather deemed the occurrence of sufficient importance to send an account of it to the Royal Philosophical Society in England, which soon after published it in its *Transactions.*

Darkness produces a peculiar feeling, probably from the mystery which is involved in it. Unnatural darkness, or what seems to be such, usually produces a weird and gloomy feeling in the average person. It often turns a superstitious mind into channels of fear and alarm. And the inhabitants of colonial New England were subject to such fear and alarm.

Perley tells us that the next dark day, Friday, May 19, 1780, is recorded in New England annals as "The Dark Day." On that occasion the light of the sun was almost completely obscured, and a strange darkness filled the hours that "should have been brightest," bringing fear, anxiety, and awe into the minds of the people.

There are many explanations given, but the most reasonable involves forest fires. From about the first of the month, great tracts of forest along Lake Champlain, extending down to the vicinity of Ticonderoga, were ablaze. Also new settlements were being made in northern New Hampshire and in Canada near the New Hampshire line, and the settlers were burning over the forests preparatory to cultivation.

The early settlers of the northern and northeastern portions of New England cleared their land by fire. In the autumn they would select the ground to be cleared. When winter came, they would cut every tree on the lot halfway through waist high, leaving the forest standing. The men then patiently waited for the strong winds of March to sweep through the woods, blowing down the half-cut trees. If they wished to have them fall sooner, the choppers at one end of the area would cut a tree entirely off, letting it tumble against the next one, and that against the next, and in a minute or two, rows of immense trees would be crashing to the earth. In April one end of the huge pile would be set on fire. It would burn until the boughs and the great logs were almost entirely converted into ashes, which proved an excellent fertilizer.

This procedure was good for clearing the fields, but it often covered New England with soot. On the Piscataqua River on one occasion the soot in certain areas was six inches deep, and the air had been thick and heavy with smoke while the fires existed.

At Melrose, Massachusetts, a high hill only two miles from the center of the village could not be seen from Monday till Thursday of the week in which the dark day occurred. Through this period the sun seemed unusually red, as it often appears when the air is dense with smoke. In Greater Boston, on the afternoon before "the dark day," a breeze sprang up, driving all the smoke to the south. This caused the air the next day to be free from dense clouds of smoke, fog, and haze, making it relatively pure, though the sky was just as dark. At sunset a very dark cloudbank appeared in the south and west, where it remained all night. In southern New Hampshire on the same night, the wind changed from the west to the east, and a dense fog came in off the ocean.

When the dark day itself arrived, the wind was from the east. The sun rose clear and continued to be visible for a short time. Then it became overcast. Changing to the southwest, the wind set in motion the foliage of the trees and brought back the clouds.

"Lightning shot its livid tongues, thunder rolled, and rain fell." The thunder and lightning occurred principally in southern New Hampshire, hardly being noticed in Massachusetts. Considerable rain fell as far north and east as Berwick, Maine, but very little south of New Hampshire.

Toward nine o'clock the clouds began to disperse. As the sun burned through, they grew thinner and thinner, and a peculiar yellow tinge settled over everything. Some described it as of a brassy color, while others spoke of it as having a coppery appearance. Doubtless it resembled the "yellow day" that New England would experience in 1881, but without question that of 1780 was much more intense. The earth, rocks, trees, buildings, and water were "robed in this strange enchanting hue," which seemed to change the aspect of everything. A few minutes after nine a dark dense cloud gradually rose out of the west and spread itself until the heavens were entirely covered, except at the horizon, where a narrow rim of light remained.

A few minutes later the sky was as dark as it usually is at nine o'clock on a summer evening. At that hour in the morning the women of Ipswich, Massachusetts, were busily at work weaving. They were compelled to postpone their work for want of light.

Ten o'clock brought rain to Melrose, Massachusetts. The heavens grew very dark, the light that had been seen at the horizon all morning vanished completely. Standing on their thresholds, women looked out upon the dark landscape with anxious, curious expressions upon their faces. Children held onto their mothers' skirts, "their hearts filled with fear." Husbands and sons returned from the fields where they had been engaged in planting and noticed candles in the windows as they entered their homes.

Carpenters left their tools, blacksmiths their forges. Schools were dismissed and children went home for answers to their confusion, but there were none. Travelers put up at the nearest farmhouse until the weird darkness would pass.

"What is it? What does it mean? What is coming?" queried everyone of himself or of his neighbor. One of two things seemed certain to most minds—either a hurricane such as was never known before was about to strike, or it was the last day when the "elements shall melt with fervent heat, the earth also and the works that are therein shall be burned up."

The darkness reached its height shortly after eleven o'clock, and for hours New England was enveloped in gloom. Candles were a necessity to carry out ordinary business transactions and to light dinner tables. At noon it was as dark as evening. Common print could not be read by the best of eyes, time could not be ascertained from clock or watch faces, and domestic work of the household had to be done by candlelight.

Fires on the hearth shone as brightly as on a moonless evening in the late autumn, and the candlelight threw distinct shadows on the walls. At Haverhill, Massachusetts, a person one hundred yards away could not be seen, and one man in a room with three large windows could not see another in the same room a short distance away.

Animals acted as though night had come. Chickens went to roost, tucked their heads under their wings, and went to sleep as quietly as if it had been sunset. Cattle lowed and gathered at the pasture bars, waiting to be let through so they might return to their barns. Sheep huddled by the fences or in circles in the open fields. Frogs peeped as they usually do at sunset, and birds sang their evening songs. The whippoorwills appeared and gave their calls, woodcocks whistled, and bats came out and flew overhead.

Men and women knew that night had not come and that the darkness was due to some other cause, but they were not sure whether that cause was natural or supernatural. In Boston one of the Reverend Dr. Byles' congregation sent her servant to ask what was going on.

"Give my respectful compliments to your mistress," replied the doctor, "and tell her I am as much in the dark as she is."

Ignorant and learned alike feared that it might be a token of the dreadful day of universal destruction. Many were of the opinion that the "sun of mercy had set, and the night of despair, of judgment, and the end of all things was at hand," according to historian Perley. It was popularly believed that the Revolutionary War, which had been in progress for five years, might be to blame. It could be the fulfillment of the prophecy that announces "wars and rumors of war" as coming before "the great and dreadful day of the Lord."

The dark day influenced the minds of all classes. The more excitable persons ran about the streets exclaiming, "The day of judgment is at hand!" almost convincing many that it was true. In several cases those who believed they had wronged their neighbors visited them and confessed, asking their forgiveness. Others dropped on their knees in the fields and prayed, perhaps for the first and last time in their lives. Some sought to hide themselves, thinking thus to escape the "great day of God's wrath."

A party of sailors landed in Salem. Noticing the gloom around them, they went noisily through the streets with bravado.

The legislature in Connecticut was in session that day. The deepening gloom surrounded the capital city, and the State House grew dark. The journal of the House of Representatives reads, "None could see to read or write in the house, or even at a window, or distinguish persons at a small distance, or perceive any distinction of dress, etc., in the circle of attendants. Therefore, at eleven o'clock adjourned the house till two o'clock afternoon." The council was also in session, and several of its members exclaimed, "It is the Lord's great day!" There was a motion to adjourn, but Stamford member Colonel Abraham Davenport quickly arose and with great moral courage and reason said, "I am against the adjournment. Either the day of judgment is at hand or it is not. If it is not there is no cause for adjournment. If it is, I wish to be found in the line of my duty. I wish candles to be brought.*

At Salem, Dr. Nathaniel Whitaker's congregation came together at their church, and he preached a sermon in which he maintained that the darkness was divinely sent to rebuke the people for their sins. In many other towns church bells were rung to call people together for religious services and crowds attended. Parishioners sought their pastors for some explanation and were almost invariably answered by reference to Bible passages such as the following from Isaiah xiii:10:

> For the stars of heaven and the constellations thereof shall not give their light; the sun shall be darkened in his going forth, and the moon shall not cause her light to shine.

The sermons also were founded upon such texts. In the middle of the day, with their families around them, devout fathers reverently read aloud from the Bible and then knelt and prayed. Pious men were sought out by their neighbors for advice.

At about two o'clock in the afternoon, when a moderate rain fell at Norton, Massachusetts, the horizon began to grow lighter. The day still remained as dark as a moonlit night for some time, and housekeepers could not see to perform their ordinary work without the aid of candles until later in the afternoon. As the sky grew lighter, the yellow brassy appear-

* John Greenleaf Whittier relates the incident in his *Tent on the Beach*.

ance of the morning returned, and remained until an hour or two before sundown, when the sun was finally seen again, shining through the murky air with a very red hue.

After sundown the clouds again came overhead, and it grew dark very fast, "the evening being as remarkable as the day." The moon had become full the preceding day and rose at nine o'clock; but in spite of that the night was the darkest that the people of New England had ever seen. It was as nearly totally dark as could be imagined. A person could not see his hand when he held it up, nor a sheet of white paper held within a few inches of his eyes, and the sky could not be distinguished from the earth. Those who were away from home, though well acquainted with the roads, could only with extreme difficulty and great danger reach their own houses, and several persons lost their way in familiar places. Some, totally bewildered, shouted for aid only a few rods from their own doors.

Many of those upon the roads, being unable to see in the darkness, refused to continue. The rising of the moon did not lessen the darkness, which continued complete. About eleven o'clock a slight breeze sprang up from the north-northwest, and a faint glimmer of light appeared. At midnight it was considerably lighter.

When morning came, light erased the gloom and "fear passed away." The people gratefully welcomed the light of another morning, though the sky was obscured by clouds and unusually dark, the temperature low, and a northeast wind blowing.

The darkness had extended over the middle and southern portions of New England, but it varied in density in different localities, being thickest in Essex County, Massachusetts. It was noticed as far west as Albany, New York, north as far as Portsmouth, New Hampshire, and out on the ocean for a score of miles.

What caused the extraordinary darkness of the dark day in

1780? Some people still hold the opinion that it was supernatural, but the great majority conclude that it was the effect
of several natural causes coming at one time. I believe that
the smoke that had spread over the area remained for several
weeks and joined a dense layer of cloud and another thick
layer of vapor that had been driven by a lower air current
blowing in an opposite direction under the stratum of smoke.
Beneath this vapor more smoke had arisen in such quantities
that another stratum was formed, held stationary by a heavy
fog coming in from the sea. All of this made a thick covering
blocking out the light of the sun. Where the darkness was
deepest, more soot and cinders were precipitated than in other
sections.

Over a century later, on Tuesday, September 6, 1881, another darkness covered New England almost from sunrise to
sunset. It was similar to the famous "dark day" of 1780, but
on account of the intense brassy coloration in the atmosphere,
reflected everywhere, it has gone down in history as "the
yellow day."

Today, with pollution from many sources, we are familiar
with smog. In 1881, smoke from forest fires was often blamed.
On that particular Thursday the smell of smoke had filled the
air for several days, indicating its presence in large quantities.
Writers in 1881 generally had little doubt that all the dark
days were caused by smoke.

Various opinions were given on the source of the smoke.
Perley believed that it came from forest fires which, it was
said, were then raging in Canada and the West. Others thought
it might be due to an active volcano in the interior of Labrador. Still others supposed it came from the immense peat bogs
of the Labrador barrens, which in dry seasons burn to the
rocks, the fire actually running over them faster than on a
prairie. In two or three days' time such fires sometimes swept
from Hudson Bay to the Gulf of St. Lawrence.

On the "yellow day" of 1881 there was one difference from that of 1780. In the morning there was no apparent gathering of clouds such as occurred in 1780. Early in the morning the sun and sky appeared red, and toward noon every part of the sky assumed a yellow cast, which tinged the entire landscape— buildings, ground, foliage, and verdure—with its peculiar copper shade. All things were beautiful, strange, and weird. It seemed as if nature were passing into an "enchanted state." It was at first intensely interesting, but as the hours dragged on, the sight became oppressive and almost monotonous. Nevertheless, those who witnessed the "yellow day" did not forget it for the rest of their lives.

The day was warm and the air close and still. In certain areas the air was unusually charged with moisture. It was not until almost the end of the day that the red sky and sun reappeared and the darkness lifted.

During the day, lamps were lighted in shops and offices to enable people to work or read or write. Work was suspended in many places, and in scores of schools a recess was taken during the darkest part of the day. In several instances the scholars were dismissed.

In some New England areas people were considerably excited, thinking that a hurricane, tornado, or some type of heavenly activity would follow. It was even conjectured that the earth was passing through the tail of a comet. There were also those who believed that it might be the last great day of darkness before eternity, that the end of the world was approaching when they would meet their Lord. Few of them believed it strongly enough to make any preparation for the event, however. There were also those who suggested that it was a token of divine sympathy for President James A. Garfield, who was then dying at Elberon, New Jersey, after having been fatally wounded by Charles J. Guiteau on July 2, 1881. Garfield passed away on September 19, 1881.

The darkness prevailed over a large part of New England, being noticed as far north as White River Junction in Vermont, some distance into Maine, westward to Albany, New York, and south into Connecticut, where it cleared early in the afternoon.

In October 1917 Mary Fifield King of Boston stated that she remembered the "yellow day" perfectly. Writing about the subject more than a third of a century later, she stated that there was "such a strong color and a brilliant stillness! The big bed of red geraniums in the yard looked almost white. The horse as my father drove into the yard shied at the strangeness."

PART THREE

At Sea

CHAPTER 1

~~~~~~~~

THE *FAIRFAX–PINTHIS* DISASTER

The disaster that befell the *Fairfax* and the *Pinthis*, even after forty-six years, is still so involved in controversy that just what happened during and after the collision can probably never be determined.

At five o'clock in the evening of June 10, 1930, the 5649-ton steamship *Fairfax* of the Merchants and Miners passenger line sailed from Boston Harbor on her regular run down the coast to the south. A heavy fog soon settled over Massachusetts Bay, and Captain A. H. Brooks ordered the steamer to proceed at a speed of from ten to twelve knots.

The first warning of trouble came at 6:58 that night when the Shell Oil tanker *Pinthis*, of 1,111 tons, suddenly hove in view from out of the fog half a point off the starboard bow of the *Fairfax*.

Captain Brooks, hearing one blast of the whistle, ordered the helm hard-a-port and backed away at full speed. The *Fairfax* quivered from stem to stern as the engine fought to reverse the steamer's direction, but it was too late to avoid a collision.

153

Coming together with a sickening crash, the two ships became entangled in each other's girders and plates. The *Pinthis*, with eleven thousand barrels of oil on board, caught fire almost at once. Blazing oil spouted high into the air, sprinkling flaming fuel down on the two steamers. The *Fairfax* also caught fire and most of her decks were soon a mass of roaring flames.

The *Pinthis* started to sink at once. As she began her final plunge into the foggy sea off Scituate's Fourth Cliff, the blazing tanker slowly pulled away from the *Fairfax*. All nineteen aboard the *Pinthis* perished.

Captain Brooks now cleverly maneuvered the *Fairfax* in order to get the fire on her decks into the lee, thus preventing it from spreading. The crew fought their way to the burning section with the ship's fire apparatus, and after superhuman efforts, extinguished the blaze. Several marines and sailors who were aboard as passengers helped the ship's company beat out the flames and then assisted in maintaining general order.

Immediately after the collision, the captain ordered an SOS sent out. Then he anchored the *Fairfax* in a position off the shores of the Third and Fourth Cliff in Scituate a considerable distance from the mouth of the North River. The 5,649-ton steamer had sustained substantial damage. Her bows were seriously damaged above the waterline, but it did not prevent the *Fairfax* from reaching port later under her own power. Although the *Pinthis* had gone to the bottom, blazing oil from the tanker lighted the sea for miles around. The Coast Guard cutter *Tampa* was a short distance away, but Captain Brooks did not request her aid, because with the sea on fire the cutter would be unable to approach. Also in the area was the *Gloucester*, the sister ship of the *Fairfax*. Alerted by the *Fairfax* radio operator, she had proceeded to the disaster scene.

Quartermaster John V. Eubank, nineteen years old at the time of the tragedy, told me years later of the horror that followed the sinking of the *Pinthis*. He believed that if a boat had been launched after the collision, many more people could have been saved. At the Coast Guard inquiry in Boston it was stated that there were men qualified to go out to the scene of the disaster from both North Scituate and Brant Rock stations. When I interviewed him, Eubank was particularly bitter against the Scituate and Marshfield Coast Guardsmen at each station, who claimed that they had no right to go out through the fog to the scene of the wreck and leave the station shorthanded without a direct order from a district officer in charge of the area. Boatswain's Mate James McIntyre testified later at the hearing that their North Scituate motorboat could be used only against rumrunners. Eubank believed this assertion was ridiculous, and in this opinion he is seconded by no less than six captains of the Boston Marine Society, of which I, holding Certificate #2738, am a member.

Eubank's remarks at the Boston hearing were the most dramatic of the day. When questioned by Mr. Lyons, chief federal steamboat inspector, about what happened after the collision, Eubank answered in his soft Virginia accent.

"I just came off watch. I was relieved two minutes of 7 and went to my room. Went down on deck and went up to the main deck door where you go down to the main deck. I looked again and I saw the smokestack of the other ship.

"There was a marine on deck and I told him 'We are going to have an accident, look at that ship.' By that time she struck.

"I went up to my room. Tried to get to my room to call some of the quartermasters that were asleep. Didn't get any further than the boat deck. Almost got to the dance hall when smoke and flames came along.

"I started to my lifeboat, which was No. 9, the last one on the starboard side and tried to get the gripes off of her. As soon as I got to her the flames were going over her and I went down to the promenade deck. The mate came and I asked him did he call the quartermaster. He never answered me. The other quartermaster came and I asked him had he called the other quartermaster and he said, 'Yes, he is up on deck, he is all right.'

"We both walked down the steps together and walked over to the rail. I started forward to go to my stateroom and get a life-preserver. The smoke and flame was heading me off again. I went back and it got so dense I couldn't see anybody. I began to strangle in the smoke. I started to go over the rail but somebody held me back. A woman threw her arms around me and tried to get me to jump overboard and carry her with me. I loosened her hold. Broke loose from two of them and got over to the rail and got down to the hurricane deck.

"I tried to go forward again. Just as I started forward my clothes caught fire. Then I went to the rail and tried to stay there, but couldn't, so finally I jumped overboard. I used the log line on the starboard side. I got on it. Five or six were on it then. I knew it was going to break with so many on it, so I let go and tried to get on the rudder.

"I missed the rudder the first time. Something struck my feet. It was the propeller. I was sort of dazed. When I came to I saw a blaze about my head and I saw the rudder. Climbed up on it. I was all right then and I hollered to somebody to come and get hold of my feet and hang on. Nobody came. One boy started up but he went down before he got to me. I stayed on the rudder until the ship started ahead.

"Engines started ahead and went through all this fire and it got so bad it burned me and I had to let go. The fire was burning so bad I had to dive. I dove and swam under water for five feet and came up. I came up in a place two feet square to get some air. Closed in with fog and I went down and swam under water for five more feet and I came up again and it was all clear. I didn't have any life preserver of my own to use. I saw those people about 50 feet away from me. I made for them. I got to them and it was this navy officer with his wife. I asked him before I got to him would he give me a life preserver and he said 'yes.' When I got where the lieutenant was I gave up and went down. He pulled me up and got me in this life preserver.

"Floating in the water. I next came to a man who struggled with me. I told him to get away from me. I knew if I had stayed there I would drown, so I left him and got away five feet or so. I noticed there was somebody else, and saw the waiter with his white coat on. I laid his face up and looked to see who it was and it was one of the boys named Seeley. I shook him to see if he was alive, but he didn't move, so I took his life preserver off. It took me twenty minutes.

"I saw this lifeboat afire. I told the sailor and his wife and these other two, 'All hands go to the lifeboat.' The only chance we had. He said, 'No, sir, we are going to stay here; we won't go to the lifeboat.' I said, 'Well, I am going.' I made for the lifeboat. Took an hour and one-half to get there. After I got there two waiters, two boys, were hanging on. I told them both to hang on. One of them let go before I could help him. I managed to get in. Boat was in a light blaze. Took my hand and threw water all around. Then she was almost sunk and I started to bail her out. The boy was screaming to me to help him from drowning. I told him to wait until I got some water out. If I tried to get him in then we would sink. I got about half the water out and got him in and told him to bail. He couldn't bail any.

"We bailed until I got sick and lay down in the bottom. I fell unconscious. I don't know what time it was when I came to, but I heard the *Fairfax* blowing four long whistles. Then we discovered that the lifeboat had started leaking again, for a rubber bailer had burned out.

"I tore our shirts off and put them in the hole. She had a wooden stem and was burned through. The water was coming in. I didn't bother with that. That would make it all the worse. So I took the tanks, some of them, and threw them overboard, some of them half full with water, and I put them back on the stern and got back in myself and kept her bow out of water. Then we started to yell for help.

"One ship passed us and didn't hear us. Then we drifted until about 12 o'clock, when I took a hatchet, ripped a can open and made a sail, a sort of sail which I put up in the bow. I ripped some boards at the bottom that were burned and tried to make some paddles. They broke when I started to use them.

"While I was thinking what to do then, I looked up and saw this Gloucester fishing smack named *Dacia*. I started to shout. Joe started hollering. He was too hoarse. I couldn't yell either. So we took a hatchet and threw it on the can and tried to attract attention. Then they lowered a dory from the fisherman and took us out of the lifeboat and brought us in to Boston."

Captain John Stewart of the government investigating board then asked Eubank if a boat passing within a mile radius from the *Fairfax* would have found them, and the boy answered in the affirmative.

Harry E. Kipp was another who testified at the hearing. A marine sergeant who helped man a fire hose, Kipp stated that as he worked with the hose he noticed passengers and crew members jumping overboard.

"I saw at one time a lifeboat containing eight or nine men," he explained. "Five could easily have handled the boat, and I do not think they were members of the crew of the lifeboat, for they were sitting in the seats. It had been partly lowered. None of the ship's officers was near the boat.

"Other men were running about the deck creating greater panic among the passengers, yelling and shouting. They lost their heads. None of them had been hurt and they would have been saved had they remained aboard the ship.

"I saw no trouble between officers of the ship or between

officers and crew. Most members of the crew did very well, but the passengers rendered great assistance in fighting the fire and their extra help may have saved the ship.

"Considering that there were 23 fire lines on the boat and a crew of 80, I don't think the lines could have been fully manned, with nine men in a lifeboat and others below decks in the engine room.

"There was a panic among the passengers from the smoke and fire. Women could hardly be expected to retain their nerve under such conditions. But the nurses were very efficient and the ship's nurse worked very hard. I saw one lifeboat full of passengers but that was ninety minutes after the collision."

A *Fairfax* passenger, Lieutenant J. A. Nash of the U.S. Navy, commented that the officers and crew "handled themselves as efficiently as possible under the circumstances." Nash's wife was badly burned in the flames that enveloped the starboard side of the liner but later recovered.

Passenger Robert French told how at the time of the collision he heard the *Fairfax* sound a long blast but did not hear another whistle. There was no confusion in the engine room when it filled with smoke, according to members of the "black gang" who talked with him later. French explained how he fought the fire on the port side of the *Fairfax*, assisted by an oiler and a wiper.

Able Seaman M. Silvia, a Portuguese sailor from Baltimore, recalled going on deck to get the fire hose and seeing the seamen and mates there. He declared that a woman helped with the hose. The woman, he said, was a passenger.

Able Seaman Frank Grace said briefly that he was not frightened, saw no one who was, saw none leap from the decks, and saw no sailors or marines about. Grace was in his bunk when the crash came. Although the fire bell was but eight feet from his head, he failed to hear it ring. After going to his station at lifeboat No. 3 and finding no one else there, Grace joined the other crew members fighting the flames, until the blaze was extinguished thirty minutes later.

Miss Nellie Toddel, senior hostess on the *Fairfax*, said she saw no evidence of panic but had observed officers and members of the crew assisting passengers to the lifeboats in an orderly manner. Her story was corroborated by Miss Alice Mannix, a passenger; and two maids, Martha Hennaman and Mabel Hermanson.

The assistant chief of the Boston fire department expressed the opinion that there must have been efficient discipline to have accomplished the saving of the steamship.

The officers of the *Fairfax* testified that no ship could have aided them immediately after the collision because the sea was on fire, and ships could not have approached near enough to perform rescues.

The inspectors stressed the importance of establishing the facts regarding the sending out of the SOS call. Entries that should have been made in the ship's radio log were not in the log. There was no entry of any SOS having been sent out within a minute or two of three minutes past seven, the time of the crash. Captain Brooks testified that he gave verbal orders for such a message, and the inspectors called the chief radio operator, J. Wesley Geweken of Baltimore.

The youthful radioman said he was licensed and had been in service on the *Fairfax* for several months. He was questioned concerning the sending of the SOS and stated that Captain Brooks gave him a verbal order that he attempted to carry out, but he discovered that the aerial had been burned off. By the time it was repaired, about twenty-five minutes later, he believed the danger was over. He admitted that the captain had not ordered him to cancel the SOS, but he didn't call the navy yard because he knew the *Gloucester* was right behind the *Fairfax*. He reported to Chatham at the time and later talked with the *Tampa*.

Geweken admitted that it was his own decision not to send out the SOS after reestablishing communication, but insisted that he had flashed out the call eight or possibly ten times before he discovered that his antenna was out of commission, and that he couldn't tell whether it had gone out or not.

He said he didn't keep a record of all messages and that he didn't make a notation at the time he talked with the *Tampa*, but did later. His own log showed that the *Tampa* called and asked if everything was O.K., that he radioed back that everything was O.K., and that the *Gloucester* was to take off the passengers. He said the message was signed merely "Coast Guard," and that no name came with it.

"What did you mean by 'O.K.' when the ship was afire and lives had been lost?" shouted Inspector Lyons at the hearing. "Conditions were far from O.K., weren't they?"

The witness answered, "I meant there was no further danger to the ship."

Captain Brooks was then summoned to the stand and questioned as to his qualifications as a mariner. He offered his credentials and stated that he was licensed and was in command of the *Fairfax* on Tuesday, June 10. The captain was asked to tell in his own words what happened aboard the *Fairfax* the night of the disaster.

"At 6:58 a vessel loomed a half-point off the starboard bow," stated Captain Brooks, "and at the same time there was one blast of a whistle. I ordered the wheel hard a-port and reversed the ship full speed. Some 30 seconds later we collided. Almost immediately the *Pinthis* burst into flames. I tried to back out, and couldn't until she sank.

"I was backing all the time, then went ahead to get the wind on the starboard. All men were ordered to their positions."

Later in his testimony Captain Brooks said that some members of the crew had jumped overboard.

"What caused members of the crew to jump overboard? Fright?"

The question was direct. So was the answer.

"Yes."

Captain Brooks was asked by Captain Lyons, "Who was in the pilot house with you at that time?"

"Captain Robertson, the pilot for the Cape Cod canal; A. J. Powell, chief officer; J. W. Brooks, the quartermaster; and myself."

At no time during the collision, declared Captain Brooks, was there any conversation in the pilot house.

The captain of the *Fairfax* then stated that there were seventy-six passengers on board and eighty in the crew. He transferred fifty-six to the *Gloucester*. Twelve passengers died in the sea, and eleven crewmen leaped to their death.

Captain Brooks' testimony shows that he traveled the 21 miles from Finn's Ledge near Graves Light to the point of collision at 11.2 knots an hour, not a moderate speed in the fair tide then being experienced. Low water was at 5:00 P.M.

The questioning of Brooks continued.

"Now, you had a full complement of crew?"

"Yes."

"How many men did you have on lookout?"

"I had one man in the bow."

"How often are fog signals required?"

"One per minute, sir."

"How long would it take you to stop the *Fairfax?*"

The captain said he could stop the *Fairfax* in 300 feet at the speed he was then going.

Upon further questioning, Captain Brooks stated that when he heard the fog signal from the *Pinthis*, and he heard it only once, he reversed immediately.

"How much time would you say there was between the signal and the time of the collision?"

"Thirty seconds."

"The time of the whistle was at 7:08?"

"That is the engineer's time."

"How do you fix the time you heard the fog signal at 7:03?"

"I got it from the engineer's log."

"Now, were there some statements in the newspapers as to conditions of panic?"

"I never saw any cooler people than were aboard that ship."

"You were in the pilot house?"

"Yes."

"The officers were on the ship where their duties called them?"

"Yes."

"Fire signals were given?"

"Yes, all bells were sounded."

"All members of the crew went to their stations?"

"Yes."

"Did every man aboard know his station?"

"Yes."

"Were the stations posted about the ship?"

"Yes."

"Were you given any assistance by the passengers?"

"Yes, I saw some marines there getting out the fire hose."

"Now, you went about the passengers to see if you could assist them?"

"Yes. Everybody was made comfortable."

"Now, did you hear any criticism among the passengers of the crew?"

"No."

"Did you hear any praise?"

"We heard plenty."

"Do you feel that everything was done by the crew and officers in this emergency?"

"Yes."

"For what reason did they jump overboard?"

"I presume they came on deck and saw it covered with flames and that was the only thing they could do."

"Looking at it now, as the accident happened, can you think of anything you could have done to avoid collision?"

"Not a thing in the world."

"Do you think that if any vessel responded, it could have done anything?"

"No. The *Fairfax* was covered with flames and the water was afire."

Captain F. A. Gower of Fall River, master mariner and representing the owners of the *Pinthis,* expressed the opinion that the prow of the *Fairfax* plowed through the bulkhead of the *Pinthis* and that the damage on the port side of the *Fairfax* was due to her striking the engines of the tanker. He said there were between 11,500 and 12,000 barrels of oil and gasoline aboard the *Pinthis* when she left Fall River, intending to discharge half her cargo at Portland, Maine, and the balance at Chelsea, Massachusetts.

Captain Gower attributed the fire to a spark caused by the steel prow of the *Fairfax* plunging through the tanker's steel sides, followed by the ignition of oil and gasoline after the *Fairfax* went through the bulkhead that separated the tanks from parts of the vessel where there was fire. He discounted the theory that the oil and gasoline reached the boilers of the auxiliary engines on deck.

Acting on orders from Washington, Howard Wilcox, commander of the Provincetown Coast Guard area, which includes the stations at Brant Rock and North Scituate, later investigated charges that the men in charge of the stations were indefensibly lax in their duty in not sending boats out to rescue survivors of the *Fairfax-Pinthis* crash.

He queried Boatswain's Mate James McIntyre, who was in command of the North Scituate station. McIntyre, who had spent many years in the Coast Guard service, insisted that they could not begin any rescue movement until they received a "definite signal of distress" or were ordered by district officers. He defended his inaction by saying that he had talked by telephone with the Provincetown and Boston offices of the Coast Guard and had not received orders. Despite the fact that six reporters were at his station and newspaper offices were continually calling him to find whether he had started a boat toward the scene, McIntyre said that until he read the morning newspapers the crash was "just a rumor" to him.

Harbormaster Gerald Dwyer and James L. Rothery, a well-known resident of Scituate, were bitter in their denunciation of the Coast Guard for not helping those attempting to swim through the burning oil. They sent a telegram to Congressman Charles L. Gifford demanding a "full investigation." The telegram said:

In view of the revelations made by newspaper investigation, we believe a full investigation of North Scituate Coast Guard is called for. The incompetency and inefficiency of the official life saving agency of the United States has been bared by fact that patrol boat 2360 did not proceed to disaster 10 miles away, although Coast Guard station knew of disaster before midnight. Two lives and perhaps more might have been saved if crew had acted within reasonable time and not waited until 5 o'clock Wednesday to proceed to scene of wreck.

Rear Admiral Frederick C. Bullard, commandant of the Coast Guard, immediately ordered Commander Wilcox to start an investigation and to give the press all the facts. Commander Wilcox, questioned at the Manomet station, gave out this statement:

The district commander had no information whatever of the disaster until he heard it over the radio at 8:05 A.M. (Wednesday), twelve hours after the collision. The radio said all passengers had been transferred to the steamer *Gloucester* and that the passengers had been landed at Boston. There was no information that any of the passengers had left the *Fairfax* in small boats at the time of the collision. Had there been a call for assistance sent out and the definite position of the collision given at least four boats from stations in the vicinity, North Scituate, Brant Rock, Gurnet, and Manomet Point, could have reached the scene in ninety minutes or less.

Bosn's Mate McIntyre, who was in charge at North Scituate station, received calls from several Boston newspapers late on the night of the collision. Nothing definite could be learned as to where the two ships came together. The newspapers that called stated that there was a report in Boston that there had been a collision at sea. No authority was given for the statement, merely that the collision was "off Scituate."

McIntyre did not want to go because he had no definite information and he deemed it best to wait for this information as to position. At no time did the station receive any word of the collision from a steamship or steamship company.

About 4 A.M. Wednesday McIntyre received a call from a Boston paper stating the *Fairfax* was in a collision somewhere off Scituate. Lacking information as to position, McIntyre waited until 4 P.M. that day until the fog lifted and then went out in a picket boat with a crew and searched from 4 to 10 P.M.

The course of the boat was north and south from Minot's light to the mouth of the North river, approximately six miles offshore. All they found was an expanse of oil burning near gas buoy No. 4, approximately twelve miles southeast of Scituate.

No wreckage was sighted. Observation was one to two miles, and the only things they sighted were two fishing boats. The search continued Thursday. The nearest station to the accident was Brant Rock, approximately eight miles from the scene. This station had no information of the disaster until the next morning when the crew heard it over the radio.

Later, at North Scituate Station, Bosn's Mate McIntyre admitted to newspapermen that absolutely no attempt was made to ascertain the position of the wreck following the calls from the Boston newspapers. He had two surf boats at his command, in addition to a motorboat usually used for rum patrol duty. When asked why he had not used this motorboat, he said it was used exclusively for rum patrol duty.

"If anything happened while we were trying to find the wreck," he said, "we'd get the devil for being away from our station." He declined to give his reasons for waiting until the fog lifted, when newspapermen, chartering a fishing boat, left early in the morning, hours before he attempted to get to the scene. When pressed for a definite reason for not ordering his crew of ten men into boats, McIntyre said, "We didn't go because we didn't feel like it."

He later said that survivors in the water "might have been struck by us, run into, ground up by our propeller. One couldn't see out there. Any survivors might have been mangled."

Wreckage from the *Pinthis* eventually drifted ashore on Hen Island near the mouth of the North River in Marshfield, but the submerged fire on the bottom of the sea near what is now H buoy burned for seven days and seven nights before going out.

Scuba divers in 1974 visited the *Pinthis* hull but never reported on their findings.

All that I shall or should say concerning the *Fairfax-Pinthis* disaster has been recorded in this chapter. It is the task and privilege of the reader to make his own conclusions as to who should have done what and when.

Those who experienced and survived the holocaust of June 10, 1930, will never forget the terror they endured in the inferno of blazing oil that surrounded them that frightful night.

CHAPTER 2

THE LOSS OF THE *ROYAL TAR*

During the summer of 1836, a circus and menagerie toured the Canadian province of New Brunswick. At the close of a successful season the entire circus embarked on the *Royal Tar,* a steamer bound from Saint John Harbor, New Brunswick, to Portland, Maine. It was a new vessel built at Saint John that spring and named the *Royal Tar* because of King William IV's deep interest in the British navy.

Captain Thomas Reed was in command of the *Royal Tar* as she sailed out of Saint John Harbor on Friday, October 21, 1836, with her strange cargo of assorted animals, which included horses, two camels, Mogul the elephant, two lions, one Royal Bengal tiger, a gnu, and two pelicans. The circus brass band was also on board.

When the steamer began her voyage that Friday morning, the weather had been fine in every respect, but before the sun set a high westerly wind started to blow. The wind continued several days and forced the *Royal Tar* to seek shelter in Eastport Harbor, Maine, where she remained until the following Tuesday afternoon. Shortly after she left Eastport, rising winds again forced her to seek shelter, this time behind Fox Island. While the vessel was anchored about two miles off Fox Island Thoroughfare, the order was given to fill the ship's boilers.

Evidently the water in the boilers was much lower than had been believed, for when the pilot's son tested the lower cock he found it dry. The boy told his father, who mentioned the fact to Mr. Marshall, the second engineer in charge. Both father and son were informed that they were mistaken in believing the boilers dry, as everything was in order. However, it was the engineer who was in error, for a few minutes after the discussion, the boiler—empty—became red hot, setting fire to two wedges supporting the elephant stall. The fire gained headway rapidly, and by the time Captain Reed looked down the grating, the flames were beyond control. Realizing that the *Royal Tar* was doomed, he ordered the men to slip anchor, hoist a distress signal, and lower the boats. (It was later learned that the regular engineer had been up all night working on the boilers. Tired, he had entrusted his position to the second engineer, who in turn had given the task of watering the boilers to the fireman—and the fireman had not done it.)

Captain Reed took charge of the stern boat and came alongside the *Royal Tar,* where two able men, Mr. Sherwood and Mr. Fowler, joined him.

Sixteen other men jumped into the longboat, cut the ropes to drop their craft into the water, and started for shore. The strong wind rapidly swept them leeward in the direction of land, which they reached safely four hours later.

A revenue cutter, the *Veto,* was seen in the distance, approaching rapidly. When the cutter drew near, Captain Reed ordered his men to row over to her where she lay to windward. The men refused, infuriating Captain Reed.

"If any man refuses to run for the cutter, I'll throw him overboard," the captain threatened. The boat then made for the cutter, where the passengers received treatment.

The revenue cutter's pilot arrived near the *Royal Tar* with the *Veto*'s gig, but the flames of the burning vessel so frightened him that he dared not approach closely enough to effect the rescue of anyone. Passing around in back of the stern, the pilot saw passengers and members of the crew clinging to the ropes hanging over the sides. Terrified by their cries for help, he lost his nerve and steered back to the cutter without saving a single person. The cutter itself, with a heavy deckload of gunpowder, was unable to approach any closer to the burning steamer.

Working desperately to construct a substantial raft from the deck boards of the *Royal Tar,* a group of men aboard the burning ship managed to launch a makeshift float that supported them fairly well. However, just as they were about to push off from the vessel, the huge form of the elephant loomed directly over them, balanced for a terrifying moment at the taffrail, and smashed down through the air to land on the raft, sinking the float and drowning the men. The body of the elephant was found floating a few days later near Brimstone Island. It was said that every animal belonging to the menagerie was lost. Other accounts mention that when the horses jumped overboard they swam round and round the burning vessel until they sank, instead of making for shore where they might have been saved.

As the regular captain was not aboard, Captain Reed took charge of the revenue cutter. He steered the cutter in closer to the *Royal Tar* and then went across in a boat for those still left on board. By this time some of the passengers on the wreck had been hanging to ropes in the water for almost two hours. One by one the ropes would burn through, dropping the victims into the sea to their death.

One of the passengers, Mr. H. H. Fuller, clung to a rope over the stern until his strength failed him; then he twisted the line around his neck to prevent slipping into the sea. Four others, desperate to hold themselves above water, grabbed hold of his body, causing terrific pressure on his throat. Lifting his leg high out of water, in some way Fuller transferred the rope from his neck to his leg. A woman grabbed hold of his other leg and clung desperately to him. They were still in this awkward position when rescued a short time later.

Of the ninety-three persons on board, thirty-two passengers and members of the crew perished. One of the most unusual deaths was that of a man who lashed his small trunk to a plank, which he slid off into the sea successfully. Then he fastened a money belt containing $500 in silver around his waist, mounted the taffrail, and leaped into the sea. He did not realize the significant weight of the $500 in silver! He plummeted down through the waves and never rose to the surface again.

The passengers were high in their praise of the acts of Captain Reed, who did much to reduce the loss of life aboard the *Royal Tar*. One of the prominent passengers on board was quoted as follows:

> Captain Reed took charge of the stern boat, with two men, and kept her off the steamboat, which was a very fortunate circumstance, as it was the means of saving from 40 to 50 persons, and to him all credit is due for his deliberate and manly perseverance throughout the whole calamity.

> It is impossible to describe the appalling spectacle which the whole scene presented—the boat wrapped in flames, with nearly 100 souls on board, without any hope of relief, rending the air with their shrieks for help; the caravan of wild beasts on deck, ready to tear to pieces all that might escape the flames.

Shortly before sunset the last rescue boat, with a single survivor on board, left the *Royal Tar*. The passenger was a woman who had seen her sister and daughter perish before her eyes. After taking the unfortunate woman aboard, the revenue cutter started for the Isle of Haut to land the survivors. There the passengers obtained a schooner to take them to Portland, while the master and crew went to Eastport on another vessel.

On November 3, 1836, Captain Reed was presented with a purse of $700 for his heroic work during the fire. A few years later he was appointed harbormaster at Saint John. He became a picturesque figure around the Saint John waterfront, where he was often seen with his faithful dog walking at his side.

CHAPTER 3

THE WALKER EXPEDITION

One of the most awesome tales of the North Atlantic is so little known that I never met any person who could tell me the complete story of the catastrophe, although more than two centuries and a half ago it shocked the entire English-speaking world.

I first learned of this terrible multiple shipwreck in 1935 when I was preparing my book on Boston Harbor. Miss Carolyn E. Jakemann was assisting me at Harvard's Houghton Library when I came across Sir Hovendon Walker's journal of his expedition against Quebec, written in the year 1720. I could not resist digging into the pages of this fascinating account.

The reader may recall that Sir William Phips, who at one time found more than a million dollars in the sea, was not quite so fortunate when he made the first attempt to capture Quebec in 1690. Phips returned to Boston in defeat after over a thousand of his men had drowned and thirty-eight ships had been lost. The English smarted under this defeat for some years, and then in 1708 prepared another expedition. General McCartney planned to lead his troops against Quebec that year, but then took his regiments to Portugal instead. The Quebec expedition was not revived again until three more years had elapsed.

England was at war with France and Spain in the War of the Spanish Succession, fought from 1702 to 1713 and sometimes called Queen Anne's War. On April 11, 1711, Queen Anne, who dreamed of achieving naval successes to match the sweeping land victories of her dazzling army leader Marlborough, called Sir Hovendon Walker and General John Hill into her palace at St. James and handed Walker sealed orders, which she told him to open after he had sailed for Boston.

On April 29 Admiral Walker and his English fleet sailed from Great Britain. Upon opening his orders at sea, he learned of the details for the assault on Quebec. There followed a long, trying period of minor disappointments and mishaps, but Walker was determined to carry out his royal mission. He dreamed of winning a greater victory against the French at Quebec than that won by Sir Francis Drake against the Spanish Armada in 1588.

Walker's fleet reached Massachusetts Bay on June 24, and the flagship *Edgar* soon sighted the beacon on Boston's Great Brewster Island. Sixty-one ships, the largest fleet that had ever entered Boston Harbor, anchored in the roadstead. Two impressive reviews under General Hill were later staged on Noddle's Island by picked regiments of Marlborough's finest soldiers.

Although eager to succeed in his mission, Walker had not underestimated the dangers ahead. After much effort he secured Captain Phips' original journal of the disastrous 1690 expedition against Quebec. Thus fortified, he laid plans carefully so he would not duplicate the treasure finder's failure. In fact, everything was done to make the capture of Quebec an easy conquest.

After the final parade on Noddle's Island was concluded and almost every soldier, sailor, and passenger was at last aboard his assigned vessel—a substantial number of deserters remained in Boston—the fleet sailed from Nantasket Road, Boston Harbor on July 30. Aboard the sixty-one transports and men-of-war were 9,385 men, with hundreds of women and children as well. The confident English leaders, not even considering the possibility of defeat this time, had made plans for the soldiers and their families to be quartered in the conquered citadel at Quebec.

Off Cape Breton, the lookouts on the flagship sighted a small French transport, the *Neptune,* on which a French captain named Paradis was transporting reinforcements for the very Quebec garrison that Admiral Walker would have to overcome before he subdued the French city. The Admiral delegated Captain Matthews of the *Chester* to withdraw from formation and capture the *Neptune,* which Matthews did handily.

When brought before Admiral Walker, the French captain proved ready and willing to answer the questions the anxious Admiral fired at him. His tongue loosened by payment of five hundred pistoles, Paradis told Walker many important facts concerning Saint Lawrence Bay, through the waters of which he had successfully completed forty trips. He then talked in great detail about the dangers of the Labrador Coast. In fact, Captain Paradis made such an impression on Admiral Walker that the Englishman decided Paradis could pilot the entire expedition, in spite of the fact that several Boston pilots, including the eminent John Bonner, had been brought along for precisely that purpose. How much the French captain, as pilot, was to blame for the events that followed is a matter of conjecture.

Paradis did not minimize the perils of navigating the Gulf of Saint Lawrence. Walker's Journal mentions his telling the Englishmen that there were possible dangers ahead that might leave "brave men famishing with hunger, drawing lots to see who should die first to feed the rest." It was often true, according to the talkative French sea captain, that men "were left dead in the march and frozen into statues for their own monuments." If Paradis hoped by this discouraging talk to make the Admiral turn back, he failed.

On August 16, 1711, while off Cape Gaspé, the flagship *Edgar* sighted Bonaventure Island. The fleet continued on up Gaspé Passage. Walker, carried away by his ambitious plans, made tentative arrangements to secure his ships at Quebec for the winter. Several of the men-of-war were dispatched to destroy the fishing fleet at Bonaventure Island, but a dead calm prevented this action. They did reach Gaspé Harbor, however, and burned a fishing craft and several fishermen's dories there. A dozen or so huts were also set afire.

By this time Admiral Walker's worries were many. The various craft of the fleet seemed to be scattering, and he felt it necessary to issue definite orders for procedure:

> No commodore is to suffer any ship of his division to go ahead of him, and in case any do, to fire at them; and the men-of-war in his division, or next to that ship that goes ahead, shall make up sail to get up with her and cause that shot to be paid for by the master.

Shortly afterward a stiff breeze pushed the mighty fleet up through the Gaspé Passage and toward the shores of Labrador at a rate much faster than Paradis appeared to think

possible. And so it was that at ten o'clock on the night of
August 22, 1711, in foggy rough weather, over forty miles
beyond the point where Paradis had indicated they were, the
fleet entered an area of extreme danger. Before they realized
what was happening, one after another of the vessels smashed
into Egg Island. Eight great transports were ripped apart on
the rocks and broke into fragments. It was a scene of great
confusion as the other ships of the fleet attempted to sail
away from the dangerous island. The men-of-war all escaped,
but the eight transports that were shipwrecked carried over
1300 officers, soldiers, and seamen to their deaths, together
with an appalling number of the men's families, the actual
count of which will never be ascertained.

The transports that piled ashore were the *Marlborough,
Smyrna Merchant, Chatham, Content, Colchester, Isabella
and Catherine, Nathanial and Elizabeth,* and the *Samuel and
Alice.*

In this mighty disaster, the Windrasse and the Seymour
Regiments, together with two complete companies of the Royal
Guards, identified by their scarlet coats, were entirely wiped
out. At least 1342 men drowned, and their families numbered
hundreds more.

Admiral Hovendon Walker was simply overwhelmed by
the disaster, and on August 25, 1711, he brought together as
many ships as possible for a conference of their captains.
Here are the details of that conference in the St. Lawrence
River, in the very words recorded at that time:

The following Minutes were taken by Mr. Gordon,
General Hill's Secretary.

Minutes taken at a Consultation of Sea Officers in
the River of *St. Laurence,* the 25th of *Aug.* 1711. abord
her Majesty's Ship the *Windsor.*

Present

Sir Hovenden Walker Knt. Rear-Admiral of the White, etc.

Captain			
Soans			Swiftsure.
Mitchel			Monmouth.
Arris			Windsor.
Walton	}	of the	{ Mountague.
Gore			Dunkirk.
Paddon			Edgar.
Cockburn			Sunderland.
Rouse			Saphire.

The Admiral told these Gentlemen that he had called them together, to ask their Advice what was now to be done in the present Juncture of our Affairs; that we had lost many Transports, with a great Number of Men in the Entrance of the said River.

Several of the Captains said, that they not having been sooner consulted touching the Navigation of the River, could not now determine.

The Admiral said, that the Pilots, *viz. Paradis* and *Bonner*, had been consulted, and did agree in their Opinions, in what was done; but the Question was now, What was to be done? and if there was any thing wrong in his Conduct, he seemed to hint he was to answer it in another Place. And then he desired their Answer to this short Question, whether it was practicable to go up the River *St. Laurence* as far as *Quebec*, with the Men of War and Transports or not.

Captain *Mitchel* said, his Pilot had told him the 22d of this Month, that we steer'd too far Northerly.

All the Captains did agree that the Pilots were very ignorant, and not to be depended upon.

The conference came to an end. Although hopelessly stunned by the enormity of the catastrophe, Walker ordered Captain Cook of the *Leonard*, and other masters to cruise in the vicinity in an attempt to save life and property, while the captain of his flagship, the *Edgar*, did likewise.

It is true that the various craft of the squadron sailed briefly about the waters around Egg Island, supposedly on the alert for survivors. What Admiral Walker never found out, however, was that had they been more thorough, the sailors could have rescued scores of officers, men, women, and children who were still alive, either on the island or on the Labrador mainland. If they had gone ashore and organized search parties instead of confining their efforts merely to sailing around the bays and inlets, they could have saved scores upon scores of lives.

Several hundred of the survivors had floated ashore to the mainland on fragments of wreckage. Having lived through the catastrophe of the shipwreck, they set out bravely for help, poorly clothed and with no way of obtaining provisions. However the early winter caught them before they could get very far, and their footprints in the snow, found later, led for miles into the interior of Labrador. Some of the unfortunates had secreted themselves in hollow trees for warmth; others had sought protection under piles of hay and wild herbs; but all perished sooner or later, and their bodies were eventually discovered by the natives.

Mère Juchereau, writing of the French who visited the island the following fall, tells of the way in which the people of Quebec learned of the disaster. It was not until October 19, 1711, almost two months later, that they heard of the shipwrecks at Egg Island and the proposed British invasion of their city. It was Monsieur de la Valtrie, returning to Quebec from Labrador, who brought the first news. When the joyous tidings of deliverance from the hated English fleet became known, the entire populace poured out into the streets. To commemorate this second escape from the British in twenty-one years, the name of the small church in the lower town, already known as *Notre Dame de la Victorie,* was changed to *Notre Dames des Victoires.* Everyone at Quebec spoke of the miracle that had saved their city, and more than a hundred poems were written of the glorious shipwrecks that had prevented the English from capturing them.

Five ships were outfitted at once from Quebec, with forty men, a pastor, and provisions, to winter at Egg Island. There they planned to salvage as much property as possible from the shipwrecks. Those who spent that winter on the island saw sights terrible to behold. By actual count over two thousand naked men, women and children from the stricken vessels were strewn along the shores. Some of the dead bodies looked as though they were gnashing their teeth; others seemed to be tearing out their hair; a few were joined in final embrace. One group of seven women was discovered with their hands locked in a fatal circle.

The spoils from the wrecks were many. Heavy anchors, chains, cannon balls, guns, plate, bells, rigging, and every type of ironware were brought up to Quebec. In a few days over $20,000 worth of material had been obtained as souvenirs of the "British Armada," and later another $50,000 worth of spoils was brought from the island.

Two days after the shipwrecks the survivors of the British fleet held a council of war. Captain John Bonner of Boston spoke out plainly to the effect that pilots of worth had never been consulted at any time during the trip, implying that in any case the French Captain Paradis should not have been trusted.

Additional grief awaited Sir Hovendon Walker when he reached England. Leaving the *Edgar* at Portsmouth after the remainder of the expedition's forces had returned home, he arrived in London only to learn that the *Edgar* had blown up, with all aboard lost! His account follows:

October 16. Being come to *London*, soon after I received a Letter from *Portsmouth*, with the melancholy *News* of the *Edgar's* being blown up; whereby as to my own particular, I sustain'd a very considerable Loss, my Household Goods, Stores, and most of my Publick Papers, Books, Draughts of *Quebec* River, Journals, Charts, Sir *William Phips* Journal of his *Canada* Expedition, all the Officers original Demands, Supplies and Receipts, my own contingent Accounts, with several other Papers of Consequence.

In the Evening I waited upon Mr. Secretary *St. John*, who seemed very much concern'd at the Disappointment of the Expedition.

17. This Forenoon I waited upon the Admiralty, where was an account of the *Edgar's* being blown up and not one Man saved.

19. I came to *Windsor* last Night, and this Morning was introduced by his Grace the Duke of *Shrewsbury* Lord Chamberlain, to the Queen: Her Majesty was pleased to receive me very graciously, and told me when I kiss'd Her Hand, She was glad to see me. I said, I was very sorry my Power to serve Her Majesty in the late Expedition, had not been equal to my Zeal, and mention'd the great Loss I had by the *Edgar's* being blown up.

When I returned to *London*, I apply'd myself to the obtaining the Bills to be paid that had been drawn from *Boston*, and to get my own contingent Accounts pass'd.

But other blows were to fall. Ridiculed and abused, Hovendon Walker was practically chased out of London by his former associates, the Lords of the Admiralty. He finally found the humiliation too great and sailed for America.

During his declining years he spent much of his time reading the works of the ancient Roman poet Horace, finding serenity in Horace's admonitions concerning action in the face of adversity.

"Show yourself brave and undaunted in the face of adversity," Horace said. "Also if you are wise, you will furl your swelling sail, though the wind seem too favorable for it."

Horace's words gave Walker peace and tranquility during the remaining period of his career, in which he spent many hours writing his journal. Published in 1720, the lengthy volume defended his actions, quoting Horace's words which are translated above:

REBUS ANGUSTIS ANIMOSUS ATQUE FORTIS APPARE: SAP-
IENTER IDEM CONTRAHES VENTO NIMIUM SECUNDO TUR-
GIDA VELA

CHAPTER 4

THE STORM OF OCTOBER 1804

One of the outstanding October gales of all times swept across New England on the morning of October 9, 1804. The tempest brought heavy rain in the southern part of New England, while the people in Massachusetts and to the north experienced a snowstorm. First the wind blew from the southeast, and then early in the afternoon it veered to the north northeast, increasing in intensity until sunset, when its terrific force blew down houses, barns, trees, and hundreds of chimneys. Before midnight the worst of the gale had passed, although the snow and wind continued for two days.

It was one of the worst October storms ever witnessed in Massachusetts, with snowfall averaging from five to fourteen inches. At Concord, New Hampshire, the snow was two feet deep, but in Vermont only five inches fell. Farmers were among the worst sufferers. Fruit orchards were blown down everywhere. Cattle and sheep died by the hundreds, and thousands of fowl perished. At Thomaston, Maine, a sixty-acre timber lot was almost completely blown down. Such great sections of timber were destroyed that entirely new views were possible; houses and other buildings never before visible from a distance could be seen across valleys and townships.

The change was so pronounced in certain sections that the surroundings seemed to have become entirely different. People felt that they were in a strange place.

In Massachusetts the South Church in Danvers lost its roof, while in Peabody over 30,000 unburned bricks were ruined by the gale. The spire of the Beverly meeting house broke off.

In Boston, the wind blew the battlements from a new building onto the roof of a residence occupied by Ebenezer Eaton, who had left his house just in time. Four others were caught in the ruins, one dying later. The roof was ripped off King's Chapel and dropped to the ground two hundred feet away. The handsome steeple of the Old North Church was toppled into the street, landing partly on a building nearby and demolishing it. No one was inside. The buildings over Paul Revere's copper furnaces were destroyed.

Shipping in the harbor suffered considerably, with several persons losing their lives. The schooner *Dove* was wrecked on Ipswich Bar, all seven on board perishing. The sloops *Hannah* and *Mary* were driven on the beach at Cohasset at about the same time. Captain Gardner of the *Hannah* was swept off the deck and drowned, but the others aboard were saved. The crew from the *Mary* were successful in reaching shore alive. The ship *Protector*, with a cargo valued at $100,-000, was wrecked on Cape Cod five miles south of Cape Cod Light. Only one man was lost.

The Reverend William Bentley of Salem said that this gale was the heaviest blow ever known in that town. He recorded the storm in his diary as follows:

9. This morning the wind was in the South & the weather uncertain. About 7 it shut down & it began to rain at S.E. & soon the wind rose & the wind changed to N.E. Its violence increased till sundown & continued all night. The barn belonging to Perkins on the Neck,

was blown down & one horse killed. Beckets barn down, all the vessels drove from their anchors. Chimnies were blown down, roof & windows injuried & trees destroyed in great number.

The fences suffered so much that in the eastern part of the Town which I visited it was easy to pass over any lot in that part of the Town. The damage is so equally divided that few have special cause to complain. It was the heaviest blow ever known in Salem & it will be remembered as the Violent Storm of 9 Oct. 1804. We had thunder & lightning all day. We lost the Railing from the top of the house in which I live. It was totally destroyed.

10. We are every moment receiving accounts of the injuries done by the Storm. The Vessels in Cape Ann & Marblehead that were at anchor are ashore. The damage done in Boston is great. The celebrated Steeple of the North Church is blown down. Mr. Atwater Phippen who for many years has noticed the fall of rain, distinguished the rain of yesterday as the greatest he ever knew, four inches fell in the day & three inches in the night.

11. Continued account of the Storm. From the Coast, accounts general only as yet. Roads everywhere much obstructed by the fall of trees, &c. Revere's Buildings over his furnace destroyed. Not of great value. Covering of Chapel Church tower blown down. Mr. Eaton at Boston, new brick walls tumbled upon his old house from which he had just time to escape. The woman who lived with him killed, servants wounded.

The spire of Charleston steeple bent down. The top of Beverly steeple blown off. The dome of the Tabernacle in this town uncapped, & shattered & Lantern. A Vessel from Cape Ann harbour, belonging to Kennebunk, lost her anchor & split her sails & drove up over our Bar into the Cove within the Beacon upon Ram Horn

rock. This is the only Vessel ashore on our coast not in
the Harbour. The Boston account is an almost total destruction of all small boats at the wharves. The damage
to Houses, buildings, trees, fences, &c. is incalculable,
but such losses not heavy to individuals, but a distressing
loss to the public.

12. This day I rode through south fields & Marblehead farms to Nahant. Every where trees are blown down
& barns unroofed & the road in several places would
have been impassable had it not been cleared. Even at
Nahant Great head, Wood lost part of the roof of his
new Barn erected this year.

The reports are endless, but we cannot distinguish
truth from falsehood at any distance from home at present. But the reports shew the state of the public mind.
The quantity of seaweed driven up is beyond any former
example. I had a good opportunity of examining a rich
variety on every part of Nahant. The most common there
in deep water is the Kelp, the seagrass & the wrack as
they are called. The *Dulce Conpici,* &c. were in less
abundance. It would not have been imagined that the
beaches over which we passed had ever been used for
pleasure had they been seen only after the late storm.

13. I cannot refuse to adopt the belief that the late
storm was the most severe ever felt in this part of America. All the accounts which I have seen represent nothing like it. In Boston, the old people are said to represent
that a storm like it happened 16 September 1727. As
yet I have found no tradition of such a storm among our
old people or upon record or any report of its consequences. I suspect as our winters have less horrour we
partake more of a southern climate from the great quantity of heat & consequently have more stormy weather
of this kind & therefore may expect more of it in future

years. I can find no history of wharves, ships, trees, houses, fences, out houses which lead to suspect great calamities from high winds.

From Cape Ann we learn that many of their boats were lost entirely & some greatly injuried by the storm. But we have hopes from the news from Plymouth & Portland, that the storm was much more limited than we have expected from its great severity here & near Boston.

CHAPTER 5

~~~~~~~~~~

THE *NANCY*

A substantial number of present-day residents of Massachusetts can recall the year 1927, when the five-masted schooner *Nancy* was stranded in the same storm that brought death to eight members of the Coast Guard rum chaser *CG 238* off Cape Cod, a tale I relate elsewhere in this book. Just as people numbered the years after the great Boston Fire of 1872, then later after the Chelsea Fire of 1908, so it has come to be that many now alive enjoy figuring out how many years have passed since the *Nancy* came ashore at Nantasket Beach.

The story of the *Nancy* is one of the sagas of New England maritime history. It all began on February 19, 1927, when the *Nancy* anchored off Boston Light to ride out an expected gale or blizzard.

Captain E. M. Baird of Floral Park, Long Island, New York, had sailed the *Nancy* away from Nickerson Wharf in South Boston late in the afternoon of February 18, but on reaching the Boston Lightship he decided to find out what the weather ahead might be. He turned on his five-tube radio set and learned that a storm was on the way. Interviewed on February 20 at the Point Allerton Coast Guard Station, he told this story:

189

"I decided it was best to drop our anchors near sight of the lightship. There was a strong wind, but our big and little anchors made us safe until afternoon. Yesterday at noon I believed that the storm was abating. The barometer was at 30:15 all morning long and began to go down at the time we lost our big anchor. The chain parted about 2:30 P.M. Immediately the flag was hoisted, union down, but no one noticed that we were in distress.

"Then for about three hours all aboard worked like beavers hauling in about ninety fathoms, preparatory to putting on a reserve anchor, and after this was done the distress flag was pulled down again for the time being.

"After dark the storm had grown so desperate that we became alarmed. We would have liked to have had a cutter then, but try as we did, our signals to the lightship received no response. Apparently they had no means of communication with the mainland, and so we had to suffer out the night, few of the men getting any sleep.

"Everything went along O.K. until the chain on our starboard anchor parted again at 7:30 this morning, although throughout the night I was afraid that we were going to be carried into Harding's Ledge. But we escaped that fate, only to avert it again by the narrowest of margins when the chain parted about one o'clock this afternoon, and then all three of our anchors had dropped into the sea.

"There was easily a seventy-five knot gale whipping up the seas as the chain parted the third time. The water was drifting like snow in the howling wind, and it was necessary to raise the staysail, a jib next to the foremast, to steer us clear of Harding's Ledge off Nantasket.

"For a time it really looked as though we would be dashed to pieces on the ledge, but I worked hard and managed to bring her up here on the beach. I should say that we were within two hundred yards of Harding's Ledge, when knowing of the clean stretch of beach here, I decided to steer for this place, as I knew that we would not be damaged too much.

"I have been sailing the seas for thirty-three years, and this is my first experience of being beached. I have been in some very tough storms during those years, but yesterday's was as tough as any I have ever encountered," were his concluding remarks to those of us who listened to him at the Point Allerton Coast Guard Station.

As she fought her losing battle, the huge five-master came slowly in, her great hulk constantly battered by towering waves that fell over each other in endless profusion. Captain Baird watched the giant billows as the *Nancy* drove her keel on the shore. The wind filled the air with biting sand, and the surf pounded relentlessly as the schooner neared the end of her voyage.

With the bellying skysail tugging at the bolt rope, the five-masted craft drove high on the beach at Surfside, Hull. Ned Blossom, patrolman at Surfside, was the nearest to the oncoming *Nancy*, and he telephoned to the Hull police station. A volunteer crew of rescuers was quickly rounded up.

The men rolled out the surfboat of the Massachusetts Humane Society. A truck mounting a snowplow pulled the surfboat across to a position opposite to where the *Nancy* was pounding ashore. Driven diagonally toward the shelving beach, the ship had her starboard bow closest to the shore.

It was then high tide, with about a hundred and eighty yards separating the *Nancy* from the railroad tracks. Even then a few hardy souls were on the shore, with the sleet and sand driving against them, but when word reached the townspeople of Hull, crowds soon began to congregate.

There has always been controversy as to which residents and coast guardsmen of Hull assisted in the rescue of the crew of the *Nancy*. No one knows how it started, but it can never be settled, as several of those claiming participation in the actual rescue effort are now dead. The story below is as close as we can come to the truth in 1976, almost half a century after the incident.

As the men ashore watched the *Nancy* successfully avoid hitting Harding's Ledge, they prepared for the eventual beaching of the great schooner.

Captain Osceola F. James of Center Hill organized the lifeboat crew, which consisted of Captain Adelbert Nickerson of the Nantasket steamer *Mayflower*, formerly of the Point Allerton Coast Guard Station, Captain Edward Hatch, John Sullivan, Louis Hurley, Robert Blossom, Clifton Jaeger, Burgess Ruderham, and Joseph James.

Another crew arrived by automobile. Organized under the leadership of Coast Guard Captain Ralph C. Rich, they started for the breeches buoy and the gun, although they soon found that neither was necessary.

Soon the lifeboat was launched into the breakers. It was drawn up under the *Nancy's* starboard rope ladder, where the crew members caught suitcases and dunnage dropped from above. Boatswain Alexander Holmberg of Brooklyn, carrying the ship's mascot, a black cat, was the first to reach the surfboat. The others were Captain Baird; Engineer Charles M. Rathburn, New York; Steward S. A. White, Norfolk; Carlin Burrell, Lynn; Ruby Hatfield, Revere; Frank Combs, Charlestown; and Carl Michaelson, Norfolk.

There were several exciting moments as the heavily laden lifeboat was rowed ashore, but the landing on Nantasket Beach was successful. Within an hour rescuers and rescued were enjoying coffee at the Coast Guard station.

For one of the *Nancy's* crew, Ruby Hatfield, it was his sixth mishap at sea. Previously he had been wrecked off Black Rock, Nova Scotia; again off Carr's Beach; still later stranded on Christmas Day at Beaver Harbor, New Brunswick. On two other occasions Hatfield had abandoned sinking fishing schooners.

The *Nancy* did not break up, as many expected, and she became the goal of hundreds upon hundreds of sightseers from all over New England, as happened similarly in 1956, twenty-nine years later when the 441-foot Italian freighter *Etrusco* beached at Scituate. There was one great difference, however. No sightseers were able to get aboard the *Etrusco* because of her high sides and her position half in and half out of the water. In the case of the *Nancy,* a ramp was soon arranged for boarding, and payment of a relatively small fee allowed visitors who wished to board her to tour certain areas of the schooner.

Every so often during high runs of tides, efforts were made to float the *Nancy*, but as the years went by she became a fixture at Nantasket Beach. One day, when the tides were accompanied by a moderate storm, the five-masted schooner slipped a short distance toward the sea but grounded again. In another later gale she went up the beach ten feet higher than previously.

Finally it was agreed that she be broken up. Her towering masts were sold to the Hitchcock Quarry in Quincy. Residents of Hull took much of the lumber. Gradually her huge bulk disappeared from the beach, and the keel area was eventually buried in the sand. No one ever expected to see her again, but in the winter of 1940, during a nor'easter, the keel of the *Nancy* washed out of the sands at Nantasket Beach. The next storm buried her again. Without question, tons of her bottom and keel are still below the surface of the sands of Nantasket.

Built at Portland, Oregon, in 1918 for the French government, the *Nancy* had cost $650,000. Originally constructed as an auxiliary steam schooner, she was rebuilt for sailing in 1925, when she was sold to S. C. Forde of Philadelphia for the coal trade. Her gross registration was 2100 tons and her cargo tonnage totaled 3500.

Captain Baird had taken over command of the *Nancy* shortly before the last week in January, at Norfolk, Virginia, from which port he sailed the schooner to Boston with a load of coal for South Boston.

Only a handful of residents witnessed the beaching of the *Nancy* at Nantasket, and of those few three are still alive today.* However, those who saw her and read about her through the years are many. They look back at her as an old friend associated with the glamour of the days of sail.

* Oliver Olson, Charles Short, and Louis Hurley.

CHAPTER 6

A STRANGE PREMONITION, OR THE LOSS OF THE RUM CHASER *CG 238*

On February 21, 1927, Mrs. Joseph Maxim of Westville Street, Dorchester, experienced a tragic dream concerning her boy Joseph. In the dream she saw her son, a Coast Guardsman aboard rum chaser *CG 238*, struggling for his life, after which she was approached by her sister, who told her to put on mourning clothes.

Mrs. Maxim awakened in a shaken state. Several hours later a messenger brought the news that her son was among those missing from the wreck of the *CG 238,* and word soon followed that he had drowned.

Actually, every member of the crew aboard the *CG 238* perished in what was the first trip her commander had ever made as officer-in-charge. All eight went to their deaths in the surging seas off Provincetown on Cape Cod.

Early the night before, on February 20, 1927, the 75-foot rum chaser had sent her first message of distress by the blinker system. Every Coast Guard station in the area was alerted, but a seventy-five-mile-an-hour gale and blinding snow blocked all attempts to save the eight men. The blizzard was possibly the worst since the steamer *Portland* sank in the storm of 1898. It had been in progress about thirty hours when the *CG 238* dropped two anchors about three miles off shore.

Highland Light crewman Clarence Carlos picked up the blinker message that the rum chaser was in distress, her engines broken down and her radio out of commission. The SOS message came immediately afterward.

Carlos notified his commanding officer, who informed other stations by telephone and radio of the *CG 238*'s peril. All night long the crews from three Coast Guard stations along the shore stood by, awaiting a possible lull in the storm, which never came. Every so often the lights of the *238* were sighted.

With the coming of dawn the wreck of the *CG 238* could be seen. She had hit the bar and broken in pieces. Bits of the wreckage washed up along the shore.

Later that day two bodies were sighted about halfway between Peaked Hill Station and Highland Light Station. A watch was found in the pocket of one man, the hands stopped at 4:57, indicating the time when the patrol craft began to break up. The remains were those of Boatswain's Mate Raymond H. Clark of Dorchester and Boatswain's Mate Charles H. Freeburn of Philadelphia. The other members of the crew were Boatswain Jesse K. Riberbank of Oak Bluffs, commander of the craft on his first trip; Chief Mechanic Cornelius Shea of Roxbury; mechanic Joseph Maxim; cook Clarence Alexander of South Carolina; coxswain Leo Kryzabowski; and Fred C. McCausland of Portland, Maine. A ninth regular member of the crew, Edward F. Cronin of Lynn, was a patient at the Chelsea Naval Hospital when the storm hit, and so escaped being a victim of the disaster.

Apparently the *CG 238* broke up shortly before five o'clock in the morning, but what happened in the twelve-hour interval between the sending out of the first blinker message and the actual destruction of the craft is a mystery that will never be solved.

According to the surmise of Captain E. B. Andrews of the Highland Light Coast Guard Station, the rum chaser had been anchored until 2:30 in the morning, when she either broke adrift or began dragging her anchor. She probably passed over the outer bar and her anchors may have caught again, to subject her to the giant breakers that battered her to pieces.

Because of the tremendous surf, Captain Andrews could not launch his surfboat for rescue work. The Lyle gun, which sends a projectile a quarter mile or more to ships in distress, could not reach the vessel, as she was then about a mile from shore. At least four rescue craft were in the general vicinity, including the revenue cutters *Tuscarora*, *Redwing*, *Pauling*, and *Cummings*, but the *238* was in water too shallow for their draft.

A statement that a coastal merchant steamer was within a short distance of the *238* and did nothing to help has been circulated, but what the captain of the steamer could have done will never be known.

CHAPTER 7

~~~~~~~~~

THE *ACTIVE* AND THE *BETSY*

The meeting of the Casco Bay schooner *Active* and the Marblehead schooner *Betsy* took place off the white tower of Cape Cod's Highland Light and proved to have not only historical but literary significance as well.

At midnight on Friday, October 28, 1808, Keeper Isaac Small of Highland Light heard the sound of a gunshot some distance offshore from the lighthouse. Peering into the darkness, he was able to detect the source of the firing.

At that identical moment Captain Benjamin "Floyd" Ireson, who had been fishing off the Grand Banks, was sailing toward his home port of Marblehead aboard the schooner *Betsy*. He heard the same gun firing off Highland Light and found it to be a distress signal from the Brunswick, Maine, schooner *Active*, then sinking. He decided to give what assistance he could. However, the waves that night were mountainous, and the crew aboard the *Betsy* protested when the captain announced he would attempt to rescue the unfortunate sailors on the *Active*. Nevertheless, Ireson approached the foundering schooner and called encouragement to those aboard.

"We'll stand by," he shouted, but the sea was far too high to launch a dory. The *Betsy*'s crew became frightened and rebellious, urging the captain to sail for Marblehead, but he insisted upon waiting for the dawn to make a final rescue effort. After several hours of arguing, his sailors asserted their rights, claiming that they had been asked to do something beyond the usual call of duty of Marblehead fishermen, and Ireson finally gave in to their demands. However, after leaving the sinking vessel, the crewmen grew apprehensive about their reception when they arrived at Marblehead. They began to talk among themselves, stirring up false courage and blaming the captain for their own reluctance.

The *Betsy* reached port on Sunday, October 30. Ireson and his crew went to their respective homes after telling a brief story of their encounter with the sinking schooner. On hearing the news of a boat in distress, two different craft, manned by eager volunteers, left for her position off Highland Light. When they returned, they announced that they had found no signs of vessel or men. By this time the crew of the *Betsy* had let word circulate that Captain Ireson had been the one who was unwilling to wait around for dawn to attempt rescue work, while the captain maintained a stolid silence.

A day later the sloop *Swallow* sailed into Marblehead Harbor with four survivors from the *Active*, Captain Given— whose name is erroneously spelled Gibbons in some accounts —and three passengers. Given explained that the *Active* had sprung a leak at eleven o'clock that Friday night and that he had fired his distress gun shortly afterward. Then he related how Captain Ireson had brought the *Betsy* alongside and had called across to inquire if he could help, after which he had sailed away without giving any assistance.

Captain Given told how a Mr. Hardy of Truro had rowed out in a whaleboat, taking off the four who were saved, but that he was unable to rescue four other persons, who perished in the wreck when the storm returned with renewed fury that Saturday morning. Captain Given and his men had then been placed aboard the revenue cutter *Good Intent,* which sailed them across to Boston. From there the sloop *Swallow* took them over to Marblehead.

When the survivors were landed at Marblehead, a great feeling of resentment developed against Captain Ireson, whom people erroneously believed responsible for the loss of the four crew members aboard the *Active.* This antagonism was soon transformed into hostile action. A crowd went to Ireson's home. After causing a commotion outside his house, they gained courage and entered his residence, where they manhandled him and pulled him outside. They had placed a dory in the street, and they bound him to the thwarts and tarred and feathered him.

Their next step was to drag the dory through the streets of Marblehead, with a great multitude of men and boys following and jeering. When the strange procession arrived at Workhouse Rocks, the bottom of the dory collapsed, and Captain Ireson finished his trip in a cart.

The parade was stopped on the outskirts of Salem by the residents there, and the men turned around and marched back into Marblehead, where Ireson was finally left at his own door. He had remained silent during the entire trip, but as he stood in his doorway he looked out over the assembled mob:

"I thank you for my ride, gentlemen," he remarked, "but you will live to regret it!"

Wondering just what he had implied, several leaders of the mob talked with the members of his crew. Explanations by the embarrassed sailors soon made the others realize that a great injustice had been done. An act of violence and shame had been perpetrated on an innocent man.

To the credit of the townspeople of Marblehead, it must be admitted that from that day on, they accepted Captain Ireson as a true citizen, who was blameless for his crew's reluctance to risk their lives.

Unfortunately, a native of Marblehead was later a classmate of poet John Greenleaf Whittier at Haverhill Academy. Whether Whittier's friend left Marblehead before learning the truth, or just did not care about the facts will never be known, but Whittier took account of the incident as the people of Marblehead originally thought it had happened, and composed therefrom his famous "Skipper Ireson's Ride," excerpts from which are quoted below:

> Of all the rides since the birth of time,
> Told in story or sung in rhyme,—
> On Apuleius's Golden Ass,
> Or one-eyed Calendar's horse of brass,
> Witch astride of a human hack,
> Islam's prophet on Al-Borák,—
> The strangest ride that ever was sped
> Was Ireson's, out from Marblehead!
> > Old Floyd Ireson, for his hard heart,
> > Tarred and feathered and carried in a cart
> > By the women of Marblehead!
>
> *   *   *
>
> Small pity for him!—He sailed away
> From a leaking ship in Chaleur Bay,—
> Sailed away from a sinking wreck,
> With his own townspeople on her deck!
> "Lay by! lay by!" they called to him:
> Back he answered, "Sink or swim!
> Brag of your catch of fish again!"
> And off he sailed through fog and rain!
> > Old Floyd Ireson, for his hard heart,
> > Tarred and feathered and carried in a cart
> > By the women of Marblehead!
> Fathoms deep in dark Chaleur
> That wreck shall lie for evermore.

Mother and sister, wife and maid,
Looked from the rocks of Marblehead
Over the moaning and rainy sea,—
Looked for the coming that might not be!
What did the winds and the sea-birds say
Of the cruel captain who sailed away?—
 Old Floyd Ireson, for his hard heart,
 Tarred and feathered and carried in a cart
 By the women of Marblehead!

*   *   *

Then the wife of the skipper lost at sea
Said, "God has touched him!—why should we?"
Said an old wife mourning her only son,
"Cut the rogue's tether and let him run!"
So with soft relentings and rude excuse,
Half scorn, half pity, they cut him loose,
And gave him a cloak to hide him in,
And left him alone with his shame and sin.
 Poor Floyd Ireson, for his hard heart,
 Tarred and feathered and carried in a cart
 By the women of Marblehead!

*   *   *

In 1880 Samuel Roads, Jr., writing in his *History and Traditions of Marblehead,* gave the true story of "Skipper Ireson's Ride." Roads tells of the arrival of the *Betsy* and Captain Ireson, and of the falsehoods spread by the crew. The account is essentially as I have narrated it above. Excerpts from the Roads tale follow:

The excitement and indignation of the people on the reception of this news can be better imagined than described. . . . On the following day, the sloop *Swallow* arrived having on board Captain Gibbons [Given] the master of the ill-fated schooner. He corroborated the story told by the crew of the *Betsey* and stated that the *Active* sprung a leak at about eleven o'clock on Friday night. An hour later the *Betsey* was spoken, "but contrary to the principles of humanity" she sailed away without giving any assistance. On Saturday Captain Gibbons [Given] and three of the passengers were taken off the wreck by Mr. Hardy of Truro, in a whaleboat. Four other persons were left on the wreck but the storm increased so rapidly that it was found impossible to return to their rescue. Captain Gibbons [Given] was placed on board the revenue cutter *Good Intent* and afterward on board the sloop *Swallow* in which he came to Marblehead.

This statement by one who had so narrowly escaped a watery grave made a deep impression on the fishermen and they determined to demonstrate their disapproval of Skipper Ireson's conduct by a signal act of vengeance. Accordingly on a bright moonlit night the unfortunate skipper was suddenly seized by several powerful men and securely bound. He was then placed in a dory and besmeared from head to feet with tar and feathers, was dragged through the town, escorted by a multitude of men and boys. When opposite the locality now known as Workhouse Rocks the bottom of the dory came out and the prisoner finished the remainder of his ride to Salem in a cart. . . .

When too late to make reparation for the wrong they had committed, the impulsive fishermen realized that they had perpetrated an act of the greatest injustice upon an innocent man.

Roads sent a copy to poet Whittier. After he read the story, Whittier wrote to Mr. Roads as follows:

Oak Knoll, Danvers
5th Mo., 18, 1880

Samuel Roads, Jr.

My Dear Friend:—I heartily thank thee for a copy of thy "History of Marblehead." I have read it with great interest and think good use has been made of the abundant material.

No town in Essex County has a record more honorable than Marblehead; no one has done more to develop the industrial interest of our New England sea-board, and certainly none have given such evidence of self-sacrificing patriotism. I am glad the story of it has been at last told, and told so well. I have now no doubt that thy version of Skipper Ireson is a correct one. My verse was solely founded on a fragment of rhyme which I heard from one of my early schoolmates, a native of Marblehead.

I supposed the story to which it referred dated back at least a century. I knew nothing of the particulars, and the narrative of the ballad was pure fancy. I am glad for the sake of truth and justice that the real facts are given in thy book. I certainly would not knowingly do injustice to any one dead or living.

I am truly, thy friend,
JOHN G. WHITTIER.

New England poet Charles Timothy Brooks wrote a vigorous plea for the maligned captain, but mispelled Ireson's nickname.

Old Flood Ireson! all too long
Have jeer and jibe and ribald song

Done thy memory cruel wrong.
Old Flood Ireson sleeps in his grave;
Howls of a mad mob, worse than the wave,
Now no more in his ear shall rave!
Gone is the pack and gone the prey,
Yet old Flood Ireson's ghost today
Is hunted still down Time's highway.
Old wife Fame, with a fish horn's blare
Hooting and tooting the same old air,
Drags him along the thoroughfare.
Mocked evermore with the old refrain,
Skilfully wrought to a tuneful strain,
Jingling and jolting he comes again
Over the road of old renown,
Fair, broad avenue leading down
Through South Fields to Salem town.
Scourged and stung by the Muse's thong,
Mounted high on the car of song,
Sight that cries, O Lord! how long
Shall Heaven look on and not take part
With the poor old man and his fluttering heart,
Tarred and feathered and carried in a cart?
Old Flood Ireson, now when Fame
Wipes away with tears of shame
Stains from many an injured name,
Shall not, in the tuneful line,
Beam of truth and mercy shine
Through the clouds that darken thine?

~~~~~~~~

CHAPTER 8

THE SLOOP *TRUMBULL*

On the morning of November 30, 1880, the patrol from the Peaked Hill Bars Life-Saving Station on Cape Cod discovered a shipwreck on the outer sandbar a half mile south of the station. It was the stone sloop *Trumbull*, manned by a crew of five and carrying a deck load of granite from Rockport, Massachusetts, to New York. She had left Rockport the previous afternoon.

Captain David H. Atkins, in charge at the station, launched the lifeboat into the surf and six men soon were rowing out to the wreck.

Upon reaching the scene, Captain Atkins found that he could not approach too near for fear of swamping his craft, so he shouted to the *Trumbull*'s crew to jump into the water, from where they could be picked up. Three of the sailors leaped into the water, but the captain and mate refused to take the chance and remained on the sloop.

The lifeboat returned to the beach with the three sailors, although the captain was troubled by the thought of the two men still out on the sloop. Finally he announced that he was going to make another attempt to rescue them and began his second trip. All went well until he reached the sloop, when the boom and loosened main sheet of the *Trumbull* caught the lifeboat and overturned it.

The surfmen clung desperately to the bottom of the boat, but their leader, Captain Atkins, weakened by his efforts earlier in the day, gave up and sank to his death. Two surfmen, Elisha Taylor and Stephen Mayo, followed him shortly afterward. Three others began the long swim to shore, where they were hauled out of the water by the man on patrol, John Cole.

The ocean almost always performs the unexpected, and the incoming tide brought a moderating wind that allowed the stone sloop to free herself from the dangerous Peaked Hill Bars and continue her journey on down the coast. But the captain and mate of the *Trumbull* must have carried to their dying day the realization that had they obeyed the captain of the lifesavers and jumped for the lifeboat, the second trip of the surfmen would not have been necessary.

Later the same afternoon Captain Atkins' own son helped to recover the bodies of the three drowned men. As he carried his father's remains along the beach, a heartbroken but proud son knew that his father had died carrying out the stern code of the Life-Saving Service.

CHAPTER 9

~~~~~~

LONGFELLOW AND
THE *HESPERUS*

The wreck of the *Hesperus* is forever associated with the Maine coast—incorrectly. Of course, there are reasons for this misunderstanding. The actual craft in Longfellow's poem "The Wreck of the *Hesperus*" came from Wiscasset, Maine, and she was named *Favorite*, not *Hesperus*. Longfellow, using poetic license, changed the story to make it more dramatic for his readers.

One of the most entertaining visits I ever made to the Craigie House in Cambridge, where Longfellow lived for many years, took place on the day I was allowed by the poet's grandson, Henry Wadsworth Longfellow Dana, to examine the diary in the family vault where Longfellow's journals are kept. Many of us have read the ballad "The Wreck of the Hesperus," and I quote below some of the twenty-two stanzas he wrote:

It was the schooner Hesperus,
    That sailed the wintry sea;
And the skipper had taken his little daughter,
    To bear him company.

208

Blue were her eyes as the fairy-flax,
    Her cheeks like the dawn of day,
And her bosom white as the hawthorn buds,
    That ope in the month of May.

                    *   *   *

Down came the storm, and smote amain
    The vessel in its strength;
She shuddered and paused, like a frighted steed,
    Then leaped her cable's length.

"Come hither! come hither! my little daughter,
    And do not tremble so;
For I can weather the roughest gale
    That ever wind did blow."

He wrapped her warm in his seaman's coat
    Against the stinging blast;
He cut a rope from a broken spar,
    And bound her to the mast.

                    *   *   *

And fast through the midnight dark and drear,
    Through the whistling sleet and snow,
Like a sheeted ghost, the vessel swept
    Tow'rds the reef of Norman's Woe.

                    *   *   *

She struck where the white and fleecy waves
    Looked soft as carded wool,
But the cruel rocks, they gored her side
    Like the horns of an angry bull.

                    *   *   *

At daybreak on the bleak sea-beach,
    A fisherman stood aghast
To see the form of a maiden fair,
    Lashed close to a drifting mast.

The salt-sea was frozen on her breast,
   The salt tears in her eyes;
And he saw her hair, like the brown sea-weed,
   On the billows fall and rise.

Such was the wreck of the Hesperus,
   In the midnight and the snow!
Christ save us all from a death like this,
   On the reef of Norman's Woe!

I have always enjoyed reading Longfellow's poems aloud, especially before an open fireplace with the burning logs crackling and a storm raging outside. "The Wreck of the Hesperus" is one of my favorites. Therefore, whenever I visited Gloucester, I enjoyed climbing over the rocks leading to Rafe's Chasm. From the chasm itself, I would look over at Norman's Woe in the general direction of Gloucester's harbor. Then I would try to remember as much as I could of the poem and shout it aloud so that the verses would mingle with the roar of the heavy surf at that location.

As time went by I wasn't satisfied merely to look at the reef from a distance, and one day I went over to Ten Pound Island Light where Keeper Edward Hopkins allowed me to take his motorboat and cross the bay to land at the reef itself. I recall one incident in particular when young Ed Hopkins, Richard Clark, and I spent the afternoon exploring the ledge. On the seaward side of Norman's Woe, we found a great pulpit with a cavelike depression under it. Richard climbed to the top of the rock, and I photographed him against the sky. After that pleasant afternoon I was determined to learn all I could about the poem by Longfellow.

It was the following year that I visited Henry Wadsworth Longfellow Dana at Craigie House, where he took me down into the family vaults to see his grandfather's diary and journals. There we read the entries that told in detail what was in

Longfellow's mind before he wrote "The Wreck of the Hesperus." Mr. Dana had already done considerable research into the background of the story itself and was able to give me several bits of information never published before. A short time later I reviewed all of the newspapers of that year of 1839 and was able to piece together the true story of the *Hesperus*.

Henry Wadsworth Longfellow wrote "The Wreck of the Hesperus" as a result of the series of terrible hurricanes that swept New England within a two-week period during the month of December 1839. The first two weeks of that December had been unusually mild, suggesting September or October weather, but at midnight on December 14 snow began to fall heavily, and the wind veered to the southeast. Boston became a temporary island because of an unusually high tide sweeping across what was then known as Boston Neck. Before the storm hit Gloucester, there were sixty schooners swinging at anchor in the harbor. During the hurricane seventeen were broken into kindling wood, three sank at their moorings, and twenty-one others were pushed ashore. When the gale went down, the remaining nineteen were still at their moorings, but only one had her sticks or masts still in her. Forty lives were lost around Gloucester alone, but the worst disaster took place at Pigeon Cove, where twenty persons from one schooner were drowned. Not until 1898, when the steamer *Portland* was lost, was such a storm recorded.

Of course, the next day the columns of Boston's newspapers were crowded with tales of the storm. Since the *Morning Post* was Longfellow's favorite, it was probably in its pages that he read the story of the gale. I quote from the December 17, 1839, issue:

The Gale—On Sunday morning, about 3 o'clock, a N.E. snow storm commenced, occasionally intermingled with heavy showers of rain. . . . The height of the gale was between half past 3 and 4 o'clock on Sunday, but fortunately had subsided considerably about 6 P.M. and continued moderate nearly an hour, when it recommenced and veered to the Northward. . . . At 11 P.M. on Sunday night, the gale was as high as at any period since its commencement and so continued until daylight when it somewhat abated. This second gust drove the schooner *Hesperus*, at anchor in the stream, from her moorings against the ship *Wm. Badger*, at the North Side of Rowe's Wharf, which parted her lines, and both drove up the dock together.

The *Hesperus* drove her jib boom across the street into the third floor of a building, and her bowsprit was soon carried completely away.

In the same column of the *Post* that carried the account of the *Hesperus* and the *Wm. Badger* is the following news from Cape Ann:

> *Disasters at Cape Ann*—We have conversed with a gentleman who left Gloucester this morning, from whom we learn that the destruction of life and property in the vicinity has been very great. Our informant saw seventeen dead bodies lying on the beach. Among them was the body of a woman, found lashed to the windlass bits of a Castine schr. Two of this vessel were also lost.

That Tuesday night, writing in his diary, Longfellow mentions both the storm and the incidents associated with Gloucester. He also refers to the *Hesperus* but does not indicate that he realized the *Hesperus* was wrecked inside Boston Harbor. The excerpt from his diary follows:

> Tuesday, Dec. 17—News of shipwrecks horrible, on the coast. Twenty bodies washed ashore near Gloucester.

One female lashed to piece of a wreck. There is a reef called Norman's Woe, where many of these took place. Among others the schooner *Hesperus*. Also the *Sea-flower* on Black Rock. I must write a ballad on this.

Later, the *Post* carried a correction in the story of the woman washed ashore lashed to the wreck of a Castine schooner. As it turned out, the woman, Mrs. Sally Hilton, fifty-five years old—no "maiden fair"—had been lost from the schooner *Favorite* of Wiscasset,* not from a Castine schooner, as had been previously reported.

The second of the triple hurricanes hit the coast on Sunday, December 22. During the gale, the brig *Pocohantas* crashed against Plum Island several miles north of the place where the ship *Deposit* had hit in the hurricane of the week before. Two people from the *Deposit* had drowned; eleven aboard the *Pocohantas* were lost. Then came the third hurricane, said by many to be the worst of all. It struck with terrific fury on December 27, causing widespread damage. In Boston the ship *Columbiana* went completely through the Charlestown Bridge and demolished the drawtender's house on Warren Bridge.

On the night of the third storm, Longfellow sat up until one o'clock smoking by his fireside. I quote from his journal:

> Suddenly it came into my mind to write the ballad of the schooner *Hesperus*; which I accordingly did. Then went to bed but could not sleep. New thoughts were running in my mind; and I got up to add them to the ballad. It was three by the clock. Then went to bed and fell asleep. I feel pleased with the ballad. It hardly cost me an effort; flowed easily from my pen. It did not come to my mind by lines, but by stanzas.

* The wheel of the *Favorite* has been preserved by an insurance company in New York City.

The disparity between the true story and Longfellow's account of it should not detract in the least from our pleasure in "The Wreck of the Hesperus." Longfellow had a perfect right to convert a fifty-five-year-old woman into a "maiden fair" for poetic purposes and to utilize the ship and locale that most appealed to his imagination. But for those of us who enjoy the story behind the poem, it should be remembered that the *Hesperus* was wrecked at Boston during the hurricane, and that it was from the Wiscasset schooner *Favorite* that the body of Mrs. Sally Hilton was washed ashore—possibly at Norman's Woe, but probably on the mainland.

Sidney Perley, the New England storm historian, said that upwards of three hundred vessels were wrecked and a million dollars' worth of property destroyed, with more than 150 lives lost, in the three December hurricanes of 1839.

In 1878 Longfellow journeyed to Gloucester and went out to Eastern Point for a very special reason. He found a heavy fog on his arrival. Returning home, he wrote in his journal the significant lines with which I end this chapter:

> I did not stay long enough at East Point to see the fog lift and Norman's Woe rise into view. I have never seen those fatal rocks.

CHAPTER 10

ST. ELMO'S FIRE

St. Elmo's Fire has lately come into prominence because several pilots of airplanes and many masters of ships have seen the elusive glow close at hand.

John R. Herbert, who has studied the phenomenon for many years, tells me that under ordinary conditions St. Elmo's Fire is fairly harmless, but that under certain circumstances it can ignite flammable gases. Mr. Herbert, while flying with his son Robert from Boston to Miami in February 1972, actually saw St. Elmo's Fire moving inside the plane's cockpit, lighting up the instrument panel in spectacular fashion. A reddish color, somewhat similar to the glow of a short circuit, bounced from place to place.

In January 1974, Mr. Herbert's other son, John A. Herbert, was able to help me record the words of Jörgen Jensen, a flyer for the Scandinavian Airlines System.

Chief Navigator Jensen informed me that "the jets are usually able to avoid the electrically charged clouds, but I have seen St. Elmo's Fire a few times at the nose of a DC-8. On the propeller aircraft operating at lower levels, St. Elmo's Fire was much more frequent. From the time when I was stationed in Rome and flew the Far East with DC-6's, I remember a great number of occurrences over India. The propellers were a very impressive sight when lighted with St. Elmo's Fire."

John A. Herbert himself observed several demonstrations of St. Elmo's Fire while flying in Thailand.

John R. Herbert also mentioned that for a while St. Elmo's Fire was considered a possible cause of the explosion of the dirigible *Hindenburg*; later indications, however, suggested sabotage.

A technical explanation of St. Elmo's Fire is offered by the United States Government Hydrographic Office:

> When the charge on the aircraft exceeds the dielectric strength of the adjacent air, the accumulated charge leaks off, resulting in a corona discharge. Under some conditions this becomes visible, when it is called St. Elmo's Fire. This can sometimes be seen at the wing tips, nose, propellers and the extremities of the vertical and horizontal control surfaces.

The 1943 edition of the *Encyclopaedia Britannica* tells us that "St. Elmo's Fire is the glow accompanying the brushlike discharges of atmospheric electricity which usually appear as a tip of light on the extremities of pointed objects such as church towers or the masts of ships during stormy weather. It is generally accompanied by a crackling or fizzing noise."

There are those who believe that many of the flying saucers seen through the years could be written off as instances of this natural phenomenon. In my opinion, however, the possibility of St. Elmo's Fire and an unidentified flying object being one and the same is remote indeed.

The mysterious light of St. Elmo's Fire, whether atop a church steeple, on the masts and spars of ships at sea, or on airplanes, has always interested mankind.

Quintus Horatius Flaccus, or Horace as we have come to

know him today, was born in 65 B.C. Even then what we call St. Elmo's Fire was observed and talked about. In describing the conditions surrounding this phenomenon, he offered the following in his *Carmina*:

> Soon as their happy stars appear,
> Hushed is the storm, the waves subside. . . .

In this thought Horace does not agree with Longfellow, who, centuries later, stated that St. Elmo's Fire meant foul weather.

Pliny the Elder, in his *Natural History*, speaks of the sight of

> . . . during the night-watches of the soldiers, a luminous appearance, like a star, attached to the javelins on the ramparts. They also settle on the yardarms and other parts of ships while sailing, producing a kind of vocal sound, like that of birds flitting about. When they occur singly, they are mischievous, so as to even sink the vessel, and if they strike on the lower part of the hull, setting them on fire.

In Columbus's journal of his second voyage we read that

> On Saturday, at night, the body of St. Elmo was seen, with seven lighted candles in the round top, and there followed mighty rain and frightful thunder. I mean the lights were seen which the seamen affirm to be the body of St. Elmo. . . .
>
> Whatever this is I leave to others, for, if we may believe Pliny, when such lights appeared in those times to Roman sailors in a storm, they said they were Castor and Pollux.

Writing on his voyage from Goa in 1588, Linschoten informs us that

> the same night we saw upon the main yard, and in many other places, a certain sign, which the Portuguese call *Corpo Santo*, or the holy body of the brother of Peter

Gonsalves, but the Spanish call it *San Elmo*, and the Greeks (as ancient writers rehearse, and Ovid among the rest), Helle and Phryxus. Whensoever that sign showeth you the mast, or main yard, or in any other place, it is commonly thought that it is a sign of better weather. When they first perceive it, the Master or Chief Boatswain whistleth, and commandeth every man to salute it with "Salve Corpo Santo," and a *miseracordia*, with a very great cry and exclamation.

In Antonio Pigafetta's history of the voyage of Magellan, we find this account:

In stormy weather we frequently saw what is called the Corpo, or St. Elmo. On one very dark night it appeared to us like a brilliant flambeau, on the summit of the mainmast, and thus remained for a space of two hours, which was a matter of great consolation to us during the tempest.

At the instant of its disappearing, it diffused such a blaze of light as almost blinded us, but the wind ceased immediately.

At another time Pigafetta said, "In this place we endured a great storm, and thought we should have been lost, but St. Elmo appeared, and immediately the storm ceased."

A storm at sea on July 24, 1609, hit a fleet bound for America. One of the craft was the *Sea Venture*. The account of William Strachey, secretary-elect for Virginia, describing the storm was later read by William Shakespeare, who is said to have used the description in *The Tempest*. I quote excerpts from Strachey below:

During all this time, the heavens look'd so blacke upon us, that it was not possible the elevation of the pole might

be observed; not a starre by night, no sunnebeame by day
was to be seen. Onely upon the [third] night Sir George
Sommers being upon the watch, had an apparition of a
little round light, like a faint starre, trembling, and
streaming along with a sparkeling blaze, half the height
upon the mainmast, and shooting something from shroud
to shroud. . . .

Halfe the night it kept with us, running sometimes
along the maine yard to the very end, and then returning. . . .

The superstitious seamen made many constructions of
this sea-fire. It might have strucken amazement.

An unusual event concerning St. Elmo's Fire occurred in
Quincy, Massachusetts, a dozen or so years ago. News Editor
Richard Carlisle of the Quincy *Patriot Ledger* recalls that he
and his family were sitting in the living room of his home at
the head of Whitwell Street near the Quincy City Hospital one
night when a fireball of St. Elmo's Light came out of the chimney, rolled across the room, and snapped into nothingness
near a radiator, vanishing completely.

It is believed that the poet Longfellow saw St. Elmo's "stars"
during a voyage returning to New England from abroad. This
is a quotation from his "Golden Legends."

Last night I saw St. Elmo's stars,
  With their glimmering lanterns all at play,
On the top of the masts, and the tips of the spars,
  And I knew we should have foul weather today.

~~~~~~~~

CHAPTER 11

FORBES AND THE *EUROPA*

Many buildings of downtown Boston around the general vicinity of Washington Street still contain, in the upper rooms above the first floors, literary treasures of value. Early in February 1975, while exploring on the fourth floor of a relatively ancient building at 5 West Street, I came across a torn, mutilated manuscript wedged into the secret drawer of an old desk that at the time was overflowing with books. In that West Street building were almost a third of a million volumes that bookseller George Gloss had crowded together, but he knew nothing of the background of the manuscript I had discovered.

I studied the readable fragments of the manuscript, which apparently was written in the year 1850. Essentially, the material told of a particularly unfortunate shipwreck that occurred on June 27, 1849, in which well over a hundred persons lost their lives. There had been a collision between the mail steamer *Europa* and the emigrant carrier *Charles Bartlett*. What more than interested me was the mention in the manuscript that a resident of Boston, Mr. R. B. Forbes, saved lives by leaping overboard and bringing back victims of the disaster.

I wondered if Captain R. B. Forbes, who had lived in Milton, Massachusetts, could have been the same man mentioned in the manuscript. I had written about Mr. Forbes back in 1944 in my *Romance of Boston Bay*, but I didn't remember the details of the story.

Studying through *Romance* that night, I came across my mention of Forbes' first voyage, taken when he was six years old. I also had written that later he was one of the heroes of the Irish grain famine of 1847 when he crossed the ocean on the *Jamestown* in fifteen days with a load of grain for the starving inhabitants of Ireland. For years afterward Irish children were named Forbes, Boston, and Jamestown.* I had not mentioned the *Europa* disaster, however.

Forbes had written a book, *Notes on Wrecks and Rescues*, and I decided to read through my copy for mention of the *Europa*. When I finished it several hours later I had found not a word of the accident, although the book is meticulous in listing scores upon scores of wrecks. I decided it was a reasonable assumption that if he didn't mention the *Europa*, he couldn't have been aboard.

Evidently the question of whether or not Forbes had been on the *Europa* was weighing on my mind more than I realized. A few nights later, when I returned from giving a lecture at Pease Air Base in New Hampshire, I indulged in far too much of a midnight snack before bed. I then experienced a dream. During the dream my senses told me that I was in the midst of a nightmare involving Robert Bennet Forbes and a person named Crosby. I also realized in the dream that I'd probably forget it on awakening, and my subconscious mind was demanding that in some way I write it down.

Mumbling to my wife, Anna-Myrle, the words *Crosby* and *Forbes*, I promptly went back to sleep. In the morning Anna-

* My own great-grandfather, Captain Richard Henry Keating, now buried at Calcutta, India, was master of a similar grain-carrying craft that same year. As he entered the harbor of Cork and guided the *Jenny Pitts* up to the pier, hundreds of grateful Irish men and women knelt on the wharf in prayers of thankfulness.

Myrle explained to me that she had written down *Crosby* and *Forbes.*

I began thinking about the name Crosby, and remembered that not long before that time Editor Arthur Morris Crosby of the Nantucket Historical Association had sent me a shipwreck story he had written for his association's quarterly. Could it have been of the *Europa*'s collision? Then I recalled that Editor Crosby's article had been about the 1952 shipwreck of the tanker *Pendleton*, whose shattered bow can still be seen, in 1976, off Chatham.

I began to ponder again. My thoughts turned to the great-grandson of R. B. Forbes, Henry Ashton Crosby Forbes, who is now in charge of the Robert B. Forbes Museum in Milton. Talking with him, I explained what I wished to know about his great-grandfather. I found that he could solve my problem.

Yes, the Mr. Forbes mentioned in the manuscript was indeed Captain Robert Bennet Forbes, and in an earlier book Forbes had written fully about the *Europa-Bartlett* disaster. His comments on this terrible marine accident follow, taken from his book *Personal Reminiscences*, published many years before his later volume on rescues came out.

I sailed on the 20th June, 1849, in the *Europa*, Captain Lott, for England. On our way to Liverpool, we met with a fearful experience. On the 27th June, while running at full speed in a thick fog, we ran into the American ship *Charles Bartlett*, Captain Bartlett.

The collision occurred about 3 P.M. I was reclining on my couch in the forward cabin, where I had gone to accommodate Mr. Augustus Thorndike, and to get rid of a lot of small children, who made day and night hideous by their squallings. I felt a sudden shock, and knew at once that we had struck an iceberg or a vessel.

I hastened on deck, and on arrival there I found a scene

of horror and confusion which beggars description. Rushing to the port bow, where the ill-fated ship was in the act of heeling over and sinking, and where lay the wreck of our fore-topmast with all the sails attached, I looked over and saw the crew and the passengers filling the fore and main hatchways in a general rush to get on deck. The afterhatch and the side of the ship abreast of it were crushed in, the steam was blowing off with a noise that drowned the shrieks of the people.

Our ship, with all the sails on the mainmast drawing, was forging ahead slowly. All our people were at the bow, trying to save the other crew and passengers. Seeing that I could do nothing there, I rushed aft on the port side to endeavor to clear away a boat.

Only two or three servants and firemen were near, and they seemed to be paralyzed. While trying to clear the boat, I saw a woman and a child come up just abaft the port-sponson. I jumped down, crying out for a rope, and by the time one was thrown to me, a man appeared clinging to a piece of timber. The rope was thrown over him, and he was hauled up more dead than alive.

By this time, the ship had drifted over the woman and the child, who were lying face downwards without any signs of life; and realizing that I could be more useful on the weather side, I mounted and ran over to the sponson just in time to see a man moving slowly by.

I cried out for a rope, and, one being thrown to me, I jumped for him; and, as the ship at the moment rolled to windward, I succeeded by a desperate effort in getting it round him, and taking a turn or two round its own part I contrived so to hold it that, as the ship lurched the other way, we were jerked out of water, against the ship's side, and when the ship came back we went under again.

I cried out whenever above water to "haul up," "haul

up"; but it appeared subsequently that the rope I had hold
of was fastened to the side below the gunwhale, probably
a short main-sheet hooked into a bolt in the bends, and
considerable delay ensued before another rope was bent
on to it, and we were hauled out of water.

In the meantime, I had taken in more than was agreeable and had become somewhat tired of holding a slippery
hitch with the weight of two men hanging to it; so that
at the moment when we were fairly out of water I could
hold on no longer, and down went my man.

I cried, "let go!" and went again under water, but could
not reach him. By this time, one of the boats came round
the stern, manned by the third mate, a couple of sailors,
and some firemen and stewards. Seeing my situation, they
took me in. I seized an oar, and we pulled off to windward where the debris of the wreck could be seen, among
which I perceived some persons struggling for life.

Approaching one of them, I being at the bow-oar, I
laid it in, and, seizing a boat-hook, made fast to his clothes
and pulled him on board. While doing this, the boat fell
off before the sea, and not being very well handled, by
the time we got her going in the right direction, another
man disappeared.

We pulled round for a short time seeking for more, but
seeing none, and those we had requiring immediate attention, and the ship nearly out of sight in the fog, we
pulled for her and soon got on board. Before taking me
in, she had picked up the man I had been aiding, and one
or two others.

We immediately turned our attention to restoring these
apparently drowned persons, and with the help of the
ship's surgeon and Mr. Francis Peabody, who was very
efficient, all save my first man were brought to. Every
means was resorted to, and I think if he had any life left

in him it would certainly have been rubbed and rolled out of him by our unscientific manipulations.

The man who was hooked up came out all right, and was very grateful. The *Europa* did not leak, and after clearing away the wreck of the top-mast, and hoisting up the boats, we pushed on again.

Only one woman out of about forty was saved, and not a single child out of about the same number. One poor man was nearly frantic over the loss of wife, six little ones, and all his earthly possessions. The passengers generally were of the better class of Germans.

It is a singular fact that nearly or quite all the watch below of the *Bartlett* crew were saved, and nearly all the watch on deck were lost. Most of those saved sprang for the bows and bowsprit of the steamer, Captain Bartlett among them; and most of the forty of the immigrants saved were hauled in over the bows by ropes. About one hundred and thirty of the steerage passengers, and eight or ten of the crew, went down with the ship. I can only account for the loss of the watch on deck, by supposing that they turned their attention to saving others, while the watch below, coming up half asleep, sprang for the steamer.

The one woman, Mrs. Bridget Conroy, who was saved, was hauled in by a bowline. A stout blacksmith was hauled up by one arm, during which process some one caught him by the leg, and the strain was such as to pull his shoulder out of joint. Great exertions were made to set his limb, but as he would not take ether, it could not be done, so that he was taken into Liverpool in great suffering.

Immediately after the accident, a committee was formed, electing Mr. Bates as its chairman, and Mr. Peabody secretary, for the purpose of giving a tangible form to the benevolence of the gentlemen and ladies on board. Subscriptions to the amount of £352 5s. were collected on the instant.

By the latter gentlemen, we were politely favored with a full report of the accident and the whole proceedings, up to the close of the collection of the subscriptions.

At one of the committee meetings on board the *Europa*, the following resolution passed unanimously:

> That we have witnessed, with feelings of intense interest, the bold and rapid movements of Captain Forbes, of Boston; that his self-sacrificing and daring leap into the sea to save the passengers of the "Charles Bartlett," commands our admiration; and we rejoice that these deeds were performed by the missionary of the "Jamestown."

The following statement was given of the unfortunate collision by Captain Bartlett:

> The "Charles Bartlett" was a first-rate ship of our hundred tons register. She left the Downs from London, bound to New York, on the 14th June, with a general heavy cargo, of about four hundred and fifty tons weight, and one hundred and sixty-two passengers in the steerage, one cabin passenger, and fourteen souls of the crew; had fine weather, with light easterly winds, up to the 19th. From that time to the 27th, had S.W. and W. winds and foggy weather.
>
> At noon it cleared up a little; observed the latitude 50 48 N., and estimated the longitude at 29 W.; all well on board, and every thing looking prosperous. Soon after noon, a dense fog set in, wind W. by S., ship heading to

the N.W., close hauled, all sail set. At three o'clock, ordered a good look-out from the topgallant forecastle; also directed the man at the wheel to look sharp to windward. At 3.30 P.M., being on the weather side of the poop deck, heard a rumbling to windward like distant thunder; turned my ear to windward, and my eye to the horizon. The man at the wheel, noticing that I was listening, looked to windward and cried out, "Sail ho!" I at once saw what I supposed was a ship about one point forward of our beam, about four hundred yards distant. I ordered the helm up, thinking she did not discover us, and that we should have time to clear her before she could come into contact. All hands shouted at the same time to alarm the ship, and I ordered the bell to be rung, and called to the ship to "port her helm," as I saw that was the only chance of escape. There were nearly one hundred passengers on deck at the time.

All was of no avail; for, in one minute from the time we saw the ship, she was upon us, going at the rate of twelve knots, striking us abreast of the after mainshrouds. The crash and the terrible scene which ensued I am not adequate to describe. I was knocked to leeward with the man at the wheel. I recovered myself in a moment, shouting for every person to cling to the steamer as their only hope. I caught hold of a broken chain on the bow, and hauled myself up, shouting at the same time to the crew and passengers to follow. I had barely time to get on the steamer's bow; and, while getting up, I noticed that her bow was into the ship within a foot of the after-hatch, and that she was stove clear to the lee side, and that full twenty feet of her side was stove in.

There must have been nearly fifty persons killed by the collision, and every exertion was made by Captain Lott, his officers and crew, and the passengers on board the steamer. Unfortunately, only about ten were saved by the boats; the balance, making thirty-three, more or less, saved themselves by hanging to the bow. The steamer lay by the scene as long as there was any hope of saving any. Of the crew, Mr. Thomas Parker, of Charleston, S.C., aged twenty-two years; George Parsons, of Portland, Me., aged eighteen years; and William Rich, of Gravesend, England, aged twenty-five years, were lost. A list of the passengers and crew saved will be found in the public prints. We were most hospitably entertained by the captain, officers, and passengers of the steamer.

I will notice that all due exertion was used by Captain Lott, and officers and crew of the "Europa," as well as all the passengers. I particularly observed one passenger using the most noble exertions; I saw him let himself overboard, and clench a man in his arms, and, finding him dead, let him go. I next saw him on the bow of a boat, hauling a man from under water with a boathook, who was afterwards restored to life on board. I afterwards found that person to be R. B. Forbes, of Boston.

I cannot express myself as I feel for the noble and generous conduct of all on board in contributing to the wants of the surviving sufferers, and for the sympathy felt by all, particularly by the ladies.

Yours, with gratitude,
WILLIAM BARTLETT.

SEA DISASTERS AND INLAND CATASTROPHIES

TO
MARGARET HACKETT

*whose personal aid in unearthing
elusive facts at the Boston Athenaeum
we should never forget*

Contents

Part Four: 1850–1900

Part Five: 1900–1940

Part Six: 1940–Present

Preface

In almost every one of the stories or books I have written,
including the smaller booklets, pamphlets and maps I have
turned out since 1935, it has been my plan never to offer you a
tale you can discover in one of my volumes still in print. Quite
often I receive letters asking that a particularly unusual tale be
inserted into an upcoming book so that those of younger generations can read it. As the years go by, these stories seem to
take on new meaning for those who have read my earlier volumes and continue to read my work.

In *Sea Disasters and Inland Catastrophes* it is once again
my pleasure to include tales of storms, pirates, buried treasure,
ghosts, lighthouses and shipwrecks—the subjects which have
attracted me the most. I trust that this year's selection will
intrigue and entertain you.

I would like to thank my wife for her help and the many
institutions of learning which have been great sources of in-
spiration: the Ventress, the Scituate, Hingham and Boston
libraries, the Boston Athenaeum, the American Antiquarian
Society and the Bostonian Society. Individuals who have
helped me, in addition to those who plead anonymity, include
Philip McNiff, Susie Withol, Bernard L. Spy, Irwin Smith,
Dorothy Snow Bicknell, Eunice Snow, Victoria Snow, Donald
B. Snow, Winthrop Snow, Len Bicknell, Laura Bicknell, Jessica Bicknell, Charles Wood, Melina Herron Oliver, William
Pyne, Frederick G. C. Clow, Richard Carlisle, Arthur Cun-

ningham, Marie Hansen, James Douglass, Walter Spahr
Ehrenfield, Jean Foley, Trevor Johnson, Joseph Kolb, Joel
O'Brien, Larry Molignano, Richard Nikashian, Charles Marks,
Elva Ruiz, Helen Salkowski, Frederick Sanford, Chester Shea,
Alfred Schroeder, William Smits, Cheryl LaBrecque and
Caroline Phillips. John R. Herbert, Quincy banker and histo-
rian, again has given me important suggestions of vital inter-
est.

Edward Rowe Snow
Marshfield, Massachusetts

Part One

1600s

1

Bendall, America's First Scuba Diver

The name Edward Bendall often comes up in correspondence to me. Without question, scuba expert Bendall found substantial treasure in Boston Harbor in the seventeenth century, although in a strange way he also put it there. And he left far more than he removed.

More than 3¼ centuries ago a Puritan galleon holding a delightful amount of treasure blew up and sank in Boston Harbor, in the area between Charlestown and the North End. This terrible explosion aboard the *Mary Rose*, the first great marine calamity in Massachusetts history, caused underwater explorer Edward Bendall to carry out plans for constructing a diving bell. He used this device successfully to go to the bottom of Boston Harbor and remove the wreckage of the *Mary Rose*. The manner in which Bendall did this gave him the honor of being America's first diver to use a method that could be compared to the self-contained underwater breathing apparatus—scuba—of today.

In the summer of 1914, while exploring the stacks at the Boston Public Library under the watchful eye of Pierce Buckley, I discovered information concerning the explosion of the galleon *Mary Rose* and Bendall's diving apparatus. At the time I had been diving and experimenting with staying underwater. In my hometown of Winthrop I was possibly the only person interested enough in underwater exploration to go overboard using rubber hose and five-gallon cans. I was anxious to stay on the bottom, under the small schooners then bringing granite into the town's Crystal Bay landing at Lewis Wharf, in back of Merryman's store. I never thought of treasure in those days. But the story I gleaned at the library activated my lifelong interest in what riches might possibly be buried on the ocean floor.

In 1642 Boston Harbor had a very different appearance than it does today. The North Street area included a pier and a stone landing at the harbor end of the street. It was there that shoemaker George Burden placed a huge wooden barrel to hold water, so that he could moisten the leather he employed in his work. Farther down North Street was the slaughterhouse of Richard Nash, who often annoyed his neighbors by killing and dressing his beasts in the street. A short distance away was the home of Edward Bendall, who owned the town dock.

Bendall probably arrived in Boston on one of the four craft brought into Massachusetts by John Winthrop. (His name is spelled at least three different ways in the records.) Within two years of arriving in Boston he had so far advanced in the community that he is mentioned twice by the clerk of the colony, William Pynchon.

The first item involves the *"lighterage of ordnance."* Bendall was paid fifteen shillings for this, and received payment of two pounds, six shillings for taking "280 *bullets out of the Griffen, being 4 tides."*

Four years later the General Court Records show that it was *"Ordered that there shall be 20£* [20 pounds] *gyven Edward Bendall out of the treasury towards the loss of his lighterman."*

And about six months after that: *"Whereas Edward Bendall*

*had 20£ yielded toward the loss of the lighter, and the lighter
was recovered, the court allowed him 12£ of the 20£ which hee
should have had if it had not been lost towards his charge and
hindrance."*

There was so much trade in Boston at this time that the
business of lighterman (now called longshoreman) was large
enough for a man to support himself by it alone. Every available foot of wharfage was needed, and so the lighters were
employed to unload cargo from ships anchored in the harbor.

Ferries to and from Boston have been given much business
down through the years, and in 1633 Bendall signed a contract
that he would "keepe a sufficient ferry boat to carry to Noodles
Island [East Boston] and to the shipps ryding before the
towne, taking for a single person iid. [twopence] and for twoe
3d. [threepence], and if there be more id. [onepence] a peece."

Edward Bendall belonged for a while to the first church, but
along with many others he later fell under the influence of
Anne Hutchinson, antagonist of John Winthrop. Church and
state strode hand in hand in those days, and because of Mrs.
Hutchinson, Bendall was deprived of his rights as a citizen. He
was also fined 40 shillings for an offense, the nature of which
has not come down to us.

In 1634 he became one of the freemen of the colony. Under
the charter the power of electing the governor was given to the
freemen, plus the privilege of deliberating on other subjects.

On March 21, 1636, Bendall was elected one of Boston's
fence viewers, a relatively important position. He and John
Button were to oversee the fences in the millfield, what is now
known as the North End.

On Christmas Day 1637, barely a year after his wife, Anne,
gave birth to a son they named Freegrace, she died. Some time
later he remarried. Bendall then built a new storehouse down
by the Town Cove and also purchased the wharf at the end of
the Cove, calling it Bendall's Dock.

Then occurred what must have been the greatest achieve-
ment of his lifetime, the raising of the sunken galleon *Mary*

Rose. Blown up by gunpowder as she was riding at anchor before the town, she is mentioned in the *Journal of Governor Winthrop,* who described the accident that took place July 27, 1640:

"Being the second day of the week, the *Mary Rose,* a ship of Bristol, of about 200 tons, her master one Captain Davis, lying before Charlton [Charlestown], was blown in pieces with her own powder, being 21 barrels; wherein the judgment of God appeared, for the master and company were many of them profane scoffers at us, at the ordinances of religion here; so as, our churches keeping a fast for our native country, etc., they kept aboard at their common service, when all the rest of the masters came to our assemblies; likewise the Lord's day following; and a friend of his going aboard next day and asking him, why he came not on shore to our meetings, his answer was, that he had a family of his own, etc., and they had as good service aboard as we had on shore.

"Within two hours after this (being about dinner time) the powder took fire (no man knows how) and blew all up, the captain and nine or ten of his men, and some four or five strangers. There was a special providence that they were aboard at that time, and some were in a boat near the ship, and others diverted by a sudden shower of rain, and others by other occasions.

"There was one man saved, being carried up in the scuttle, and so let fall in the same into the water, and being taken up by the ferry boat, near dead, he came to himself the next morning, but could not tell anything of the blowing up of the ship, or how he came there.

"The rest of the dead bodies were found, much bruised and broken. Some goods were saved, but the whole loss was estimated at 2000 pounds. A 20s. [shilling] piece was found sticking in a chip, for there was above 300 pounds in money on her, and 15 tons of lead, and 10 pieces of ordnance, which a year after were taken up and the hull of the ship was drawn ashore."

The church members of Boston considered the disaster ret-
ribution for the past sins and offenses of many seafaring men.
John Endicott, who cut the cross from the English flag, wrote
to John Winthrop concerning the disaster:

> Dearest Sir,—Hearing of the remarkable stroak of God's hand
> uppon the shippe and the shippe's companie of Bristol, as also of
> some Atheisticall passages and hellish profanations of the Sabbaths
> and deriding of the people and ways of God, I thought good to
> desire a word or two of you of the truth of what you have heard. God
> will be honoured in all dealings. We have heard of several ungodly
> carriadges in that shippe as ffirst in their way overbound they
> would constantlie jeere at the holie brethren of New England, and
> some of the marriners would in a scoff ask when they should come
> to the holie Land? That the last ffast the master or captain of the
> shippe, with most of the companie would not goe to the meetings,
> but read the book of common prayer so often over that one of the
> companie said he had worn that thread bare, with many such pas-
> sages.
> Now if these or the like be true, as I am persuaded some them
> are, I think the truth herof would be made knowen, by some faith-
> full hand in Bristoll or elsewhere, ffor it is a very remarkable and
> unusuall stroake.
>
> Yours ever assured.
Jo. Endicott.

Salem the 28th of the 5th month, 1640.

Thomas Lechford, the Boston lawyer, considered the case
"not so much as a special providence, being by no means a
friend to the Puritans and their ways." He notes in his diary
the fact of the explosion, and the death of one James Smith.
Later, he wrote to a friend:

"And now, Worthy Sir, what news can I write you from us,
but such as is heavy and sad in every respect? Yesterday being
the 27th of July, a tall ship riding at anchor before Charles-
towne, that brought hither provisions from Bristoll, called the
Mary Rose, was (most part) blown up with gun powder which
she had in her for her defence, (and the rest sunke downe
immediately,) through some careless rummaging with candle

light in the hold: wherin died a brave mariner Captain Davis, with ten others, seamen, and two or three of the country being on boarde. Fourteen others of the ship's company being on shore, through the mercy of God escaped: I never hear such a fearful blow: it shook the house wherein I was being a mile off, as an earthquake. A sad and doleful accident, and much laid to heart by me. This was at one a clocke in the afternoone. God of his mercy grant that we the living may lay it to heart and repent indeed, lest we likewise perish."

As a result of the explosion the General Court contracted with Bendall to rid the river and harbor of the wreck.

". . . If he cleare the harbor, hee is to have all wch he can get up; if not he is to have one halfe and the country is to have the other halfe. For the clearing of the harbor he hath liberty till the first of the 8th M, 1642; and he is to give account to the treasurer, from time to time, and to leave the full haulfe, or give good security.

"Edward Bendall hath liberty to make use of any of the cables, and other things belonging to the worke, as he needeth, allowing hurt of them."

Although cables were necessary, it was not by them alone that the galleon *Mary Rose* was relieved of her cargo, ordnance and lead. Edward Bendall invented and constructed diving bells, "two great tubs, bigger than a butt, very tight, and open at one end, upon which there were hanged so many weights as would sink it to the ground (600wt)." Bendall so carefully laid his plans that he could go down and make fast the "cables and other things" to the ordnance, and put the ballast and the lead into a net or tub so that they were easily drawn up into the great lighter on the surface.

As the giant cannon came to the surface, the lightermen were very curious, for there was a rumor that substantial treasure had been hidden in some way among the guns. Many believed it to be inside the giant mouth of one of the guns, but others scoffed at the idea.

Bendall had heard the rumor. After a casual search of each

cannon, he decided it was false. From one gun he removed a large padding of rope yarn that felt unusually heavy, but it had been underwater more than two years and was soggy and foul.

Actually, the rope yarn concealed the great treasure. But Bendall, who could not quite understand how the galleon's commanders would ever put valuable gold and silver coins inside a cannon's mouth, ordered that the rope yarn be "flung aside."

Then came the day Bendall decided to test the cannon. He rammed the rope yarn inside the gun as a firing wad. At high tide the cannon was fired. Myriads of coins shot out from the wad as it described a parabola, raining down into the water in both deep and shallow areas.

The next day at low tide those walking along the sandy beach in the vicinity of the firing were amazed to see gold and silver coins glistening in the sand. During the next few days hikers picked up no less than fifteen pounds of the gold and silver. When Bendall learned of this, he rightfully claimed the money as his. The finders would not give up the treasure. "Whereupon," says Winthrop, Bendall brought "his action and the money was adjudged to him." *

Evidently Winthrop was quite impressed with Bendall's ability. In Volume II of *Winthrop's Journal* he explains the inner workings of the bell. Bendall would go down in the diving bell and would sit inside, "a cord in his hand to give notice when they should draw him up, and another cord to show when they should remove it from place to place, so he could continue in his tub near half an hour, and fasten ropes to the ordnance, and put the lead, etc., into a net or tub. And when the tub was drawn up, one knocked on the head of it, and thrust a long pole under water, which the diver laid hold of, and so was drawn up by it; for they might not draw the open end out of water for endangering him, etc."

---

* In today's values, possibly $100,000 is still on the bottom of Boston Harbor, where it landed after the gun fired centuries ago.

Having done so well with the diving bell, Bendall asked the General Court for a patent. He was refused, although no one in America had ever constructed such a device before.

All the material Bendall brought up was stored at Castle Island. On September 7, 1643, "it was ordered by the court that Edward Bendall should fetch away the ordnance, ammunition, lead and other utensals from the Castle Island and deliver what is granted to Charlestown, and rest to Boston."

The name of Edward Bendall is not found in the records after 1660. He died about then, but it is not known where or precisely when. Bendall's son, Freegrace, and his wife Mary were lost at sea, leaving five children "soe small not able to shift for them selves" to be cared for by the town.

2

Mount Agamenticus

Lofty Mount Agamenticus, not far from York, Maine, is the highest mountain in the region. It is the outstanding landmark for sailors sixty miles up and down the coast, rearing its giant back almost at the edge of the sea, into which it seems to be advancing. Its form is at once graceful and imposing.

As Samuel Adams Drake related in 1891, Mount Agamenticus is the extreme outpost of the great White Mountains. No mariner could ever mistake Agamenticus for any other location, for it stands as the solitary guidepost of a natural harbor, actually the only real harbor for some distance around.

Poet James Russell Lowell in his "Pictures from Appledore" makes this reference to Agamenticus, the sailor's mountain:

> He glowers there to the north of us
> Wrapt in his mantle of blue haze,
> Unconvertibly savage, and scorns to take
> The white man's baptism on his ways.
> Him first on shore the coaster divines
> Through the early gray, and sees him shake
> The morning mist from his scalp-lock of pines:
> Him first the skipper makes out in the west,
> Ere the earliest sunstreak shoots tremulous,

Flashing with orange the palpitant lines
Of mutable billow, crest after crest,
And murmurs *Agamenticus!*
As if it were the name of a saint.

The name is in fact a legacy of the Indians who dwelt at its foot, and who always invested the mountain with a sacred character. From this circumstance comes the Indian legend of Saint Aspenquid, whom some writers have identified with the patriarch Passaconaway, the hero of so many wonderful exploits in healing and in necromancy.

The Indian name of the pond at the source of the York River is Añghemak-ti-koos, or Snowshoe, as the pond is in the shape of a snowshoe. For countless centuries before the white man came, the entire area around the mountain was called Agamenticus, but now the name is confined to the mountain itself.

Early in the seventeenth century, as far as can be proved, Sir Ferdinando Gorges established a colony at the mouth of the Agamenticus River, now known as York. He bought twenty-four thousand acres of land, half on each side of the small tidal river, and gave his grandson management of the colony.

Edward Godfrey, who settled on the Agamenticus River in 1632, petitioned the General Court in Massachusetts in 1654 that he had been a "well wisher, encourager, and furderer of this colony of New England, for forty-five years past, and above thirty-two years an adventurer on that design, twenty-four years an inhabitant of this place, the first that ever bylt or settled ther." Two years later he obtained from the Plymouth council a grant of twelve thousand acres of land on the north side of the River Agamenticus.

The York area was made into a city by Sir Ferdinando Gorges on March 1, 1641; the first election of mayor and aldermen was held March 25, 1642. The city of three hundred residents was called Georgeana, and Thomas Gorges was elected mayor.*

Thus, according to Edward C. Moody, Agamenticus became "the first incorporated English city on the American continent, with the graceful name of Georgeana." Unfortunately, in 1652 the Massachusetts Puritans found that two factions were attempting to run Georgeana, and intervened to annex the Agamenticus area to Massachusetts.

Gorges's complicated machinery was thus overthrown in a short time. The province became a county with the name of Yorkshire, while the metropolis of Georgeana from that moment on was called York.

York had many problems in the seventeenth century. One embarrassing situation was finally solved when an erring, amorous preacher, the Reverend Mr. George Burdett, was shipped back to London. An idea of what Burdett stood for can be gained by the remarks of Samuel Adams Drake:

"On looking about him Deputy Gorges found neither law, order, nor morality prevailing,—a state of things not to be wondered at when it is known that the minister himself, George Burdett, not only set his parishioners an example of unchaste conduct, but easily distanced them in the number and shamelessness of his amours."

Scarcely had the memories of Burdett faded when the terrible King Philip's War was upon New England. This was followed fifteen years later—on February 5, 1692—by the Abenaki uprising.

A violent snowstorm was falling that day. At the height of the storm three hundred Abenaki Indians attacked the village, bursting into the homes one by one. Ransacking the houses, they ripped up the beds and set fire to them, so that shortly twenty houses were ablaze. When the slaughter ended, only

* The aldermen were Edward Godfrey, Roger Garde, George Puddington, Bartholomew Bartness, Edward Johnson, Arthur Bragdon, Henry Simpson and John Rogers.

eighty people were still alive, many of whom were carried off into captivity. The Abenaki killed about seventy-five residents and left only four buildings standing: the garrison houses of Alcock, Harmon, Norton and Preble. Cotton Mather called the Indians "bloody Tygres," and he also mentions the shooting of the Reverend Mr. Shubael Dummer, who lived on the seaside near Roaring Rock. While his wife and son were carried off into captivity, "one of the hell hounds" strutted amidst the prisoners wearing the minister's clothing.

A boy of four survived the massacre. Many years later he led an avenging band against the same Abenaki Indians, exterminating both the Kennebec tribe and their mission. His name was Jeremiah Moulton.

More than a century before the Abenaki uprising, the gallant Saint Aspenquid, an Indian, was born in the region of Mount Agamenticus in 1588. He was about ninety when he died. Converted to Christianity and baptized when he was about forty years old, he dedicated his life to active ministration among the people of his own race, to whom he became a saint and a prophet. For more than forty years he is said to have wandered east to west, north to south, preaching the gospel to no less than sixty-six different Indian nations. Saint Aspenquid healed the sick and performed many miracles that gave him the character of a prophet appointed by Heaven. Even the white man agreed that he was endowed with supernatural powers.

Finally came the period of extreme old age. The venerable patriarch knew that he must soon be gathered to his fathers. Saint Aspenquid at last came home to spend his final days among his own people. When he died, all the sachems of the different tribes came together to attend the funeral of this greatest of all Maine Indians. They carried the body of their prophet to the summit of Mount Agamenticus.

Before burying the patriarch there, following the sacred customs of the period, the hunters of each tribe spread through-

out the forests to catch wild beasts—among them deer, rabbit,
bear, buffalo, moose, porcupine, woodchuck, weasel, otter and
mountain lion—and to slaughter them as a sacrifice in honor
of the departed saint. Even the fishermen of the region made
their contributions.

Poet John Albee wrote:

SAINT ASPENQUID

The Indian hero, sorcerer, and saint,
  Known in the land as Passaconaway,
And after called the good Saint Aspenquid,
  Returning, travel worn and spent with age
From vain attempt to reconcile his race
  With ours, sent messengers throughout the East
To summon all the blood-bound tribes to him;
  For that upon the ancient meeting-place,
The sacred mountain Agamenticus,
  When next the moon should show a new-bent bow,
He there would celebrate his funeral feast
  With sacrifices due and farewell talk. . . .

Light not the fires of vengeance in your hearts,
  For sure the flame will turn against yourselves,
And you will perish utterly from earth.
  Nor yet submit too meekly, but maintain
The valorous name once ours in happy days.
  Be prudent, wise, and slow to strike.
Fall back; seek other shores and hunting grounds,—
  I cannot bear you perish utterly!
Though, looking through the melancholy years,
  I see the end, but turn my face away,
So heavy are my eyes with unshed tears;
  And yours too I would turn, warriors and braves!
And mind not my prophetic vision much,—
  Th'unhappy gift of him who lives too long;
But mind the counsel many years have taught,
  The last I give: remember it, and live!

3

The Gorges
of Maine

When I authored *Fantastic Folklore and Fact* several years ago, I dedicated it to Dr. Robert E. Moody. On December 27, 1977, he wrote to tell me that the Maine Historical Society was about to publish his book *The Letters of Thomas Gorges, 1640–1642*.*

Dr. Moody sent along a copy of one of the letters that tells about a shipwreck of which I had never heard. Although colonial Governor John Winthrop mentions the wreck, Dr. Moody said it was .iis pleasure to give me all the details for the first time. "I take great pride in being able to tell Edward Snow things he doesn't know about wrecks."

The narrative of the disaster is included in a letter written by Thomas Gorges to Sir Ferdinando Gorges, his cousin, dated May 19, 1642 (original spelling retained):

"We have had a most intollerable peircing winter that the like was never known by Inglish or Indian. It is incredible to relate the extremity of the weather. Fouls & fish lay frozen

---

* The letters were written from York, Maine, where on my 1978 Flying Santa trip I landed for the first time in a helicopter, to say hello to the people of Cape Neddick Nubble.

Flotinge thicke on the waters in the sea. For 10 weeks not a boat caught a fish, the Isles of Shoals excepted, where they have had the best fishinge that ever was there known, some 10, some 11,000 of fish & upward to a boat, the largest that ever was seen.

"I will relate you one sad story of the extremity of the weather by which you may beleeve the rest. On the 23 of January, Alderman Longe his eldest son, with our provost martiall named Robert Sankey, Will Cutts, brother to the litle boy, one brown, Gibbins, Lacy & Heard went to sea & soe wer driven in a storme till the 27, cast all theyr victualls over board except one side of porke & a little meal in which tyme . . . neither ate a bit nor drank a drop expecting every hour to sinke, The water soe Frose in theyr boat, but by Gods goodenss they got a shore on Monhigun an Iland to the eastward, wher they lay frozen in most miserable case, not one able to help another, having lost all theyr victualls, one side of porke & a little meal. 5 days after, Cutts died next Lacy, then Sankey, last Heard. The rest wer brought hither by a boat that [was] goinge a fishinge . . . [whose?] own boat was spared . . . spied them after 5 weeks time. Mr Longe & Gibbons are thoroughly recovered, Brown hath lost 3 Joynts. To relate all that passed of theyr misery would seem rather some things fained than reall."

On many occasions I have written about Sir Ferdinando, to whom the preceding letter was addressed. A most interesting figure in the Maine-stream of history, he was leader of the Plymouth Company and proprietor of Maine. He was also one of the two chief backers of the Sagadahoc colony.

The expedition to found that colony was fitted out by Sir Ferdinando. The *Gift of God,* captained by George Popham, and the *Mary and John,* under the control of Raleigh Gilbert, sailed May 1, 1607, and June 1, respectively. They dropped anchor north of Monhegan Island August 7, then sailed to Popham Beach on the Sagadahoc River, which is the lower

Kennebec, on August 14. Here they built a fort and established the colony. Because of idleness and factionalism, the settlement failed on the death of George Popham the next year.

Sir Ferdinando died in 1647. On March 13, 1677, John Usher, agent of Massachusetts, bought out the rights to Maine from the Gorges heirs for 1250 pounds. Maine stayed incorporated with Massachusetts until March 15, 1820.

Richard B. Morris, in his *Encyclopedia of American History* (page 36), includes this letter written in 1642: "Despite the attempt of Gorges to govern Maine through his cousin Thomas Gorges and the establishment of a provincial court at York, (25 June 1640), Massachusetts persisted in its expansionist aims."

4

Treasure in Byfield, Massachusetts

I have spent scores of years, gone hundreds of miles and suffered crushing disappointments to produce this chapter. The stories of John Winthrop, Mary Sholy, William Schooler, Orin Arlin, Dr. Griffin and Stearns Compton span different generations and even different centuries. The unifying thread is the rock marked *A*, which probably still exists in Byfield, Massachusetts. But whether or not any of us shall ever see it is another question. Despite my intense efforts to garner more details from several generations of writers and oral storytellers, the key moments lack the completeness they deserve.

John Winthrop, writing in his 1637 Journal, tells us that William Schooler was a common adulterer who "had wounded a man in a duel" and had been forced to flee "into this country, leaving his wife (a handsome, neat woman) in England." Winthrop goes on:

> He lived with another fellow in Merrimack, and there being a poor maid at Newbury, one Mary Sholy, who had desired a guide to go with her to her master, who dwelt at Pascataquack, he inquired her out, and agreed for fifteen shillings to conduct her thither. But two days after, he returned, and, being asked why he returned so

soon, he answered that he had carried her within two or three miles of the place, and then she would go no farther. Being examined for this by the magistrate at Ipswich, and no proof found against him, he was let go. But, about a year after, being impressed to go against the Pequods, he gave ill speeches, for which the governor sent warrant for him, and being apprehended (and supposed it had been for the death of the maid, some spake what they had heard, which might occasion suspicion,) he was again examined, and divers witnesses produced about it. Whereupon he was committed, arraigned, and condemned, by due proceedings.

John Winthrop relates that not only had Schooler lived a vicious life, but he was then living as an atheist. He had sought out the maid, and taken her to a place where he had never been, and had crossed the Merrimack three miles from the usual path. But he claimed that he had gone close to Swamscote, where he left her. When he returned he had blood on his hat and clothes, which he claimed "was with a pigeon" that he killed. He had a scratch on the left side of his nose and claimed it was from a "bramble, which could not be," as the scratch was too wide, and he then said "it was with his piece [gun]."

About half a year later the body of the maid was found by an Indian in the depths of a thick swamp, "ten miles short of the place he said he left her in," and about three miles from the place where he crossed the "Merrimack, (and it [the body] was after seen, by the English,) the flesh being rotted off it, and the clothese laid in a heap by the body."

Schooler afterward claimed that he met with a bear and thought the bear might kill her, yet would not go back to save her.

Put in prison, Schooler escaped but later was apprehended near Powder Horn Hill. Winthrop writes, with little detail (he completely left out the hanging incident), the conclusion of Schooler's unhappy life:

[Schooler] hid himself out of the way, for fear of pursuit, and after, when he arose to go forward, he could not, but (as he himself confessed) was forced to return back to prison again.

At his death he confessed he had made many lies to excuse himself, but denied that he had killed or ravished her. He was very loath to die, and had hope he should be reprieved; but the court held him worthy of death, in undertaking the charge of a shiftless maid, and leaving her (when he might have done otherwise) in such a place as he knew she must perish, if not preserved by means unknown. Yet there were some ministers and others who thought the evidence not sufficient to take away his life.

Winthrop indeed makes quite a case against Schooler, stressing in his Journal eleven points against him, a few being the peculiar summing up of the money the two had: "He had about ten shillings in his purse, and yet he said she would give him but seven shillings, and he carried no money with him" (Winthrop's Journal, Volume 1, pages 236–238). Another point against Schooler was his incorrect description of the road he was supposed to have taken. A third was the peculiar fact that Schooler did not mention to "anybody of her, till he was demanded of her." And so it was that he was "committed, arraigned, and condemned, by due proceeding."

Mary Sholy, who was murdered, had a strong group of followers north of Boston who firmly believed that the money mentioned by John Winthrop and connected with her death was buried along the Parker River at some unknown time between the landing of the Puritans and the publication of the *Massachusetts Spy* for March 5, May 7 and August 20, 1800. (These newspapers are available in several New England libraries.)

In the Parker River area in Byfield, Massachusetts, there is a rock marked *A*, near which many people believe a substantial treasure has been buried. The tidal river only covers the trap-granite boulder at the highest of tides, probably two or three times a year. The distinctive mark is the letter *A*, approximately six inches in height. At least a dozen stories involving the rock have been told to me orally by North Shore residents of former generations.

Miss Grace Bixby, Newburyport historian, believed that the rock was a marker to indicate the location of a hoard buried nearby, but she had no idea who had concealed the treasure or where it was. Mary Sholy may have had considerable wealth, but probably never the large number of coins so many residents who knew about the rock thought of as a possibility.

Fred Dudley Pearson wondered if the two pirate chests brought to Newburyport after the Gonaïves incident could have any connection with the rock marked A.

The tale of the pirate chests off the island of Gonaïve begins in the West Indies. Captain Roger Hayman, renegade Englishman, was in command of a pirate stronghold with headquarters at the western end of the island of Haiti. Bold and aggressive, he never worried about attacking American men-of-war when they were becalmed in the Gulf of Gonaïve. Pirates easily overcame merchantmen caught in the vicinity.

Late in December 1799, in order to halt Hayman's piracy, the United States sent a small fleet into the area. The armed schooner *Experiment,* commanded by Lieutenant William Maley, was ordered to convey four merchantmen by the island of Haiti.

On January 1, 1800, a dead calm set in. Hayman decided to attack. Ten pirate barges, each manned by forty to fifty desperadoes, set out from Haiti with Captain Hayman in command. Hayman first boarded an American merchantman and took her strongbox, then went aboard an English vessel of the convoy and took the purser's chest of sovereigns.

Before anything else could happen, the *Experiment* sailed into the area, sank three pirate craft and killed almost eighty pirates. Hayman was badly wounded; aboard the *Experiment,* one American was wounded and two injured. The frigate *Boston* came along and also attacked the pirates, crippling five more pirate vessels.

Later many Massachusetts newspapers, especially the Newburyport paper on March 5, May 7, and August 20, 1800,

gave details of the pirate battle off Gonaïve. But few Newburyport citizens realized it would have lasting repercussions
in nearby Byfield, Massachusetts.

Captain Hayman kept the two chests acquired in the recent
fighting and divided the remainder of the booty among his
followers. Soon he gained possession of another trim schooner
of 295 tons to take him to England. His wounds were very
severe, and he reached Liverpool more dead than alive.

Greatly disappointed to find that his family had emigrated to
New York, Hayman decided to start for America. He sold his
schooner and took passage on a brig that would make its first
stop in Newburyport. With great secrecy he made arrangements for the two chests to be brought on board and hidden in
the captain's cabin. A passenger on the brig, Dr. Griffin,
treated his wounds and learned of the chests of treasure.
Realizing that Hayman had only a few more days to live, the
doctor let Stearns Compton, another passenger, in on the secret. The two made plans to get the chests when they reached
port.

Compton hired a sturdy team as soon as they arrived in
Newburyport, surreptitiously transferred the treasure to the
wagon, and gave a signal to the doctor that all was ready.
Griffin jumped into the wagon and seized the reins. Compton
was soon beside him.

"I know the way," Griffin exclaimed. "We'll keep on this
road."

Two hours later they reached a small inn known as the
Pearson Tavern, situated by the side of the highway in the
parish of Byfield. The inn was run by Jeremiah Pearson, the
great-great-grandfather of Fred Dudley Pearson, whom I mentioned earlier. Pearson agreed to give Griffin and Compton
lodging for the night. The two men took turns watching the
barn where the treasure was concealed to make sure it was
safe.

Morning finally came, but with it arrived a man on horseback who rode up and told the news. "Have you heard the latest? Two men got away from a brig in Newburyport Harbor with all the purser's money and are on the way to Boston." The horseman then galloped away in the morning light.

"Gentlemen," Pearson asked, "whence came you last night?"

"From Haverhill," Griffin replied promptly. Then the two men paid their bill and drove away, taking the Andover Road until they reached the Parker River. There they stopped, determined to bury the money.

This was the very morning that a bird lover, Howard Noyes by name, had climbed a tree in the vicinity. Observing some birds in a nest, he happened to glance across and see the men when they got out of the wagon near a large boulder of trap-granite. It was hard work they planned. Compton dug with a small spade until he had a pit four feet deep, whereupon they piled the money into the hole and smoothed dirt and foliage over the top again. Then they marked the boulder with a six-inch-high A and departed the area.

High in the tree, young Noyes became frightened. He climbed down and ran home to tell his story. A search at first failed to discover anything. Later the letter A was identified on the boulder by another group.

Meanwhile the two schemers reached Boston, took the New York stage and, after parting, agreed to return and claim the treasure in five years. Half a decade brings many changes. Neither man ever returned to Byfield, and both were dead by 1857. Sixty-six years later, a great-granddaughter of Compton inherited a strange pact the two men had signed in Byfield. Compton had sealed it in an envelope with information about where he had buried the treasure. Each generation had unsealed the envelope, read the instructions and done nothing but reseal the envelope. They wanted "no part of the disgraceful matter," according to one source.

Nevertheless, this particular lady, Compton's great-granddaughter, became fascinated by the document and wrote to the Pearson Tavern, thinking she would be revealing unknown valuable information.

Of course, half of the Byfield residents interested in treasure had heard the Noyes story before. Excitement developed again and more holes were dug. But no one has proof that a treasure was found at that time.

Within the last ten years the highway in the area of the Parker River has been changed so that the rock marked *A* seems to have vanished. Long before this, actually more than half a century ago, Orin Arlin's story begins when a workman was digging a well not too far from the rock marked *A*. Arlin visited the scene and spoke to the workman.

"How are you coming with the well?"

"No water yet," came the short reply.

Late the following afternoon Orin returned. The workman had vanished, and there were indications that he had discovered something very unusual. Old oak splinters and fragments of canvas lay strewn at the bottom of the well hole, and everything pointed to a hasty exit by the laborer.

Arlin never saw the well-digger again, but one day when he was over at a store on Ring's Island, Salisbury, the proprietor spoke up. "Say, Orin, your friend the well-digger was in the other day, and look what he used for money to pay for his purchases!" The merchant held up a handful of coins, still fairly bright and shiny except for a few badly tarnished places. Orin Arlin told me about it later in detail.

"Although my friend the well-digger told the store proprietor that he got the money by winning a lottery, I really believe he blundered in some way onto the money, or at least a part of it."

Arlin later gave me one of the coins, and it now has a valued place in my collection of pirate skulls, derringers and treasure. Regardless of which story it is connected with, I know the possible bloody past of the metal disk. But Orin Arlin cautioned me against placing too much significance on the coin; he rightly suggests it may have come from anywhere.

Now, after generations and generations have passed, we at least know that some treasure has appeared. The remainder, if there is a remainder, probably is buried under the highway, not too great a distance from another buried item, a trap-granite rock marked *A*, which formerly was pointed out to visitors as they wandered along the banks of the beautiful Parker River in Byfield, Massachusetts.

Part Two

1700s

1

Shipwreck
and Cannibalism

Many of the true stories I have related through the past fifty years include details or incidents that baffle understanding. This tale is in that category, for it contains the horrible act of cannibalism. It is my belief that such an inhuman deed cannot be satisfactorily explained. All a writer can do is relate the facts, leaving the reader to his own thoughts and questions regarding the meanderings of human behavior.

In February 1765 the vessel *Amiable Suzette* sailed from Bordeaux, France, to San Domingo in the West Indies. There passenger Peter Viaud was taken desperately ill.

Peter Viaud did not improve and was put ashore at Saint Louis Island, near Cuba. After several weeks at the home of a friend, Monsieur Desclou, he recovered completely. During his illness the two men planned a journey to Louisiana to trade various goods for a considerable profit, if all worked well.

They acquired the ship *Tiger*, of which Captain La Couture was master. The *Tiger* was loaded with commodities they believed would have a good sale at their destination. Several passengers were signed up for the trip, and the captain brought his wife and son David along. The ship's company amounted to sixteen in all when they were ready for sailing.

263

On January 2, 1766, the *Tiger* left Saint Louis Island but was soon becalmed. Day after day there was no wind. By January 26 they were no closer to Louisiana than the Isle of Pines, some fifty miles south of the western curve of Cuba. However, the master of the *Tiger* erroneously claimed that they had reached not Cape Pepe on the Isle of Pines, but the Cape of Saint Antonio at Cuba. This serious miscalculation led to the ship crashing against rocks forming an outlying ledge northwest of the Isle of Pines.

The crew shifted the cargo several times and finally managed to free the *Tiger* from the rocks. But she had developed a bad leak, and all hands were called out to the pumps. During this crisis it was agreed that Peter Viaud should take command.

Finally the leaking ship reached Cape Antonio and started across the Gulf of Mexico, heading for the Mississippi River. The water in the hold gained to such an extent that the vessel barely kept afloat. In her helpless, waterlogged condition, the *Tiger* was caught by the approach of a violent storm. Before the storm hit, a Spanish frigate came in sight and offered assistance. Darkness intervened, however, and when morning came the frigate was gone.

The next morning the crew of the *Tiger* discovered a new leak. Bailing and pumping continued, but all aboard realized that they should attempt to run the *Tiger* ashore somewhere along the coast of Apalachee Bay in northwest Florida.

On the night of February 16 the *Tiger* again struck heavily, this time on some jagged ledges six miles from land. The waves soon tore the stern apart. When the tide rose and the *Tiger* gradually lifted herself over the ledges, it was discovered that the rudder had been ripped off.

Desperately Viaud guided the *Tiger* by the foresail. Two hours later they approached the southern shores of an unknown island, possibly Cape Saint George's. Viaud and the captain planned to cut away the masts and build a raft on which to float ashore.

Suddenly, without warning, the *Tiger* went over on her beam ends, throwing several of the crew into the sea. Most were able to swim back to the wreck, just as the rays of the moon that had been guiding them disappeared, leaving the survivors on the upturned bottom of the *Tiger* in pitch darkness.

Rain began falling and a violent thunderstorm broke loose. Higher and higher came the waves, until they washed entirely over the shipwrecked men and women. Lightning flashes illuminated the terrible scene.

Finally dawn arrived. By its faint light Viaud surveyed their situation. The waves were running very high. Shore was but a short distance away. However, Viaud knew that an attempted landing in the seething billows would end in death for most of them, for the giant breakers were rolling up on shore with terrific impact.

No one dared move for several hours, while the wreck drifted closer to shore. Finally a Dutch sailor could stand it no longer. Sliding off the ship's bottom into the heavy seas, he struck out hopefully for shore. A wave swallowed him up momentarily. He was seen again, still swimming toward land. The next wave smashed into him, and five minutes later a great comber tossed his lifeless body with dreadful violence on a rocky ledge.

Finally the storm appeared to be dying down. The masts and cordage had all washed away, so the last hopes of making a raft and floating ashore were gone. There was a tiny boat still attached to the *Tiger*, and three sailors were able to cut it free, bail it out and start for shore. They landed safely on the beach and pulled the tiny craft above the reach of the tide as dusk fell.

A short time later the *Tiger* drifted in toward shore and lodged precariously against hidden rocks, in danger of breaking up at any time. Those still clinging to the wreck could see the sailors on the beach attempting to patch up the skiff. An old sailor, watching their efforts, asked for all available pieces of cloth. Securing the pieces to himself, he plunged into the sea and managed to swim to shore. Working feverishly, the four men stuffed strips of cloth into the many cracks of the rescue craft. It was three o'clock before the boat could be launched.

Out on the capsized *Tiger*, lots were drawn to decide who would go on the first trip ashore. The four winners soon scrambled into the boat and reached land safely. Again the tiny skiff was sent out. Meanwhile, Viaud, his friend Desclou and Desclou's servant succeeded in pulling free a large fragment of the *Tiger*'s stern. They clambered aboard; ten minutes later they floated up on the beach. A short time later the skiff brought the final four survivors to shore.

After a short period of prayer and rejoicing, Viaud decided to search for food. The tide was low, and on nearby rocks he found more than enough oysters to satisfy their hunger. One man, Mate Dutroche, was too sick to benefit from the nourishment. Becoming delirious, he was in agony by morning and died before noon. The crew buried him in the sand.

Cargo from the *Tiger* soon scattered up and down the beach, including several trunks; some casks of tafia, a type of fiery liquor made of distilled sugarcane juice; and many bales of merchandise.

The ocean had calmed down. Viaud decided to return to the wreck and see what of value was still aboard. When he asked for volunteers to row out with him, not a single man came forward. Therefore, he rowed to the *Tiger* alone. He found that the craft had partly righted herself, with one section entirely above water. Viaud was able to obtain a keg of gunpowder, six muskets, a flint, a package of Indian handkerchiefs, several blankets, forty pounds of biscuits and two hatchets. Rowing ashore safely, he was received with great admiration by the others when he landed with the welcome supplies.

Ordering the crew to collect dry wood, he struck the flint and soon produced sparks to start a warm fire, around which everyone huddled. Several men had explored the island and found a spring of water, bringing back enough of the precious liquid for all. The biscuits, which had been immersed in salt water, were soaked in the fresh water for several hours, dried out by the fire, then dipped into the tafia and pronounced entirely acceptable.

The next night the survivors gathered around the fire and discussed plans for the immediate future. They were fairly certain that they had landed at Cape Saint George's Island, one of a series of islands forming an outer barrier in a south-westerly direction from what is now Franklin County, Florida.

At the time Indian tribes and wild animals controlled Florida's forest regions. Bear, deer, fox and wolves prowled the woods. It was known that the Indians of the Apalachicola area left the mainland every winter to hunt on the islands offshore until the following April, and the shipwrecked survivors feared they would be killed by the savages. This fear was heightened because of the casks of strongly alcoholic tafia, which often left Indians with such a feeling of exuberance that a massacre followed. Thus the crew staved in the barrels of liquor one by one, until they had destroyed all but three casks. Viaud ordered these buried deep in the sand for an emergency.

On February 22 a seaman who had been a few hundred yards from the camp came rushing out of the forest crying, "The Indians! The Indians! We are lost!"

Soon two Indian men and three women appeared, walking slowly toward the survivors. The men each carried a tomahawk and a musket.

Realizing that the Indians planned no immediate harm, Viaud decided to keep on friendly terms with them. He presented the women with trinkets and the men with other little gifts. Viaud ordered a cask of tafia removed from the sand, and soon the Indians and the survivors were drinking around the fire.

One of the Indians spoke a few words of Spanish. Viaud eventually learned that he was Chief Antonio, hailing from Saint Mark in the Apalachee Bay some thirty-six miles away.

Those with him were members of his immediate family. They had been wintering on a neighboring island and had found fragments of wreckage washed up on shore. Suspecting that a ship had struck the rocks in the area, they paddled over to the island to investigate.

After several pleasant hours the Indians withdrew, taking three sailors with them and promising to return the following day. The three survivors were landed on the chief's island, and he appeared the next day with food—a bustard and a roebuck—for the shipwrecked party to eat. Later that day he agreed to carry back six more survivors, including Viaud, Captain La Couture and his wife and son David. The five sailors left near the wreck were brought to Antonio's island a few days later, after the chief had gone hunting.

The chief disappeared into the island forest for the next five days. Upon his return, Viaud offered muskets and other supplies if he would take them by canoe to the mainland. Antonio countered with the proposal that he would make only one trip. He asked Viaud to pick the passengers.

Viaud chose the three members of the Couture family, Desclou, a slave and himself. Antonio took only his wife, leaving the other members of his family with the remaining sailors as good faith that he would return. Some boiled quarters of a bear and a roebuck, together with several pounds of biscuits and a container of water, were taken aboard the craft.

The following morning the canoe passengers landed at another island. Antonio decided that more provisions were needed. After days of hunting, enough oysters and wild fowl were obtained to continue the journey toward Fort Saint Marks. That night Chief Antonio brought the canoe ashore on a sandbar, bare of all trees and other vegetation. Viaud became suspicious that Antonio was planning to abandon them there. When he expressed these fears to the others, La Couture laughed and told him to forget his worries and go to sleep.

"All will be well in the morning," La Couture promised.

Shortly after midnight Viaud woke up, feeling extremely

uneasy. He rose and looked around. The fire they had built was still smoldering, but his worst fears were realized when he looked for the native's canoe. It was gone! The muskets had also been taken, leaving the shipwrecked party with only one sheath knife, a rather blunt instrument Viaud always wore at his hip. All they had were the clothes on their backs, the blankets in which they slept and one knife. Search as they could, they found nothing to satisfy their hunger.

Viaud realized that to stay on the tiny island would be to resign themselves to death. Less than half a mile to the west lay another island, and at low tide the desperate party waded and swam across to it.

Immediately they began to search for oysters. Finding plenty, they satisfied their appetites. They also discovered a tiny stream of water not far away. The hot sun came out from behind the clouds, enabling them to dry their clothes. Relatively comfortable, the party fell asleep.

When night came it was so cold that they were unable to keep warm. They got up and walked around. They grew hungry again, but the tide had come in and they were forced to wait for low water to get oysters. The only herb or roots they discovered were some wild sorrel plants. The wind changed to the southeast, and they found to their disappointment that the oyster beds did not become bare when the wind came in from that quarter. Consequently they had to wait until the following day, when the wind died down, to get oysters. After this experience they decided to keep an extra supply in reserve.

In this manner the weeks went by. On March 22 Viaud recalled having seen an old canoe on one of the islands where Antonio had stopped while hunting. This seemed the best solution to the problem of getting to Fort Saint Marks. Viaud and Captain La Couture agreed that they and Desclou should try to find the canoe.

At low tide they were able to wade back to the barren sandbar, then set out from the other side heading in a westerly direction. They had to swim in deep water to reach the island where they had seen the wreck of the canoe. It was strenuous effort for the exhausted men, but they all arrived safely and threw themselves down to rest.

The hot sun soon brought them back to life. Within the hour they were lucky enough to find the old canoe, but it was in terrible condition. They debated whether it was really worth salvaging. Seeing it as their only hope, they fell to work repairing it with osiers, or willow twigs, reinforced with Spanish beard, a tough moss that flourished in the area.

Hunger finally caused them to cease their efforts on the canoe and to turn their attention to food, which they found in a nearby oyster bed.

"I like oysters better fried or stewed," said Viaud. "There must be some way of getting a fire."

"I've got it!" cried Desclou. "Didn't we see Antonio change his flint somewhere around here?"

"Why, I think you're right!" agreed Peter. "Let's try to find the old flint."

After eating several more raw oysters, the men walked across the island to the location of their last camp with the chief. Finding the ruins of the old fire, they searched diligently until finally Viaud discovered the vital flint.

Soon they had a hot fire burning and oysters cooking. The men then lay down and slept in happy exhaustion.

Next morning they were awakened by the rising sun and again fell to work on the canoe. It was agreed that a blanket should be sacrificed and cut into strips to caulk the cracks. All that day they worked, trying to make the canoe watertight. The following morning they placed it in the water, and La Couture agreed to ferry it across to the island where the others had been left. Gingerly he stepped aboard and began to paddle; the craft still leaked considerably.

As soon as La Couture was out of sight, Viaud and Desclou explored the other side of the island seeking another way of getting to the mainland. They were unable to advance beyond the edge of a channel at least three miles wide.

Deciding to wade back to the island where Madame La Couture had set up camp, they made rapid progress and soon reached their companions. Next morning Viaud discovered a dead roebuck on the beach. Evidently it had bled to death a short time before, and Peter was able to cut it up and cook it on a spit. All ate heartily, after which they slept in comfort until the sun rose. It was March 26, 1766.

The canoe had leaked terribly, and La Couture had barely reached the island without sinking. Still anxious to repair the canoe so that they could paddle to the mainland, Viaud decided that two more blankets should be cut up to reinforce the cracks. Three days were devoted to this project.

Finally they placed the craft in the water and Viaud tested it. Feeling the planking sink under him, and watching the water begin to seep in, he decided it was hopeless. "I shall never go to sea in this craft," he declared.

"Come on, Peter," La Couture cried. "You and I can paddle while Desclou bails. We'll reach the mainland in no time."

Viaud refused to go with La Couture and Desclou. "You'll never make it in a thousand years!" he cried, and refused to help the others as they loaded a scanty stock of provisions aboard.

La Couture bade farewell to his wife and son, then instructed his slave to remain faithfully at Madame's side. He went back to the canoe, ordered Desclou to take the bow seat, got in at the stern and pushed off.

They figured that the mainland was five to six miles away. Although the two men paddled with determination, their progress was slow, for the water pouring into the tiny craft made it heavy and unwieldy. Soon Desclou was forced to stop paddling in order to bail. Finally the canoe rounded a smaller island nearby, passing out of sight. Viaud never saw the two men again. Without question, they perished in the ocean soon thereafter.

During the following few days the wind blew from the southeast, making it impossible for the small group to get any oysters. Their only source of food was the wild sorrel, which weakened their stomachs.

Six days elapsed; there was no news from the canoe. Peter felt in his heart that his companions were drowned. That night, as Viaud got up to replenish the bonfire with a large log he had obtained during the afternoon, he suddenly sprang to his feet and shouted over to Madame La Couture, who was almost falling asleep. "What a fool I've been!" he cried. "We have the means of getting off this island whenever we wish! Look at that heavy log. There are many of them around the island. If we put them side by side, lashing them together in some way, we'll have a raft to carry us across to the mainland!"

The next morning those still able to walk began collecting the heavy logs down by the shore. Soon there were enough for a raft that would hold them. Viaud fashioned a mast from a sapling and planned to use a blanket for a sail. His next problem was binding the logs together. He found that the bark of certain trees was pliable and strong, and he cut it from the trees in long, sturdy strips. Reinforced later by pieces of cloth from another blanket, the raft was soon finished and ready for service.

They spent the next few days collecting oysters and all edible material they could find. At last they were ready for the voyage. The journey was planned for the next dawn.

During the night, however, a furious storm broke, not only wrecking and scattering the timbers of their craft, but sinking all their provisions. The four survivors despaired of ever reaching the mainland of Florida, but they knew they must try again. After painfully reconstructing the raft and gathering more supplies for the journey, they were ready once more to drift and sail across to the mainland. It was the 15th of April. Their final blanket, the remainder of their stockings and everything they could possibly spare was used to finish the craft.

Young David La Couture had become ill. When the time came to start, he was found unconscious. Plans for departure were hastily abandoned and all supplies taken ashore from the raft. David, wrapped in the blanket that had been planned for the sail, suddenly awakened and stared at them. Later, when his mother had gone down to the shore to get some food for him, he said to Viaud: "I'm going to die, and the sooner you take my mother off the island the more chance she'll have. Tomorrow I want you to take me away and then tell my mother I have died. You've got to do it, Peter. Promise me."

After much arguing, Viaud agreed to carry out David's plan. The next day, before Madame La Couture awakened, Viaud carried David into the woods until they reached a small, secluded clearing, where he arranged a litter for the boy. Working rapidly, he placed sorrel, water, the edible roots of several trees and a great heap of oysters nearby. Then he bade farewell to David and returned to camp.

Telling Madame La Couture as best he could of the supposed death of her son, Viaud announced that he had buried him in the forest, and that David's last wish was that they should start for the mainland at once.

An hour later Madame La Couture, the slave and Viaud were sailing toward the mainland. In less than twelve hours they landed there. As far as Viaud could estimate, it was April 19, 1766.

They landed on swampy ground. After a search they found an elevated spot, sheltered by leafy trees. Viaud made a fire and all three ate heartily, then fell asleep.

They were awakened in darkness by the noises of wild beasts, evidently close by. The slave fled in terror up the nearest tree, and Madame La Couture followed him. Viaud implored her not to leave the safety of the fire, but she paid no attention. Suddenly, without warning, she found herself trapped in the tree by a bear. Viaud quickly pulled a blazing timber from the campfire and forced the animal away while Madame La Couture scrambled down. When they returned to replenish the burning logs, the bear began to climb the tree after the slave, whose cries intermingled with the roar of the pursuing bear. Viaud seized several blazing logs and threw them against the base of the tree. The bear disappeared into the forest and the frightened slave descended to the ground.

There was no more sleep possible that night. The wild animals continued to surround the camp, howling and roaring until the coming of dawn sent them away.

The three survivors planned to set out at once for their destination, Fort Saint Marks, which Chief Antonio had indicated was to the east. They began to walk, but their physical condition did not allow rapid progress. Aware of the coming dangers of night, the group stopped at sunset to gather a huge amount of firewood. They arranged a dozen small piles in readiness for darkness. Next came the problem of food, but there was none to be found. They did discover water and drank it thirstily.

At night they lighted their fires. No wild animals were heard until about midnight, when they appeared to be uncomfortably close. There was no attack, however, and the welcome light of dawn soon arrived.

Still there was no food. In desperation the slave tore off handfuls of leaves from a tree and devoured them. The others followed suit, and all three were later seized with terrible cramps.

Day after day they continued to make slow progress toward Saint Marks. Finally came the morning of crisis when Viaud realized they did not have the strength to continue. All three were delirious with hunger; the mind had become "the slave of the body," as Viaud later explained. He looked across at the emaciated body of Madame La Couture, then turned his eyes on the poor young slave, who was sound asleep. His eyes met the woman's in what he later declared was perfect understanding. In order to provide food, he would sacrifice the slave.

Unable to stop his disordered mind from acting on this impulse, Peter stepped over to the fire, seized a knotted stick and approached the sleeping form. Desperately needed food was his only thought. He brought the club down on the boy's head.

The slave screamed in anguish. Viaud blindly continued his horrible pounding until the lad was dead.

For the next few days both Madame La Couture and Viaud used the remains of the slave to keep alive. Gaining renewed energy from the human meat, they continued to journey toward Fort Saint Marks. What their thoughts were as they made their way through the forest we shall never know.

The traveling was wretched, for they had to struggle through thickets, brambles and thorns hour after hour. At one time they were attacked by literally tens of thousands of mosquitoes and sand flies, which left their bodies swollen and disfigured. Each day they would return to the seashore, catching a few cockles and flounders but, as Viaud said, "Never enough for a meal."

Some time later they could find no food either along the shore or inland, but the roars and cries of the wild animals that night suggested a plan to Viaud. When morning came he set fire to the entire woods. After the flames died down, he found enough burned animals to have palatable food for several days. When they discovered two large dead rattlesnakes, one with fourteen rattles and the other with twenty-one, they were more than happy. Cutting off the heads, they devoured the meat, which tasted delicious to them.

A few days later they came upon an alligator. Killing it, Peter made shoes from its skin and masks to protect their faces from insects. They also ate the flesh, but neither enjoyed it.

Then they reached a swift-moving river they could not ford. Following its bank, they proceeded for two full days before finding and killing a ten-pound land tortoise. As Viaud prepared to cook the tortoise, he discovered that he had lost the vital flint. He could not make a fire!

Viaud believed he had dropped the flint either at the last night's camp or somewhere between the two camps. He started out alone to find it, searching every inch of their path. He soon reached the old camp, but five hours of careful investigation failed to produce the flint. In despair he flung himself on a soft bed of ferns—and touched the metal of the missing flint!

Darkness had descended before Viaud reached Madame La Couture. He could hear the crashing of wild animals as they began their nocturnal wanderings. Viaud soon had a roaring blaze sending sparks up through the tops of the trees. They broiled the tortoise, ate their meal and fell asleep.

Revived next morning by the tortoise meat, they constructed a raft and attempted to pole across the river. The raft struck a tree trunk, however, and they were thrown into the stream. Viaud used the trunk to steady himself while he pulled Madame La Couture to safety. Building a fresh fire, they dried their clothes and ate the rest of the tortoise before sleep overtook them.

The following morning they set out due east. They ran into another great horde of mosquitoes, flies and wasps. Their bodies again began to swell, and Viaud soon began to suffer from a bad fever caused by the insect bites. Madame La Couture was still able to walk.

"Go on and forget me," Viaud declared. "You have a good chance now. I can't get there."

"I will never abandon you," was her answer. Finding and killing another tortoise, she bathed Peter's body in its blood, which seemed to afford him some relief. But that afternoon he grew worse and felt that he would die soon. Madame La Couture had vanished into the underbrush in pursuit of a turkey that had appeared a few feet away.

Suddenly Peter imagined that he could hear the sound of human voices, apparently men in conversation. Afraid that they were savages, he remained quiet for a long time until sure that he recognized English being spoken. When he first attempted to sit up, it was too much for him. Again he tried to raise himself, this time reaching a half-upright position. He crept in the direction of the voices. Suddenly he saw a large boat offshore and began to tremble with excitement. Grabbing a long stick, he tied his tattered clothing to it and placed his cap at the top. Then he waved feebly at the craft, trying to shout but unable to make himself heard. Finally a soldier walked over to the shore side of the ship and noticed him.

"Hello!" the British voice cried. "We've been looking for you!"

Viaud slumped to the ground in a faint. He awakened a short time later to find the strangers pouring tafia down his tortured throat. Madame La Couture appeared at last, carrying the turkey and the turkey's nest. Her joy knew no bounds when she realized they were saved.

The British soldiers were from Fort Saint Marks, out looking for survivors from a shipwreck they knew must have occurred because they had found the dead body of a European on the beach nearby.

By nightfall the next day they were in the vicinity of Fort Saint Marks. But Viaud began to wonder about young David La Couture and if he might still be alive, though it had been nineteen days since they had left him. The soldiers agreed to sail back to the original island with Viaud and Madame La Couture to look for David.

They found the lad, apparently dead. Digging a grave, the soldiers asked Viaud to say a prayer for David. When they leaned over to lift the body into the grave, one of the soldiers gave a cry.

"Wait, men, this boy's still alive!"

When Viaud felt David's chest the heartbeat was noticeable, feeble but steady. Madame La Couture rushed forward and threw herself on the ground beside her son. Restraining her, the others raised the boy tenderly and carried him to the boat. They immediately set sail for Fort Saint Marks and soon arrived.

All three survivors eventually recovered, but the miracle of young David La Couture was discussed for many years by all

who knew of it. How a boy, left to die on a lonely island, could
live alone for nineteen days was declared one of the mysteries
of the century.

It had been eighty-one days from the shipwreck to the arrival of the three survivors at the fort. Two of the company had
perished in or near the vessel, two had drowned in the canoe
and one had been murdered. The eight seamen left at the
camp of the Indians had killed Antonio's mother, sister and
nephew in the chief's absence. Five of them had then fled in a
canoe. They were never heard from again.

If this were fiction, undoubtedly Madame La Couture and
Viaud would have married. But in reality he sailed to Saint
Augustine, then traveled to New York and eventually made his
way back to France. He never again saw Madame La Couture
after he bade her and David farewell at Fort Saint Marks,
where she waited for a ship to take her to Louisiana.

In later years Peter Viaud always carried with him a letter
written by the commanding officer of Fort Saint Marks,
Lieutenant Swettenham, verifying the strange adventures following the unfortunate shipwreck of the *Tiger*.

Whether Peter Viaud and Madame La Couture told their
rescuers of their cannibalistic act is a question that remains
unanswered. Whether or not they revealed their deed to young
David is another enigma. Eventually, however, Peter Viaud
did tell the entire story, perhaps at the urging of an anguished
conscience.

2

The Unbelievable
Siege of Louisbourg

More than forty years ago, when I was doing research for a lecture series on American coastal defenses, I found a striking illustration of unpreparedness. In 1745 the seemingly impregnable French fortification at Louisburg * on Cape Breton Island fell to New Englanders after a relatively short siege of about two months. At least 2¼ centuries after the siege, I flew over Louisburg and tried to visualize the strange, dramatic episodes that led to the final surrender of the largest artificial stronghold the French ever had in the Western Hemisphere. It was here that an ill-sorted group of American merchants, farmers, country squires and fishermen overcame the well-trained soldiers of the armies of France.

To build the fort, France expended thirty million livres and used her best engineers. Constructed from plans furnished by master bastille designer Marquis Sébastien Vauban, military engineer extraordinary for Louis XIV, the fort took more than twenty-five years to complete.

In 1744, with the outbreak of the Austrian War of Succession, Commander Duquesnal of Louisbourg sent an expedi-

* The town's name is *Louisburg,* but the fort itself is spelled *Louisbourg.*

tion against the Nova Scotia town of Canso, which he conquered. He planned to seize Annapolis Royal also, but failed.
His activity aroused not only the English but also the people of
Massachusetts, who rose up in great indignation against him.
Nova Scotia and Maine were under English rule until 1820,
and the colonists resented intervention from the Frenchman.
They were also infuriated that the fort was being used as a
base by French privateers who preyed on New England
fishermen working the Grand Banks.

The leading agitator for revenge was William Vaughan,
owner of successful fishing and lumbering enterprises around
Damariscotta, Maine. Vaughan convinced Governor William
Shirley of the possibility of besieging Louisbourg, and later he
was active in achieving this objective.

One cold January day in 1745, Governor William Shirley
privately communicated with the General Court of Massachusetts regarding the situation between Massachusetts
and Cape Breton Island. Meeting in secret session, he informed the court that he was considering the capture of
France's mighty stronghold, Louisbourg. The plan was first
voted down, but the governor persevered and won approval.

The secrecy of the scheme was violated when one religious
council member prayed too loudly for its success. Devout but
unwise, he explained to the Lord in detail the plans for the
expedition, and soon the entire countryside was aware of the
secret. When the scheme became known, public reaction was
strong against it. Another ballot was then taken in open session. The expedition won by a single vote. (The tying vote was
lost when one member broke his leg hurrying to the council
chamber.)

Governor Shirley, whose enthusiasm for the project was not
lessened by his narrow victory, wrote of his plans to other
colonies as far south as Pennsylvania. The response was amazing. Even faraway Pennsylvania sent supplies. New Hampshire provided five hundred men; Rhode Island voted a sloop;
Connecticut offered 516 men with certain conditions at-

tached; and Massachusetts planned to provide three thousand troops plus the commanding officer of the entire expedition.

The choice of the commander was a problem, however. Not in all New England, according to Governor Wanton of Rhode Island, was there one experienced military officer. William Pepperrell of Kittery, Maine—then part of Massachusetts— was well known as a prosperous trader and so was appointed to lead the expedition. The army, hastily assembled, drilled assiduously for the next few weeks. The troops were composed of outstanding men of each community: country squires, farmers, merchants and shipmasters. In many cases they had left their wives and children to enlist at twenty-five shillings a month.

Finally, when no word of approval or disapproval came from England, Governor Shirley ordained that the expedition should go forward as planned. On March 24, 1745, the fleet of 2070 men and 106 ships sailed from Nantasket Road. The final words of Reverend George Whitefield were *Nil Desperandum Christo Duce* (*No despair while Christ leads*) which became the motto of the expedition.

There was no reason the expedition should have succeeded. The troops knew nothing of military life or of the conditions they might encounter. They acted for the most part as though they were on a vacation tour. One historian claimed the siege resembled a Harvard commencement in the old days when such activities were not taken too seriously. The audacity of the entire project impressed Benjamin Franklin so unfavorably that he wrote a Boston friend asking several pertinent questions.

An idea of the military caliber of the attacking army can be gleaned from a plan made by one of its enthusiastic New England strategists. It was suggested that two men should be sent out at night to scout the area surrounding Louisburg's fortifications for the presence of land mines. One soldier was to beat on the ground with a mallet while the other placed his ear against the ground to detect any hollow sound indicating the presence of a mine. If the test was positive, the soldiers were to mark the spot with chalk as a warning to the attacking troops.

The New England regulars had only a few large-size cannon, but they brought a substantial supply of cannonballs. Knowing that the French had cannon, the Americans planned to seize the outlying areas of the fort and then use their ammunition in the captured French cannon. Believe it or not, that is what actually happened.

On Friday, April 5, 1745, the American fleet arrived at Canso, seventy miles across the water from Louisburg. They quickly overcame the small garrison of French soldiers. In Canso the men of New England completed their training for the great undertaking. The English navy also was active, capturing enemy ships and cutting communication lines to Louisburg.

The fleet sailed from Canso for Louisburg on the morning of April 29, intending to arrive at the walls of the great stronghold around nine o'clock at night. The wind fell, however, and it was the following morning before the New Englanders obtained their first glimpse of the Gibraltar of America.

The complete indifference to the arrival of the American fleet by the French soldiers is beyond belief. It is not true, as many claim, that the New Englanders surprised the defenders of Louisbourg. The Frenchmen had known for two months that American forces were planning to capture their stronghold. The mystery is why the landing and the subsequent capture of the outer defenses were not opposed; no one has yet been able to explain it satisfactorily.

The provincial forces made a creditable landing some three miles below the fort. Colonel Vaughan marched four hundred soldiers outside the walls of the mighty citadel and led them in three great cheers, which echoed strangely in the ears of the defenders of Louisbourg. What type of men could these New Englanders be, they thought, to fight their battles with cheers instead of bullets? There was not the slightest opposition to the cheering, so Vaughan paraded his four hundred men over to the northeast arm of Louisburg Harbor. There he proceeded to set fire to the naval stores.

The mightiest outlying defense of Louisbourg, known as the Grand Battery, was about a mile from town. The next day Colonel Vaughan marched his forces toward the Grand Battery, halting a few hundred yards away. Vaughan sent a scout—a Cape Cod Indian, brandy bottle in hand—to pretend that he was drunkenly staggering toward the fort. The Indian started for the Grand Battery, waving his bottle in the air, swaying from side to side. Finally he reached the outpost. There was not a single Frenchman around. The entire Grand Battery, which had cost the people of France a terrific sum to build, was empty! It was so strange that Colonel Vaughan suspected a trick.

To his surprise, Vaughan took possession of the Grand Battery without opposition. He then sent his drummer boy to unfurl a red undershirt from the top of the flagstaff as an emblem of the might of New England. Not only had the fort been deserted, but it was fortified with thirty unmanned cannon, waiting for the New Englanders.

Some cannon were not in firing condition; only a small number of troops was needed to man those that were. The remaining idle soldiers decided to hold what amounted to a Donnybrook Fair in the open ground near the Grand Battery. Lines were drawn up and measured off for a track meet, and the men of Boston raced against the men of Providence, Hartford and Portsmouth. The meets were held to the accompaniment of booming guns from the New England forces and the answering crash of French cannonballs from the main fort. When the Americans ran short of ammunition, the winners of the foot races were sent chasing after French cannonballs, which were brought back to be used by the Americans. Other groups were pitching quoits, wrestling or firing their precious ammunition at bird targets. One squad decided to go fishing nearby; several of the soldiers who strayed too far were scalped by the Indians. The whole expedition would have made excellent material for a Gilbert and Sullivan operetta.

However, the New England gunners knew what they were doing. The first burst from their cannon killed fourteen men at Louisbourg. An artillery precision test between the New Hampshire gunners in the Grand Battery and the defenders of Louisbourg was the highlight of the entire siege. The men from New Hampshire won easily.

On May 20 the mighty French man-of-war *Vigilant*, with forty-six guns and a crew of 560, sailed unsuspectingly into the bay. After a brief but hot exchange, the French surrendered.

Pleased with their progress, the New Englanders set up a battery 1600 yards from the West Gate of the main fort, another battery a thousand yards away to rake the entire town, and a third only a quarter mile from the city itself. This aroused the French forces. They attempted a sortie but were repulsed. Thirty more cannon hidden under water were discovered by scouts. Raised by the Americans from the bottom of the northeast harbor near the lighthouse, they were put in condition and turned against the defenders of Island Battery, one thousand yards away.

An attack against the French at Island Battery was attempted by a whaleboat army. It was driven back, with two hundred American casualties. Pepperrell finally conceived the plan of seizing the lighthouse. The New Englanders climbed the beacon, fired directly down on the battery and captured the island.

Another battery established against the West Gate destroyed the drawbridge. American troops surrounding the entire area prevented reinforcements from reaching Louisbourg by land. In the dead of night, the Americans sent a fireship to burn three French vessels in the harbor. The rest of the fleet, unable to enter the harbor and aid the beleaguered fort, was either captured or fled to the open sea. Finally the Americans so damaged the fortification that the French, after a defense which at first was conspicuous for its complete indifference and later developed into a bitter struggle for survival, surrendered their mighty bastion.

On June 26 Commander Du Chambon of Louisbourg asked for a truce. Two days later, at two o'clock in the afternoon, the British fleet entered the harbor in triumph. At four o'clock the same afternoon, the army marched in by the South Gate. The French soldiers, accorded the full honors of defeated troops, then marched out of the fort in orderly fashion.

Parson Samuel Moody lost no time destroying what he called symbols of idolatry in the Louisburg parish church. He had carried an axe precisely for this purpose all the way from New England. The cross was removed from the chapel and later sent to Harvard College, where it is still pointed out.

During the siege the British officers plundered the Spanish ship *Deliberanza,* taking a million pounds in all. The amount of booty probably angered Pepperrell, who spent ten thousand pounds of his own money to carry out the expedition and received nothing in return. To add insult to injury, he was allegedly charged with the ridiculous theft of the French governor's garters and six silver spoons.

The expedition had its cruel, bitter side. Many did not return from Louisburg. The colonists left to guard their prize the following winter were plagued with pestilence. No less than nine hundred of them died and were laid in shallow graves along the shore. Even today, storms occasionally wash out the skeletons of brave New England men buried there more than two centuries ago.

It was a magnificent feat of American daring. Had it occurred in the days of Chaucer or King Arthur, it would have been immortalized in saga. Why the French permitted it to happen is still a total mystery.

3

Loss of
the Packet *Antelope*

Since childhood I have heard the story of how my grandfather, Captain Joshua N. Rowe, was shipwrecked aboard the clipper ship *Crystal Palace* on the island of Mindanao in the Philippines. He and the others repaired the damage, fought off pirates and then sailed to Macao. They put out again on August 30, 1859, and after a record voyage landed at Plymouth, England, on October 27, 1859.

About three-quarters of a century before, another vessel sailing from Macao to England met disaster on a reef some 500 miles east of the island where Grandfather Rowe was wrecked. Captain Henry Wilson sailed that vessel, the packet *Antelope,* out of Macao on Sunday, July 20, 1783.

Stormy weather beset them until Friday, August 8, when the skies began to moderate, giving way to a relatively calm Saturday. Since it was then possible to throw open the ship's ports and dry out the cabin, the spirits of those aboard rose and all looked forward to better sailing conditions.

Unfortunately, heavy rain and a thunderstorm struck early Sunday morning. Suddenly breakers were reported dead ahead. Before any orders could be given, the *Antelope* struck heavily. Complete confusion ensued. The ship bilged within the hour and filled with water to the lower deck hatchways.

With his air of confidence and decision, Captain Wilson brought order out of chaos. Soon he had the gunpowder and small arms secured, the bread safe on deck and many of the other provisions protected from the water. He ordered the mizzenmast cut away to prevent excessive heeling, then gave directions for the main topmast and fore-topmast to be removed and the main and foreyards to be lowered. The boats were hoisted out and filled with provisions. Plans were made to abandon the wreck hurriedly if necessary.

The wait for dawn began. Two glasses of wine and several biscuits were doled out to each person. Everything possible was done to allay the fears of the anxious passengers.

At daybreak they discovered a small island about ten miles to the south and later made out several other islands to the east. Captain Wilson chose the smaller but nearest island to the south for their destination. The boats left the ship with orders to proceed there.

Those who remained aboard the wreck started building a raft in case the *Antelope* began to break up. In the afternoon when the boats returned, the sailors reported that five men had been left with the stores on the island and that no natives had appeared. This good news caused the captain to order another glass of wine and more biscuit for all hands, but the loss of a man overboard at this time stopped the celebrating.

Finally the raft was finished. The men loaded it with a great number of stores and then completely stocked the jolly boat and the pinnace.

The latter now started out towing the raft, with the jolly boat going on ahead. At times the pinnace crew could not even see the raft because of the giant waves. Eventually they reached the island and unloaded the cargo.

During the next few days the captain and several others attempted to free the ship. When a great wind blew up and it appeared that the packet would go to pieces, those at the wreck were able to return safely to the island.

At about eight o'clock the next morning, two canoes were observed approaching the island. Tom Rose from the Malayan Peninsula was chosen to negotiate with the natives in the canoes when they reached shore. As soon as they were within hailing distance, Tom began. The usual questions were asked concerning the presence of the white men on the island. Satisfactory explanations were given. Finally Tom called to Captain Wilson, who strode down the beach and waded into the sea waist-deep to greet the strangers.

Among the eight natives were two princes, brothers of the king of their tribe on neighboring Ternate Island. The men explained that the masts of the *Antelope* had been seen by fellow islanders fishing from a canoe.

The whites, still very suspicious of the natives, tried to conceal their feelings as they sat down to breakfast with them shortly afterward. During the meal the men talked about the area where the *Antelope* was wrecked. The Palau (or Pelew) Islands, and especially Oroolong where they had been cast away, are about 500 miles due east of Mindanao Island in the Philippines. They were first called the Palos Islands by the Spaniards, who believed the tall palm trees resembled masts of ships when seen from a distance.

The native men who sat around the breakfast table were copper-colored, admirably proportioned and quite naked. Their thighs were much blacker than the rest of their bodies because of tattooing. The chief, or prince, carried a small basket containing betel nuts and chinam, which is coral burned to lime. The natives would sprinkle the leaf of the betel nut with the lime powder and then chew the leaves, forcing the red juice between their already blackened teeth.

Finally the natives decided that they had stayed long enough at the island. They requested Captain Wilson to appoint one person to return with them for a visit of respect to their king. Wilson deliberated a few minutes about this awkward predicament, then chose his brother, Matthias Wilson. He told Matthias to ask for protection and also permission to build a vessel in which they could sail back to their own country. Captain Wilson sent the king a package of presents—broadcloth, a canister of tea, a jar of sugar candy and a bottle of rusk.

It was also agreed that the king's brother, Prince Raa Kook, and three other natives would remain with the white men and help them. The prince soon found a fine well of water on another part of the island. Then he went down to the beach with his companions and the white men to say good-by to the natives in the two canoes as they started for the island where the king lived.

Meanwhile, other natives had been plundering the wreck, as Captain Wilson found out to his disappointment. He was especially concerned when he discovered that the medicine chest had been ransacked, the costly and vital fluids emptied because the natives coveted the bottles. When the captain told Prince Kook about it, the prince was enraged and promised vehemently to kill any natives caught plundering the ship in the future.

There was a large store of choice wines and liquors on board the *Antelope*. Captain Wilson knew the relative strength of such intoxicants on the empty stomachs of his men. Therefore he suggested to the other officers that they go aboard the packet and stave in every one of the scores of liquor casks. The task was carried out at once, not one man imbibing in even a farewell glass.

On the morning of August 14 two canoes arrived, bringing Arra Kooker, the king's other brother, and one of the king's sons. A third canoe, so the natives claimed, had been delayed by the wind. Aboard that craft was Matthias Wilson. Some of the white men wondered whether he was being forcibly detained.

After introductions, everyone went over to the wreck. There they found twenty native canoes, which Raa Kook dispersed at once.

Returning to the island, Arra Kooker amused the others by

telling of Matthias Wilson's concern while visiting the king, explaining by facetious mimicry the apprehension Matthias had shown when he was the only white man in the center of hundreds of savages. Shortly afterward the canoe was sighted with Matthias aboard, and Captain Wilson heaved a sigh of relief.

Matthias told of his experiences while visiting the king. He had given the presents to the monarch in a respectful manner, and they were graciously accepted. Then Matthias had been allowed to mingle with the scores of people in the little enclosure where the king received him. The natives crowded around the white man, believing his clothing was part of him; they all were completely naked and had never seen a clothed man before. When Matthias took off his hat, unbuttoned his waistcoat and removed his shoes, their wonderment knew no bounds.

With the approach of evening, Matthias explained, he had been greatly concerned when two groups of natives lit large bonfires, one on each side of him. He wondered if they were about to roast him alive. But the king, noticing his apprehension, explained that the fires were to keep Matthias warm during the long tropical night. Matthias fell asleep shortly afterward, to be awakened by the bright sun shining in the east.

For breakfast he was given yams, coconuts and sweetmeats. A wind of great strength had come up, and the king decided that Matthias should wait till the following day before returning to Captain Wilson. The next morning two canoes were sent out ahead. A few hours later, in still calmer weather, a third canoe with a picked crew transported Matthias back to Oroolong, the island near which they had been wrecked.

Captain Wilson was highly pleased. His brother's account made him confident that the natives were going to remain friendly. The king showed no objections to the white men building a craft in which to sail for home, and the captain at once started making plans to construct a vessel large enough to transport them all.

Meanwhile, certain formalities had to be observed. The king had promised Matthias that he would soon visit the white men's settlement. When a number of canoes were seen approaching early the next morning, Arra excitedly told Wilson that the great king of the Pelew Islands was in one of the canoes.

Soon an impressive marine procession entered the little harbor. The king's canoe was easily identified as it proceeded with two other craft on each side, making a dramatic spectacle approaching the beach side by side. Trained natives pulled their paddles high out of the water, each flourish in perfect coordination. As the paddlers neared the beach, four natives in each canoe brought forward their conches and at a given signal blew the shells like trumpets to announce the arrival of His Majesty King Abba Thulle.

Captain Wilson, instructed by Arra Kooker, went down to the low-water mark on shore to welcome the king. He was brought out into the shallow water to His Majesty, who was seated on an impromptu throne built in the center of the canoe. Stepping aboard, Captain Wilson and the king embraced each other. The monarch now stated that he was ready to go ashore. Captain Wilson was carried to the beach by the natives, but the naked king walked ashore himself. Because he refused to enter any of the tents that had been set up on the island, the white people spread a sail on the ground and escorted him to the center of it.

After Captain Wilson introduced the other officers of his crew, the king asked him to identify his badge of supremacy. At a loss for an answer, Captain Wilson was aided by Chief Mate Benger, who surreptitiously slipped a beautiful gold ring into Wilson's hand. Wilson slipped it on his own finger as he stepped forward to the king.

"Your Majesty," he began, "this is typical of my symbol of authority." He pulled the ring from his finger and gave it to the king, who tried it on and was very pleased at the token of leadership Captain Wilson had shown him.

The captain now reintroduced his chief mate. The king called him "Kickary Rupack," which meant "Little Chief."

The native leader was impressed with the ship's grindstone, which had been placed on a block on shore. He took hold of the handle and turned it. Then his attention went to the muskets, and he asked questions about them. Captain Wilson promised to arrange a demonstration. In a short time the sailors conducted a drill on the lowtide beach, which they concluded by aiming their guns at a saluting angle and firing three volleys. The king and his followers were overwhelmed by the exhibition.

To press his advantage, Captain Wilson asked the chief mate to put on a special demonstration of shooting. A fowl was released to strut along the beach, and "Kickary Rupack" shot him with one blast. The natives rushed to the remains, examined them and were again dumbfounded.

That night the savages sang their customary songs, which some of the white men misinterpreted as preliminaries to a massacre. A scuffle started that might have led to serious trouble, but the king and Captain Wilson soon quieted both sides. After a few English songs were sung, the remainder of the night was spent in sleep.

Then came the first efforts to build a ship from the wreckage of the *Antelope*. The natives were anxious to watch the proceedings. But the English, not knowing how far to trust the savages, had concealed many tools and weapons from them. To the consternation of all, a native discovered one of the cutlasses, demanded it and finally stalked off in triumph as the white men let him have it. Seeing the man with the cutlass, Raa Kook angrily took it away and gave it back to Wilson. The incident caused some unpleasantness, for Captain Wilson had lost face by giving the cutlass to an inferior member of the tribe. Native protocol dictated that only royalty receive gifts of such importance.

A neighboring tribe at Artingall Island had bothered the king a short time before arrival of the white men. Abba Thulle thought a show of strength would be timely. It was arranged that five Englishmen armed with their magic guns would accompany the native warriors to the offenders' island. In the battle that followed, the neighboring tribe was first terrorized and then overwhelmed by the firearms. On September 4 Captain Wilson gave permission for a second demonstration, during which ten of his men were to fight on the side of Abba Thulle's warriors. This second battle with the king's enemies at Artingall Island also ended successfully, and the king returned to his own island well pleased.

Meanwhile, building of the vessel progressed. While the framework was being erected, Abba Thulle appeared with news that the chief minister at Artingall was suing for peace. Realizing the importance of the guns in obtaining the victory, the king requested that when Wilson completed his ship and sailed away, he leave behind ten muskets for safety. Wilson tentatively compromised at five muskets, and there the matter ended for the time being.

The vessel was breamed by October 27. The outside caulking was completed, but there was neither pitch nor tar to pay her with. The sailors burned coral into lime, mixed it with grease and used it as a substitute.

On November 6 Captain Wilson sent the jolly boat across to Pelew, requesting the honor of the king's presence within a few days. It was also announced that seaman Madan Blanchard was so impressed with native life that he was anxious to stay behind. When the king arrived at Oroolong, Wilson told him Blanchard would remain to instruct the natives in firing muskets and using the iron tools Captain Wilson planned to leave with them. The king consented gladly.

On November 9, a Sunday, in the presence of the King of Pelew, the new vessel was launched and named *Oroolong*. She appeared neat and trim as she lay at anchor in the cove.

After a happy breakfast the men began carrying aboard all their possessions. Next the ship was hauled into the basin, where there was about twenty feet of water, and the remainder of the cargo was loaded, except for the heavy guns and other weighty objects.

A short time later Abba Thulle told Wilson the local rupacks had decided to make him an honorary prince of the first rank. Giving him a circular bone standing for the rank of prince, the king said: "You are now invested with our highest mark of honor, and this bone, the signal of it, you will carefully keep as bright as possible, rubbing it every day. This high mark of dignity must always be valiantly defended, nor suffered to be wrested from you but with your life."

Then came the great surprise. Abba Thulle informed Captain Wilson that he was sending his second son, Prince Lee Boo, back with Captain Wilson so that he would get a thorough education and eventually return with knowledge he could impart to his countrymen. Overcome by the news, Captain Wilson agreed gladly and ordered quarters prepared on the *Oroolong*.

Among the ship's company was a huge Newfoundland dog that had delighted Arra Kooker. The prince was overjoyed when the captain gave him the prized pet. Arra Kooker planned to build a huge craft on the ship's ways, which Captain Wilson left on the beach.

A final act was to hoist an English pennant on a tree near the cove and put up a copper plate on the trunk of the tree with the following inscription:

> THE HONORABLE ENGLISH
> EAST INDIA COMPANY'S SHIP THE ANTELOPE
> HENRY WILSON COMMANDER
> WAS LOST UPON THE REEF NORTH OF THIS
> ISLAND
> IN THE NIGHT
> BETWEEN THE 9TH AND 10TH OF AUGUST
> WHO HERE BUILT A VESSEL
> AND SAILED FROM HENCE
> THE 12TH OF NOVEMBER, 1783

Now came an unpleasant discussion concerning firearms. When Abba Thulle renewed his request for the ten muskets, he was refused. Quick to resent this attitude, the king spoke out frankly. "Why should you distrust me? I have never refused you my confidence. If my intentions had been hostile, you would have known it long ago, being entirely in my power. And yet, at the very last, you suspect me of bad designs!"

His straightforward manner embarrassed the white men. Without further hesitation they gave the king five muskets, five cutlasses and almost a full barrel of gunpowder, with flint and ball in proportion. In this way peace and goodwill were restored, and Abba Thulle soon forgot their unkind suspicions.

During the evening Prince Lee Boo arrived from Pelew with his elder brother, and Abba Thulle presented him to all the officers. The night was spent ashore, with the king giving advice to his son.

Early Wednesday morning a signal gun was sounded from the *Oroolong* and camp ashore was broken at once. All persons left the island, the white men not to return.

As soon as farewells were made, the *Oroolong* hoisted sail and proceeded to a position outside the reef, where guns and other equipment were loaded aboard. Finally all was in readiness for the long trip back to civilization.

The king then directed that his canoe be brought alongside. Going aboard, he gave his son a farewell blessing, spoke briefly to the captain and prepared to leave the vessel. Fruit and food of all kinds were now carried aboard from the native canoes. Then Captain Wilson ordered a package carried forward for the king. It contained a brace of pistols and a cartouche box of cartridges.

Now came the final moment. King Abba Thulle stepped forward and began to speak slowly. "You are happy because you are going. I am happy because you are happy, but still very unhappy to see you going away."

The captain was so overcome that he was momentarily unable to answer, and the king was equally moved. Finally, pointing to his heart, Abba Thulle stepped over the side into his waiting canoe, which was a signal for a conch salute.

The *Oroolong* rapidly progressed out of the harbor, leaving the natives far behind within an hour. It was November 12 that the ship's company thus terminated their enforced stay at the island, which began on August 10.

Aboard the *Oroolong* Prince Lee Boo was placed in the care of Mr. Sharp, the surgeon, who taught him the fundamentals of dress and behavior during the voyage to China. On November 25 the crew sighted the Bashee Islands. This greatly pleased the prince, who was happy to see land once more. The next day Formosa was in sight, bearing northeast, and on the 29th the ship anchored near the high land called the Asses' Ears, arriving at Macao one day later. The Portuguese governor visited the captain and told him the war that had been going on was over, and peace had been established in Europe. A message was forwarded to Canton explaining what had happened to the *Antelope*.

Lee Boo was taken to visit the home of Mr. McIntyre, a friend of Captain Wilson. When the prince saw his image in a large mirror, he was amazed, supposing it to be someone else looking at him. This and other wonders of civilization kept him at a constant pitch of excitement. Arrangements were later made for Captain Wilson, Lee Boo and the officers to embark from Whampoa aboard the *Walpole,* leaving Chief Mate Benger to take over the *Oroolong* and sell her.

The crew was paid off with funds forwarded from Canton, and the next day the *Walpole* sailed away. On July 14, 1784, after an uneventful journey, the *Walpole* put into Portsmouth, England, her long trip ended.

Back in the Pelew Islands, the king had been told on the day Captain Wilson departed that it would be at least thirty moons, and possibly six more, before his son returned. The king had then knotted thirty knots into a rope, left a little space and knotted six more.

But Prince Lee Boo never returned to his father. About six

months after he arrived in England, he caught the dread smallpox disease and died. He is buried in Rotherheathe Cemetery, where a magnificent tomb was erected to his memory by the East India Company. The stone on the tomb reads:

To the memory of
PRINCE LEE BOO
A native of the Pelew, or Palos Islands
and Son to Abba Thulle, Rupack or King
of the Island Coorooraa:
Who departed this life on the 27th of December, 1784,
Aged 20 Years
This stone is inscribed
by the Honorable United East India Company
as a Testimony of esteem for the humane and kind
Treatment afforded by his Father to the crew of
their ship, the ANTELOPE, Captain Wilson,
which was wrecked off that Island
In the night of the 9th of August, 1783.

Stop, Reader, stop—let NATURE claim a Tear—
A Prince of Mine, Lee Boo, lies bury'd here.

4

The Polar Crusoe

On my first visit to Scotland in 1943 I took a brief walk around Aberdeen, where my natural tendencies took me to a book-shop. I soon discovered a score of fascinating story possibilities, one of which I found impossible to leave. Because I was about to sail on what was then the world's largest ship, the *Queen Elizabeth,* a few speedy notes were all I could manage that day. Later, as I browsed deeper and deeper, I could not believe the tale. But subsequent research has won me over.

In 1757 a vessel named the *Anne Forbes* left the port of Aberdeen, Scotland, for the Greenland whaling grounds. On board, as a seaman, was a lad by the name of Bruce Gordon. The captain was Emmet Hughes, an Englishman with the reputation of being a rash, obstinate drunkard.

On her way to the whaling area the ship had fine weather and an open sea at first. Then one day a girdle of ice was sighted, about thirty miles broad. The whaler sailed between this obstruction and Iceland. Reaching a latitude of 70 degrees North, she came upon some gigantic whales journeying rapidly northward. The crew captured one and then continued on their route for two weeks. Although the mate, an old experienced sailor, repeatedly told the captain of the danger of penetrating so far into the Polar seas, Captain Hughes only laughed and declared that they were now at the Pole and could sail to China as easily as to Spain.

There were plenty of whales, and they harpooned so many they loaded the vessel. Despite this rich haul, Captain Hughes ignored the approach of colder weather and refused to head south. He was drinking heavily, bragging about his great feat of discovering the North Pole. For the next few days the mate persistently pointed out to his commanding officer several of the worst ice floes in the vicinity, which would certainly imprison the ship if the wind should rise from that direction. Captain Hughes berated him for being a nuisance.

One afternoon the mate noticed that the vessel had entered a strong current and was drifting northward. Realizing that the *Forbes* was being swept rapidly toward danger, the mate again spoke to the captain. This time he was sobered by the situation and ordered all sails set. Taking the sun's altitude, he suddenly became terribly worried and commanded the course to be set due south.

The current was strong against them, with a light breeze on the starboard bow. The ice soon forced itself against the ship on all sides. Even worse, a whitish fog began to cover them. Staying on deck, the captain barked orders with an impatience born of fear.

Despite all their efforts the ship became completely surrounded by the relentless floes, which were still sufficiently loose to allow slow progress toward the southwest under short sail. The *Forbes* passed what the crew took to be a huge iceberg but the captain said was an island, "one of the Seven Sisters" off the coast of Spitsbergen.

After struggling on for twenty-four hours more they noticed another, apparently endless field of ice before them. The mate knew that the moment the two packs collided the ship would be crushed. Just before that occurred he ordered Bruce Gordon up to the masthead.

Within a short time the masts and the bulwarks of the *Anne Forbes* shattered under the terrific impact. The ship went over on her beam ends, throwing Bruce from the mast onto one of the fields of ice. The *Forbes* went down in less than thirty minutes, taking everyone except young Bruce Gordon.

The very next day, as a result of peculiar forces at work below the surface, the vessel rose again, capsized with keel uppermost and became imbedded in the frozen wastes.

So it was that Bruce found himself alone on a field of floating ice, far out on the great Polar ocean, without food or shelter. He happened to have a small Old Testament in his pocket, which his mother had given him when he first went to sea. From this he derived his sole consolation.

He saw at once that his only chance of survival lay in trying to reach the hulk of the wreck. The broken ice had been pushed up in heaps, and there were great gulfs between the floes that had to be crossed. But Bruce was determined to reach the ship—or perish in the attempt.

The way was perilous. After climbing over mountains of ice as firm as rocks, he came to other areas with the consistency of froth, and there he slid into water over his head. The ice was so slippery at times that he could get no hold. He knew that if he went down gradually into the soft spots he was gone. Thus, whenever he found that he was beginning to sink, he jumped in bodily to keep his momentum and managed to spring to a firmer foothold. At length, as he wondered how he could keep up his unequal flight, he reached a broken boat mast. With this for support he finally made his way to the wreck. He was completely exhausted.

The keel of the *Forbes* was uppermost, and there was no way to get inside. He had nothing to dig with save the splinter of mast. The hulk, above the ice, seemed undamaged but impenetrable.

He was terribly thirsty, but all the surrounding ice he tasted was salty. Nearly worn out from his efforts, Bruce noticed not far from him, beyond a level plain of ice, a tremendous berg that he took for a mountain. Hastening toward it, he found to his relief that the ice was fresh, not salty. This was an unexpected blessing, and he knelt and thanked God. Committing himself to His mercy and protection, he broke off sections of ice and ate them until he could stomach no more.

Although his thirst had been satisfied, the pangs of hunger were increasing. He started once more toward the wreck to search for something to eat. Among other things, he found a small boat hook used for the yawl and a harpoon fastened to a part of the shattered longboat. Returning to the hulk with difficulty, he was able to reach the cabin window and force entrance. The cabin was full of ice, with everything turned upside down.

Bruce made his way to the bread locker, broke it open and savored some biscuits. He thought he had never tasted anything so delicious. He ate and ate until he again became thirsty. Fighting through the rubble in the cabin, he reached the captain's secret store closet and broke it open in hopes of getting something stronger than ice water to drink. But every bottle was either empty or smashed.

He located knives and forks, a corkscrew and many other implements that might prove valuable. At length, below all the rubbish, he came upon an entire unbroken cask of spirits. The corkscrew was instantly applied, out flew the bung and down went his nose to the hole. It was either rum or brandy—he believed it was a mixture of the two. Taking the tube of the old ship bellows, he put in the wide end and sucked the small one. Never having tasted anything so strong before, he was little aware of its potency and was soon overcome. He fell fast asleep beside the cask.

Bruce awoke after sleeping for a considerable time, his body so numb that he was unable to get up. He turned again and again to the contents of the barrel.

At length he heard what to his amazement sounded like a great number of people muttering outside the vessel. Weak and tipsy from the liquor he had consumed, Bruce became frightened. His fright turned to terror when he thought he heard somebody enter the cabin through the hole he had made in the stern, followed by the sound of munching at the biscuits.

Vitalized by his fear, he cautiously opened the door of the closet where he had slept. In his delirium he saw what he first believed was a naked woman escaping from the cabin window. He was at least sure that he saw her bare feet and toes. Seizing a boat hook in one hand and a harpoon in the other, he went cautiously to the entrance hole.

Looking out, he saw several white polar bears prowling around the ship, all busily digging and eating. He was amazed at the holes the powerful beasts had clawed in the ice in order to prey on the blubber stored in the ship. They were also attacking the bodies of Bruce's unfortunate companions. Two bears within twelve yards of him were tearing at the corpse of his late captain, which he recognized from the shreds of clothes strewn about.

In an effort to drive the creatures away, Bruce took a speaking-trumpet and shouted through it with all his might, "Avast, ye lubbers!" They sprang up on their hind feet, standing as straight as humans. They were sleek and plump, and one appeared to be at least ten feet high. After staring about them for a time, the bears resumed their gruesome feast.

Bruce tried to frighten them with various kinds of sound. Instead of fleeing, they began to draw nearer to him. Frightened, he barricaded his entrance by fitting a large fire grate into it. He then used oakum to lash knives, forks and other sharp instruments to the grate, facing their points outward.

Thinking he was safe, he retired to the closet and swallowed a tankard of brandy. Then he took the hard, frozen blankets from the cabin bunks and made himself a couch. Locking the door on the inside, he climbed on his bed and was soon asleep. He was not disturbed again by the animals during his slumber.

The long Arctic night was setting in. The bears kept prowling about, but in a more listless manner than before, as if they were well fed. Bruce ate a good amount of salt biscuit; hoarfrost, which lay nearly two inches thick, satisfied his thirst. To warm himself he had recourse to the brandy, which usually set him sleeping for twenty-four hours, sometimes even longer.

Bruce guessed he was somewhere in the middle of the sea between Greenland and the North Cape. With ample spirits and provisions within the wreck—if he could get at them—he believed he could winter on the ice. But to do this he would have to make his way both into the hold and the forecastle, where there were coal and important stores. It would be necessary to reach the door, then work himself between the deck and the solid ice below. The fact that everything was upside down added to his difficulties. He spent many a hard day's labor making little progress. When at length he had hacked his way to the hold, Bruce found the whole weight of the cargo lying above it. At first he could not move it.

In the course of his efforts, he discovered the captain's wardrobe, with plenty of shirts and clothes, every article steeped in salt water and frozen. He also found shaving utensils, flint and materials for lighting his pipe.

Finally he reached the coal bin. It contained a moderate amount of large pieces of coal, with an old axe for breaking them into smaller fragments. From the rubbish of a boat that had been fastened on deck, he pulled out a squaresail, some smaller canvas, a good hatchet and many other useful articles.

Fire was now the only thing he needed. With it he could melt the ice, cook his food and dry his clothes. Although he had all the materials, without a chimney or smoke vent he could not start a blaze. After various experiments, he at length succeeded in carrying a flue up to the heel of the keel, and found it worked out admirably.

The Arctic winter had set in. No more did he hear the calls of swans and geese journeying southward. A few bears occasionally prowled about, but he seldom went outside. He stuffed snow up the entrance he had hacked out, and he fixed a piece of cable to a door so he could close or open it with a minimum of effort.

During the middle of one night when a great Arctic blizzard was raging, Bruce was awakened by a noise outside his cabin. He was frightened beyond measure. The sound continued. Then something came to his closet door and bumped against it. He held his breath. A creature attempted to force open the door but failed. By this time Bruce was on his feet brandishing the large carving knife he always kept beside him. Presently the intruder went away and began to attack the biscuits.

What appeared to be the sound of crunching teeth led Bruce to believe that the unwanted visitor was a polar bear. He struck a light, flung open the door and bolted out, armed with the torch in his left hand and the long sharp knife in his right. His guess had been correct. The flame frightened the creature, who tried to dash out the door with such speed that it stuck fast. Bruce ran forward and gave the animal two deadly stabs in the heart. Blood cascaded across the cabin, and very soon the brute was dead.

The carcass became stiff and began to freeze. Bruce pulled and strained until he had the beast inside the cabin. It proved to be a huge female with "milk in her dug," indicating she had been nursing recently. Bruce skinned her with great difficulty, sliced the flesh into neat square pieces and spread it on the ice to freeze. He figured that he had no less than a hundredweight of good, wholesome, fresh meat. He then cleared out the cabin and washed it with hot water; when the floor had dried, he spread the bear's skin for a carpet. After swallowing some hot punch, he once more retired to bed.

On awakening, he heard another familiar noise at the door, a plaintive grumbling. Cautiously he opened the entrance. Outside, a female polar bear cub, apparently dying of hunger, raised its forefeet as if entreating to be taken in. He helped the small creature inside, and when she found her mother's skin she seemed to utter a bleat of joy. The cub went round and round licking the skin with great fondness, looking for the milk she could no longer get from her mother.

At length the animal seemed to understand that a terrible change had taken place in her mother's body. The baby curled herself on the fur in an attitude of almost human grief. Feeling sorry for the cub, Bruce offered her some biscuit. She accepted the first piece shyly, then ate the rest so voraciously Bruce was afraid she would choke.

He recollected that there were heaps of frozen blubber lying on the ice that he had cleared below the deck of the hold. He crept away with his coal axe and a light, and brought some large pieces into the cabin. These he broke into small bits to feed the cub, patting her and speaking kindly, calling her Nancy after the only girl he ever loved. She licked his hand in return. He was ecstatic at having found a live companion. The cub fell asleep on her mother's skin and did not awaken for three days.

In the meantime Bruce was not idle. On the floor of the forecastle was a trapdoor communicating with the bilge water, into which the crew had emptied foul water without being obliged to run up constantly to the ship's side. There was likewise a trapdoor in the cabin, but that was carpeted and thus seldom opened. On pushing aside the latch of that trapdoor, which he did easily with a table knife, the door fell toward him since the deck was his ceiling.

He entered this hatch hole and discovered himself at the keel of the vessel, among the pig iron. He had a free passage into the hold, where he found more coal and additional casks of fresh water—or, rather, fresh ice—as well as the carcasses of five or six whales. He had meat for the bear cub for years to come, plus plenty of blubber to burn. The forecastle's larder yielded a large barrel half full of beef, and another more than half full of pork. There was also bacon, mutton and deer hams, and about half a cask of Highland whiskey.

He returned to the cabin in a happy mood, taking with him a good piece of solid meat, pipes, snuff and tobacco, all of which he had found nicely packed up in boxes. He tried to awaken

Nancy but in vain; only by holding burning tobacco to her nose, which made her sneeze violently, could she be prevailed upon to open her eyes.

He fed her, and her eyes lighted up. As she weighed only about forty-five pounds, he carried her into his closet and closed the door, but she would not settle down away from the skin of her mother. At last he took the mother's skin into his closet and spread it above his blankets, after which she lay down upon it, uttering the same plaintive sounds as before.

By degrees he taught Nancy to follow him in and out of the wreck. She was never weary of rolling in the snow, often scraping her claws frantically at the ice as if longing to get into the sea. She continued to thrive and soon was as plump as a calf.

She never once showed the least disposition toward anger or surliness, but seemed to consider Bruce a friend of her own species. As the months went by she answered to her name and came at his bidding. When they walked out upon the ice, Bruce dressed in his late captain's holiday clothes, he would take her paw within his arm to teach her to walk upright. He often laughed heartily at the figure they cut. She tried to imitate him in everything, including laughing. Her laugh was irresistible, with the half-closed eyes, a grin and a neigh resembling that of a wild horse.

At length the sun made its appearance above the southern horizon. Every day Bruce worked to cut a regular flight of steps to the top of a giant iceberg near the ship, which would serve as an observation post. He finally finished the rough stairway to the peak of this huge mountain of solid ice, winding it around the innumerable creeks and ravines that went far down into the body of the berg.

The Arctic spring arrived. The swans came north over his head, their weird cries piercing day and night. This, he thought, boded evil for him, for it told him plainly that the Polar seas beyond this great field of ice were open. If the ice

broke up, he was sure to be carried northward among unknown seas and frozen coasts. To prevent such a catastrophe,
he would have to start out in search of land. But he did not
know in what direction to seek either continent or island.

He still had ample food as well as a fowling piece, and he
had dried out a box of gunpowder. Bruce climbed the iceberg
almost every day. At length he resolved to dig a cavern, believing it impossible that the iceberg could melt or sink. He hol-
lowed out several comfortable apartments. One had a chimney
he fashioned with a bar of pig iron. Here he stored part of his
provisions, spirits and other supplies. He resolved to trust himself to the iceberg if he saw the ice breaking up, and leave the
rest to Providence.

For about two months he spent all his waking hours on top
of this ice mountain with Nancy, who was always at his heels.
One morning, which judging by the height and heat of the
sun must have been about midsummer, he looked out from his
observation peak and saw that the whole sea northward was
clear of ice to within a mile of him. At the same time there was
a strong current running in that direction. Everything remained as usual for several days, with Bruce and his cub
staying in one of the chambers he had cut in the iceberg.

He was awakened from a sound sleep one night by a tottering motion of the iceberg. The movement ceased in a minute,
by which time he was up and out on the platform at the top.
He saw that the berg had twisted a small degree to the west
and had separated from the great field of ice on the east, leaving an opening "about a bowsprit over." The wreck remained
on his side of the gap, and he hastened down from the
mountain to see how matters stood there.

The sea in the new opening was as bright as a mirror. As
soon as Nancy saw the water she rushed into it, vanishing
below the ice for so long that Bruce feared for her safety. She
appeared at length with a fish in her mouth, something like a
large herring. He was happy to get fresh fish and caressed her

for it; away she rushed again to the opening. Whenever she dived she brought up a fish, and every day thereafter she kept him well supplied.

Realizing that it was a strong foundation on which the wreck rested, he again began sleeping in his old berth in the cabin closet. One morning when he arose, the ice bordering the beautiful crystal gap of water was gone. They had set off on another Polar voyage, leaving the vast field of ice behind. As far as the eye could see, all was again water.

Lazy walruses rested and rolled on the ledges of the ice mountain. Seals would also have congregated on it had it not been for Nancy, who carried on perpetual and bloody warfare with them.

Bruce must have traversed the Polar seas for at least six months more without ever knowing where he was. Several times he saw mountains. Once he observed a headland or island straight before him. Anxious to see what kind of country it was, he went to the topmost point of the iceberg to watch.

He was so near land that he saw a human being, a woman he thought, moving about on the shore and staring at the floating mountain. He put his two hands to his mouth and hailed the stranger with all the strength of his lungs. But before he could establish real contact, the bear sent forth such a vibrating roar that the native was frightened and vanished among the rocks.

The iceberg, including the attached ledge of ice on which the hulk of the *Anne Forbes* rested, was moved by different currents and driven from one direction to another in that vast Polar sea. At length the fogs returned to cover the face of the ocean. The sun neared the horizon, and from that time forth Bruce saw no more around him—neither sun, moon nor stars—but journeyed on he knew not where. Unless he was busy cleaning the fish Nancy caught, he either dozed, read his Bible (most of which he learned by heart) or amused himself with the antics of his companion. Though he often slept in his ice cave in summer, he moved into his old cabin in the wreck as winter approached.

One day he was frightened when he heard a great rushing noise like a tempest. It continued for some time, although he could perceive no change in the ocean. He decided to walk around the vast mountain of ice, as far as he could go. By the time he was halfway, the mystery was solved.

The new ice had commenced, and the irresistible mass of his frozen island borne along by a strong undercurrent was breaking it up with tremendous violence. The ice continued to roll up before the mountain, and was heaped against it to such a height that finally the berg became fixed and the noise ended.

An intense frost set in one night. The fog cleared away, the stars appeared in the zenith and a beautiful blue twilight sky fringed the horizon. Bruce went to the top of the mountain to look around. Suddenly he was sure that he saw land dead ahead.

While contemplating the scene with disbelief, the report of a gun reached his ears. It sounded like a signal from a ship not many miles away. He hastened from the height, seized his fowling piece and again climbed the peak, where he fired the weapon. After his third shot a report was returned with a roar louder than before. He tried as best he could to imitate the signal of distress. After his signal had been answered, he judged that there was no time to be lost. Hastening down once more, he packed some powder and shot, food and a bottle of spirits and hurried off in the direction from which he thought the sounds came and the land lay.

When he had traveled sixteen to twenty miles, calculated by the length of time he took, he suddenly noticed the bear cub greatly interested in something a long distance to the right. He turned in that direction, and to his astonishment found traces of a company of thirty or forty men, all journeying on the same path straight for land. Thus encouraged, he continued walking for many miles. Nancy, meanwhile, had run off and left him. Straining his eyes, he perceived on high ground that must mark the shore a number of white bears—all coming toward him!

He dared not run for fear of being pursued by the whole band and torn to pieces. Since it also seemed dangerous to advance, he squatted down on the ice and "wished himself under it." The animals had discovered him, however, and they all came toward him. Then he sprang to his feet and ran, without looking back. A noise coming nearer and nearer compelled him to glance over his shoulder, and he perceived two bears in close pursuit.

Terrified, he flung away his provisions, keeping only his loaded gun and his long dirk. The two creatures paused when they came to his supplies and soon devoured the food. Bruce recognized the smaller bear as Nancy. Evidently the larger bear, a male, had become interested in her and had followed her. Realizing the other bear could easily kill Bruce, she scampered in the opposite direction over the icy wastes to lead the bear away.

Bruce knew his troubles were over temporarily, but he had fled in such haste that he had lost all traces of his path. After traveling several miles, he was hungry, thirsty and overcome with fatigue. Kneeling on the snow-covered ice, he prayed to God to direct him. Then he hurried on, he knew not where. Shortly afterward, to his great joy, he came upon his own track, which would lead him back to the wreck.

He kept going for some time. At length he heard a noise coming along the ice, like galloping horses, accompanied occasionally by a growling murmur. His strength gone, he could not make much progress. Looking back, he beheld a bear coming upon him at full speed. Soon the animal was kneeling at his feet and licking his hand. It was Nancy, and she was bleeding. She instantly turned around, then went slowly back.

He now perceived a gigantic bear standing upright, resembling a tall obelisk covered with snow. He cocked his gun and tried to run on. Nancy endeavored to stop the monster by throwing herself constantly in front of him. But the great male bear gave her a cuff with his paw to make her keep out of his way. Bruce tried several times to aim at him, but found it impossible without shooting Nancy. All he could do was stagger on. Finally, utterly exhausted, he fell flat on his face.

Instantly he found himself grasped by one of the bears. It was Nancy, trying to cover him with her own body from the attacks of the savage pursuing brute. The male struggled to reach his neck. First Bruce felt the cold nose and then the warm lips close to his throat. He called out, "Seize him!"—the words he had trained Nancy to obey in hunting. She gave the male bear such a snap that the animal desisted momentarily. Then the huge beast attacked again. Trying to reach Bruce's neck, the bear seized him by the left arm, close to the shoulder, and inflicted a deep wound. Bruce called out to his pet, who promptly seized the attacker by the throat with her teeth and paws. The beast started away, swinging her round and round like a baby, bellowing fearfully. But Nancy would not relinquish her grip. The male bear then wrapped his paws around her and threw her down.

As the two animals fought, Bruce placed the muzzle of his gun to the larger bear's ear and fired. The shot ripped away part of the beast's mouth, but his paws continued to embrace Nancy in a deadly grasp. Still she kept fast hold on his throat.

With all his waning strength, Bruce then stabbed the monster with his knife again and again. Although blood streamed through the snow as if a sluice had opened, the creature clung tenaciously to life for a few minutes. Then, with a dying gasp, he released Nancy. As soon as she got free, Bruce embraced her. Feeble and tired almost to death, they made their escape back to the old hulk.

Barricading the entrance door, Bruce fed his valiant protector, ate something himself, drank a little brandy and knelt down to return thanks to the Almighty for his strange deliverance. Having kindled a fire of coal and driftwood, he bathed and dressed his left arm, which was badly lacerated, and took a short, troubled sleep. As for Nancy, with the exertion of fighting and a hearty meal, she dozed off and on for most of the following three months, until Bruce was finally obliged to awaken her as he had done before.

It was a severe winter, much stormier than the last. By the time the sun began to show above the horizon, this Polar Crusoe had once more resolved to make a pilgrimage over the ice in search of inhabited country. Accordingly, he loaded himself and Nancy heavily with supplies. Then he left his old comfortable cabin and his mountain of ice, uncertain whether he should ever see them again.

Away they jogged together, holding a course as near as Gordon could guess to the south-southwest. At the southwest corner of the area, he unexpectedly came upon the traces of three men and a number of dogs. By following them, he arrived at a shore in a few hours.

In his attempt to overtake the men, it was necessary to leave the greater part of the supplies. He now made a muzzle for Nancy out of strong cord, for he knew she would certainly attack the dogs first and, in all probability, the men next. He set out on their track, leading his pet by a rope attached to a muzzle. She tried to get loose by pulling it off with her paws, but when he shouted at her, she stopped in bewilderment.

Fourteen hours later Bruce came to a place where the three men had evidently rested and refreshed themselves. There was a great deal of blood on the snow, and from this he concluded they were hunters and had killed game. He drank from a spring gushing out of a rock and also fed Nancy, who began scraping a spot between two rocks. He soon discovered a store of venison covered over with snow. He gathered that this spring was a hunters' rendezvous, and that to meet them he had only to remain where he was.

He soon fell asleep from fatigue and anxiety, to be awakened by Nancy struggling to get free. Hearing voices, he peeped

over the rock and saw three men. Bruce drew himself up to the
edge of the cliff and on his knees implored them to take him
under their protection, invoking the name of the Lord. They
recognized his reference to Christ, and each of them took off
his fur cap and knelt on his right knee.

When Nancy appeared on the cliff, the dogs scampered off.
The men were about to follow, but Bruce held up the cord to
show that she was muzzled and leashed. On receiving his
command, she cowered at his feet and nuzzled his hand. This
astonished the men, who stared at one another. Bruce explained the situation to them as best he could in sign language, for they did not understand his tongue.

After an hour or so the men became friendly. Bruce sat
down to eat with them. The meal over, they packed for departure. Taking as much food as they could transport, they yoked
the dogs to sealskin bags in pairs. Bruce was afraid of a row
between the dogs and Nancy. He made signs for the men to
muzzle their animals, which they did. Then they started on
their journey together in peace.

After proceeding for three days and three nights along the
level surface of the ice, they reached the open sea and came to
two canoes and a boat. Each of the men took two dogs under-
neath the leather of his canoe, and Bruce was deposited in the
bottom of the small boat. He was forbidden to move for fear of
upsetting the frail craft. Nancy obediently swam along behind
the canoe, completely dominated by the commands of her
master.

They crossed the sea and were met on shore by twelve
young women. Bruce was conducted to their living quarters,
where they were received by an old man with white hair and
beard. He was the patriarch of the little colony and their priest.
Bruce was instructed to kneel and receive his blessing, which
he did.

The home of these simple people was strangely constructed.
The outer apartments were vaulted with snow. Beside these

was a long natural cavern stretching under the rocks, with many irregular side recesses. In one of these a comfortable bed was made for Bruce.

The colony consisted of thirty-one women and ten men, including the aged father—the rest of the men evidently had perished at sea or while hunting. There were seven children, two of whom were boys. Bruce was told that he was in Old Greenland among the remnant of a colony of Norwegians, a race of simple, primitive Christians whose ancestors had inhabited that bleak shore for centuries. Here, among these surroundings, Bruce lived for several months.

Nancy soon became a favorite with the entire tribe because of her fishing expertise. She accompanied them on a long expedition they made to the hulk of the *Anne Forbes,* to bring away some of the oil, spirits and iron that had been left there. On this occasion they took eight light sledges with them, drawn by thirty powerful dogs. Four men were in charge of the party, one of whom was Bruce; Nancy followed.

From the moment they returned, the bear seemed disconsolate. Her moans disturbed the whole community. One morning, after she had spent part of the night groaning as if her heart might break, she was missing. Although they searched for her far and near, she was nowhere to be found. Bruce never saw her again.

One day at the height of the summer, reports came of whaling and sealing vessels less than 150 miles to the south. Bruce decided to attempt to reach them. There were plenty of canoes, and he was given the best. He stowed supplies at his feet and then bound the sealskin around his breast. After farewells to his many friends, he set out to sea.

He continued his voyage night and day, going along the shore and landing only to sleep. He held this course until he was almost hemmed in with ice. Then he drew his canoe ashore and climbed a hill, from which he saw open sea not far away. There, to his startled eyes, were several ships, all apparently beating southward. Was he too late?

Running downhill, he leaped into the canoe and made his way to the clear water, paddling rapidly toward the fleet. Soon he realized he was being outdistanced by even the slowest craft. He reluctantly returned to shore for the night.

Next morning, after a good sleep, he again climbed the hill. To his joy, he noticed a ship far to the north, heading south in a direction that would pass his lookout post. Down the slope he ran to the canoe.

He paddled out about a mile from shore. The ship still came on. Beating up, she passed close to the canoe on one of her tacks, and Bruce's frantic shouts were heard. Heaving to, the great vessel awaited his approach. Five minutes later he was taken aboard.

He found himself on the *Briel* of Amsterdam, homeward bound to the Netherlands. From her captain he learned that he had been gone from home for seven years and one month!

Four weeks later, off Scotland, the *Briel* hailed a small fishing vessel, which took Bruce to Scotland. He went ashore in Aberdeen and eventually reached his home.

His story was received with such disbelief that he was shunned for many years as a sort of Baron Münchausen-type Scot. But as the years went by, other Scottish sailing vessels came back from the Arctic and confirmed various topographical details he had mentioned. Bruce Gordon's account was accepted by more and more people, until finally he was in good standing in the community. One of his descendants moved to America a hundred years later, and there are still many by the name of Gordon in Massachusetts.

Part Three

1800–1850

1

Mutiny
on the *Somers*

"Do you fear death? Do you fear a dead man? Are you afraid to kill a man?" Thus spoke Midshipman Philip Spencer of the United States brig-of-war *Somers* on the night of November 25, 1842, to the steward, Mr. Wales. He had asked Wales to climb up into the booms so that they could converse without being overheard.

Cleverly and with great tact he talked, not revealing what was about to take place until Wales swore an oath of secrecy. Then Spencer told Wales that twenty of the crew were planning to take over the *Somers*. They would murder the commanding officer, Captain Alexander Slidell Mackenzie. Then, after choosing from the willing members of the crew who would be useful, they would kill all the others and become pirates!

Spencer stated that an inducement of the plan was the box of rare wines brought abroad when the *Somers* was at Madeira. The box also contained a large sum of money, a gift to be presented to the Commodore of the Navy on their return to the States.

When the mutineers had full charge of the vessel, Spencer proposed to sail to the Isle of Pines, a place frequented by

319

pirates. There he had a friend who had been "in the business" before. Their plan of action was to attack only those craft they were sure to capture. After removing everything of value, they would completely destroy the vessels. Spencer and his followers would acquire all suitable women from the captured craft, use them until the pirates' interest waned, then kill them.

Spencer said that he had written out the details of this plan on the back of his cravat and would show it to Wales early the next morning. Before parting, Spencer threatened instant death should the steward reveal even one word of what had passed.

Despite the warning, next morning Wales revealed the conversation to Purser Hieskell, so that it would be communicated to the captain. Hieskell, in turn, related the story to Lieutenant Gansevoort, who immediately informed Captain Mackenzie. Although the plan seemed utterly improbable to Mackenzie, he ordered Gansevoort to keep Spencer under the closest observation without his realizing it.

After watching Spencer narrowly and inquiring among the crew about him, Gansevoort reported that the suspect had been in the wardroom examining a chart of the West Indies, and that he had questioned the assistant surgeons about the Isle of Pines, receiving the answer that it was a place much frequented by pirates. Spencer had also been observed in secret and nightly conferences with boatswain's mate F. Cromwell and seaman Elisha Small, both of whom had received money from Spencer. Bribing the wardroom steward, Spencer got him to steal brandy from the wardroom mess, brandy Spencer and several crew members drank till they were inebriated.

Although he was "servile in his intercourse" with the captain, among the crew Spencer opined that it would be "a pleasing task" to roll Mackenzie overboard off the roundhouse. At one time he drew a picture of a brig with a black flag and asked a midshipman what he thought of it. During the early part of the cruise, he had repeatedly asserted that the *Somers* might easily be taken from the Navy.

These reports together with other circumstances made Captain Mackenzie decide that something had to be done. After due consideration he ordered that all officers should lay aft on the quarterdeck except for one man stationed on the forecastle. Captain Mackenzie now approached Spencer and asked if he aspired to the command of the *Somers*. Of course, Spencer denied it.

"Did you not tell Mr. Wales, sir, that you had a project to kill the commander, the officers and a considerable portion of the crew of this vessel, and to convert her into a pirate?"

"I may have told him so, sir, but it was in joke."

"You admit, then, that you told him so?"

"Yes, sir, but in joke."

"This, sir, is joking on a forbidden subject—this joke may cost you your life! Be pleased to remove your neck handkerchief."

When nothing was found in the handkerchief, Captain Mackenzie asked Spencer, "What have you done with the paper containing an account of your project, which you told Mr. Wales was in the back of your neck handkerchief?"

"It is a paper containing my day's work, and I have destroyed it."

"It is a singular place to keep days' work in."

"It is a convenient one," Spencer replied.

"It will be necessary for me to confine you, sir." Thus speaking, Captain Mackenzie turned to Lieutenant Gansevoort with the order, "Arrest Mr. Spencer, and put him in double irons."

Gansevoort stepped forward, removed Spencer's sword and ordered him not only double ironed but handcuffed as additional security. This done, Gansevoort was directed to keep a constant watch on Spencer and to have him put to death instantly if detected speaking to any member of the crew.

Spencer's locker was searched and a small razor case was found. It contained two papers, one rolled within the other. The inner paper was covered with strange characters, which proved to be Greek. A midshipman acquainted with that language, converted the characters to English, revealing the names of the crew arranged in separate rows: the certain—the doubtful—those who were to be kept whether they would join or not—those who were to do the work of murder in the various departments, to take the wheel, to open the arms chests.

The next day the crew was inspected at ten o'clock quarters. Captain Mackenzie took his station abaft and focused his attention particularly on Cromwell, the tallest man on the brig, and Small, the shortest. That night Cromwell was brought to the quarterdeck and questioned by the captain as to a secret conversation he had had the night before with Spencer. Cromwell denied any part in it, accusing Small. When Small was brought before the captain he also made a strong denial of any guilt. But the evidence was too strong, and both men were placed in irons.

Increased vigilance was now enjoined upon all the officers. They were to be armed at all times. The captain or his first lieutenant was always on deck, and frequently both men were there. When several acts of disobedience occurred among the ship's company, punishment was inflicted to the full extent of the law, after which Captain Mackenzie addressed the crew, explaining the general nature of Spencer's plot.

Reaction to the captain's speech was varied. Many were filled with horror at the idea of the foul play they had escaped. Others were in fear of the fate that awaited them because of their connection with the conspiracy. The entire crew was under tremendous pressure. Those most seriously involved in the plot began to gather at night. Seditious words were heard, and many assumed an insolent and menacing air. Every one of the officers of the *Somers*, from the first lieutenant to the commander's clerk, proved faithful and patriotic. They were all of the opinion that the vessel was yet far from safe, that an attempt to release the prisoners was being seriously planned.

Conditions on the *Somers* were deteriorating so fast that Captain Mackenzie now instituted a thorough inspection of the crew, with the immediate arrest of the principal suspects. On November 30, 1842, he wrote a letter to all officers on board, excepting the midshipmen, asking their opinion as to what additional measures were necessary for the security of the vessel. On receipt of the letter, all the officers met in the wardroom to examine witnesses. The witnesses were duly sworn and their testimony written down; each witness signed the evidence he had given, after hearing it read to him.

Without interruption or food, the officers spent the entire day in examination and deliberation. The unanimous result of their efforts was the decision that Spencer, Cromwell and Small should be executed.

Captain Mackenzie concurred in the justice of their opinion and in the necessity of putting it into immediate effect. The petty officers were now mustered on the quarterdeck, each armed with a cutlass, pistol and cartridge box.

After all were armed, the captain spoke. "My lads! you are to look at me—to obey my orders—and to see my orders obeyed! Go forward!"

Captain Mackenzie stated that preparations for the hanging of the three principals should be made at once. All hands were called to witness the punishment.

The after guard and idlers of both watches were mustered on the quarterdeck to man the whip intended for Spencer. The forecastlemen and foretopmen made ready for Cromwell, to whose influence they had been chiefly exposed. And the maintopmen of both watches were at the whip for Small, who for a month or more had been captain of the maintop. The officers and petty officers were stationed about the decks, with orders to cut down whoever should let go the whip with even one hand or fail to haul on it when so ordered. The ensign and pennant were bent on and ready for hoisting.

Captain Mackenzie now put on his full uniform and prepared to carry out the most painful duty ever asked of an American commander: to tell three of his own men of their final fate. Going up to Spencer, he said: "When you were about to take my life, and to dishonor me as an officer while in the execution of my rightful duty, without cause or offense to you, on speculation, it was your intention to remove me suddenly from the world, in the darkness of the night, in my sleep, without a moment to utter one whisper of affection to my wife and children—one prayer for their welfare. Your life is now forfeited to your country; and the necessities of the case, growing out of your corruption of the crew, compel me to take it. I will not, however, imitate your intended example as to the manner of claiming the sacrifice. If there yet remains to you one feeling true to nature, it shall be gratified. If you have any word to send to your parents, it shall be recorded and faithfully delivered. Ten minutes shall be granted you for this purpose."

Spencer was overcome and sank to his knees, sobbing, until Captain Mackenzie reminded him of his duty as an officer to die with decorum. The captain then spoke to Cromwell and Small. The former protested that he was innocent, and Spencer supported his claim. But Lieutenant Gansevoort and the petty officers agreed that Cromwell was guilty beyond the shadow of a doubt.

Captain Mackenzie returned again to Spencer and asked if he had any messages for his family. Spencer replied: "Tell them that I die wishing them every blessing and happiness. I deserve death for this and many other crimes. There are few crimes that I have not committed. I feel sincerely penitent, and my only fear of death is that my repentance may be too late. I have wronged many persons, but chiefly my parents. This will kill my poor mother! I do not know what would have become of me had I succeeded. I fear this may injure my father.* I will tell you frankly what I intended to do, had I got home—I should have attempted to escape. I had the same project on board the *John Adams* and *Potomac*. It seemed to be a mania with me."

Spencer questioned whether the law would justify the commander taking life under such circumstances. Captain Mackenzie assured him that it would; that he had consulted all his brother officers, his messmates included, except the

---

* Spencer was the son of the Honorable John C. Spencer, Secretary of War under President Tyler, who held that position at the time of his son's disgrace.

boys, and their opinion was just, and that he deserved death.

Spencer now asked for a Bible and a prayer book. After a short time he stated that he begged forgiveness for what he had planned against the captain, at which Captain Mackenzie shook hands with Spencer. The prisoners were then escorted to the gangway. At the break of the quarterdeck was a narrow passage between the trunk and the pump-well. Spencer and Cromwell met on either side. Cromwell was told to stop in order to allow Spencer to pass first. Spencer asked to talk with Mr. Wales, who then came forward.

"Mr. Wales," said Spencer, "I earnestly hope you will forgive me for tampering with your fidelity."

Wales, almost overcome with emotion, replied, "I do forgive you from the bottom of my heart, and I hope that God will forgive you also."

Spencer now walked on, meeting Small at the gangway. Spencer extended his hand and asked forgiveness, but Small drew back with horror.

"No, by God! I can't forgive you!"

Spencer asked again, and after a brief pause Small, at the urging of Captain Mackenzie, stated in a subdued voice that he forgave Spencer, and the two men shook hands.

Small was placed on the hammocks forward of the gangway, with his face inboard. Spencer was similarly placed abaft the gangway, with Cromwell on the other side of him.

Spencer asked the captain what was to be the signal for execution. Mackenzie answered that he wished to hoist the colors at the moment of execution, so it was his plan to beat to call as for hoisting the colors, then roll off, and at the third roll fire a gun. Spencer asked to be allowed to give the word to fire the gun, and his request was granted. He then begged that no interval might elapse between giving the word and firing the gun.

Now Small asked to address the crew. "Shipmates and top-mates! Take warning by my example. I never was a pirate. I never killed a man. It's for saying I would do it that I am about to depart this life. See what a word will do!" He turned to Spencer. "I am now ready to die, Mr. Spencer. Are you?"

Cromwell's last words were, "Tell my wife I die an innocent man. Tell Lieutenant Morris I die an innocent man."

All was ready. But then Spencer, who was to give the signal, stated that he could not give it and asked Captain Mackenzie to do so.

The signal was given, and the execution by hanging was carried out. Thus it was that three Navy men were swung out into eternity from the yardarm of the brig *Somers*.

The crew was ordered aft at once. All hands were called to "cheer the ship," as the saying went more than a century ago. Captain Mackenzie himself gave the order: "Stand by to give three hearty cheers for the flag of our country!" Never were three heartier cheers given.

On the following Sunday the captain addressed the crew, telling them that as they had shown they could give cheers for their country, they should now cheer their God in song. The colors were then hoisted and above the American ensign, the only banner to which it may give place: the banner of the cross. Then every member of the ship's company, officers and crew, joined in singing the one-hundredth psalm.

When the *Somers* eventually reached home, the mutiny and execution were investigated by a court of inquiry made up of Commodores Stewart, Jones and Dallas. Captain Mackenzie's action was fully approved. Mackenzie himself requested that a court-martial be held. Commodore John Downes was president. The trial, which lasted forty days, resulted in Mackenzie's acquittal.

Thus the insidious action of Philip Spencer in the year 1842 aboard the brig-of-war *Somers* is recorded for all generations as the first regularly organized mutiny in the annals of the naval history of the United States of America.

2

The Murdered Minister

One pleasant day in October 1827 the Reverend Mr. Charles Sharply rode into Alfred, Maine, and held services in the meetinghouse there. After the sermon he announced that he was going to Waterboro to preach, and that on his circuit he had collected $270 to help build a church in that village. Would not his hearers add to that sum? They would and did, and that evening the parson rode away with over $300 in his saddlebags. He never appeared in Waterboro or any other village or settlement again.

Various reasons were suggested by the country people, many of whom believed that possession of the money had made him forget his sacred calling and leave the State of Maine with his spoils.

On the morning after Reverend Sharply's disappearance, the church deacon, Nathaniel Dickerman, appeared in the town of Alfred riding on a horse that some believed was the minister's. The tavern hostler, however, affirmed that the minister's horse had a white star on his forehead and breast, whereas the horse the deacon was riding was all black.

Deacon Dickerman explained that he had found the horse grazing in his yard at daybreak, and that he would give it to anyone who could prove it to be his property. Since nobody appeared to demand it, he kept the animal. People soon forgot that it was not his. The deacon extended his business shortly after this and prospered. With wealth, he became sullen and averse to company.

One day a rumor went around that a belated traveler had seen a misty apparition under "the owl tree" at a turn in the road where owls were hooting, and that it took on a strange likeness to the missing clergyman. Deacon Dickerman paled when he heard the story, but he shook his head and muttered about the folly of listening to stupid nonsense.

The years went by, a decade since the minister had vanished. During that time the boys of the town had avoided the owl tree after dark. Then one afternoon a clergyman of the neighborhood was hastily summoned to see Deacon Dickerman, who was said to be suffering from overwork. He found the deacon in his house alone, pacing the floor, his clothing disarrayed, his cheeks strangely flushed. He asked the clergyman to listen to a statement he wished to make.

"My time in this world is almost ended," said Nathaniel Dickerman, "nor would I live longer if I could. I am haunted day and night, and there is no peace, no rest for me on earth. They say that Sharply's spirit has appeared at the owl tree. Well, his body lies there. They accused me of taking his horse. It is true. A little black dye on his head and breast was all that was needed to deceive them. Pray for me, for I fear my soul is lost. I killed Sharply."

The clergyman recoiled.

"I killed him," the wretched Dickerman went on, "for the money that he had. The devil prospered me with it. In my will I leave two thousand dollars to his widow and five thousand dollars to the church he was collecting for. Will there be mercy for me? I dare not think it. Go and pray for me."

The clergyman hastened to leave but was hardly outside the door when the report of a pistol brought him back. Dickerman lay dead on the floor. Sharply's skeleton was found and removed from the shade of the owl tree, and as far as is known the area around the tree was never haunted afterward.

3

Drowned at Sea

At the height of a great storm a frantic woman, faced with death and almost out of her mind from worry, clung to her baby son on the deck of a stranded bark. Wave after wave smashed into the vessel, and she realized that she could not keep up the unequal fight much longer.

The woman in mortal terror was Margaret Fuller, recognized today as one of the most brilliant and scholarly American women of the nineteenth century. In the field of female intelligence, she dominated her century as Anne Hutchinson did hers. Both were either bitterly condemned or extravagantly praised.

Margaret Fuller once stated, "If all the wicked people submitted to be drowned, the world would be a desert." Her own fate during a shipwreck was indeed a weird contrast to her remarks.

Margaret Fuller, who became Marchesa Ossoli, was an American writer born May 23, 1810, in Cambridge, Massachusetts. Early in Margaret's life her father, Timothy Fuller, recognized her brilliance and trained her to be a "youthful prodigy."

It is said that Margaret danced her way through Harvard College with members of the class of 1829. This class has been made too famous by the wit and poetry of Oliver Wendell Holmes not to be considered among the most eminent that ever left Harvard. The memory of one lady has preserved for us a picture of the girl Margaret as she appeared at a ball when she was sixteen. "She had a very plain face, half-shut eyes, and hair curled all over her head; she was dressed in a badly-cut, low-neck pink silk with white muslin over it; and she danced quadrilles very awkwardly, being withal so near-sighted that she could hardly see her partner."

Margaret Fuller became one of the backers of Brook Farm in West Roxbury, and frequently appeared at this famous head-quarters of transcendentalism. Unfortunately, about this time she incurred the everlasting resentment of Nathaniel Haw-thorne. Gentle as the great writer was by birth and upbringing, he was outstandingly harsh and bitter in his comments on Brook Farm and on the woman he called Zenobia, in reality Margaret Fuller. Elsewhere in his writings he indicated that the Marchesa was definitely not one of his particular favorites: "Margaret Fuller had a strong and coarse nature which she had done her utmost to refine, with infinite pains; but, of course, it could be only superficially changed. . . . Margaret has not left in the hearts and minds of those who knew her any deep witness of her integrity and purity. She was a great hum-bug."

Although Margaret was known as the high priestess of the transcendental movement, early in its operation she detected several of its outstanding flaws.

Then, when her father died, Miss Fuller taught languages in the Alcott School. In 1837 she became a "principal teacher" in the Green Street School, Providence, Rhode Island, to fulfill her responsibilities for her brothers' and sisters' education.

In December 1844 Horace Greeley brought her to New York to put the literary criticism of the *Tribune* on a higher plane than any other American newspaper. He also gave her an opportunity to discuss in a broad and stimulating way all philanthropic questions.

While on the *Tribune* Margaret Fuller put aside money for a journey to Europe, a trip that had been her lifelong dream. At last, on the first of August 1846, she sailed away.

Soon after Miss Fuller's arrival in Rome, early in 1847, she went one day to hear vespers at St. Peter's. Becoming separated from her friends after the service, she was observed in the church by a young man of gentlemanly address, who offered his services as a guide.

Not seeing her friends anywhere, she let the young Marchese Ossoli accompany her home. They met once or twice again before she left Rome for the summer. The following season Miss Fuller had an apartment in Rome. She often received among her guests this young patriot who had her sympathy and with whose labors in behalf of his native city she was so thoroughly in agreement.

When the Marchese proposed, Margaret refused to marry him, insisting that he should choose a younger woman for his wife. At length he convinced her of his sincere love and affection, and she married him in December 1847.

She served in hospitals while Ossoli was in the army outside the city. In September 1848 their child, Angelo, was born. The happy family went to Florence.

On May 17, 1850, together with her husband, her son Angelo and a maid, Margaret boarded the bark *Elizabeth* at Leghorn, bound for the United States. She brought with her a precious manuscript of the struggle for Italian liberty in which she and her husband had been involved.

For the twenty-three persons aboard the *Elizabeth* it was a voyage of terror almost from the beginning. Two days after the ship sailed, the captain came down with smallpox and was confined to his bunk. He never recovered, dying a few days later. The inexperienced mate took charge of the bark, and the *Elizabeth* stopped at Gibraltar before resuming her voyage.

A short time later Angelo became ill with smallpox, but Margaret was able to nurse him back to health.

By July 17 the *Elizabeth* was near New York. Late that

afternoon a gale began and the unhappy mate soon admitted that he had lost his bearings. Although Jeannette Edward Rattray * relates that the mate was reasonably certain the *Elizabeth* was off the New Jersey coast, at four o'clock in the morning of July 17 the bark was wrecked on a sandbar off Fire Island, near Point O'Woods, New York.

The bark stayed afloat for some time, but the waves were so high that no one dared launch a lifeboat. A few of the passengers and several crew members managed to reach shore on planks. Margaret Fuller, holding her child in her arms, sat on the deck at the foot of the mainmast. Clad only in her nightgown and shawl, with the wind whipping her long hair, she refused to leave the ship. The steward, noting that the mainmast was about to fall, seized the child and jumped overboard. Both were drowned, as were Margaret's husband and their maid when waves washed them out of the rigging. Margaret went down with the bark alone. Ten others were lost in the sea, while twelve saved their own lives.

A bronze tablet was erected on Fire Island near Point O'Woods in memory of Margaret Fuller, but later it too was lost because of the encroachment of the sea.

Marchesa Ossoli and her husband had been fearful as they embarked on the fated ship that was to take them to America. Ossoli had been cautioned by a fortune-teller when he was a boy to beware of the sea, and his wife had long cherished a superstition that the year 1850 would be a marked epoch in her life. In writing to a friend about her fear, Margaret said, "I pray that if we are lost it may be brief anguish, and Ossoli, the babe, and I go together."

The bodies of the parents were never recovered, but that of little Angelo was discovered and buried in a seaman's chest among the sandhills. The child's remains were later disinterred and brought to Mount Auburn Cemetery in Cambridge by relatives who never saw the baby in life.

---

* Author of *Ship Ashore*.

The letters that passed between the young nobleman and the wife he adored are still extant, having been found with her baby. They are the only things of Margaret Fuller's saved from the fatal wreck in which she and her two loved ones were drowned. Her manuscript of the Italian struggle was lost forever.

So at Mount Auburn, in the same cemetery where Longfellow, Agassiz, Booth, Winslow Homer, Julia Ward Howe and a host of others are buried, the unfortunate waif lies in a neglected area of the great burial ground.

4

Miraculous Escape from the *Adelaide*

A shipwreck with a strange aftermath quite similar to the *Cod Seeker* * occurred at Barnegat, New Jersey, on September 10, 1846. Bound out of Manahawkin, the sloop *Adelaide* was attempting to reach Barnegat Inlet before a severe gale hit the coast. Crashing into the bar, the *Adelaide* capsized. Captain James Lamson and his entire crew drowned almost instantly.

The vessel, still bottom up, pounded through the breakers and finally went ashore some distance from Barnegat Light. Lighthouse keeper John Allen, former keeper Garret H. Herring and young Charles Collins watched the wreck push in toward the beach. Around dusk, just before the tide would turn and come in, it appeared that by careful attention to safety they could probably get on the bottom of the craft and inspect it. Realizing that the captain and crew had perished, they were eager to see what could be salvaged, for the *Adelaide*'s crew were all natives of Barnegat. At almost dead low water Herring and Collins started to go down the beach; Allen had to stay behind to trim the wicks and light the lamps for the night.

After reaching the *Adelaide*, which apparently was burying

---

* See my *Tales of Terror and Tragedy*, pp. 200ff.

334

herself in the sand, they waited for a particularly huge wave to recede. Then they jumped nimbly aboard.

As the two men walked along the slippery hull, the surf roared in and out, sand and gravel scraped against the sides and the vessel rocked back and forth. But suddenly there came a different sound—a dull pounding. At first they paid no attention. Then the noise grew louder and more insistent. Could it be that someone was still inside the hull, imprisoned by the water and sand, and was thumping on the bottom to attract attention?

Just then Keeper Allen, high in the tower, turned on Barnegat Light. The two figures atop the wreck watched as the steady beam shone through the gathering darkness.

"There's someone or something still alive in there," shouted Herring above the roar of the surf. "You and I have got to break through and reach them. We'll have our hands full, what with the tide coming in and darkness coming on. You are a lot younger than I am, so you start running for the lighthouse. Get the two axes in the storeroom and a lantern, and come back as soon as you can."

Young Charlie Collins raced along the bottom of the vessel, leaped high on the sand and broke out in a fast dash for the lighthouse. Breathlessly he told his story, got the needed articles and returned to the wreck. But even the twenty minutes he had taken made it just a little harder to climb aboard the hull of the *Adelaide,* for the gathering storm was now sweeping in rapidly.

"Good work, boy," said Herring. "I've located the tapping. It's right here below me, where the cabin is. We have a chance, if we're quick."

The two fell to work with the axes by the light of the lantern. Within twenty minutes, between surges from the sea, they had chopped a hole in the bottom of the ship. Herring grabbed the lantern and thrust it inside.

"Wait just a little longer," he shouted down into the darkness.

The answer he received astounded him. "I will," said a girl's voice!

They chopped all the faster, for with the incoming tide it did not seem possible that the girl, whom they judged to be a teenager, could live under such conditions much longer.

Just then a terrific wave hit the *Adelaide,* rushing through, over and under the craft. A great spurt of water shot out of the small hole the men had made in the bottom.

"Hold on. We'll get you out in a minute!" cried Herring. He knew that if they did not hurry, the cabin would soon become a tomb.

Again and again the axes smashed into the vessel. Slowly but surely the opening widened to a point where the girl could almost clamber out.

At the moment she was about to attempt her escape, a towering wave began to build up just off the bow of the overturned vessel.

"Give me both hands," Herring shouted. A moment later two wet, bleeding arms were thrust out as far as the broken section of the hull would allow. Collins had cut a piece of line from the wreck. As Herring held the girl's hands, Collins began to secure each of her wrists.

Just then the billow struck. Smashing toward shore with terrific force, it actually jarred the *Adelaide* from her deeply imbedded position in the sand, overwhelming the craft, filling the tiny cabin and burying the men with foam. Herring clung desperately to the girl. A moment later the wave began to recede.

Now was their chance. Collins secured her wrists so that another wave would not smash her around inside the cabin.

"We'll have you out in just a little while," Herring reassured her. "We've got you tied so that whenever there is a bad wave you won't drown. For now, clamber back in the cabin away from the hole, and we'll chop away a little more of the bulkhead. Then I think you'll be able to climb out."

By the light of the lantern the men desperately crashed their axes against the hull, widening the opening. Just as another towering breaker was about to smash into the wreck, they pulled the bleeding, frightened survivor from her prison.

The three huddled there, clinging to each other and the craft as the wave inundated the hulk. After it subsided, the men guided the girl to the shore side of the wreck, helping her down through the swirling water. Ten minutes later they were at the lighthouse, where the victim began to recover from the stark terror of her experience.

She was the daughter of Captain James Lamson, a widower who had taken her along on the voyage. The *Adelaide* had turned over and was driven onto the bar after the girl's father sent her below for safety. She did not know what had happened to the others because the capsizing had enclosed her in the fearsome darkness of the upside-down cabin. Evidently the air had been compressed into a corner and she had clung there, holding on to the bunk.

As the *Adelaide* was pushed shoreward by the waves, time and again the bunk was submerged in water and Miss Lamson * had to hold her breath. The compressed air, which she could breathe every time the boat went back to an even keel, kept her alive. But the hole that was chopped in the *Adelaide* let out the compressed air, and the surf rushed through whenever a wave hit the craft. It was a miracle she was still alive.

After putting her to bed and getting word to her relatives, the keeper's wife made a hot supper. The following week a fisherman named Worden, who hailed from Forked River and was a friend of the Lamsons, proposed to Miss Lamson. The offer was eventually accepted and they were married.

The couple's little girl, Katherine, arrived two years later. She was frequently taken by her mother to the scene of her grandfather's death and her mother's miraculous escape. Katy grew up on the seashore and fell in love with a Sandy Hook pilot named Carr. They were married sometime after the Civil War. Together they often visited Barnegat Light on the anniversary of the wreck.

---

* Her first name has not come down to us.

5

Tom Dunn's Dance

Vermont's Rag Rock, in which the famous Indian Wabanowi began his long sleep in 1767, was the home of demons and sprites as late as the nineteenth century. Indian scout Thomas Dunn was aware of this, and ordinarily he would take a long maneuver to avoid contact with the creatures of the spirit world. However, one night when he had occupied himself with what historian C. M. Skinner called "keeping his spirits up by pouring spirits down," and had kissed his pretty partner at the husking bee twenty times, he decided to take a chance and cut right across the hill so famous for the demons and sprites he usually feared.

Approaching the top of the hill, he observed a glow through the trees, and soon heard a fiddle "going like mad." With determination he forced his way through the thickets to discover who was holding a picnic in the moonshine of the evening. When he listened carefully, he distinctly heard the rustle of feet.

Arriving at the edge of the glade, he saw a richly dressed and merry company surrounded by a dozen torches. Each person was dancing with extremely vivacious spirit.

Tom, who dearly loved to participate in a jig or a reel, could not possibly ignore this chance. When he entered the ring where the people were enjoying themselves, he was greeted with a tremendous shout. While sitting on a hummock of moss, he noticed a maiden fair who lacked a partner. She had snapping black eyes, rosy cheeks and lips apparently inviting. The skirts she wore were just a speck higher than the custom of the period, and her ankles were indeed acceptable to all who saw them.

Catching her by the waist, Tom started whirling with her into the middle of the gayest, most extraordinary dance in which he had ever participated. He felt himself soaring into the sky. As he glanced around the ring, he realized that all the other dancers had quit their activity to sit on the edge of the ring and watch him. Then the music of the violin, starting with an especially catchy note, made him kick his heels in the air, cracking them before he came down in an ecstasy that combined both motion and existence itself.

Round after round of applause greeted him. He and the pretty girl decided to separate half a dozen feet and dance each other down. After a strenuous twenty minutes, Tom noticed uneasily that the early freshness was vanishing from the girl's features. Her eyes, becoming harder and deeper, began to turn from black to light green. Her teeth began to push out of her mouth, turning sharp and yellow, and her lips curved in an evil grin. He realized with a shudder that he was in the company of the demon group of the hill!

He knew that if he could not keep dancing until dawn, or the setting of the moon, he was doomed. He began to fling off his clothing—first his coat, then his hat, finally his vest and tie. By this time the moon was beginning to set. In two hours he would be free.

All seemed well until a cramp caught him in the calf and he knew he could not last. With a cry of desperation, he cried, "God save me!" and fell over on his back.

That cry did save him, for no witch or spirit, it is said, can endure to even hear the name of God. All Tom saw was a brief vision of scurrying forms going in every direction, hissing, growling and uttering curses.

Suddenly a hideous shape was hanging right over him in a terribly threatening fashion. He had the feeling that his time had come, that he was going to die. The strong smell of sulphur overcame him, and then he knew no more.

Hours later he awakened in the brilliant sunshine of a new day. Wondering if the strenuous carousal of the night before had been only the imaginings of a mind befogged by alcohol, he glanced around the clearing. Everywhere was evidence of high activity. Beside him lay his jacknife. Tom picked it up and was shocked when he looked at the handle: etched in fire were two portraits of the witch with whom he had begun his dance in happiness and ended it in terror. One portrait showed her in the full blossom of youth, the other as she appeared in her final decrepitude, hanging over him in that last frightening moment.

Tom Dunn soon suffered a high fever. When it ended he decided what he should do, and he did it with a vengeance. Calling on a desirable woman of his own age, he courted her briefly and then proposed. Soon after that he began to attend church regularly, married the girl who was not exactly of his dreams, forsook all entertainments, drank tea and became a steady workman.

For the remainder of his many years he enjoyed peace of mind, eventually dying a deacon of his church. In recognition of his good character, on his gravestone was carved a cherub similar to those on the organ loft of the Old North Church in Boston. But it was different in one striking way. The cherub on Tom Dunn's stone, for some mysterious reason, suffered a sculptured toothache.

Part Four

1850–1900

1

The Inherited Curse

When Sir Anthony Brown, Knight of the Garter, centuries ago took possession of Battle Abbey and Caldray in the British Isles, awarded to him by Henry VIII for services rendered, the monks are said to have placed a curse upon him and his descendants for evicting them, vowing that fire and flood would always follow his family.

A direct descendant of Sir Anthony, Mrs. S. Fahs Smith of York, Pennsylvania, collected information that indicates the curse—if curse it was—actually did influence the lives of many of Sir Anthony's descendants. The husband of Mrs. Smith's aunt, Laura, was drowned about 1870 when getting off a ship at Charleston, South Carolina. Aunt Laura died from taking poison by mistake in 1872. Two of Charles Mitchell's nieces drowned while passengers on the S.S. *Champion*, which collided with another craft en route to Charleston, around 1878. In 1900 Charles Mitchell's nephew, Mr. Bramwell of Flushing, New York, was sitting on the shore at a resort in New Jersey. After handing his watch to his fiancée, he went into the water and was attacked and eaten by a shark. Burwell Smith's yacht was lost off Cuba in 1947. This chapter concerns the terrible affair of the steamer *Arctic,* on which Mrs. Smith's father, Charles Mitchell, sailed in the year 1854.

343

Charles Mitchell had taken his sister Caroline to London, and they were planning to return aboard the *Arctic*. On the night before they were to sail, Caroline had a terrifying nightmare. She decided it was a warning not to sail on the *Arctic;* Charles Mitchell agreed to cancel her passage. However, because he was anxious to see his family, he sailed without her. That decision almost cost him his life.

The *Arctic* was launched on January 28, 1850, at William H. Brown's East River yard. She was the third of four wooden-hull, paddle-wheel steamships of the New York and Liverpool United States Mail Steamship Company, usually referred to as the Collins Line. She was capable of breaking the transatlantic record of the period, and did so on her February 1852 crossing. On the average, all the Collins liners were much faster than the Cunarders.

The 284-foot *Arctic* was such a beautiful ship that she soon became the talk of two continents. *Harper's* magazine for June 1852 stated, "Never did there float upon the ocean a more magnificent palace." John S. Abbott, writer of the article, described the main cabin, with its carcel * lamps, highly polished satinwood and rosewood, beautiful mirrors, "stained glass, silver plate, costly carpets, marble center tables, luxurious sofas and arm chairs," plus a "profusion of rich gilding giving an air of almost Oriental magnificence to a room 100 feet in length and 25 in breadth."

It was indeed a remarkable ship. Congressman Barry of Mississippi later said: "If they had spent in lifeboats for that vessel the money they spent in gingerbread ornaments and decorations, there might have been hundreds of valuable lives saved."

The *Arctic* left Liverpool on her ill-fated voyage for New York September 20, 1854, with more than 250 passengers and a crew of 140. Among the passengers were many of wealth and distinction. The wife, son and daughter of Mr. Collins,

---

* A mechanical lamp named for its inventor, B. G. Carcel, in which the oil is pumped to the wick by clockwork.

owner of the line, were aboard, and the Duc de Gramont was one of the distinguished names on the passenger list. Captain James C. Luce, commander of the ship, had with him his crippled eight-year-old son who, it was hoped, would benefit from the sea voyage.

New Englanders aboard included a Bostonian, Mr. A. Stone, and his family. Frederick W. Gale from Worcester, Massachusetts, together with his wife, child and servant had been traveling in Italy and had lived in Florence for some weeks. A young married couple named Lang hailed from Massachusetts. Mrs. John Childe and her daughter were from Springfield. Benjamin W. Copes, his wife and child were said to have been aboard, as well as "R. S. Williams & Lady" of Salem. Mrs. Howland and her son, relatives of Dr. Williams of Boston, also made the fatal trip, together with M. M. Day, his wife and daughter of Salem.

A week passed at sea without bad weather. The Collins liner reached the Grand Banks, and all aboard were expecting to arrive at New York three days later, on September 30. September 27 was calm and hazy. Occasional low-lying fog moved into the area. Although a sailor was often stationed in the forecastle head to blow on a horn at intervals, Captain Luce did not consider it foggy enough for this precaution.

At noon the captain took his observations for latitude. All who had entered the pool for guessing the day's run were anxiously awaiting announcement of the ship's position, but Luce never finished making his calculations. Suddenly the lookout in the bow gave a shout of alarm, and almost at once the officer of the deck told the man at the wheel to change the course "hard to starboard."

"I rushed on deck," said the captain later, "and just got out when I felt a crash forward and at the same moment saw a strange steamer under the starboard bow. In another moment she struck against the guards of the *Arctic* and passed astern of us. The bows of the strange ship appeared to be cut off literally for about ten feet. Seeing that in all probability she must sink in a few minutes, after taking a hasty glance at our own ship and believing that we were comparatively uninjured, my first impulse was to try to save the lives of those on board the stranger."

Immediately Captain Luce ordered two of the *Arctic*'s lifeboats lowered. His chief officer, Robert J. Gourlay, and six seamen rowed over to the vessel to see if help was needed. Later it was found that the craft with which the *Arctic* had collided was the 200-ton French steamer *Vesta*, on the way back to France from the island of Miquelon with 197 fishermen and sailors aboard. She suffered appalling damage but was able to stay afloat.

Just when the lifeboats were lowered, Captain Luce heard that the *Arctic* herself was in serious trouble. The collision had not been felt at all on the *Arctic*. No one in the engine room realized what had happened when they received the sign for "full astern." A few minutes later, however, Chief Engineer J. W. Rogers saw an ominous flow of black bilge water beginning to swirl around the engine bed plates. He opened the bilge injector at once, allowing the giant jet condensers of the main engine to suck water from the bilge. But the flow continued to gain, and soon Mr. Rogers realized that the *Arctic* was doomed.

In addition to water pouring into the engine room, it was also coming into the ship through several holes in the bow, the largest of which was more than five feet long and eighteen inches wide. No less than a thousand gallons a second were swirling into the hull.

Captain Luce ordered a sail passed over the bow to cover the leaks, but a large part of the *Arctic*'s stem and her broken iron anchor prevented a snug fit. Carpenter George Baily volunteered to go over the side in a boatswain's chair to attempt stuffing pillows and mattresses into the holes. By the time they began to lower him, the *Arctic* was so far down by the head that the operation was abandoned as impossible.

Inside the hull Boatswain Thomas Wilde was also desperately attempting to plug the leak. When the water reached the cargo, he realized he could do nothing more.

Captain Luce was now faced with a terrible decision. Should he continue his attempt to stop the leaks, or put all efforts toward a mad dash for the nearest land, fifty miles away at Cape Race, Newfoundland? He finally decided on the latter alternative. By this time Gourlay's lifeboat had disappeared in the fog, and the steamer *Vesta* had also vanished. Luce believed she had already gone down.

Now occurred one of the terrifying incidents of the disaster. The *Arctic* had just begun her desperate dash for shore when a horrifying scream pierced the air. Coming out of the fog, directly in the *Arctic*'s path, was a lifeboat that had been launched by the *Vesta*. Before anyone could do anything, the boat was caught under the *Arctic*'s paddle wheel and eleven men were ground to pieces. Only one of the twelve occupants was saved: François Gajoick, a French-Canadian fisherman. He was hauled aboard, then the *Arctic* continued through the icy seas in a desperate gamble to reach land.

Meanwhile, in the *Arctic*'s hold, the seawater was rising higher and higher. When it reached the ash pits and the bottom grates, the lower fires were extinguished one by one and the firemen were forced to flee topside to save their lives. The paddle wheels continued to turn rapidly. The upper fires soon went out as well. This was the beginning of the end, for the paddles began to slow down. Then, with a last indecisive churning, they stopped.

Only an hour had passed since the two craft had come together. Captain Luce's gamble had failed, but he had developed other plans for saving the women and children in the five remaining lifeboats. When the paddles stopped, however, uncontrolled panic broke out. A group of men leaped into the stern boat and cut her loose at once. What happened on the next lifeboat was written by a passenger, Mr. F. DeMaeyer:

"The boat was then ordered to be lowered, but before letting it down to the water, the passengers were placed in it to secure it against seizure of the ship's crew. Twenty-five passengers, of whom eighteen were ladies, and among them Mrs. Collins, were placed in it, when one rope at the stern end of the boat gave way, hanging it by the bows and precipitating all into the ocean except two men (one of them was Thomas Stinson, officer's steward) and Mrs. Craig, who clung to the boat. The lady was again taken on board the ship, and the boat with the two men in it was immediately put afloat. As soon as it was on the water a rush was made for it, passengers and crew together jumping from the ship, some falling in the water and others into the boat."

All but one of the remaining lifeboats were taken over by mobs of men and cut adrift. In the last boat the chief engineer placed a group of fifteen and rowed it out to a position near the *Arctic*.

Captain Luce now decided to make a raft on which many of the survivors could find refuge, and he gave all the women passengers life preservers. Along with examples of cowardice among the men, there were many instances of courage and even heroism. A young apprentice engineer, Stewart Holland of Washington, had been given the task of firing the signal gun at minute intervals. This he did continuously until the ship sank beneath him. His last act was the final firing of the gun as he was engulfed by the sea.

When the raft was almost ready, an alarm went around the ship that the *Arctic* was about to go under. This created a terrifying rush for the raft. Captain Luce almost tore the shirt off Fireman Patrick Tobin's back, attempting to restrain him.

"It was every man for himself," said Tobin later. "Life was as sweet to us as life to others."

At 4:45 that afternoon the stern dipped under the water, the bow rose in the air and the ship began her fateful plunge stern first. Passenger George Burns remembered "one fearful shriek . . . but the most terrible noise of all, which drowned other sounds, was the ship's own death moans as air trapped below made its final escape through the smokestack with an all but human-sounding wail, awful to hear."

Captain Luce, holding his little boy, went down with the ship but floated up to the surface. After struggling with the child in his arms, he was sucked under for a second time.

When he came to the surface once more, he had a terrible moment in which he could not find his son. Then he, too, reappeared. The captain later reported: "A most awful and heart-rending scene presented itself to my view; women and children struggling together amidst pieces of wreckage of every kind, calling on each other and God to assist them. Such another appalling scene may God preserve me from ever witnessing—I was in the act of trying to save my child when a portion of the paddlebox came crashing up edgewise and just grazed my head and fell with its whole weight on the head of my darling child. In another moment I beheld him a lifeless corpse on the surface of the waves."

Although the raft had been put together in the best possible way under the circumstances, it was not a perfect job. Seventy-two men and four women boarded it after the *Arctic* went down. Only one, Peter McCabe, managed to live through the following twenty-six-hour ordeal. Later, from the sanctuary of Sailors' Snug Harbor on Staten Island, New York, McCabe made the following statement:

"I swam to the large raft which had about seventy persons clinging to it. The sea, though not strong, was rough, and the waves, as they dashed over it, washed away a portion of its living freight. I shall never forget the awful scene. There we were, in the midst of the ocean, without the slightest hope of assistance, while every minute one or more of our unfortunate fellow passengers were dropping into their watery graves from sheer exhaustion. Those who had life preservers did not sink, but floated with their ghastly faces upward, reminding those who still remained alive of the fate that awaited them.

"In the midst of this, thank Heaven, I never lost hope, but retained my courage to the last. One by one I saw my unfortunate companions drop off; some of them floated off and were eaten and gnawed by fishes, while others were washed under the raft and remained with me till I was rescued. I could see their faces in the openings as they were swayed to and fro by the waves, which threatened every moment to wash me off. The raft at one time was so crowded that many had to hold on by one hand. Very few words were spoken by any, and the only sound that we heard was the splash of the waters or the heavy breathing of the poor sufferers as they tried to recover their breath after a wave had passed over them. Nearly all were submerged to their armpits, while a few could with great difficulty keep their heads above the surface.

"The women were the first to go. They were unable to stand the exposure more than three or four hours. They all fell off the raft without a word, except one poor girl who cried out in intense agony, 'Oh, my poor mother and sisters.'

"When I was about eighteen hours on the raft there were not more than three or four left. One of these gave me what appeared to be a small map, but which I understood him to say was a sort of title deed to his property. In a few minutes after I took it, he too unloosed his hold and was added to the number that floated about the raft.

"I endeavored to get the paper into my pocket, but found this impossible on account of my cramped position, so I placed it between my teeth and held it there till I was overwhelmed by a wave, when I lost my hold of it, and it was washed away. Another, who had an oiled silk coat on, called on me, for Heaven's sake, to assist him as his strength was rapidly failing and he must fall off if not relieved. As he was about four or five feet from me, it was difficult to reach him, but after considerable exertions I succeeded in doing so and helped him with one of my knees until I became quite faint, when I was obliged to leave him to his fate. Poor fellow, he promised me if he ever got to New York alive he would reward me well. He clung with terrible tenacity to life, but he too dropped off in his turn. I was now left alone on the raft; not a solitary being was alive out of seventy."

McCabe was eventually rescued by the ship *Huron* of St. Andrews, New Brunswick, bound for Quebec.

Henderson Moore, one of the passengers of the *Arctic*, had watched several others jump overboard into the water to get a place on one of the lifeboats. He was picked up by a lifeboat that had about fourteen people aboard. "We soon drifted out of sight of the steamer," Moore explained later. "After laying on our oars a few minutes, we went towards the steamer, being directed by the sound of her bells. While approaching her we fell in with another boat containing twenty-five persons in charge of the purser. Including those picked up, our boat now contained twenty-six persons in all, under the direction of Mr. Baalham. The boats being together, put it to vote and appointed him captain of both. We had at first six oars and the purser's boat three. We broke one of our oars and gave the purser one, which left us only four.

"We then headed for Cape Race, supposing it might be about a hundred miles distant, being guided by the wind and the sun which shone out for a few minutes. The compass taken on aboard failed to traverse and was of no use owing probably to the fact that Francis' lifeboats are made of iron. After pulling in company with the purser's boat all that night and the next day and night or until about one o'clock A.M. on the Friday following, we discovered land and which we reached about 4 P.M. the same day and landed at Broad Cove, a little bay and the only one within several miles where it was considered safe to effect a landing. Providentially a fisherman's hut was found near the spot, where we obtained some crackers and water, the first we had tasted after leaving the ship, as we had taken neither water nor food in either boat."

The first lifeboat to leave the *Arctic* vanished and was never heard from again.

The *Vesta* arrived at St. John's, Newfoundland, on September 30, just before the weather turned bad. At the time of the collision she had launched two lifeboats, one of which was run down by the *Arctic*. The other had returned to the ship, and its occupants were taken aboard again. Captain Duchesne of the *Vesta* had ordered 150 mattresses stuffed behind the bulkhead and fastened with timbers. The foremast was cut away and the vessel set out for St. John's under "small steam," according to the *Illustrated London News*.

One of the strangest consequences of the *Arctic* tragedy,

according to Alexander Crosby Brown, was the case of Mr. Fleury of New Orleans, who had supposedly perished on the liner. His young wife mourned for him and then married his chief clerk, by whom she had three children. Mr. Fleury had been taken aboard a whaler after the disaster and was then wrecked on an island, from which another whaler saved him. He finally arrived at New York six years later; on October 4, 1860, he wrote a letter to his wife.

Estimates as to the number saved and lost aboard the *Arctic* indicate the confusion common to this sort of statistics. Kennedy in *Steam Navigation* lists 87 saved of 365 on board. Angas in *Rivalry on the Atlantic* says 86 survived and 322 were lost. The U.S. Government reported that 305 disappeared. John G. Dow estimates that 106 were saved and 283 lost. Alexander Crosby Brown compiled a list of 83 saved from the *Arctic:* 4 officers, 57 crew members, 22 passengers; and one fisherman from the *Vesta.* Of course, the 11 men in the *Vesta*'s lifeboat must be added to the casualties.

No disciplinary action was taken against any of the survivors of the *Arctic,* some of whom had cowardly fought other men and even women to gain space in the lifeboats. Nevertheless, many of the surviving crew members decided to remain in Canada until the episode was dimmed by the passage of time and they could return home quietly without attracting attention. Alexander Crosby Brown relates that when Mr. W. W. Gilbert, a member of the New York Stock Exchange, arrived in New York alive and well, there was an "indescribable chill which ran through the entire community." In his own defense Gilbert said that he had gone to secure and hold seats for the lady members of the Brown family, but the inrush of the crew prevented him from getting out again. When he told his story it was believed that all witnesses who could contradict him had gone down with the ship. Later, George F. Allen, to the astonishment of all his friends, was picked up alive at sea. He did not confirm Mr. Gilbert's story, but what Mr. Allen did say was never made public.

When the crash occurred, Charles Mitchell, Sir Anthony's descendant, took momentary comfort in the realization that his sister Caroline was not aboard. Then the task of keeping alive occupied all his thoughts. He reached the ship's railing and grabbed a rope, from which he lowered himself and then jumped the remaining distance into the icy sea. Temporarily stunned by the fall, Mitchell was revived by the shock of the freezing water.

Feebly he swam to a lifeboat. Coming alongside, he was grasped by those aboard and hauled to safety. Minutes later the fog enveloped them, and they drifted away from the sinking ship. It was discovered that there were neither rations nor water aboard the lifeboat. There was no compass; they were adrift about forty-five miles from the nearest shore with no means of determining direction. During the next day two of the men gave in to their intense thirst and drank seawater; both died within twenty-four hours.

Two days later the fog lifted enough to allow the occupants of the lifeboat to see about a mile around them. Soon a schooner was sighted, but it sailed away without observing them. A brig came into view but also disappeared.

One of the crew then noticed what he believed was a land bird flying overhead. Assuming that it disappeared in the general direction of the shore, the occupants of the lifeboat started rowing after it. Hours later they landed at a small fishing village, Broad Cove, Newfoundland, twelve miles north of Cape Race.

Charles Mitchell was taken to the hut of a fisherman, where he had to remain for "a month before he recovered sufficiently from his exposure so that he could leave his benefactors and return to Charleston." *

---

* I have been permitted to quote from the pen of Mrs. S. Fahs Smith in recording the story of Charles Mitchell. Walter Ehrenfeld of York, Pennsylvania, also deserves special mention for making much of this chapter possible.

2

Blizzard
of '91

Unknown to most weather experts in the United States, in the year 1891 England suffered a blizzard of monumental proportions. The winter prior to the blizzard had been strange indeed. Europe was frozen from the Baltic to the Adriatic. Every major river of the Continent was blocked, and the port of Antwerp was closed by ice. The lakes of Zurich and Constance were frozen solid. Five inches of snow covered the streets of Naples. Then, on January 20, a sudden thaw occurred, the east wind turned westerly and the temperature went up to 40° F. Serious flooding resulted.

The great frost in England set in toward the end of November 1890. By Christmas the Serpentine in Hyde Park, the Welsh Harp at Hendon and the ponds around Hampstead and Highgate were covered with six inches of ice.

January 1891 remained cold, but February was characterized by fine, genial, springlike weather, so warm and dry that there was a drought in parts of Cornwall and Devon. Spring flowers bloomed and butterflies fluttered about. By the end of the month the *Royal Cornwall Gazette* reported that "agriculturalists have seldom had a fine February for spring

354

sowings and seldom have they got so much grain into the ground by March 2nd, as they have this year."

With the arrival of March, the weather became unsettled but still remained dry. Friday, March 6, dawned fair, but the barometer was falling and it was getting colder. On Saturday much-needed rain fell fairly steadily until evening. By Sunday the cold front had moved south, although a small depression passing across the western counties of England caused frequent rain. During the night the wind changed from west to east, and throughout the day it strengthened and steadied at northeast. It became very cold, but still there was no anticipation of the unprecedented blizzard that was to come.

Monday, March 9, 1891, was fair. According to a contemporary report, "the barometer had been rising slightly, and . . . the day 'promised to be fine' . . . nothing was said about a great fall of snow, accompanied by a hurricane fierce enough to send it down in powder, without even allowing time for the formation of snowflakes."

By evening "the streets were deserted, all the traffic stopped; neither horse nor man could stand against the thick driving snow and the piercing wind." The blizzard of 1891 had arrived.

What made the storm a killer was not the snow itself but the easterly wind of hurricane force that rose at noon, March 9, and raged unabated until dusk the following day, making the snow fall "in blinding sheets . . . fine, powdery snow that . . . gradually piled up its tiny pellets into huge masses of a solid character many feet deep."

The blizzard claimed over two hundred lives, the majority at sea. Sixty-three ships foundered between the Goodwins and the Scilly Isles. Over half a million trees were brought down; many forests and woodlands took generations to recover.

Because of the suddenness of the storm, many farmers were caught with their flocks and herds up on the moors and high fields. In the driving wind it was impossible to round them up.

More than six thousand sheep and lambs were lost in Cornwall and Devon alone.

Incidentally, in 1891 *blizzard* itself was a new term, imported to England from the United States only a month before when a severe snowstorm was reported in Nebraska. The Union Pacific Railroad between Cheyenne, Wyoming, and Sydney, Nebraska, was blocked, and six mail or express trains with more than five hundred passengers were snowed in for two days. Little did anyone dream that the British railways would soon face similar conditions. Strangely enough, on the same March 9 another blizzard swept the states of Ohio, Illinois, Iowa and Minnesota.

It may behoove us all to be more wary than were those Englishmen on days our weather forecast reads as the *London Times* did that Monday, March 9, 1891: "North-easterly winds, moderate; fair generally."

3

Copper King
Thomas W. Lawson

In 1978 I wrote the history of the world's greatest schooner, the seven-masted *Thomas W. Lawson*. I used information from an interview with the last survivor of the *Lawson*, Engineer Edward Longfellow Rowe, shortly before his death. when the book * containing the *Lawson* chapter came out, I was amazed at the number of people anxious to obtain information about Thomas W. Lawson. This chapter explains more of the man himself and the reasoning behind his actions.

Probably there will never be another financial genius to equal Thomas W. Lawson, the so-called Yankee wizard of the stock market. Born in Charlestown, Massachusetts, in 1857, the son of Canadian parents, he spent his childhood in Cambridge. When twelve years old he ran away from school to obtain a position with a Boston investment firm; even at that tender age he was fascinated with the stock market.

Traced down, he was sent back to school. Within a short time he again escaped to Boston and got a job as an errand boy. This time his parents thought the matter over and allowed him to keep his position.

* *Adventures, Blizzards, and Coastal Calamities*, pp. 226–239.

When he reached the age of seventeen, Thomas Lawson
began to show signs of the genius that was to make it possible
for him to amass $53 million by 1900. He studied hard at home
and concentrated on the intricate ways of the financial world,
soon rising from errand boy to clerkship. At the age of eighteen
he was installed as a clerk at the sedate Globe Bank of Boston.
The next year he made a substantial killing in the stock market, then lost the relatively large sum by unfortunate manipulations within twenty-four hours.

Four years later the financial expert of twenty-two was actually established as an operator on "The Street." That same
year he proposed marriage to Jeannie Augusta Goodwillie and
was accepted.

At twenty-four Lawson began to sit at directors' tables in
large corporations. He had made his first million dollars before
reaching the age of thirty. A newspaper of that period states
that Lawson was "a speculative factor of dominant influence,
with a spirit of daring unusual, if not startling, in conservative
Boston, and a surprising capacity for doing the seemingly impossible and the ultra sensational."

George Corliss, an inventive genius, believed Lawson would
have been a great inventor if he had put all his energy into that
particular field. "There is probably not another," said Corliss,
"who possesses to such a marked degree the inventive genius
combined with the thorough businessman; he is one of the
very few who can quickly perceive the necessity for a new
invention, who can make the invention, who can invent
labor-saving machinery to produce the invention, who can
manufacture that machinery, and who can then organize all
these inventions into a business; and not only successfully
conduct that business, but can personally interest all the capital which is necessary to make such a business a success."

When a lad in his teens Lawson invented a substitute for
playing cards, which many held in disrepute. He soon put his
game on the market and it had a long, successful run. Shortly
after he was twenty he wrote, printed and produced a booklet
on the national game of baseball.

During the Harrison-Cleveland presidential campaign of 1888, Lawson compiled and published more than 350,000 copies of his views on the Republican party leaders whom he favored. The Republicans were elected, although Lawson's part in the victory was said by some to have been relatively small.

Lawson's first great financial undertaking was successful reorganization of the Lawson Service Company. His second venture proved to be a disaster in a completely new field. Then he set Westinghouse Electric Company on its feet with several new inventions, making millions for himself as well.

Some time later he started dealings in copper stocks. He sold Butte and Boston stock short all the way down from $16 to 75 cents. Then he participated in reorganizing the company, being so successful that he became known as the Copper King.

As his wealth increased, he acquired a town house in Boston and a summer residence in Cohasset. By 1900 he was living in Winchester, and also occupying a large edifice on the water side of Boston's Beacon Street at Charlesgate East.

His property in Cohasset at the Dr. John Bryant estate consisted of about fifty acres. There he had stables for thirty-two horses and kennels for forty dogs. He also had magnificent gardens; in 1899 alone there were 15,000 cuttings, with 2800 hydrangeas stored in the stable cellar for the winter.

The story of the $30,000 pink carnation is a South Shore epic familiar to many people two or three generations ago. When Mrs. Lawson became an invalid shortly before the turn of the century, Thomas Lawson decided that only a particular type of carnation was worthy to decorate the rooms in which his wife now was forced to spend much of her time. The carnation was grown by Peter Fisher at Ellis in Norwood. Lawson bought the entire output for several years, then decided that it should be offered in competition with other flowers. The carnation was then named the "Mrs. Thomas W. Lawson Pink." It won a silver cup in the competition, the cup offered by Lawson himself.

In January 1899 Lawson competed with a Mr. Higgin-
botham of Chicago for the right to own the pink. He offered
$30,000 for eight thousand plants of the pink, an offer that
was accepted. There has been controversy whether this transaction ever took place. These are Mr. Lawson's own words of
explanation: "I made my offer . . . on the spur of the moment,
because I was touched by the pathos of the picture. In my
mind's eye as I read of the Chicago and New York offers, I saw
great circus posters blazoned with cabbages of a brilliant pink.

"And bye the bye, some of the dealers and growers say that
no flower is worth what they term the extravagant price I have
paid. Sentiment aside, I know a little something about flowers,
and know considerable about carnations, and I will say to my
critics that I can realize more than double the amount I have
invested for my eight thousand plants.

"To anyone who can produce a finer carnation than 'The
Mrs. Thomas W. Lawson' before February 1, I offer the sum of
$5000."

The offer was never accepted, and the carnation, in the
opinion of many Norwood growers, was never exceeded in
beauty.

In 1899 Thomas Lawson added the 182-foot yacht *Dreamer*
to his possessions. It was a splendid vessel, rich and tasteful in
furnishings and decorations.

When he became interested in the America's Cup races, he
became embroiled in a situation that was to divide yachtsmen
all over the world into two camps.

The America's Cup was won at Cowes from an English fleet
on August 22, 1851, by the yacht *America*, which had sailed
across the ocean for the competition. The Cup has been accepted as representing the world's blue ribbon of yachting.
Thomas W. Lawson decided he would like to compete in the
America's Cup Race in the 1901 season. On December 31,
1900, he ordered work to begin on a new sailing craft at the
Atlantic Works in East Boston.

The keel of the new challenger, *Independence*, its base a

bronze casting made at East Braintree, was put in place on January 26, 1901. The vessel was fully in frame on March 6, and by April 25 all her body plates were in position so that burnishing could begin. The challenging craft was launched May 18, 1901, with full ceremony and great pride.

It was a tremendous blow to Lawson when he was informed that the *Independence* would not be allowed to compete for the right to meet the British challenger unless he joined the New York Yacht Club, which in all previous Cup races had represented the United States. The issue was basically whether anyone other than a member of the New York Yacht Club could compete for his country in defense of the America's Cup. After many arguments and bitter words, the New York Yacht Club ruled that "no American other than a member of the New York Yacht Club has the right to take part in the defense of an international cup."

Thomas Lawson was thus not allowed to compete. He issued the following statement: "My refusal, as owner of the American-built and American-named yacht *Independence*, to recognize the right of the custodians of the America's Cup to compel me, or any American, to join any club in order to compete for the honor of defending an American National trophy, led to this extraordinary ruling, which dazed the yachting world."

The sails of the *Independence* had been hoisted for the first time off Boston Light on June 3. On September 3 Lawson realized that the New Yorkers were not going to permit him to compete. With an admirable show of defiance, he lowered her sails for the last time in the same locality off America's oldest lighthouse. Wasting no time, Lawson began the work of breaking up the challenger at once; within a month she was reduced to a conglomerate pile of metal in a Lawley Yard boatshop.

Designer B. B. Crowninshield in 1902 surveyed with great pride Lawson's gigantic seven-masted schooner *Thomas W. Lawson,* launched that year at the Ship and Engine Building

Company in Quincy. Some people believe the magnificent craft was built to sail coal to Manila from this country—the *Thomas W. Lawson* did sail in the coal trade for almost four years. Then she was converted into a tanker, but her total effective service was limited to five years. This steel seven-master only had two rivals as a steel schooner; the six-masted *William L. Douglass* was the only one strictly New England-built.

In 1900 Thomas Lawson had become interested in moving into Scituate. There were several hundred undeveloped acres in the vicinity north and west of what is today called the Lawson Tower. He soon was visiting Scituate weekly, and at times daily, to make his plans for an unsurpassed estate. "Dreamwold," when completed, would make his name famous almost wherever the Massachusetts South Shore was mentioned.

Lawson succeeded far beyond his fondest dreams. Dreamwold was the most perfect example of its type in all eastern America. According to many Scituate residents, the only comparable place anywhere in the United States was Leland Stanford's great establishment across the country in California.

Dreamwold took many years to build, and during its construction the Town of Scituate erected a water tower that interfered with the pleasing panorama from the Lawson home.

Always a person to attempt to overcome difficulties whenever they presented themselves, Lawson at once visited the local water company and obtained permission to enclose the 153-foot tower with a wooden wall and conical roof. Thomas Lawson sent an architect to Europe to find an appropriate design that would be both attractive and historically correct in the tower and turret effect he wanted.

His ultimate choice was an edifice shaped like a Roman tower, with a separate turret at the side of the original water tower. The turret enclosed a spiral staircase of 123 steps that rose to a bell room in which were mounted ten bells. The bell ringer could operate the bells either from a music room on the ground floor or from the bell room itself.

Above the bell deck is a clock room in which a large clock used to strike the hours and play the Angelus automatically at seven in the morning and six at night. Nowadays, beginning in June, the custom of the Angelus is continued throughout the summer.

William Tecumseh Sherman, formerly of the Scituate Water Department, was responsible for the statement that the Lawson Tower, a New England landmark for mariners for years and years, is the most beautiful, most expensive, most photographed water tower in the entire United States.

Carol Miles, a librarian at the new Scituate Public Library, which is situated fairly near the Lawson Tower, told me that in 1907 Lawson wrote a book, *Friday the Thirteenth*. His daughter, Dorothy Lawson McCall, also wrote about her life in the book *The Copper King's Daughter*.

The turning point in Thomas W. Lawson's life probably occurred at the death of his wife, whom he adored. Jeannie Lawson died on August 5, 1906, and Lawson was never the same after that day. He did not noticeably lose his financial touch until several years later. It is said that his clash with the New York interests, involving the loss of millions of dollars, was the first indication that he was no longer the Tom Lawson of the turn of the century. His death on February 8, 1925, came only after he had lost almost his entire fortune.

4

Mary Had
a Little Lamb

Mary had a little lamb;
Its fleece was white as snow;
And everywhere that Mary went
The lamb was sure to go.

About fifteen years ago I took a canoe trip with several carries to a place near Sterling, Massachusetts, where stood the schoolhouse attended by Mary Sawyer, who had a little lamb. That trip aroused my interest in the nursery rhyme.

The story of the lamb was told by Mary herself when she was an elderly lady. I have here quoted from her whenever possible. For well over a century the story of Mary and her lamb has been repeated with various conclusions and opinions. I believe I can gain no further information by postponing the story and referring again to the various authors, locations and inferences.

"Well, if I had known," Mrs. Tyler smilingly said to a visitor at her home, "that the interest I took in my little pet was to have given me so much notoriety, I do not know that I should have carried out the plan I did; but I think I should, for then I was too young to understand about notoriety, though not too young to take an interest in dumb animals, especially when I saw them suffering."

At first Mrs. Tyler, formerly Mary Sawyer, was somewhat loath to talk for publication. But when informed that it was youngsters for whom the story was to be told, she related the tale as follows:

"I was always very fond of animals, and from the time I could toddle out to the barn I was with the dumb beasts not a little of my time. I think there was not a horse, cow, sheep, ox or any other animal upon the place but knew me. It was rare sport for me to pluck clover tops and make the horses follow me about the fields for them. By calling to them, or to the cows, I could get them to come to me, and I always intended to have something for them when they came.

"One cold, bleak March morning I went out to the barn with father. And after the cows had been fed, we went to the sheep pen and found two lambs that had been born in the night. One of them had been forsaken by its mother, and through neglect, cold and lack of food was nearly dead.

"I saw it had still a little life, and I asked to take it into the house. But father said, 'No, it is almost dead anyway, and at the best it may live but a short time.' I couldn't bear to see the poor little thing suffer, so I teased until I got it into the house. Then I worked upon mother's sympathies. At first the little creature could not swallow, and the catnip tea mother made, it could not take for a long time.

"I got the lamb warm by wrapping it in an old garment and holding it in my arms beside the fireplace. All day long I nursed the lamb, and at night it could swallow just a little. Oh, how pleased I was! But even then I wasn't sure it would live, so I sat up all night with it, fearing it wouldn't be warm enough if there was not someone at hand to look out for its comfort. In the morning, much to my girlish delight, it could stand. From that time it improved rapidly. It soon learned to drink milk, and from the time it could walk about, it would follow me anywhere if I only called it.

"My little pet was a fast grower, as symmetrical a sheep as ever walked, and its fleece was of the finest and whitest. I used to take as much care of my lamb as a mother would of a child. I washed it regularly, kept the burdocks picked out of its feet, and combed and trimmed with bright-colored ribbons the wool on its forehead. When that was being done, the lamb would hold down its head, shut its eyes and stand as quiet as could be.

"From the time it could walk until the season came for the sheep to go to pasture, my lamb stayed in the woodshed. It did not take kindly to its own species. When it was in the field, it preferred being with the cows and horses instead of with other sheep.

"The lamb was a ewe and became the mother of three lambs, a single one and twins. Her devotion to her little family was as strong as could be.

"We roamed the fields together, companions and fast friends. I did not have many playmates outside the dumb creatures on the place. There were not many little girls to play with, and I had few dolls. But I used to dress up my lamb in pantalets, and had no end of pleasure in her company. Then I had a little blanket or shawl for her; usually when that was on, she would lie down at my feet, remaining perfectly quiet and seemingly quite contented.

"The day the lamb went to school, I hadn't seen her before starting off. Not wanting to go without seeing her, I called. She recognized my voice, and soon I heard a faint bleating far down the field. More and more distinctly I heard it, and I knew my pet was coming to greet me. My brother Nate said, 'Let's take the lamb to school with us.'

"Childlike, I thought that would be a good idea, and quickly consented. The lamb followed along close behind me. There was a high stone wall to climb, and it was rather hard work to get her over. We got her on top, then clambered over to take her down. She seemed to understand what was expected, and waited quietly for us to take her off the wall.

"When the schoolhouse was reached, the teacher had not arrived, and but few of the scholars were there. Then I began to think what I should do with the lamb while school was in session. I took her down to my seat—we had old-fashioned high boarded-up seats then. Well, I put the lamb under the seat and covered her with her blanket. She lay down as quietly as could be. By and by I went forward to recite, leaving the lamb all right. But in a moment there was a clatter, clatter, clatter on the floor, and I knew it was the pattering of the hoofs of my lamb.

"Oh, how mortified I felt! The teacher was Miss Polly Kimball, who was afterward married to a Mr. Loring and became the mother of Loring, the circulating-library man of Boston. She laughed outright, and of course all the children giggled. It was rare sport for them, but I could see nothing amusing in the situation. I was too ashamed to laugh, or even smile, at the unlooked-for appearance of my pet. I took her outdoors and shut her in a shed until I was ready to go home at noon. Usually I did not go home till evening, for we carried our lunch with us; but I went home at noon that day.

"Visiting the school that morning was a young man by the name of John Roulstone, a nephew of the Reverend Lemuel Capen, who was then settled in Sterling. It was the custom then for students to fit for college with ministers, and for this purpose Mr. Roulstone was studying with his uncle. The young man was very much pleased with the incident of the lamb. The next day he rode across the fields on horseback to the little old schoolhouse and handed me a slip of paper, which had written upon it the three original stanzas of the poem. Since then three additional stanzas have been added to it. Here is the little poem as I received it:

> Mary had a little lamb;
>   Its fleece was white as snow;
> And everywhere that Mary went,
>   The lamb was sure to go.

It followed her to school one day,
    Which was against the rule;
It made the children laugh and play
    To see a lamb at school.

And so the teacher turned it out;
    But still it lingered near,
And waited patiently about
    Till Mary did appear.

"From the fleece sheared from my lamb, mother knit two pairs of very nice stockings, which for years I kept in memory of my pet. But when the ladies were raising money for the preservation of the Old South Church in Boston, I was asked to contribute one pair of these stockings for the benefit of the fund. This I did. The stockings were raveled out, pieces of the yarn being fastened to cards bearing my autograph, and these cards were sold, the whole realizing, I am told, about one hundred dollars. After the first pair were thus sold, the ladies wanted more yarn. They were so anxious to have the other pair raveled out, that I gave them also. Now all I have left in remembrance of my little pet of years long ago is two cards, upon which are pasted scraps of the yarn from which the stockings were knit.

"I have not told you about the death of my playmate. It occurred on a Thanksgiving morning. We were all out in the barn, where the lamb had followed me. It ran right in front of the cows fastened in the stanchions, running along the feed-box. One of the creatures gave its head a toss, then lowered its horns and gored my lamb, which gave an agonizing bleat and came toward me with blood streaming from its side. I took it in my arms, placed its head in my lap and there it bled to death. During its dying moments it would turn its little head and look up into my face in a most appealing manner, as if it would ask if there was not something that I could do for it. It was a sorrowful moment for me when the companion of many of my romps, my playfellow of many a long summer's day, gave up its life. Its place could not be filled in my childish heart."

Mrs. Annie E. Sawyer, Mary's niece and a Somerville schoolteacher, made Mary's declining years peaceful and happy. Mary died December 11, 1889, and is buried in Mount Auburn Cemetery.

Henry S. Sawyer deposes and says:

That he is a relative of Mary E. Tyler, née Sawyer, deceased; that he lives in the same house in which she was born and married, and in which she lived at the time the incidents referred to in the poem of "Mary Had a Little Lamb" occurred. That he attended school at the same schoolhouse where she attended school at the time referred to in the poem, and that he knows the facts as published here to be true.

Henry S. Sawyer

Sworn and subscribed before me, a Notary Public in and for the Commonwealth of Massachusetts, this sixth day of May, A.D. one thousand nine hundred and one.

William A. Wilcox
Notary Public

Several incidents or stories that have developed during the years should be told in this chapter. In 1927 a large gathering of friends met at Llangollen, Wales, to celebrate the eighty-sixth birthday of Mrs. Mary Hughes. She tells us that her father, John Thomas, had a pet lamb named Billy that went to school with Mrs. Hughes, and was removed by the teacher as he had "frisked and gamboled about the room in a way to cause a commotion among the children." In some way Sarah Josepha Hale of Newport, New Hampshire, toured Wales in 1849 and immediately wrote the nursery rhyme that included the following stanza:

And you each gentle animal
In confidence may bind,
And make them follow at your call
If you are always kind.

In December 1931 Mrs. Hughes died in Worthing, England. Senator Horatio Hale, who married Sarah Buel, was staying with the Hughes family at Ty Issa Farm in Vale Llangollen, North Wales. Miss Buel set the lamb incident in verse.

Sarah Josepha Buell Hale, who was just mentioned but with a slightly different spelling of her middle name, was born in 1788 and died in 1879. Without Mrs. Hale, Bunker Hill Monument never would have been finished. In the *Ladies Magazine* she began her active literary life, writing about half of each issue herself. She initiated the Seaman's Aid Society and raised enough money to finish the laggard plans for Bunker Hill Monument, for which work she should receive full credit. Her magazine for women provided a periodical that was "a beacon-light of refined taste, pure morals, and practical wisdom."

Late in life her part in the "Mary Had a Little Lamb" story was told to her son, and she stated to him that she had written the volume, as is explained in *Century* for March 1904. Nevertheless, she does not mention Mary and her lamb specifically, and she titled the book *Poems for Our Children* (it was reprinted in 1916). It is believed that she wrote the last three stanzas of the nursery rhyme.

There are four people in the last twenty years who have written me concerning Mary. Mrs. George Walker writes that the school was moved and is now located on the Wayside Inn estate. Larayne Gallagher says that the school was rebuilt and still has "the same desks, stove, etc. as it had originally." I also heard from Sarah Jacobus, Mary's great-aunt, and from Miss Amy Stone, whose father's relatives recalled Mrs. Tyler selling yarn from the lamb's wool.

5

The *Portland* Legacy

When the first piercing winds of a chill November gale swirl into the harbors and inlets along the New England coast, the thoughts of many mariners turn to the night in 1898 when the *Portland* sailed out of Boston Harbor, never to return.

The *Portland* left Boston on Saturday evening, November 26, 1898, on her regular trip to Maine. As she backed out from India Wharf, it was beginning to snow. Later that evening, during the snowstorm, she was seen by men at Thacher's Island, off Cape Ann, and was also sighted by sailors aboard four different vessels in the vicinity. The storm soon became a hurricane, and the great seas probably disabled the *Portland,* battering and pushing her across Massachusetts Bay toward Cape Cod.

Early the next morning Captain Samuel Fisher of the Race Point Life Saving Station at Cape Cod heard several blasts from a steamer's whistle. Later that morning the weather changed completely and the sun came out for a short time. It was then that District Superintendent Benjamin C. Sparrow noticed two steamers and a fishing schooner off the Cape Cod shore. The fishing schooner was the *Ruth M. Martin,* whose captain, Michael Francis Hogan, was steering his damaged craft under jury rig for Provincetown Harbor, which he reached some hours later.

Around eleven o'clock that morning the storm shut in again and, a short time later, was as severe as before. Evidence points to the foundering of the *Portland* at a point five miles northeast of the High Head Life Saving Station on Cape Cod that Sunday evening at about 9:30. Watches found later on the victims were stopped between half-past nine and ten o'clock. Not one of the 191 persons aboard the ship ever reached shore alive to tell his story of horror. Wreckage began to come up on the great Cape Cod beach as early as seven o'clock that evening; by Monday morning the shore was littered with debris for miles in each direction. Thirty-six bodies were recovered from the wreck of the *Portland*.

On July 1, 1945, Diver Al George, working on a clue I received from Captain Charles L. Carver of Rockland, Maine, located the *Portland* in 144 feet of water 7½ miles out to sea from Race Point Coast Guard Station. He brought up a key from one of the staterooms, plainly marked PORTLAND. His words follow:

"It would seem as though the *Portland* had hit bottom on her beam ends and then through the years had worked her way into the sand until she is buried almost completely. Only the bare hull of the ship seems in position.

"All superstructure evidently has been spread around the ocean bed long ago. The boulders are much higher than my head. I could not tell whether I had found the foremast or the mainmast. Going down on my hands and knees, I could make out the ripples of sand on the bottom of the sea and could see little shells from time to time.

"It was a strange experience standing there alone with the ill-fated *Portland* and probably what remained of the passengers and crew still imprisoned in her sand-covered hull."

Part Five

1900–1940

1

The Chelsea Fire
of 1908

On Palm Sunday, April 12, 1908, a group of us who had been attending Sunday School in Winthrop, Massachusetts, were returning home to various parts of Cottage Hill, where the Winthrop water tower stands today. We all separated at the fire alarm box at the corner of Cottage and Hillside avenues, where I lived.

Suddenly as we were calling out farewells we saw a great yellowish-brown, funnel-shaped cloud of smoke in the air. It crossed diagonally over Cottage Avenue, about 150 yards to the west of us, near the Harrison Gray Otis estate. We ran to the area where the billowing clouds were rushing through the sky at more than a mile a minute.

A moment later, as we looked upward, we were astonished to see a good-size fragment of wood in the midst of the smoking funnel, being carried along toward the sea. I have never forgotten that wooden timber, which must have weighed three or four pounds, so high in the sky above us.

The following story by William J. McClintock is presented here through the kindness of Helen J. McClintock, his daughter.

375

"I am going to take you back to April 12, 1908, in my old home city of Chelsea, Massachusetts. It was Palm Sunday—a beautiful day in the spring, but with a fifty- or sixty-mile gale blowing from the west.

"Many residents were preparing to attend services in their various places of worship, not dreaming that within the next few terrifying hours our city would be reduced to rubble and ruin by one of the greatest fires ever to occur in this country. I was then a resident of Chelsea, and it was my privilege to witness events from the actual start of the fire, through the next twelve hours and for two weeks on relief work. Because of the terrific speed and widespread action of this event, no one person could possibly have seen it all. The following is simply a story of my own experiences and observations during those twelve terrifying hours.

"Shortly after ten on that memorable morning, an alarm of fire sounded. Now, I belonged to that great fraternity called 'sparks,' and we loved to 'follow the engines.' There were several box numbers that did not merit our attention. This was one of them. However, upon looking out my window and seeing a cloud of smoke scudding along with the gale, I decided to go. The fire was about a mile from my house in a small wooden factory which was pretty badly burned. The firemen had responded in good time, and in spite of the gale had 'knocked the fire down.' Some of the apparatus had returned to quarters. One hose company was standing by, 'playing a stream' on the ruins as a precautionary measure. The last engine company was preparing to leave. As there did not seem to be any further excitement, I started for home. Meeting a friend, we walked along together.

"About one hundred yards from the original fire, and to the north, was a comparatively new wooden building. . . . As we rounded the corner and crossed the street, I glanced at this building, noticed a peculiar orange-red glow in the second-story window and called my friend's attention to it. . . .

"At that moment a small wisp of smoke issued from the side

of one of the windows. We decided that the building was on fire. I started for the nearby box to pull in the alarm just as Engine 3 rounded the corner on the way back to its station. I stopped it and told the driver that I thought the building was on fire. . . . Turning to his engineer, he shouted, 'Blow your whistle and call that hose wagon back. . . .'

"The hose wagon returned with only two or three men on it, as many of the call men had gone home by horse and carriage or bicycle. I told the captain of our discovery and they started to throw the hose out into the street. Now, when this hose was picked up at the original fire, it was disconnected, rolled into coils and thrown loosely into the wagon. This all had to be made up into a single line. They were shorthanded so we pitched in to help. . . .

"At this moment Chief Spencer arrived. More smoke was appearing now. He sent a man to pull in the alarm. The hoseman was alone at the pipe, so I gave him a hand. He shouted, 'Play away three,' the old-time call for the water to be turned on. We directed the stream, and when the water hit one of the windows there was a muffled explosion caused by the accumulated gas and hot air. All the windows were blown out. Blazing rags from the factory, borne by the gale, soon filled the air and headed toward home. We could see them landing on roofs, in dry grass, in litter. The Chelsea fire had started on its way.

"Now Chief Spencer had always dreaded the conditions which existed on that day—an outside fire, a strong wind in the right direction and acres of shingled roofs, tinder dry. He immediately sent a messenger to Police Headquarters with the request that they call Boston for help as quickly as possible, for a conflagration threatened.

"Local apparatus and men were now returning . . . and I was soon relieved from my duty on the pipe. It was not long before several streams were working on blazing roofs, dry grass, paper and other litter. As fast as one fire was put out, others started.

"My friends and I started up toward town. There was confusion everywhere. People were beginning to move furniture and household goods out into the street. They were crying, screaming, looking for lost children, relatives and pets. Nobody seemed to know what to do or how to do it. We stopped at numerous houses to warn residents to seek safety. As many of these people did not speak our language, we had difficulty with them. In one such situation, with the roof afire, we had to forcibly drag an elderly couple out of the house. A neighbor took them in charge.

"The call for outside help was now being answered and apparatus was coming from several directions. Fires were so widely scattered that a central command was impossible. Each company arriving on the scene had to select a position best suited for conditions. Some streets were so blocked with household goods that apparatus could not get through.

"With help pouring into the city, it now seemed possible that the fire might be checked. But with the strong gale that was blowing, these hopes gradually faded. The fire was making great jumps and the people were in a state of panic. As street after street burst into flames, it became certain no human force could stop the fire.

"I arrived at the corner of Chestnut and Fourth streets in front of the Universalist Church where the Reverend Mr. R. Perry Bush was standing on the steps with some parishioners. He asked me what the prospects were. I told him they were very bad, and if he had any valuables inside which he would save, he had better get them out and leave in a hurry. I then went up into the steeple to observe the fire from there. When I arrived on the bell deck, the wind was terrific. The last time I saw my hat it was sailing over the rooftops. Flames were leaping in great tongues, smoke was thick, sparks and embers were falling in showers and the heat was intense. It was an ominous sight.

"At this time a Boston fire company stopped at the corner. They had seen a fire on the roof of a house directly behind the church and stopped to take care of it. I had no hat, so I borrowed a fire helmet from the wagon and started to help the firemen. There was a ladder against the house, which we used to take care of the fire. We soon extinguished it.

"Two elderly women stood at the corner opposite the church. I went to them, warned them of the danger and advised them to leave for safety. One of them said she could not go until her husband returned. It seemed that he was out with his wagon helping some friends move goods from the danger zone. He never returned. He was one of the seventeen known victims. . . . The two women were taken to the Cary Avenue Church for safety.

"I went down Fourth Street to Broadway, which was alive with excitement. Businessmen were trying to save goods, fire engines were at work and streams of water were wetting down the buildings. . . . The fire had not taken hold of Broadway but had jumped several blocks and was raging in Division and Hawthorne streets.

"I arrived at Bellingham Square and stood talking to a policeman as we looked up Hawthorne Street, a roaring mass of fire and smoke. As we watched, a flaming board came out of the smoke like an arrow and pierced the roof of a house. I was interested to know how long this house would last so I timed it. In eighteen minutes there was nothing left.

"During this period there suddenly appeared out of that seething mass of smoke and fire a fire engine, horses galloping. It was then that I saw demonstrated the affection old-time drivers had for the animals in their care. The man got down from his seat, went around and hurriedly examined the horses to see if they were injured and burned. He stroked them and hugged them around the neck as much as to say, 'Boys, you saved our lives.'

"From here I went down to the common, now called Union Park, about two blocks away. This was a small area covering a city block, planted with grass and trees and adjacent to the Boston & Maine Railroad, which up to then had served as a barrier to help keep the fire from the northern part of the city. This park, like all other vacant spots, was piled high with household goods; even a few carriages and two or three horses were tied to trees.

"At a time like this one may see human nature in many of its moods: sorrow, terror, fright, panic—even comedy. These manifestations appeared in so many cases that to enumerate them all would be impossible. At one point a Negro preacher stood on a box loudly calling upon the Almighty to stop the fire. Not far away a local character, noted for his Shakespearean endeavors, removed his hat and cried, 'Burn on ye fiery demon, burn on. . . .'

"The streets were full of refugees. Everybody was carrying something—articles of value and some of doubtful worth— apparently the first thing that was snatched up when they were suddenly driven from their homes. I saw one man carrying a parrot cage containing a very frightened cat. Another carried an empty tin pail, and another embraced an armful of framed pictures.

"The fire had now been raging for about two hours. It had jumped to Bellingham Hill and had started to attack the oil tanks in East Boston. Gradually the engines were forced out of the fire zone.

"About this time I returned home. It was not until then that my wife learned that part of Chelsea was in ashes. After a consultation we packed a few necessities and closed our house. Through the kindness of a neighbor, my wife and the baby were driven to her parents' home in Everett until conditions for housekeeping were more favorable. I went up onto Powderhorn Hill with a camera and got a panoramic view of the fire from there.

"I returned home and was about to pick up a lunch when a messenger arrived from my father with a request for the loan of my fire extinguisher. There were a few doughnuts and cookies in the pantry which I tucked in my pocket, and taking the extinguisher, I returned with the messenger. On the way back I laughed out loud when I thought of my puny extinguisher going to face that roaring inferno ahead.

"My father's house was not in direct line of the fire. It was on the north side of the railroad opposite St. Rose Church buildings. When I arrived a squad of soldiers had just finished tearing down the wooden fence along the railroad location. One of my brothers was in the cupola on the stable with a supply of water; another brother with a group of friends and other volunteers was deployed along the railroad bank with water, brooms and other equipment, watching for any stray spark that might cross the very important safety zone. There did not appear to be anything to do at the moment, so I sat down on my pony tank and ate doughnuts and cookies. This was my Sunday supper.

"The fire was now coming up Chestnut Pocket, a dead-end street stopping at the railroad. This was a crucial spot now and the fire-fighting forces, concentrated on the Washington Avenue and Broadway bridges, were making a desperate stand to keep the fire from crossing the railroad. . . . The armory, St. Rose Convent and school were in flames, and St. Rose Church was beginning to burn. Across Broadway the car barns of the Boston Elevated Railway were in flames. Adjacent to them across Gerrish Avenue, Cobb's Livery Stable was being deluged by several streams of water, with the result that only one corner containing the office was burned. The car barns were destroyed. . . .

"My father's house was a busy place. Several of his friends who had been burned out had sought refuge there. . . . My brother, a practicing physician, had an office adjacent to the house, and this too was a scene of activity. A continuous line of policemen, firemen, soldiers and others came in for emergency treatment of burns, cuts and other injuries. All serious cases were sent to the hospital at the Soldiers' Home.

". . . In the latter part of the afternoon the wind abated. The fire in Chelsea was practically under control, although it was still raging among the oil tanks, bridges, pumping station and other buildings in East Boston. The fire-fighting forces now massed along the perimeter of the fire were striving to extinguish the last remaining threat. There was an intermittent screaming of whistles as engines called for more coal. There were thirty-nine engines at work in Chelsea on that day, three of which were trapped by the fire, abandoned and destroyed.

"Seventeen thousand people had been burned out of their homes. Many of them had been taken in by the more fortunate. Others were being sheltered in the few remaining schools and churches. Many were in tents brought in by the Army and the Red Cross. The great majority, however, had left town to be with relatives or friends. Army kitchens were being rushed in to feed the soldiers and refugees.

"In the evening a group of city officials and prominent citizens met in the high school for the purpose of formulating relief plans. This meeting was held by light of kerosene lanterns sent in by a neighboring city's highway department. A committee was organized and started to work immediately. Food and clothing were needed at once, and a call was sent out for these supplies.

"At two o'clock that morning, I stood in a window of the high school and saw the last building burn in Chelsea. I could see two or three illuminated spots in the sky and could hear the distant humming of the engines as the last remaining fires were being extinguished. The continual roar and whistling of the pumps had been gradually diminishing since late afternoon. Much of the apparatus had returned to their home stations. The city was now in darkness and comparative quiet, as if exhausted from its stunning blow.

"Shortly after this my father, who had been selected as chairman of the relief committee, requested that I accompany him to the courthouse on the southerly side of the burned area. We found a military guard posted along the edges of the area, with orders not to allow anyone through. We were trying in vain to explain our mission when Captain Whiting, in charge of that detail, appeared on the scene. As he could vouch for us, we received permission to enter. However, he insisted on a military escort, for the sentries had received orders to shoot, if necessary, anyone ignoring the order to stay away.

"We started out on what proved to be a weird trip. There was no light except that shed by the kerosene lantern that I bore. The pavement, mostly of granite blocks, was still uncomfortably hot in places, littered with rubble and other noncombustible material and a tangle of wires of all sizes. My father was a former city engineer, and he and I had roamed the streets for thirty years. But we were lost in that utter desolation. We finally reached the courthouse. Our errand completed, we started the return trip over the same route. We were challenged at the sentry line, but our escort finally convinced the sentry that everything was in order and we continued the trip. The remains of numerous coal piles in cellar holes were burning, some of the gas pipes in the cellars were still emitting flames and there was a faint sound of water from broken pipes. The gas from the burning coal and the dust was choking in that awesome stillness. As we approached the ruins of City Hall, we were again challenged by two men in uniform. One of them proved to be Captain Whiting, who quickly let us through so that we could return home.

"The call for food and clothing had been spontaneously answered, and these necessities were now coming into the high school. Bread lines were formed and people waited patiently in line for this welcome commodity. I saw one bread line nearly half a mile long. A corps of volunteers were kept busy unpacking, sorting and dispensing these goods.

"A stupendous task now faced the city and public utilities. The fire had caused complete destruction. Hundreds of water and gas service pipes had to be shut off, sewer connections attended to, streets cleared, fire and police signal systems restored, and dangerous walls torn down. The telephone, electric and street railway companies lost all their wires, poles, meters and telephones. Heat was so intense that wooden poles were burned two feet down into the ground. Early Monday morning crews of workers arrived to start this task. Many of them came from distant points. A military guard was surrounding the area with sentries, patrolling within that line to keep all unauthorized persons out in order that the work would not be impeded. Chelsea had started on the road to recovery.

"I'm going to give a few statistics in order to show the enormous destruction wrought by this disaster. There were 490 acres burned over, more than three thousand shade trees were destroyed and most of the granite curbing in the city was ruined, seven hundred business and professional men were burned out and two bridges were destroyed. Seventeen persons lost their lives, the majority of these being trapped by the fire. Among the public and other buildings destroyed were the City Hall, the Board of Health, eight schools, thirteen churches, Frost General Hospital, two fire stations, the public library, armory, Masonic Temple, Post Office, Y.M.C.A., three bank buildings and four newspaper plants. The insurance losses paid amounted to approximately $8,840,000."

The following excerpts are from a letter written by Paul McClintock, son of the first writer.

"At 10:30 A.M. the fire alarm rang, and Frank [his chum] and I went down to see the fire. Our way led us along the B & M R.R. track toward Everett. The wind blew a gale, and looking ahead was almost impossible, on account of things flying in the air. We walked three fourths of a mile up to the fire.

"It was not a very exciting fire, for the firemen kept the flames inside, and so in about twenty minutes we walked around to the other side to see if anything was doing there. We had been standing directly to windward before, and the smoke hid everything from sight to leeward. But when we reached the tracks again to one side, we were surprised to see a big three-story rag shop, six hundred feet down the line, ablaze all over, and in a minute one wall had burned through and fallen in.

"Five hundred feet from this new fire, and about the same distance from the original one, another and much larger rag shop was covered with flames, and things began to look interesting.

"The continual calls on the fire alarm finally brought engines from Boston (about nineteen), Malden, Melrose, Saugus, Somerville, Medford, Lynn and possibly other places.

"I ran back home to get a camera, but mine was out at Tufts, Sam's was not to be found and there was only one in the whole house—the little Brownie of Sam's that had a film in it two years old I guess. I was mad at that, for the smoke was making a beautiful sight, and the flames could be plainly seen from our house. However, I took what I had to and ran back to the Boston Blacking Company's plant (where it started) and passed through the smoke to the other side of the fire from the house.

"By that time there were about eighteen buildings going (that I was aware of). The wind was carrying huge sparks through the air, spreading the fire almost as fast as one could walk. I walked toward Chelsea Square as far as Fourth Street, where I turned up and walked up Everett Avenue toward the fire again.

"Very soon I passed the fire line and struck a dense stream of smoke so black that I had to use my handkerchief (which was black with pitch) to breathe with, and trust to my knowledge of the street and my sense of direction to tell where I was. After I once got in I was not so sure about getting out, but finally I did and stood in the shelter for a moment to cool off and get some fresh air. My clothes were so hot I thought they were on fire. The smoke hid everything so I could take no pictures, and I started for home again to leave my camera and put on old clothes so I could get into the game and be of some help.

"From each house and tenement articles of cheap furniture

were being carried out and piled on the sidewalk, where, if it belonged to someone fortunate to have a horse at his disposal, it was carted away, or else left to be burned. As I passed by Union Square I saw it being filled with all kinds of furniture, none of which was destined to be saved.

"At home I went up to the billiard room (third floor) where I took in the situation. The course of the nearer edge of the fire seemed directed toward Bellingham Square, or slightly this side of it. But even though we seemed to be out of danger, a change of five degrees in the wind would have settled our fate without argument.

"I kept one eye on the progress of the fire. It had crept up Chestnut Street and up Broadway, settling on the large Catholic Church one hundred feet from us. The church was a brick edifice with a slate roof, as was the convent and the school next to it. I had taken up my post on the stable roof and had a large rope made fast to the cupola, by which I could cover the whole roof. The house and stable are both slate-roofed, but the wooden cupola and wooden walls were excellent places for a fire to get a foothold.

"I could look down on the railroad, and I saw a train of flatcars being filled with all kinds of articles. Lying across two rails was a piano with the legs unscrewed. I learned later that almost all this assortment belonged to the Blisses.

"The church kept blazing up until my position was too warm for comfort. The woodwork was almost unbearably hot, and the wind, the strongest I ever experienced, made it hard to wet the hot woodwork, because it blew the water right out of the saucepan I was using. Just then I looked toward Everett and saw that the fire had crossed the tracks and all indications pointed toward our being driven out in a short space of time.

"I looked on the other side, and there was the nozzle of a hose pointing at me. I thought it was time for me to vacate, so I climbed down. The yard was full of people. I followed up the hose to see where it came from. It led toward an engine on the corner of Lawrence Street and Clark Avenue, but stopped fifty feet short because of scarcity of hose.

"I went back to the house, where I learned that Bliss's house was gone. None of us expected to remain long where we were, but soon the church began to burn out, and in twenty minutes we were assured that all danger was past. (I then thought it was about one o'clock, but on looking at the clock saw it was five-thirty.)

"Had the fire in Fairfield's place, near Spruce Street on this side of the railroad, not been controlled, probably twice as many houses, including our own, would have gone. But a hard fight was put up there, and a successful one. We did escape, but it was a mighty close call. I thought they might dynamite our house to save the section this side of the track. I did, in fact, give the people warning, at one time, that they would have five minutes to get out with what they wanted.

"Around six o'clock we made about fifty sandwiches and over a gallon of coffee for the firemen and soldiers, who had arrived early at the scene of the fire. Most of us had eaten nothing since eight-thirty, but excitement killed our appetites.

"That night I learned that Raymond Bliss had saved almost all of his furniture. A train of flatcars backed from Revere to where it could be loaded with things to be saved, but strangely enough the Blisses were about the only ones to profit by it. There was a small army of people in the Bliss house ready to help, and Raymond, by judicious management, got them to take almost everything out that he wanted, without breaking anything to speak of. The train was pulled to Revere, where Raymond and I shortly went with a wagon and removed the furniture to our stable. We got two double-horse loads that night, and got in bed by two. At six we were up and made another load. The amount they saved in so short a time was wonderful."

2

Hermit Mason Walton

More than two thirds of a century ago a man by the name of Mason Walton was slowly wearing away because of his unsuccessful bouts with civilization. Deciding to do something about it, he eventually moved from his home in Boston to Cape Ann.

The world has not heard much about Mason Walton, although in my opinion his writing puts him in a class with Henry David Thoreau and John Burroughs. Some of his thoughts, penned in 1903, follow.

"Eighteen years ago I was in sore straits. Ill health had reduced my flesh until I resembled the living skeleton of a dime show. I realized that a few months more of city life would take me beyond the living stage, and that the world would have no further use for me except to adorn some scientific laboratory.

"A diagnosis of my case would read as follows: Dyspepsia, aggravated, medicine could give but slight relief. Catarrh, malignant, persistent. A douche was necessary every morning to relieve the severe facial pain. A cough that had worried me by day and by night, and thrived on all kinds of cough medicine. Also my lungs were sore and the palms of my hands were hot and dry. I thought that I was fading away with consumption, but the doctors said my lungs were sound. I was advised to go into the woods and try life in a pine grove. As there was no money for the doctors in this advice, I looked upon it as kind and disinterested, but my mind ran in another direction.

"When I was young and full of notions, the idea entered my head that I should like a change from fresh to salt water. It resulted in a two months' trip on a fishing schooner. During the trip I had been free from seasickness, and had gained flesh rapidly. The memory of that sea voyage haunted me, now that I had become sick and discouraged. It seemed to me that a few weeks on salt water would save my life.

"With high hopes I boarded the little steamer that plied between Boston and Gloucester. I thought it would be an easy matter to secure board on one of the many vessels that made short trips after mackerel. For three days I haunted the wharves in vain. The 'skippers,' one and all, gave the same reason for refusing my offers. 'We are going after fish,' said they, 'and cannot be bothered with a sick man.' At last one 'skipper' discouraged me completely. He said to me, 'I once took a sick man on board, and because we did not strike fish, the fishermen called the passenger a Jonah, and made his life miserable. Three days after we returned he died, and I swore then that I never would take a sick man to sea.' This 'skipper's' story, and my fruitless efforts, caused me to abandon the salt water cure. I turned now to the hills around Gloucester. In the end I selected Bond's Hill, because it was surrounded by pine groves.

"I found the hill covered with blueberry and huckleberry bushes, the latter loaded with fruit. On the brow of the hill the soil had been washed away, leaving great masses of bed rock (granite) towering above the cottages that clung to the base of the cliff. On the extreme brow of the hill I found a spot where the soil had gathered and maintained a grass plot. Here I pitched my little tent. Here I lived from August to December. I called the spot the Eyrie, because it reminded me of the regions inhabited by eagles. A visit to the spot will disclose the fitness of the name."

On this spot eighteen years of hermit life began for Mason Walton. At first he made it a practice to go to town every day for one meal, bringing back supplies enough to last until another day. But he soon found the huckleberries, crab apples and occasional grapes good wholesome food that did not aggravate his chronic dyspepsia.

Two weeks of outdoor life brought a little more color to Walton's cheeks and made him feel like a new man. About this time he awoke one morning to realize that he had not coughed during the night. The cough that had harassed him night and day for two years left then and there, never to return. Before long his other complaints were also gone.

From his Eyrie, Walton looked out over the panorama, entranced with the ebb and flow of the tide through the marshes, the view of the outer harbor with its variety of fishing craft, and the city of Gloucester sprawling out across the way to Magnolia and Manchester. There, too, was Dogtown Common,* a boulder-covered region of pasture land choked by huckleberry and blueberry bushes.

Sunsets seen from the Eyrie were often beautiful beyond description. Whenever a massive bank of clouds hung above the western horizon, the setting sun illuminated the city from Riverdale to Eastern Point, and every window in sight glowed like burnished gold. Such glorious moments contributed a sense of well-being that Walton had never known before.

Well satisfied with his new way of life at Cape Ann, Walton constructed a substantial hut in a clearing. One April morning he found a flock of fox sparrows in the dooryard. It is more than unusual that for the three years following they reappeared on the same day of the month. On April 2, 1887, the

* See my 1978 book *Adventures, Blizzards, and Coastal Calamities,* p. 240.

hermit awoke early to find three feet of snow in the dooryard, and he was obliged to shovel the snow away in order to feed his good friends the sparrows on bare ground.

Mason Walton describes the bird as follows:

"The fox-sparrow is two-thirds as large as a robin, and may be classed with the beautiful birds both in form and coloration. The sexes are alike. The color above is a rich rusty red, deepest and brightest on the wings, tail, and rump. The head, neck, and shoulders are a dark ash color, more or less streaked with rusty red. Below the groundwork is snow-white, also thickly spotted with rust red. It could be called a wood-thrush by a careless observer. These birds are migrants with us, and pass through the State to their breeding grounds in April, to return in October. It is usually six weeks from the time the first flock appears before the loiterers are all gone. The flock that called on me was a very large one, numbering over a hundred birds. Mornings they made the woods ring with their delightful music."

With the coming of spring, Walton found that he was a trespasser on the nesting grounds of many woodland birds. Robins, thrushes, towhee-buntings, catbirds and numerous warblers nested around his cabin.

By this time Mason Walton had settled down to hermit life in earnest. He had tried the experiment of "Nature versus Medicine," and Nature had triumphed. With good health, with strange birds and flowers to study and identify, Walton decided he was content to spend a portion of his "rescued life" in Nature's company.

When younger, Walton had caught and caged many small animals such as deer mice, woodchucks, flying squirrels, stouts, mink and red and gray squirrels. His first captive in the cabin area was an artful old coon Walton named Satan. He was caught in a steel trap, the jaws of which had been wound with cloth to protect the animal's foot.

Satan's den was under a boulder near the cabin. Walton set the trap at the mouth of the den and covered it with leaves.

The next morning the trap, with clog attached, was missing, but Walton easily followed the raccoon's trail in the dead leaves. All the time he was in plain sight of the coon, who remained quiet until he realized that he was discovered, then made frantic efforts to escape. The clog, however, had anchored him securely to some witch hazel shrubs. The animal was full of fight, and Walton had to look out for his wicked teeth and vicious claws. The hermit brought along a stout piece of canvas, which he wrapped around the raccoon, trap and all, thus securing the animal's teeth and claws. Then he carried the raccoon to the cabin.

It took Walton two hours to get a strap on the raccoon's neck. The struggle was a desperate one, and without the canvas it would have been a victory for the raccoon. With the strap securely fastened and a dog chain attached, the trap was removed from the animal's foot and he was staked out near the cabin. For two weeks he tried night and day to free himself from collar and chain, then suddenly appeared contented.

As Walton says, "Instinct plays no part in coon lore. A coon can reason as well as the average human being. My captive proved to be as artful and wicked as Beelzebub himself."

Whenever unwatched, Satan would be up to all sorts of mischief. When caught red-handed, he would put on a look of innocence that made his master laugh. By the end of the first month he had learned about the hermit's way of life. If Walton went into the woods with his gun, on his return Satan would tear around in his cage, anxious for the squirrel he had not seen but was sure to get. When Walton went away without the gun, the raccoon paid no attention to his return. In this the animal was not guided by scent, for sometimes the wind would not be right. Without doubt he connected the gun and the squirrel in his mind, and perhaps he knew more about a gun than the hermit realized.

Satan did not take kindly to confinement, although his cage was under a small pine tree. When Walton was at the cabin he chained Satan to a tree and let him run outside. However, the hermit put him into the cage every day before going to the city for his mail. The raccoon resented this and would run up the pine tree when he saw his master lock the cabin door. One day Walton pulled him down and whipped him while the animal lay prone on the ground, his eyes covered. The hermit also took away his food and water. The raccoon never forgot the lesson. After that, whenever he saw Walton lock up, he would sneak into his cage, fearful that if found outside he would be whipped and starved. According to Walton, Satan preferred food in the following order: insects, eggs, birds or poultry, frogs, nuts, red squirrel, rabbit, gray squirrel and fish. This undoubtedly was the bill of fare of his wild state. He would not touch green corn or milk until Walton had crushed the former into his mouth and had dipped his nose into the latter. After this introduction, Satan would leave everything for the taste of milk.

One morning Hermit Walton opened up his cabin door to discover that a winter storm had left at least two inches of snow. A veritable mass of fox tracks surrounded a choice piece of meat he had nailed just too high to the trunk of a large pine tree. The tracks led away from the tree in an unusual trail: only three feet. Walton had seen these particular tracks before, for the animal who made them was no stranger to the area. Months before the hermit had appropriately named the fox Triplefoot.

After a short breakfast the hermit started on Triplefoot's trail. He followed the tracks all the way to a location where there were two ruined cellars and an ancient cultivated orchard. Triplefoot evidently had been foraging under some barberry bushes, for a drop or two of blood indicated she had caught and eaten a field mouse.

At that moment, far in the distance, the sound of two hounds could be heard in the area known as Solomon's Orchard. From their tone Walton knew that they were hot on the trail of the fox. Triplefoot's tracks now led the hermit across Magnolia Avenue, below the lily pond, along the ridges to

Mount Ann and then down to Coffin's Beach. There the sand dunes and the melted snow caused him to lose the trail. He noticed that the hounds also had been baffled at that point.

Hermit Walton realized that he probably should give up the effort, for there was not a track in sight in the shifting white sand or skirt of the woods near where Triplefoot's trail had left the beach. But he decided to backtrack toward the fox's den. Within ten minutes he located the trail again and found that the fox had crossed Magnolia Swamp south of Solomon's Orchard, then followed the ridges to the old quarry area.

Triplefoot's den was actually less than an eight-minute walk from the hermit's cabin. It was dark when Walton first located the den, and it reminded him for all the world of the den the great general Israel Putnam had entered when he pulled out the legendary wolf at extreme danger to his own life.*

One season Triplefoot reared a family. In April she stored two hens and a grouse in the den so that she would not have to hunt when her cubs were born. Later, when the cubs came out to play, the hermit spent hours watching them with a telescope. Once one of the three cubs suddenly appeared, saw Walton and coolly looked him over. Then he vanished, only to appear a moment later with another cub. Not over six feet away, they appeared fat and stocky "as two young pigs."

That fall Triplefoot's cubs were killed by hunters, leaving her childless. Her mate probably had been shot as well, for she did not rear a family the next year.

One item always puzzled Walton: the fact that Triplefoot did not go after poultry every day. Walton finally decided the fox reasoned that a wholesale slaughter of fowl would attract attention, and the irate farmers might make it a business to hunt for the fox den.

Walton and Triplefoot often met while tramping in the woods, and the fox soon understood that the hermit did not covet her glossy pelt. She frequently led pursuing hounds

* I cover the episode in my *Legends* volume, page 93.

through his cabin yard, always fooling them completely. Nevertheless, the hounds had a good scent, and matters finally became dangerous.

The end of Triplefoot's career came when a group of hounds evidently united in the chase after her, bringing her within reach of the gun of a hunter often seen by Hermit Walton. Triplefoot was hit by a bullet near Magnolia Swamp. Walton followed her into the swamp, where he found her under a boulder slowly dying from her wound and from exhaustion. Walton buried the body of his friend, glad that her beautiful robe and her mutilated body would not be separated in death.

Without question, Mason A. Walton, author of many articles in the famous *Youth's Companion, Forest and Stream* and the delightful 304-page book *A Hermit's Wild Friends*, was a great woodsman. During his eighteen years of real "hermiting," he put on paper many discoveries that should not be forgotten. He made for himself a permanent place among the world's outstanding naturalists.

3

Tragedy
of the *Eastland*

At a few minutes before 7:30 A.M. on the fateful morning of
Saturday, July 24, 1915, the excursion steamer *Eastland*, with
more than 2000 men, women and children aboard, overturned
while tied to the dock at Clark and South Water streets in
Chicago. Within minutes 812 people were dead; 23 more died
of their injuries shortly afterward. Twenty-two families were
totally wiped out. It was the worst disaster in terms of loss of
life in Great Lakes history.

It had all begun as a festive occasion, the fifth annual picnic
and excursion boat trip to Michigan City, Indiana, for employees of the Western Electric Company. It was sponsored by the
Hawthorne Club, an educational and recreational organization
for the workers. A contract had been signed between the
chairman of the picnic committee, Charles J. Malmros, and
the Indiana Transportation Company for five lake passenger
steamers to accommodate the expected crowd.

The club indeed intended to have a crowd, for the contract
provided for a substantial rebate to the organization on a sliding scale, the amount of rebate rising with the number of
tickets sold at seventy-five cents each. With 9000 employees
as potential purchasers, the club was in a position to add a

great deal of money to its treasury, and efforts to sell tickets were more than enthusiastic. In fact, after the disaster more than one tale was told of coercion to buy tickets under threat of job loss. Peter Frisina, after identifying the body of his nineteen-year-old wife, cried out, "Oh, if I hadn't taken tickets, even if it cost me my job!" The father of drowned Agnes Kasperski later stated, "Agnes's fear of the water had been conquered by her fear of losing her job."

Many others, of course, were eagerly looking forward to the outing. Thus on the morning of July 24 thousands of families from Chicago and the suburbs of Cicero and Hawthorne were heading to the Chicago River near the Clark Street bridge, where the five steamers were moored. Departure times were staggered as follows: *Eastland,* 7:30 A.M.; *Theodore Roosevelt,* 8 A.M.; *Petoskey,* 8:30 A.M.; *Racine,* 10 A.M.; and *Rochester,* 2:30 P.M.

The *Eastland* * was the craft on which most of the excursionists wished to travel, for it was claimed she had a speed of over thirty miles an hour, making her the fastest ship on the lakes. A trip on the *Eastland,* leaving the earliest and going the fastest, meant the longest time at the picnic—or so those who boarded her thought.

Not one of the excited crowd knew that sailors on the Great Lakes were calling the *Eastland* a "cranky ship." On several occasions her instability had been demonstrated when she listed badly to port. On July 17, 1904, with 2142 passengers sailing from South Haven to Chicago, those aboard were ordered to shift to the starboard side to correct her imbalance. For some reason, perhaps fear, they refused to move until the fire hose was turned on them. This method proved effective.

---

* As furnished by the *United States Shipping List of Merchants for 1906,* the *Eastland* had the official number 200031 and was steamship-rigged. She had been built in 1903 at Port Huron, Michigan, with a horsepower of 3000. Gross tonnage was 1961, with a net tonnage of 1218. Her length was 265 feet; breadth, 38.2; depth 19.5. Her crew numbered seventy four plus the captain. The *Eastland,* with Chicago as her home port, was in service to carry passengers.

Ignorant of these facts, Western Electric employees happily jostled each other in their efforts to get on board the doomed ship.

A short time before seven o'clock several of the earliest arrivals noticed a slight list to port. Observing this list himself, Chief Engineer Joseph M. Erickson decided to open the starboard ballast tank and seacock. Unfortunately not only was the list corrected, but soon the vessel began a list toward starboard. Helping Erickson at this time was John Elbert, a survivor of the *Titanic*. The listing condition continued, changing several times from side to side. At 7:16 there was a slight list to port; two minutes later the *Eastland* heeled in the opposite direction, then listed slightly to port again; at 7:23 she listed sharply to port. Erickson now sent men to the main deck to tell the passengers to go to starboard, but only a few obeyed.

Captain Harry Pedersen was alarmed. Realizing the potential for disaster because of the listing, he shouted down from the starboard bridge to open the inside doors and let the people back onto the pier. Unfortunately he was a few seconds too late, for the *Eastland* began her ominous fatal swing to port. Tons of water poured through the open ports and gangway doors. A weird mass of popcorn machines, candy boxes, entire refreshment stands, picnic baskets, crushed and leaking lemonade barrels, ship bulkheads and furniture, together with men, women and children, slid into the portside pilings as the *Eastland* rolled over on her side on the bottom of the river. Less than eight feet of her starboard side remained above water, giving the *Eastland* the look of a massive whale.

One man who survived, Theodore Soderstrom, later described the scene on board the *Eastland* at the terrible moment the vessel went over: "The passengers were crowded on the outer rail from ten to thirty deep in places. I noticed the boat beginning to career slightly, but at first it gave me no uneasiness. Then just before we pulled out, several hundred passengers who had been saying good-bye to persons on the dock came over to the outer [port] rail. Almost instantly the boat lurched drunkenly, righted itself, then pitched once more.

"By this time passengers knew there was something wrong. But it all happened so quickly that no one knew just what to do. For a third time the boat lurched, this time slowly, and there were screams as everyone tried to get to the side of the vessel next to the dock. Many were beaten down to the deck unconscious in this mad rush. Probably a dozen persons—it might have been more—jumped into the water. But they were crushed under the side of the boat before they had a chance to swim away, for after the boat got part way over, it seemed to drop on its side like a stone."

Traveling over the Clark Street bridge on his way home from market, Mike Javanco, his wagon loaded with vegetables, could not believe what he saw. Knowing nothing about ships, he instinctively realized something was terribly wrong. Leaning far over the bridge, he called to the crowd of young men on the bow to get off the boat. They jeered at his accent, and chose death. Javanco jumped from his wagon, ran across the bridge and soon was on the dock helping to rescue scores of passengers.

A few hundred people, most of them from the upper deck, managed to climb over the starboard rail to find relative safety on the exposed side of the craft. But the water around the steamer was teeming with men, women and children desperately struggling for their lives.

Seeing what was happening, the lineman on the tug *Kenosha* had cut the towline between the two craft. The tug's captain realized that the powerful propeller of his craft would cause terrible injury to the hundreds of people thrashing in the water. He backed the *Kenosha* against the now horizontal bow of the *Eastland,* forming a bridge by which many of the passengers reached shore.

After the initial shock of seeing the *Eastland* roll over, witnesses on shore quickly began throwing all available objects that would float into the water. Every craft on the river raced to the scene. Passengers on the *Theodore Roosevelt* threw the lifesavers from their vessel to the people in the water.

N. W. LeVally, manager of the Oxweld Acetylene Company, rushed his men to the exposed side of the *Eastland,* where they could hear the cries of trapped passengers who were hammering for release from what had become an underwater prison. To the amazement of torchman J. H. Rista, he was ordered by Captain Pedersen to stop his work of cutting an escape hole. Rista refused to obey him, and eventually forty people were pulled from certain death through that very hole. A few more passengers were taken out alive through other holes torched in the hull.

Not a single member of the crew was lost, many of them having clambered over the rail and jumped to the dock before the final list. But for 835 passengers, this was their last excursion.

Free funeral service was provided for families left destitute, and plans were completed for community funeral services in the various churches of Cicero and neighboring suburbs. So many funeral processions passed through the streets of Cicero on the Wednesday following the disaster that the day has since been known as Black Wednesday.

Victor A. Olander, secretary of the Lake Seamen's Union, aroused governmental and public outrage with his statement that many other ships on the lakes were as dangerous as the *Eastland* because of faulty construction. He held that the *Eastland* was not properly designed, and that the water ballast system was not the main fault. He charged that United States inspectors under Captain Charles H. Westcott of Detroit, chief of the lake district, had played into the hands of ship owners at the expense of sailors and passengers. He said this was shown by the fact that thirty-one ships, passed by the inspectors, had sunk in the Great Lakes since 1905, several of them taking all on board to their deaths.

The announcement by detectives from the State Attorney's office that they had seized tickets taken from the passengers boarding the *Eastland* further increased public outrage. They asserted that these tickets numbered 2550 and did not account for children, musicians and the seventy-two crew members. They estimated that the total number of persons aboard the steamer might have been 2800 or more. The lessees of the ship asserted that 2408 passenger tickets had been collected.

According to records, the temporary inspection certificate issued June 4, 1913, by U.S. inspectors at Cleveland allowed the *Eastland* to carry 2000 passengers. A later temporary certification, dated June 15, 1915, permitted the craft to carry 2253. But a third certificate, issued only twenty-two days before the disaster, granted permission for the *Eastland* to carry 2570 passengers.

State Attorney Hoyne seized correspondence between officers of the Hawthorne Club and the Indiana Transportation Company, and the issue of overcrowding the boat was added to a growing list of questions about the disaster. Hoyne declared that Captain Pedersen of the *Eastland* told him that federal sanction for increasing the carrying capacity without change in construction was "arranged," and that Pedersen was told to go to Grand Haven, Michigan, and get the certificate.

When actual rescue operations had ceased and the dead were still being identified, the coroner's jury was assembled to find out what had happened and how. The inquiry, under Cook County Coroner Peter Hoffman, took six full days.*

Victim Kate Austin was chosen as typical of the 835 who perished as a result of the *Eastland* disaster. The evidence given applied to all lives lost.

The inquest began on Tuesday, July 24, 1915, in Room 811 of the County Building in Chicago. Starting the proceedings, the coroner spoke slowly and clearly:

"Gentlemen, I shall ask you to keep as quiet as possible during the hearing and during this investigation, in order that

---

* The *Transcript of Testimony* of Coroner Hoffman's investigation, an impressive booklet of 156 pages, is available today at the Boston Athenaeum.

the jurors and all interested may hear the evidence given here. I shall ask the Chief of Police and the Sheriff to keep absolute order. I don't want anybody around the aisles unless they can be seated, and unless they are absolutely interested they will have to leave the room, outside of the Police and Sheriff. It is hot in this room and close, and absolute order will be necessary so the jurors may hear the testimony."

The coroner went on to explain that the State of Illinois was represented by Mr. Hoyne and Mr. Sullivan, plus several assistants. He also explained that the State Attorney was cooperating with the coroner, and that it was his privilege to question the witnesses "because I may not be able to bring out the full facts."

Congressman A. J. Sabath now told the coroner that "at a meeting of Bohemian-American citizens of the City of Chicago, a nationality which has suffered a great deal in this disaster, I have been requested by the General Committee to represent it in any way possible."

The first witness was R. J. Moore, a passenger on the *Eastland*. When he arrived at the *Eastland* at about seven o'clock that July morning and started down the stairs to board the boat, "there was a long line, five or six abreast." His testimony continued as follows: "As I was going along the side of the boat, I saw water coming out of there; I saw it by the ton—I remarked to a gentleman, they were taking out a lot of ballast; he said, 'It isn't ballast, it is exhaust steam.'

"I thought it was throwing out a lot of steam. It was about 7:10, and the first indication of the boat listing was about eight or nine minutes before it went down, when the refrigerator in the bar was thrown over with all the bottles and made a terrific crash. I was on the second floor and could see the bottles on the floor from that end. The boat started to list north, and if they were given a signal at that time, I think most of the people could have gotten off the boat.

"From that time on, the boat kept listing. I tried to get on the south side; there were a little batch of ladies and children, and

I took a chance and went with the crowd. I went through the staircase, and just as I struck the floor, the water struck me. I got up in some part of the boat and worked my way through—I suppose about the width of this umbrella and maybe fourteen feet long; it was filled with women and children. They were all saved. I don't know if any of them are here or not.

"I was pulled out second to last by one of the firemen. I think he belonged to a tugboat. I hung on down in there for thirty-five minutes before I was taken out. When I came out, I wandered away; my clothes were all torn and I was dazed."

The question was now asked how long it was from the time the boat began to list to the port, or north side, up to the time it toppled over. Mr. Moore answered that it was from eight to ten minutes, and the boat was "going all the time." Mr. Moore was asked to estimate how many people were on the upper deck; he answered "about 800 or 900 people." When asked about children on board, he stated that there were "a lot of boys and girls there from the age of eight up to fifteen, running around, having a good time, trying to locate themselves," and he agreed with the coroner that there were many children below the age of five.

Another witness was Algernon Richey, a solicitor. At the time of the disaster he stood with the bridge tender of the railroad company at the north end of the Clark Street bridge from seven o'clock until she went over. "I saw her start to list. We commented upon it in every way, commented upon it until it got to the top of the middle deck doors. She got to the top of that and commenced to list more, fast, and the crowd on the boat deck, the hurricane deck, started to the south; they ran to the south rail, starboard side. They ran over and it seemed their feet—probably the boat went faster; she went down quick after that. It seemed as if she were overbalanced at the time.

"The bridge tender and I ran down on the pier on the bridge. We threw in everything we could find that was loose. We went down on the dock on the south side of the river; the ship chandlers there threw out coil after coil of rope. We made them fast and threw them into the river, and pulled out three, four and five at a time. I am a good swimmer myself, even with one hand, but I didn't dare go into the water."

Adam F. Weckler was harbor master of Chicago. His duties included wharves, bridges, moving of vessels and everything to do with the harbor and river. He had arrived at the Clark Street bridge at 7:10. According to Weckler's testimony, "The boat at that time was listed to port, just coming over, about a five- to six-degree list. I stood down on the dock and called to Captain Pedersen on the bridge, and I asked him to put in his water ballast and trim her up. He said he was trimming all the time. In the meantime he had given the 'stand-by' order and cast off the stern line. The dockman ran forward to see what line he wanted thrown off. I would not let him throw off the line. I told Captain Pedersen to trim her up. He held up his hand to state that he was trimming as fast as he could. He stepped out to the outside of the bridge. The boat kept turning, and he shouted to the people to get off the best way they could, and the boat, I should say, around in eight or ten minutes' time, laid right on the side."

Weckler was asked for his opinion, as a harbor master with seventeen years' experience in navigation and boat building, what he believed caused the boat to go over. He responded, "I don't think there was any water in their tanks, to start with."

Congressman Sabath then asked him, "Is it your opinion, if the Government limited the capacity of the boat to 1200 instead of 2500, that the accident would not have happened under the circumstances that it happened?"

Weckler answered, "Well, I do not think it would."

Harbor Master Weckler was then asked how he knew that the *Eastland* did not carry water. He replied, "On account of the way she trimmed, she is always lunging on the side, she is never ready until the moment she ships off, she always gives a lunge according to the side she is tied, but I know the boat so well, I never was much—I know she doesn't carry water, that is why I have been trying to find out why she did not carry water, the only satisfaction that I ever got was they did not need any water."

Joseph R. Lynn, assistant harbor master, stated that on the day of the accident when he was at the *Eastland*'s midship gangway, "it appeared to me she had considerable of a side list, more so than I had seen her have at any other time that I have been down to the dock at the Rush Street bridge.

"The list was to the out, the port, and the starboard means the river side, and I walked along there to where her spring line was, and met Mr. Weckler, the harbor master, and I made the remark, 'Ad, she has got quite a list,' and he says, 'Yes, it is a shame to let that boat go out with that load on her.' And I looked down the bridge at the same time, about, and saw Captain Pedersen there, and I says, 'Good morning, Captain,' and he answered me back, and Captain Weckler said, 'Are you taking in your water ballast?' He nodded and said, 'Yes, I am trimming,' and he left the starboard side of the boat and walked out of our sight. I noticed that the spring line was particularly tight, and I tested it with my foot; and I walked to her waist line. It wasn't in line forward, and I noticed that it had a considerable of a side list. I went forward to the head line, and it didn't seem long, and came back again. I think that I had walked over the after gangway the third time, and back to the spring line again, and she had gone over four inches to my idea, what I had seen her former mark, for the water had gone down again, and I would say then she was very close to an eighteen-inch list, from observation. She was down; her bow was pretty near off the dock, and her stern was in close to the dock to take the passengers down there.

"I went forward again to where I could look across her stem, and I leaned against the building and looked up at her so that I would be perfectly firm, and wouldn't be swaying, and I saw her going. I hollered to Mr. Weckler, 'The boat is going over, get off. If she goes, we are going with her.' At that Mr. Weckler appeared by the stairway and I heard him holler, 'Ed!' I looked up and saw him coming out of the gangway, and my first impulse was to get back to a telephone, which I did.

"I ran up the stairs on the approach of the bridge, south to the iron bridge, and goes [sic] back to the City of South Haven dock, and, arriving on the first floor, I had to go west 150 feet, then back to get up another flight of stairs, and then came in here and got into the South Haven steamboat line's office. I got a telephone and immediately telephoned the City Hall and had them send all the ambulances and pulmotors and lung motors, and to notify the police department and the fire department that the *Eastland* was turned over.

"That is an interval of nine or ten minutes from the time I landed on that dock, and I set the telephone down and looked out, and saw that the tug was in close under her bow, and that they were jumping onto that, and the people were climbing over her side—the starboard side—in over the side, and some were jumping out into the river, and throwing life preservers and other things, and the dockmen were throwing everything. I grabbed a telephone book, hunting for the city boat company, to come and cut holes in her—upon her—between what you would call her second, you would call that the second main deck—that is, her cabin deck. An opportunity to get out would have to be through those portholes—those on the starboard side were going over the rail to get on her side and stand on them, and I tried to look at it, and I didn't know where to look for it, for those ox-welders, because they had to cut places for them in order to get down into the cabin. I tried the big phone—the regular day company's phone. . . . I was unable to get this tug company on the phone."

John H. O'Meara of the tug *Kenosha* was dispatched to help the steamer *Eastland* at 6:55. "When I got there I tied up to a cluster of piles just south of the abutment on the south side of the bridge. I put a line over and let the tug drift, drift so she would lay out of the way of all water craft passing back and forth there.

"I went up in the pilot house and sat down there and the tug laid in this position with a slack line, and I should judge about 7:25 or so—maybe not that late—someone hollered on the deck, 'All ready, Captain,' and something about a bridge.

"Then I lay there without the engine working waiting for the 'All right' signal from the captain. After a considerable length of time, I couldn't say how much—I should judge five to seven minutes—I began to get uneasy. The signal wasn't coming; the captain didn't work his stern out. . . . The boat listed slowly to port and she hesitated. I didn't think there was anything wrong at the time. I began to notice the boat more closely and she began to list more gradually. She kind of hesitated and kind of seemed to stay there; I couldn't say how long, and I heard someone say something—I don't know whether it was the captain or not. Then there was a roar and a scream and screeching of people and over it went."

The controversy and litigation involving the *Eastland* went on for twenty years. Finally, on August 7, 1935, the decision was handed down that the owners of the *Eastland* were not to blame. The Court held that the boat was seaworthy, that the operators had taken proper precautions and that the responsibility was traced to an engineer who neglected to fill the ballast tanks properly.

Thus ended the story of the *Eastland* disaster, a catastrophe that claimed 835 lives—585 more than were lost in the Chicago Fire. This tragedy has always interested me strangely because to those who perished "the sea" was only a romantic dream, far away and unknown. Yet they met their deaths in a watery grave as final as any the ocean has ever opened to the unsuspecting.

4

The Disaster-Prone
Circassian

As I walked along the New York State beach from Shinnecock Light, Long Island, on September 11, 1937, toward the last resting place of the iron ship *Circassian,* I thought how she had been hounded by disaster time and time again.

This 280-foot vessel was originally built as a steamer in England, the country whose flag she flew. At the time of the Civil War she was captured under humiliating circumstances while running the blockade for the South. The Fulton ferryboat *Somerset,* with her double ends, had been remodeled and fitted with heavy guns by the United States.* Encountering the *Circassian* off the coast of Cuba, the *Somerset* ordered her to come about. Inclined at first to disregard this order from a renovated ferryboat, the captain of the *Circassian* hastily changed his mind when a few shots impressed him with the caliber of the guns mounted on the *Somerset's* deck. The *Circassian* hove to at once and surrendered, yielding to her captors a rich haul of badly needed goods valued at $315,371.29.

After the war the *Circassian* was purchased by shipping

---

* Because the *Somerset* had been built to withstand the hard knocks of ferry service, it was believed she would make an effective gunboat.

interests, only to be wrecked a short time later at lonely Sable Island. The famous New York wrecker, Captain John Lewis of the Columbian Wrecking Company, succeeded in pulling her off the treacherous sands on which she had grounded.

Sailing later for New York, the *Circassian* went ashore again at Squam, New Jersey, in December 1869. Refloated once more, she was put in drydock. During most of the next three years she was repaired and made over into a sailing vessel. Finally the proud *Circassian* was seaworthy again and set out under a full spread of sails.

In November 1876 she was making a return voyage from Liverpool to New York with a crew of thirty-seven. A week after sailing down the Mersey River, she sighted a dismasted wreck at sea. Captain Richard Williams ordered a boat put over, and twelve survivors were taken from the waterlogged craft.

Unknown to the captain at this time, there was a substantial error in his ship's compass. On December 11, while approaching the American coast, the *Circassian* ran into a heavy snowstorm. Around midnight, with visibility reduced to a few yards, she entered an area of heavy seas where the sound of breaking waves was plainly heard. Before her course could be changed, the great ship ran upon a bar one quarter mile from land, near the Shinnecock Life Saving Station on Long Island, New York.

Although the *Circassian* was sighted at once, it was impossible for Captain Baldwin Cook of the Life Saving Station to launch a lifeboat because of the mountainous combers that the northeast gale was sending toward the beach. At the same time the ship's great draught of almost twenty feet prevented these breakers from working her in toward shore over the bar.

She was too far out to be reached by breeches buoy, for the shot line would never have crossed the four hundred yards to the ship against the teeth of the gale. Even if it had, there was no assurance that the survivors could find the line in the blackness of night. Therefore the lifesavers could do nothing but wait for dawn, when the tide would go down and the apparatus could be set up much closer to the vessel.

Lifesavers from the two nearby stations, Numbers 9 and 11, were on the scene when dawn broke. All hands pitched in to make ready the first shot. Whistling through the air, the projectile fell short. Again the gun was loaded; again failure resulted. Finally, on the third try, the weight fell squarely on the deck of the *Circassian*. The sailors quickly made the line secure. All was put in readiness to send out the lifecar, but at low water the storm relented and the waves subsided so rapidly that the lifecar was no longer necessary.

The surfboat was promptly launched. In seven trips all forty-nine shipwrecked sailors and passengers were taken safely ashore. After being shipwrecked twice on one crossing of the Atlantic, they finally felt firm ground under them. After arrangements had been made, they dispatched with gratitude to New York City.

Still the old *Circassian* was not finished. Although every one had been landed safely, wreckers in the vicinity believed there was a good chance of salvaging the rebuilt iron ship that already had so much unusual history.

The Coast Wrecking Company of New York sent its representatives down to Long Island to save the unlucky vessel. Captain Perrin cooperated with the local agent, Captain Charles A. Pierson of Bridgehampton. Captain John Lewis, who had pulled the ship from the sands of Sable Island, was given the task of doing his work again under more difficult circumstances.

As soon as the gale subsided, Captain Lewis started salvage operations. He hired three engineers from New York, ten members of a nearby Shinnecock Indian tribe and two other local men. In addition, sixteen of the original crew returned to the *Circassian* and were ready to hoist sail and take her away from the dangerous sands once she was afloat.

The ship had been swung around broadside to the waves by the storm. Most of her weight was supported amidships, with her bow and stern under constant strain. Heavy anchors were sunk far to seaward and immense hawsers ran between the anchors and ship, with continuous tension being kept on these lines. It was hoped that eventually the combined forces of high tide, hawsers and heavy ocean swells would lift the *Circassian* and gradually pull her out of the sand. Within fourteen days she had actually moved 295 feet; at dead low water she rested 308 yards from the beach.

It is easy to say what should have been done after a disaster has occurred. Hindsight indicates that a line ought to have been stretched from ship to shore as a precaution for those who were gambling their lives in order to free this vessel. The *Circassian* required a brisk northeasterly gale so she could be taken out to sea. Unfortunately, as every lifesaver knew, such a wind might well develop into a bad storm, and the ship would then be in exactly the same trouble as when she was originally stranded. The wrecking company decided that no line should be stretched between the ship and the shore because they anticipated that once the wind developed, the Shinnecock Indians, as well as the sailors, would use it to flee prematurely to safety. The *Circassian* would then never get off the beach. To be fair to the wreckers, they also felt that the great iron ship would never break up and that the thirty-two men living aboard her were perfectly safe.

The storm they awaited began to develop on December 26, a good northeasterly blow with threatening weather. The winds increased daily until, by December 29, the lighters that had been alongside removing cargo fled for shelter. The last cargo gang, led by Captain Luther D. Burnett, came ashore at ten o'clock that morning. From then on there was no communication with the *Circassian*.

People gathered up and down the shore to watch the so-called second launching of the ship. Everyone believed she would float at high water and go to sea under canvas. But by noon the wind developed into a gale, and snow mixed with biting sleet began to sweep the vicinity. By four o'clock in the afternoon tremendous seas were crashing against the hulk of the *Circassian*, which began to roll and pound heavily on the bar. Probably her iron hull was already beginning to break.

Then onlookers watching from shore noticed that her great hawsers were being slackened. It appeared as if those on board realized the futility of attempting to free her from the bar and were giving the waves a chance to push the *Circassian* nearer to the beach, where they might be rescued. Until this time there had been no sign from the *Circassian* that anyone aboard was trying to get to shore.

Around seven o'clock distress signals went out from the stricken craft, but it was too late to try to send a boat for the men. Crews from Life Saving Stations 9, 10 and 11 were called; Captain Baldwin Cook made initial preparations for rescuing men from the luckless *Circassian* for the second time within eighteen days.

The ocean beach sidesaddling the ship presented a strange spectacle that night. The sea had come up across the higher part of the shore, sweeping in around the hummocks and sand dunes, even reaching out for the distant beach hills and pouring through their sluiceways. Because of this, Captain Cook was forced to retreat seventy-two yards farther back, almost to the shelter of the dunes.

A hurricane was now blowing. Giant billows cascaded across the decks of the *Circassian,* and every sailor was perched high in the rigging. No lifeboat could maneuver in the awesome cross-sea that enveloped the *Circassian* from all points, creating a veritable caldron of foam and water.

The ocean flooded the beach still higher. The combination of surf and wind, rain and sleet, freezing cold and a hail of wet sand became almost unbearable for the lifesavers. Then they found they had to change their location in order to reposition the shot-line gun. A change in wind direction necessitated moving westward of the stranded ship, which took considerable time. Trouble next developed in getting match rope to burn.

Finally the gun was ready to fire. Three times the shot left the gun, described its parabola in the sky and fell short of its goal. Each time the long lines were hauled back and made ready again. At last it became apparent that no shot could reach the *Circassian*—even if it did, it would be physically impossible for the survivors to use the line.

Around midnight the tide began to go out. Lights were observed on deck, indicating that the hull still held together, but the wreck must have been cleared of everything by the fearful sea. At two in the morning survivors who had been in the foremast were seen taking refuge in the mizzen rigging.

Ninety minutes later the *Circassian* snapped completely in two. Her forepart settled down outside the bar, while her stern beat across the shoal closer to shore.

Still the iron mizzenmast stood erect, the rigging crowded with men whose shouts of despair could be heard even above the roar of wind and waves. A short time later the tall spar began to dip and swing as it worked loose from its supports. The frantic lifesavers could only watch the gyrations of that mast crowded with anguished humanity, realizing that they were about to witness one of the great tragedies of the sea.

Back and forth the great pole swung, until finally it bent far over to port with its heavy load. Beyond recovery, it gradually lowered and began to submerge in the giant seas. One by one the men were pulled away and washed toward shore, drowning in the breakers. Those who remained in the rigging perished alongside the ship as the mast settled under water.

Superintendent H. E. Huntington, in charge of all lifesaving stations on Long Island, organized a lantern squad of twenty men to search for bodies or possible survivors, although there was little hope that anyone could get to shore alive. The current ran with great force in an easterly direction outside the breakers, which made the chance of reaching shore extremely remote.

Suddenly, however, a group of lifesavers noticed a strange weaving mass caught in a huge breaker just about to crash on the beach. What they actually saw was a large cylindrical piece of cork, five feet long and eleven inches in diameter, fitted with straps and beckets for use in salvage work. The first and second mates had noticed the object aboard the *Circassian* and had grabbed it when they were about to be washed overboard. They were submerged in the cross-sea for a time, but then the buoyancy of the cork brought them to the surface. The ship's carpenter and one of the seamen hired by the wreckers quickly grabbed onto the floating buoy.

The first mate realized that four men could swamp the cork and cause everyone to drown unless they were careful. "Lock your legs together with mine and with each other!" he shouted in a voice of authority above the roar of the storm. They obeyed at once, thus stabilizing the rocking buoy and maintaining a safe equilibrium with each other. They were now a single mass of buoy and humanity, battered by the waves but slowly being pushed away from the ship. Watching the action of the sea, the chief mate ordered the men to begin kicking slowly toward the shore as they clung onto their handholds. Despite the reverse action of the easterly sweep, they made slow progress toward the shore.

Just before a wave swept over them, the mate would give the order to hold their breath. By the time the surf had passed, they would be able to refill their lungs with air. Then came the moment when they were sighted at the crest of a breaking wave.

On the beach a great shout went up when the buoy was seen. A human chain rushed into the water to meet the great breaking billow head-on as it collapsed and swept up the shore.

Kicking hard every moment against the dangerous undertow, the men rode the buoy until they were only waist-deep in water. As the wave paused momentarily before receding, the lifesavers reached them. Soon the entire mass of twirling buoy and shouting men was slowly making progress toward the beach.

Finally the men and the buoy were beyond reach of the next wave. The four survivors were carried to the nearest guard station, where they were put to bed at once. Because of the cleverness and bravery of the first mate, four men had been saved from almost certain death. But they were the only ones rescued of the thirty-two aboard ship at the start of the gale. The *Circassian* had ended her career.

Part Six

1940–Present

1

Spies from
U-Boat Landings

Shortly after dawn on Saturday, June 13, 1942, four German saboteurs disembarked on the American shore. They landed unopposed at Amagansett on Long Island, barely one hundred miles from New York City.

Jeanette Rattray, gifted author from nearby East Hampton, writes in *Ship Ashore!* that within twenty-four hours of the arrival of the spies, the entire East Hampton township was alerted. However, many people did not take the landing seriously until FBI Director J. Edgar Hoover announced it was a fact weeks later.

Not only did German U-boats send ashore those four saboteurs, they also landed four more at Ponte Vedra Beach in Florida. In both cases the men had come ashore in collapsible rubber boats with substantial sums of money, clothing and explosives, which they buried at once above the waterline. They had a complete two-year plan of destruction aimed at American industries and utilities.

On the evening of June 12, 1942, "Den Mother" Mrs. Jeanette Rattray took her Cub Scouts for a late afternoon picnic at East Hampton. One of the Scouts down on the beach heard the sound of a Diesel engine. He wondered why, for he knew no beam trawler would venture inside the bar just offshore. The entire group went to the shore to look out over the water. They could see nothing because of the breakers and the foggy weather.

Later, around eight o'clock that night, a summer resident drawing blackout curtains heard the sound of an engine where the saboteurs actually landed. A Coastguardsman patrolling the area stopped by and told her it was probably one of the new Navy patrol craft. At about this time Lothar-Gunther Buchheim * was in the general area aboard a submarine.

Shortly after midnight on June 14, Surfman 2nd Class James Cullen of the Coast Guard began his six-mile patrol along the beach from the Amagansett station. When he had walked a relatively short distance, a stranger dressed in civilian clothes came up the beach out of the fog. A short distance away two men in bathing trunks were wading out of the water, followed by a fourth man carrying and dragging what he told the Coastguardsman was a bag full of clams.

Cullen was not convinced and continued to question them. The "civilian" then got tough. He told Cullen they would not kill him if the Coastguardsman could "keep his mouth shut"; $260 was offered as bribe money.

"Would you know me if you saw me again?" asked the saboteur.

Cullen answered in the negative. The two men then parted.

Cullen went back to his station at Amagansett, breaking into a run as soon as he had covered enough distance so that the Germans could not see him. At the station he turned over the bribe money to the man in charge, Carl Jenette. Immediately the station was electrified with activity. Jenette telephoned Warrant Officer Oden and Chief Boatswain's Mate Warren Barnes. They began a visual search of the ocean and before long actually saw the submarine through a rift in the fog,

* His book *U-Boat War* cannot be surpassed.

observing that the U-boat was on a course to the east.

Four members of the Coast Guard then took rifles and began intensive exploration of the area on foot. As soon as the Army and Navy were put on alert, soldiers joined in systematically searching the dunes. They discovered German cigarettes as well as a pair of wet bathing trunks. Freshly disturbed sand caught the attention of the searchers; they dug out four wooden, tin-lined cases of explosives. More German clothes and an overseas cap with a swastika then were unearthed.

The saboteurs had purchased four tickets to Jamaica, Long Island, at about 6:45 that morning from Station Agent Ira Baker at Amagansett. A search turned up clothing left by the saboteurs under a hedge near the station.

On June 20, 22, 23 and 27 the eight saboteurs who had landed from U-boats at Amagansett and at Ponte Vedra Beach were arrested. After their capture, two confessed. Six of the men were executed, the seventh was sentenced to thirty years in prison and the eighth received life imprisonment.

Following the U-boat landing at Amagansett, men of the Coast Guard carried rifles, revolvers and flashlights in addition to their standard Coston signals and regulation time clocks for the duration of the war. Before this they had been unarmed.

James Cullen of the Coast Guard was later promoted to coxswain and given a medal for his handling of the situation on June 14, 1942. In Washington, D.C., the FBI has an exhibit of mementos from the saboteurs' landing.

At least four U-boat landings along the Atlantic coast occurred during World War II. The one at Amagansett and the one in Florida, not far from Jacksonville, have been reported fully by Allen Hynd in *Passport to Treason* and by Colonel Vernon Hinchley in *Spy Mysteries Unveiled*.

A Cape Cod World War II landing from a U-boat was revealed to me by C. Graham Hurlburt, Jr., of Cohasset, Massachusetts. The landing was said to have been on Cape Cod's Dennis Beach between Lighthouse Inn and the entrance to

Bass River. German radio equipment was later found there.

The fourth U-boat incident took place on the coast of Maine in the town of Hancock. American-born William Colepaugh and German national Eric Gimpel came ashore there in a rubber raft from Nazi U-boat *1230*.

Actually, FBI records on one of the spies went back several years. William Curtis Colepaugh had been under observation for some time. In June 1940 an FBI special agent in Boston was informed that customs officers had observed Colepaugh from May 2 to May 27, 1940. During that time he visited the German tanker *Pauline Friederich*, which was tied up at Battery Wharf in Boston.

The customs official stated that Colepaugh claimed he was engaged as a painter aboard the vessel. While visiting the German tanker, he often spoke of going to Germany to study engineering. It was also reported that he expressed dissatisfaction with conditions in the United States and was interested in leaving this country.

It occurred to customs officials that because of Colepaugh's dissatisfaction the FBI might wish to conduct inquiries concerning him. Thus a case was opened on William Colepaugh. Instructions were issued to make necessary checks to determine whether he was engaged in subversive activities.

Investigation revealed that William, born March 25, 1918, had been a student of naval architecture and engineering at Massachusetts Institute of Technology. Records of this college show that he entered in September 1938 after attending secondary school in Toms River, New Jersey. His home address was listed as Niantic, Connecticut.

Because of scholastic difficulties, Colepaugh left MIT on February 6, 1941. The name of one of his former roommates was obtained. This young man advised investigators that Colepaugh often received mail containing propaganda publications from the German consul in Boston and also from German news agencies in New York. He indicated that Cole-

paugh showed more than ordinary interest in these publications.

Customs guards stationed at the wharf where the *Pauline
Friederich* had been docked remembered Colepaugh. One
guard indicated that Colepaugh claimed he was living on
board. When asked if he was a crew member of that ship, he
replied that he was not but lived on board because he liked the
crew members.

Another customs guard said that he once stopped Colepaugh attempting to board the ship and asked what his business was on board the vessel. The suspect replied that he had
permission from the chief officer to spend a few days aboard
the *Pauline Friederich*. When questioned by the customs
guard why he wanted to go on a German ship, Colepaugh
answered that the persons on board were treating him well
and that he liked them better than the people in the United
States.

A retired customs guard remembered seeing Colepaugh in
the company of the first officer of the *Pauline Friederich*. He
said he also had seen him in the dining room with the captain
of the ship. The FBI also learned that in August 1940 William
Colepaugh had two German sailors from the *Pauline
Friederich* as weekend guests at his home in Niantic, Connecticut. Colepaugh's current address was unknown. One individual advised that he might be in South America as a crewman aboard a merchant vessel.

It was not until fourteen months later that Colepaugh again
attracted the attention of the FBI. One afternoon in August
1941 a young midshipman from the United States Naval
Academy walked into the FBI field office in Washington, D.C.,
and reported that he had roomed with William Curtis Colepaugh at a secondary school in New Jersey from September
1937 to June 1938. He was anxious to let the FBI know about
him. He said that he visited Colepaugh in March 1940 at MIT
and was taken to the German tanker *Pauline Friederich*. It

appeared to the midshipman that his former roommate was well acquainted with the officers on board that ship. As they were leaving the ship, Colepaugh stated he was in favor of Germany and that he wanted to go there on the *Pauline Friederich*.

The midshipman further related that in June 1940 Colepaugh visited him in Groton, Connecticut. During a discussion of the war, Colepaugh was asked where his affiliation would lie if the United States went to war against Germany. His reply was that his affiliation probably would be with Germany.

The midshipman stated that he never had an occasion to meet Colepaugh after this incident, but what had been said bothered him. He felt that Colepaugh's attitude toward Germany warranted investigation.

All this time the FBI was building up data concerning Colepaugh. They learned he had either sold or given a radio receiving set to a former attaché at the German consulate in Boston. Reportedly Colepaugh had built this set himself.

Information was also received that Colepaugh often dropped in at a German tavern frequented by members of the German consulate in Boston. On one occasion Colepaugh stated that he had just returned from England on a British freighter.

On July 23, 1942, the *Scania,* a Swedish vessel, arrived at Philadelphia from Buenos Aires. The crew list of that vessel indicated that William Colepaugh was aboard as a seaman. He was questioned by local naval officers, at which time he presented a draft card indicating he had registered under the provisions of the Selective Training and Service Act on October 16, 1940. During this interview he admitted that he had not communicated with his local draft board, explaining that he had never received any communications from that board. This information was immediately turned over to the government, and Colepaugh was interviewed by FBI agents.

A check of draft board records in Boston, where Colepaugh had registered, revealed he had failed to return a completed questionnaire and had also failed to keep the board advised of his address. These were violations of a federal law under the investigative jurisdiction of the FBI. Accordingly, FBI agents in Boston contacted the local United States attorney. On July 25, 1942, a complaint was filed against William C. Colepaugh, charging him with violating the Selective Training and Service Act. A warrant was issued for his arrest.

Colepaugh was returned to Boston, where he was interviewed by FBI agents. He said that he was born in East Lyme, Connecticut, and claimed that his father was a native-born American. His mother, however, was born aboard the German ship *The Havel* en route to the United States. The suspect explained that while he was a student at MIT he met the captain of the German tanker *Pauline Friederich* and was invited to visit the ship. He did so on several occasions, becoming acquainted with a man he knew to be a Nazi party leader on board the vessel. On two occasions Colepaugh took this party leader home as a guest.

Colepaugh said that he had purchased a radio set and subsequently received a telephone call from the secretary to the German consul, who was interested in the radio. Colepaugh denied building the set but admitted selling it to the German official for sixty dollars. He stated that he had visited the German consulate in Boston on numerous occasions during early 1941.

From January to April 1940, Colepaugh was employed at Lawley's shipyard in the Neponset section of Boston as a laborer on yachts. One of the officials at Lawley's in the year the suspect worked there stated in February 1965 that Colepaugh probably was one of the men who left the yard at once when told they would have to be fingerprinted and photographed. "Several men left in a hurry on learning this information, not even stopping to get their pay," the official explained. Colepaugh is remembered as a thin, mild-mannered youth who would not attract more than average attention.

On May 7, 1941, Colepaugh went to Canada and shipped

out as a seaman on the *Reynolds*. The boat went to Scotland and returned to Boston in the latter part of July 1941. He subsequently landed in New York City and, on September 5, 1941, obtained a job as a deckhand on board the *Anita*, sailing from New York City for Rio de Janeiro. He was at Buenos Aires in October 1941.

On December 8, 1941, the day after the Pearl Harbor attack, Colepaugh secured a position as deckhand on the tanker *William G. Warden*. He made a few trips on this craft in South American waters, and on March 25, 1942, was again in Buenos Aires. On April 5 of the same year, he worked as a deckhand on board the *Scania*.

Colepaugh stated that he had written to the German Library of Information in New York City for publications, and he added that he had attended a birthday celebration in honor of Hitler at the German consulate in Boston. The secretary to the German consulate, according to Colepaugh, had discussed with him the possibility of going to Germany to study at marine engineering schools there.

The United States attorney in Boston advised that he would not authorize prosecution in the case against Colepaugh if he would enlist for military service. Colepaugh promised to do so, and on October 2, 1942, enlisted as an apprentice seaman in the United States Naval Reserve. When he became a member of the armed forces, under the jurisdiction of the Navy, the FBI's case on William Curtis Colepaugh was closed administratively. Copies of Bureau reports were furnished Navy officials.

On June 28, 1943, the FBI received information that Colepaugh had been discharged from the Navy "for the good of the service." Once more he was in civilian life, and again the FBI became interested in his activities.

On March 26, 1943, Colepaugh commenced employment at the Waltham Watch Company in Waltham, Massachusetts. Three months later he was working for a poultry farmer in Concord, Massachusetts.

A check with the local draft board indicated Colepaugh telephoned them on January 10, 1944, that he was going to enter the merchant marine. Five days later the draft board received a letter from him postmarked New York enclosing a note on Swedish American Steamship Line stationery certifying Colepaugh was employed on board the *Gripsholm* as a messboy.

The FBI had been informed that the *Gripsholm* was carrying individuals who were to be repatriated to Germany. It was not known whether Colepaugh would return to the United States as a crew member aboard the same ship. The FBI therefore asked several government agencies to advise the FBI in the event Colepaugh reentered the United States.

On February 15, 1944, the *Gripsholm* sailed. Within a few days of her arrival in Portugal, Colepaugh phoned the German consulate in Lisbon but was advised that the consul was not in. At noon the following day Colepaugh went to the consulate in person. He told the doorman that he was from the *Gripsholm* and wanted to see the consul, explaining that he was a friend of the former German consul in Boston.

Within a relatively short time Colepaugh was interviewed by the German consul and taken to Germany. He was then transported to Security Service headquarters at The Hague in Holland. Here he met Eric Gimpel, who was to become his partner. Gimpel had been an instructor in 1943 at a fascist academy for young boys in Madrid, Spain, after which he returned to Berlin as a prominent member of the Security Service. In Berlin he had been given a private office and a secretary.

Gimpel and Colepaugh began training for the dangerous mission ahead, a mission that would involve crossing the Atlantic in a German submarine and landing on American soil. Courses included radio work and use of firearms and explosives. The American was given a tremendous amount of athletic training to build up his relatively weak body, and he learned to drive a motorcycle. He was taught how to handle explosives and was shown the most effective way to derail a train. He was shown how to handle Thermit, which could burn through metal.

In August Colepaugh and Gimpel went to Berlin for a photographic course, using a Leica camera, that included developing and printing special photographs. Then they went to Dresden, Germany, to study microphotography and learn to work with microphotographic apparatus. They soon were able to reduce regular Leica negatives to sixteen-millimeter film.

In Dresden and later in Berlin, Colepaugh did not know what his assignment would be. Eventually he learned that he was to go to the United States. Two days before Colepaugh and Gimpel left Berlin for Kiel, they were advised that their objective in the United States was to obtain information from periodicals, newspapers, radio and all available sources regarding shipbuilding, airplanes and rockets. Gimpel was to build a special radio that would send information out of the United States. In an emergency they were to use American prisoners of war as "mail drops." Letters sent to these captives were to be written in secret ink. In sending radio information out of the United States, they were to use specific code-wave lengths and times.

Their final instructions included the code for sending radio messages to Germany. It was based on the words, "Lucky Strike cigarettes, it's toasted." They were also furnished wristwatches and two small compasses, as well as two kits of concentrated food taken from captured American pilots.

Gimpel received a blue onionskin paper packet containing about one hundred small diamonds. These were to be used to provide funds in the event the money given to them was found to be worthless or dangerous to use.

Gimpel and Colepaugh signed various identification papers. Those for Colepaugh carried the name William C. Caldwell. The papers consisted of a birth certificate showing Colepaugh to have been born in New Haven, Connecticut; a Selective Service registration card showing him to be registered at Local Board 18, Boston, Massachusetts; a Selective Service classification card from the same draft board; a certificate of discharge from the United States Naval Reserve; and a motor vehicle operator's license for the State of Massachusetts. There were also several duplicate papers, completely signed and filled out except that names and addresses were omitted to permit Colepaugh and Gimpel to assume other names if necessary.

About September 22, 1944, Gimpel and Colepaugh went to Kiel and spent two days waiting aboard the Hamburg-American liner *Milwaukee*. Subsequently they went aboard German submarine *1230*, which left immediately and remained off Kiel for about two days awaiting a German convoy going up the coast of Denmark. They proceeded with this convoy to Horton, Norway, where the submarine was tested for about six days. The next port was Kristiansand, Norway: two days to take on food and fuel.

Colepaugh and Gimpel had received expense money of $60,000, a sum determined when Colepaugh pointed out that the American cost of living had taken a sharp turn upward. He estimated $15,000 a year living expenses for one man in the United States. Based on this, $60,000 was given to them as expenses for two men for a period of two years.

On October 6, 1944, the submarine left Kristiansand bound for the United States. The transatlantic trip was made under conditions of extreme caution.

On November 10, 1944, the Nazi U-boat approached the Grand Banks of Newfoundland. At that point the crew took radio bearings on Boston, Massachusetts, and on Portland and Bangor, Maine. Later they established a position off the Maine coast at Mount Desert Rock. They lay off that point until about 4:00 P.M. on the afternoon of November 29, 1944.

During the day the submarine rested on the ocean bottom. At night it charged its batteries by using Diesel engines. Through listening devices the crew could hear fishing boats on the surface nearby. Throughout one day they had listened to a fishing boat anchored above them. About this time word was received by radio from Berlin that a submarine had been sunk in Frenchman's Bay, Maine. The Captain of the *1230* was instructed to land Colepaugh and Gimpel somewhere other than Frenchman's Bay.

Colepaugh, Gimpel and the captain * of the submarine discussed landing places in Rhode Island, New Hampshire and Maine. Eventually the captain disregarded the instructions from Berlin. On the night of November 29, 1944, the submarine, completely submerged, started for Frenchman's Bay.

About half a mile off Crab Tree Point the captain ordered the craft to be raised until the conning tower was just above water. In this fashion they proceeded to a point about three hundred yards from shore at Crab Tree Point, which is near the peninsula of Hancock Point.

During the trip across the Atlantic, Colepaugh and Gimpel had worn regulation German naval uniforms. About half an hour before the submarine came to its offshore position, they removed the uniforms and donned civilian attire.

The submarine turned to face the south, and the crew made ready a rubber boat with oars. Attached to this boat was a light line to pull the rubber boat back to the submarine after the saboteurs rowed ashore. But when the boat was launched the line broke. It was necessary for two crew members to row the agents to shore and then return in the craft.

At the landing point there was a narrow beach approximately six feet, with a bank above it. In the stillness of that cold November night on the Maine coast, Nazi agents Colepaugh and Gimpel stepped from the rubber boat onto the shores of the United States. The German sailors also went ashore so that they could return to their homeland and brag that they had touched American shores. When these sailors departed they saluted, "Heil Hitler."

With all their equipment, Colepaugh and Gimpel climbed

---

* H. Hilbig, captain of the *U 1230*, surrendered his submarine June 24, 1945, at a time when many others were giving up.

the bank and walked through the woods adjacent to the shoreline until they reached a dirt road. They did not bring any explosives ashore, nor did they bury anything on the beach. In fact, they did not even bring the microphotographic apparatus from the submarine because it was extremely heavy. Gimpel claimed later they were weakened because of their long stay aboard the submarine.

On that night, five months before VE Day, Colepaugh and Gimpel came up a path leading through woods to the road along the west side of Hancock Point. They started on foot down the road toward Hancock shortly before midnight, muffled by a moderate snowfall.

Two Americans soon became aware of their presence. Mrs. Mary Forni, wife of a Franklin, Maine, schoolteacher and the mother of three children, was driving home from a gathering of neighborhood women. She saw two men laden with bundles walking along the high road. Although the men were strangers, she noted nothing suspicious about their actions. A little later Mrs. Forni saw Ellsworth High School senior Harvard M. Hodgkins in his car as he drove home from a dance at Hancock Village. After Mrs. Forni reached home she began to wonder why two strangers should be trudging along late at night in the Hancock Point area at that time of year. If it had been July or August, the height of the summer season, she would not have "given it a second thought."

The more she thought the more it worried her. Finally Mrs. Forni decided to call the Hodgkins's residence the following morning. The lad's father, deputy sheriff Dana Hodgkins, was away on a hunting trip. Mary Forni talked with his wife and asked her to question her son regarding the two men. Harvard Hodgkins confirmed their presence, saying that without question he saw the tracks of the men along the road as he drove home.

That afternoon Deputy Hodgkins returned and immediately began investigating the incident. He followed tracks in the snow down a path at Hancock Point to the water's edge, where he saw enough to convince him that the men had landed from the sea. At first he wondered if the pair could be hunters. But when he saw that the tracks ended at the ocean's edge and noted evidence that a rubber raft had landed, he decided to contact the FBI in Bangor.

Four days after the landing FBI agents questioned Mrs. Forni and the Hodgkins boy. They set in motion machinery that led to the eventual capture of Colepaugh and Gimpel.

The two spies did reach Boston and then New York. But Colepaugh decided to surrender. He aided in capturing Gimpel, after which both were tried and sentenced to be executed as German spies. Their sentences were reduced to imprisonment. They were freed after serving a substantial number of years in prison.

It is believed that later Harvard Hodgkins spent a whirlwind week in New York as guest of a New York newspaper and a radio program of that era. This was at least partly a reward for reporting the spies on November 30, 1944.

I visited Mrs. Forni up on the Hancock Point peninsula. She took me to the very location where the saboteurs from the *U 1230* landed on the beach. Mrs. Forni and Harvard Hodgkins helped make history on that memorable night in 1944 by thwarting one of the most daring spy plots hatched in World War II.

2

Loss
of the *Lakonia*

All seemed in readiness for the cruise ahead. It was December 1963. The location was Southampton, England, where three liners were tied up at Berth 107. Two of the ships were familiar to me—the *Queen Elizabeth* and the *Queen Mary*. The third craft, between the Queens, was the *Lakonia*.

Although the weather was not perfect, it was an average winter day in the British Isles. The 20,314-ton *Lakonia* bore the sea trident as symbol of the liner's company. Ironically, one circular for the cruise ship stressed that the trip was to be a holiday with all risks eliminated.

The 658 passengers were eager to escape England's cold climate in favor of the Canary Islands and Madeira. With the crew of 383, there were 1041 in all, from all walks of life— stewards, chefs, carpenters, hair dressers, electricians, stockbrokers, honeymoon couples, a model, a well-known actor, a schoolmaster, an architect, a baronet, a dentist, army officers, a football club manager, a bookmaker, students, babies, pregnant women, widows and wealthy retired couples. Both the strong and the crippled were aboard.

Most of the passengers knew little of the *Lakonia*'s past history. The Greek liner had been a troubled craft since her

431

launching in 1930. Formerly the Dutch liner *Johan van Ol-denbarnevelt,* she had been constructed by the Nederland Shipping Company. On her maiden voyage, with Queen Wilhelmina aboard, she collided with another craft in the North Sea. On one voyage in 1951 six small but dangerous fires broke out. In 1962 she was sold to the Ormos Shipping Company, a Greek firm, which changed her name to *Lakonia* and put her in drydock for refurbishing so that she would be ready for the cruise trade.

The ship and its complement of excited passengers sailed from Southampton with few cares. As a precaution, the captain ordered a fire and boat drill December 22, 1963, while the ship was sailing at a speed of 17 knots. The drill was executed successfully.

At eleven o'clock that evening a steward walking by the barber shop, which was closed, noticed smoke seeping under the door. When he forced entrance to the barber shop, he discovered a wall of flame about to engulf him. Running for help, he found that the fire had already gained terrific headway in the hall, and that the conflagration was heading toward the staterooms.

Meanwhile the skipper, Captain M. N. Zarbis, detected an odor he could not believe—the terrifying, overwhelming smell of smoke. He immediately set about to find the cause of this most feared danger at sea. The alarm was soon sounded, and crew members as well as passengers were seized with some degree of confusion and concern.

A ship's warning system, alerting and in many cases overwhelming each person aboard, is an appalling, startling, frightening noise. In conjunction with the emergency it heralds, the alarm often creates panic. Some on the *Lakonia* did nothing, appearing dazed; others thought of life preservers; still others realized that they were already in immediate danger from the flames. In the dance hall the orchestra tried to keep playing to calm the crowd, but in split seconds the screams and shouts drowned the music.

In the radio room Operator Kalogridis had been flashing out Christmas messages over the airwaves. Suddenly a message from the bridge told him of the blaze. Forgetting the holiday greetings, he ripped out over the air a distress signal, telling all other ships in range that the *Lakonia* desperately needed assistance because the fire was out of control. He gave the ship's position: latitude 35 degrees North, longitude 24 degrees West.

There was panic aboard the *Lakonia*. The lifeboat deck was crowded with crew and passengers scrambling for the rescue craft, stumbling around in every possible attire. Women in evening gowns and men in tuxedos, others in nightgowns and pajamas, forgot everything but the possibility of saving their lives. Great sections of the burning ship were rapidly becoming a blazing inferno. Some lifeboats were launched, but the great swells and December cold jeopardized those lucky enough to be on board. Four of the *Lakonia*'s survival craft could not be dropped to the sea because of the flames and heat. Many discouraged passengers who despaired of getting into lifeboats jumped into the ocean wearing lifejackets. Soon it became a question of how long they—and the lifeboats— could stay afloat.

The first rescue craft was the *Montcalm*, one of the passenger ships called to the scene. Others included the Coast Guard cutter *Mackinac*, the *Salta*, the *Gertrude Frizen*, the *Stratheden*, the British aircraft carrier *Centaur*, the two American liners *Independence* and *Rio Grande*, as well as the Belgian ship *Charlesville*.

As soon as the *Montcalm* reached the scene, searchlights were zigzagged across the water, giving courage and hope to victims in the sea. The rescue ship picked up many people from the water and from the lifeboats. By early dawn the *Montcalm* radioed that 240 had been taken aboard, with 12 dead. Shortly afterward came the *Stratheden*'s report that they had saved 300.

With the coming of morning rescue planes looked down

upon a gruesome sight. One airplane pilot recalled later a dead baby floating all by itself in a lifebelt; the incident simply overwhelmed him.

Except for part of the stern, flames were sweeping the entire *Lakonia*. About a hundred people were crowded around the taffrail, including Captain Zarbis. Then, one by one, they leaped into the sea. Some drowned; others were picked up by one of the eighteen boats helping in the rescue work.

Finally word came that many of those who had been rescued—both members of the ship's company and passengers—were on the way to Casablanca aboard the *Charlesville*, the *Mehdi* or the *Montcalm*. It was Christmas Day when they arrived, and they were given the choice of hotel rooms or air transportation to their homes. Other survivors were taken to Funchal in Madeira. Most were dazed or weeping after suffering hours in lurching lifeboats. Several refused to go on another Greek ship, the *Arkadia*, which was waiting to rush them to Southampton.

The disaster claimed 155 lives; 886 passengers and crewmen survived after very difficult rescue operations. In the tradition of the sea, Captain Zarbis was the last to leave the burning liner.

What caused the fire? There are many different opinions, but overloaded fuses probably were to blame. The countless mistakes by individuals on the ship, timing errors, communication failures and simply bad luck all contributed to the tragedy of the *Lakonia*. The Marine Ministry investigating the fire discovered that when the ship was refurbished, she was not fitted with automatic water sprinklers for use in a fire. This may well have been the deciding reason for her loss.

It was arranged to have the *Lakonia* towed into Gibraltar. But when two tugs, the *Herkules* and the *Polzee*, attempted to tow her, the *Lakonia* went down in two thousand fathoms 250 miles from her destination. This sinking, of course, meant that the exact cause of the blaze would never be known.

Later came the usual charges, complaints, accusations and

denials, as is almost always the case in marine tragedies of this sort. One man said that there were orders and counterorders. Another saw twenty people leaving the ship in a lifeboat built for seventy-five. Still another observer charged that Greek seamen, in panic, fought with passengers for places in the lifeboats.

A passenger stated that members of the crew often did not seem to know what to do in the emergency, and said that they even thought of taking passengers back to the burning vessel. Another testified that almost every member of the crew managed to get aboard the rescue craft before the passengers.

The final decision of the Marine Ministry investigating the actual reactions of the crew who ran the *Lakonia* was that they acted in faultless manner and in accordance with Greek tradition. This is ridiculous.

3

Burning
of a Lighthouse

One of the greatest Englishmen of all times stated more than a quarter century ago that the lifeboat "drives on as a proof, a symbol, a testimony, that man is created in the image of God." Sir Winston Churchill, when he made this statement, said that the lifeboat "drives on with a mercy which does not quail in the presence of death."

Coastguardsmen and lifesavers all deserve great commendation. Two of the most outstanding are Americans Joshua James, who saved 636 lives in his career, and Coxswain Henry Blogg of Cromer, England, who went out on service 387 times and rescued a total of 873 people.

As grateful as anyone for the work of lifesavers were the three keepers of England's Chickens Rock Lighthouse. Off the tip of the Isle of Man lies an island called the Calf of Man. To the southwest is a reef where the Chickens Rock Lighthouse was built more than a century ago. Extending 149 feet into the air, the tower was surrounded by water at high tide.

On December 23, 1960, the British Admiralty sent out a warning to all vessels that disaster had struck that lighthouse, extinguishing the light. Exact details of what caused the fire

436

were never made clear. But it is known that at approximately ten-thirty in the morning a terrific explosion occurred at the Chickens Rock Light, setting the inside of the tower ablaze within minutes. At the time of the explosion all three keepers were high in the tower in one of the upper rooms. They were trapped by the flames below. It looked as if they would be burned alive.

Means of escape were present, however. The three keepers tied a rope to the ironwork of the upper balcony where they were imprisoned, then used the long line to reach relative safety at the base of the tower. One of the men sustained ugly burns sliding down the line.

Although they had reached temporary safety, matters grew dangerously critical as time went by. The force of the wind was increasing, which would make rescue impossible. And the men realized that the coming high tide would inundate them.

Minute by minute the wind was growing stronger. Above them the flames sweeping the lighthouse were approaching the storage tanks, which meant that another blinding explosion was imminent. Half-dressed, the keepers were suffering from the bitter cold and swirling surf.

Then the three keepers saw a boat approaching, tossing in the gathering wind. The craft was the Royal Navy National Lifeboat Institution's *R. A. Colby Cubbin*.

The *Cubbin* had steamed away from Port St. Mary at 11:10 that morning after hearing of the trouble. At first the authorities did not know quite what had happened and what could be done. Then came word that the three keepers were safe temporarily at the burning lighthouse but had to be rescued almost at once because of the rising tide. The *Cubbin* lost no time in getting to the tower.

Watching carefully as the red, white and blue lifeboat with the servicemen dressed in their yellow oilskins approached the lighthouse, the keepers wondered how they could possibly save their lives before the rising wind, waves and tide made it too late.

By now the three men had been forced to climb back onto the lower part of the tower. They clung to a small emergency landing stage, the water just a few inches below, spraying them with every wave. Since the boiling surf as well as the hidden boulders prevented the *Cubbin* from getting closer than three hundred feet, Coxswain Gawne readied his gun to fire the line in such a way that the three keepers could be saved.

Then the loudspeaker from the *Cubbin* advised the men imprisoned at the base of the burning lighthouse to secure one end of a sturdy line to the tower and attach the other end to a board they would throw into the sea. When this was done the board rapidly floated away from the tower. Another line fired from the lifeboat landed in the water across the one the keepers had sent out. Within a short time the men in the lifeboat had pulled the rope in so that they were connected to the tower.

The keepers now hauled back the original line, bringing back the lifeboat line and the breeches buoy as well. The end of the breeches buoy rope was then strapped to the iron lighthouse ladder.

The men had agreed that the keeper who had burned his hands should be given the first trip across to safety. Within ten minutes the two other lighthouse men had strapped him safely to the buoy and started him off for the lifeboat. Unfortunately, when he was halfway across to the *Cubbin,* a giant wave smashed against the breeches buoy, capsizing it and throwing the keeper into the water. With great difficulty the men from the *Cubbin* managed to reach him. Pulling the keeper aboard, they wrapped him in a blanket and took him below, where they kept him warm near the engines. He suffered severely from his burns, exposure and general shock.

There was still the problem of rescuing the two remaining lighthouse keepers. The captain of the *Cubbin* decided to send for help. Not trusting the breeches buoy after the capsizing, he radioed for assistance from the Port Erin lifeboat *Matthew*

Simpson. She was launched at once. Meanwhile the *Cubbin* made for Port Erin as quickly as possible to land the rescued keeper, who required immediate medical attention.

The *Matthew Simpson* soon reached the scene of the smoking tower. They found the situation even worse than before but could only stand by in case the two keepers should need emergency assistance before the *Cubbin* returned.

It was now decided to dispatch an Air Force rescue helicopter from Anglesey. The craft was soon hovering near the burning tower. The pilot realized that the only safe way he could remove the men was to lift them off the upper lighthouse balcony. But he also knew there was no way the keepers could climb again through the flames to the top of the structure. With deep regret he returned to his station.

Thus the only solution was for the lifeboats to find some way to take the men off Chickens Rock.

By this time a sizable gathering had assembled on a hill on the Isle of Man. They stood staring out at the tall tower with smoke billowing through the windows. At the base every wave brought white seething foam, which now covered the lower part of the light where the men clung desperately to the ladder. By this time the two lifeboats had arrived back at the reef. The lifesavers could do nothing as the waves roared in around the structure, swirling over the dangerous rocks. The two craft, the *Cubbin* and the *Matthew Simpson,* maneuvered helplessly off the light for the next three hours, unable to approach closer than a hundred yards.

Then came the change of tide, and the lower area around the base of the lighthouse began to reveal itself. The weather also had moderated. With the Port Erin lifeboat, *Matthew Simpson,* standing by, the *Cubbin* cautiously approached the base of the tower, came alongside and managed to rescue the two keepers. The men had been on the burning tower and reef for more than eight hours, half-dressed, with wind and spray numbing them. Now, wrapped in heavy blankets, they were placed below near the engine's warmth.

Still burning away, the lighthouse faded into the distance as the rescuers returned to shore with the keepers. All night the Chickens Rock Lighthouse sent up wisps of smoke from the blackened windows, the tower standing lonely and forgotten on the location it had protected for more than eighty-five years.

Two days went by, and then the lighthouse tender *Hesperus* * arrived off the burned tower, sailing to the area from Oban. She placed a flashing beacon in the vicinity of the fire-blackened tower to warn all shipping away from the reef. The tower itself stood as a reminder of the explosion and of the catastrophe averted by so narrow a margin. The incident proved once more the statements of Sir Winston Churchill.

* Whether or not the *Hesperus* was the same tender that participated in the strangest incident ever in the history of the service is unclear. On December 26, 1900, the tender *Hesperus* stopped at Eileen Noors Lighthouse in the Hebrides and discovered that the three keepers were missing. Although search was made for months, they were never found.

4

Trapped Aboard
the *Kaptajn Nielsen*

The rescue of people trapped under the ocean's surface is always noteworthy and fascinating. The miraculous escape from the *Adelaide*, capsized near Barnegat Light, is told in Part III of this book. Here is the tale of the giant dredge *Kaptajn Nielsen*, which sank to the bottom of Australia's Brisbane Harbor in September 1964. Thirty-three men were imprisoned at the bottom of the sea under circumstances rarely equaled in the world's marine history. Eight of the victims died almost at once. Efforts were made to rescue the others, who were kept alive by air trapped inside the craft.

The disaster that befell the Danish dredge occurred late in the evening of Friday, September 18, 1964. First sign on shore that something was amiss was at 11:30, when vacationer Bob Anthony was gazing out from the Tangalooma tourist resort. He saw "what looked like searchlights" and a long cigar-shaped vessel in the channel between Moreton Island and the mainland. He dismissed it as a "submarine" and went to bed.

It was not until 3:00 A.M. Saturday morning that Seaman Eric Poulsen, after an incredible four-mile swim followed by a two-mile staggering run on the beach, reached Moreton Island in Brisbane Harbor to report the tragedy and ask for help.

Dressed in only his soaking wet underpants and a polo shirt, his feet cut and bleeding, Poulsen stumbled to the first cottage he saw and knocked on the door. "Boat overturn . . . many drown . . . telephone," he said in broken English to the occupant, Mrs. Bennett, when she answered his knock.

"I thought he was a drunk," Mrs. Bennett later recalled. "I was a bit scared, so I closed the door and went to tell my husband. But Poulsen kept knocking, and when we had a good look at him we realized something terrible had happened."

Mr. William Isherwood, at the Tangalooma tourist resort, reported to the Water Police that a man named Eric Poulsen was reporting that the great dredge in the harbor had turned turtle.

"We thought it was a joke," said Sergeant Jim Schofield of the Water Police. "But I checked it out and found the dredge was overdue. We immediately organized rescue operations." Word had reached him at 3:05 A.M. Saturday.

In a short time the air was filled with police appeals broadcast on every radio station in the vicinity. Owners of outboard motorboats, cabin cruisers and work boats were beseeched to go out to the disaster scene. Sergeant Les Clark of the Water Police notified all civilian skin divers that they were desperately needed.

The response was amazing and gratifying, the start of a massive rescue operation. Dozens of craft, including launches, speedboats, trawlers and tugs, soon converged on the area. The most vital move was made by a scuba diving organization headed by Joe Engwirda, thirty-two, a professional who ran a school for underwater divers in Brisbane. Arriving on the scene with great haste, he actively supervised the rescue. It was a situation no scuba diver had ever faced before.

In nighttime's pitch darkness, under the surface of the ocean, the divers explored the overturned craft foot by foot. With the help of electric torches, they discovered that the steel plates had burst in two when the giant dredge capsized, and several doors had broken from their hinges. Fighting their way through the overturned craft, Engwirda and the other scuba divers reached the survivors in cabins that were half-filled with water. There was still enough trapped air to keep the sailors alive.

"They were panicky when I first got there," explained Engwirda. "I had to spend about a half hour talking to the sailors before I brought them out. Fortunately I speak a bit of Danish.

"We got Aqualungs for the trapped men to come up with. I gave the crewmen a quick lesson on using the Aqualungs and let each one have a short workout in the cabin before we tried to get out.

"We had to take the men out through a skylight only three feet wide. In the middle of the skylight was a steel bar that we could not get through with our Aqualung equipment on. We had to take off our Aqualungs to pass through and then put them back on again. We had trouble pulling the men through the skylight. One chap was too fat to get through and he panicked, but he finally escaped. On the average it only took two minutes to get each man from his cabin to the surface. We used air hoses for panicky ones who could not be given Aqualungs." Air was also sent into the hull to replenish the supply.

Senior Constable Ivan Adams also covered himself with glory that September morning, bringing up several survivors. He said, "Trouble was that most of the trapped men had not used underwater gear before. One of the men refused to use gear at all. I grabbed hold of him, told him to take a breath, and got him out as quickly as possible. The door of the cabin had been smashed, and we had to tear it away to get into that particular cabin. We had to rip furniture from around another man who was trapped in his cabin."

After being underwater for more than four hours, the constable collapsed. It was found that he had developed a severe carbon dioxide headache from the impure air in the ship. He and Engwirda had been the first skin divers on the scene. Adams said later that the superstructure and bridge of the dredge were buried in the sand, and the ship was fast on the bottom.

At 2:00 P.M. the afternoon following the disaster, Water Police Sergeant Schofield, in overall charge of rescue work, gave up all hope of finding more survivors and announced discontinuance of operations. Sergeant Schofield said: "There is definitely no one left alive on board. A dozen skin divers have just searched the length and breadth of the ship. They went into every nook and cranny, every cabin, every alleyway, dining room and engine room. They tapped in each section of the ship but got no response. Then they repeated the search, just to make sure. They are satisfied there is no person alive aboard the ship."

Sergeant Schofield emphasized the fact that fifteen crewmen escaped. It was "the greatest stroke of good luck I have seen in many a day," he said. When the tragedy occurred, he reported, the dredge was taking on sand and had almost completed a capacity loading. Schofield added that it was his opinion the dredge turned over suddenly. "It just went 'whoof.' "

The survivors later related what their thoughts and actions had been while they were imprisoned in the dredge. Electrical engineer Kim Petersen, thirty-six, the last to leave the underwater tomb, told his rescuers the following day that there was no panic. This seems to contradict what diver Joe Engwirda reported; possibly conditions varied in different parts of the submerged craft.

"Even when things looked the worst," said Petersen, "we were confident you would get us out somehow. I promised the boys that we could stay alive at least two days. Maybe I was a bit optimistic."

Petersen praised the spirit of all the survivors, particularly several young crew members. Even when the water was rising and the air getting stale, they kept their heads and managed to tell a joke or two.

"I was sitting on my bunk," said Petersen, "when the dredge lurched over. I managed to drag myself through the cabin door. Just as the lights failed I saw James Madsen, a young Danish apprentice, madly scrambling up the living quarter steps.

"Madsen was met by a wall of water and disappeared. He drowned. I and eight others managed to climb into an up-turned cabin that contained a trapped air bubble. When the water settled, clusters of phosphorescent organisms gave us a little light to see with.

"I tapped a chair leg on a table for three hours to let anyone outside the hull know that we were still alive. After three hours my prayers were answered when a tap-tap-tap rang through from outside the keel. Incidentally, several of the men had been bruised when the barge capsized, and were bleeding; some were worried that the blood might attract sharks.

"All the time we were peering into the water waiting for divers to reach us. It was a terrific feeling when the first frog-man came through a skylight under us in the cabin roof."

The first survivor to be rescued was Per Wistensen, a fifteen-year-old cabin boy. Then came oiler Gurg Jakobsen, fifty-eight, the oldest man in the cabin. Others followed. Petersen was the last to be rescued, for he had volunteered to show young crew members how to use the air equipment.

For the *Kaptajn Nielsen's* chief cook, fifty-two-year-old Aage Hansen of Rudkjobling, it was the third time he had been lucky. Hansen, one of the men entombed for eight hours in the flooded cabin, had a previous record of shipwrecks at sea.

Waiting to have a gash on his forehead treated at the General Hospital, Hansen showed a large scar on his right arm. "Mussolini gave this to me when one of his planes bombed our ship out of the water during the Spanish civil war. Then in 1942, during Hitler's war, my boat went down off Greenland after it struck a rock, and we were stranded in Greenland for three months. But last night was easily the worst experience I had at sea.

"In my bunk when the dredge turned over, I was stunned by a blow on the head. One of the cabin doors flew off its hinges, and I found myself floating down a passageway. I swam and paddled into another cabin where there was not so much water, and there were my mates.

"The spirit of the boys was wonderful, especially that of the young ones. During the night they sang songs and some even told jokes." Hansen said he would be going back to sea as soon as he returned to Denmark. "It's my living," he asserted.

Deckhand Dion Jorgensen, seventeen, from Aarlborg, Denmark, said he heard three men drown shortly after the dredge capsized. "They were calling for help, but we couldn't do anything." Jorgensen said nine seamen crammed into his cabin as a wall of water bore down on them when the dredge went over. "We thought we were going to die. Nine of us stood in water about four and a half feet deep. We were in that room for eight hours."

Rescue from the deathtrap hull came as a birthday present for Gurg Jakobsen, an oiler from Copenhagen. "Today is my fifty-eighth birthday," Jakobsen said at the General Hospital.

Engineroom-hand Christian Reinholdt arrived at the Brisbane General Hospital semiconscious from immersion and shock. Others taken to the hospital were the captain of the dredge, Karl Albert Flindt, and the second officer, Niels Sonne. Reinholdt and Sonne were picked up by a helicopter piloted by Captain Ray Hudson. The chopper landed on the water near the disaster scene, then sped the survivors to a hospital.

Two survivors, Svend Frederiksen, twenty-six, and Borje Hanson, forty-four, missed certain death by a bare six inches. They climbed out through a pipe and were sitting on the overturned hull when help arrived.

"In seconds," Frederiksen explained later, "the water rushed in and then all the lights went out. I found myself down in the main engine room, swimming in the darkness. The water was covered with oil from the Diesel and lubricating tanks. I swam over to Hanson, and we climbed up on one of the engines to try to get out of the water. It was dark and cold, and the water was rising all the time.

"I found one of the engine room tools and banged on the hull, but there was no answer. The stern end was getting deeper, so we swam forward. We heard hissing as air trapped in the compartment began escaping. It came from one of the big tubes through which sand is pumped when dredging. We decided to get into the tube. If we opened it and it was full of water, we would drown for sure.

"Our air was nearly gone and the water was up to our chests, so we risked it and tore it open. We could see the end of the tube about eighteen feet ahead. Most of it was underwater, but the top of the tube was six inches clear. We crawled along it, keeping our heads out of the water, then ducked down and swam out. We sat on the keel waving the flashlight but could not attract anyone's attention, though we could see people on shore. Finally we were rescued."

A three-day hearing was held later in the year before shipping inspector Captain R. Hildebrand and a battery of legal and shipping representatives. First there was an announcement that the body of one of the two men still missing had been found by a private launch in Moreton Bay. It was identified as James Madsen.

Master of the *Kaptajn Nielsen,* Captain Karl Albert Flindt, forty-three, was the first witness heard. "About 11:15 P.M. I left the bridge to go to my day room," he said. "I heard the sound of the winches commencing to raise the suction pipe on the starboard side. The ship started to hang over slightly. This is usual when the suction pipe is being raised. Normally the ship settles back again. This time she didn't.

"She did not stop going to starboard. At first she moved only slightly, then faster. I became alarmed. I decided to go back to the bridge to see what was happening."

Captain Flindt said that he reached the door of his day room and was "thrown back inside by a wall of water."

The officer of the watch, First Mate M. Munt, and the winchman, Mr. Eschen, both of whom were on the bridge, were killed. Mr. Eschen, who had been operating the dredging controls, had twenty years experience.

Captain Flindt said he did not believe the dredge was overloaded. He had looked at the load meter before leaving the bridge, and it indicated that the loading was nearly completed. Captain Hildebrand asked Captain Flindt if he had ever known a loading meter to "go wrong." Flindt said it had happened once on the *Kaptajn Nielsen*, but a long time ago. "I don't think it went wrong on this occasion," he added. Captain Flindt said he had no idea why the dredge capsized.

Professional skin diver Joe Engwirda, in testifying before Captain Hildebrand, said that he believed the capsizing of the *Kaptajn Nielsen* took no more than ten seconds. He based his opinion on observations he made while diving into the semisubmerged dredge. Engwirda found that furniture drawers which could have moved to starboard had not had time to slide out of position. He tested the drawers and they moved easily. He added: "Another reason for my opinion is that the ship filled with water so quickly that a lot of the crockery was still unbroken." The water came in so fast that when the crockery shifted at the moment the dredge capsized, the dishes fell into water instead of onto the metal deck.

Engwirda said he also considered that from the time the dredge began to capsize to the moment it completely turned over, it had not moved more than ten feet from the location over which it was working. He deduced this from the debris beneath the ship on the sea bottom.

Engwirda said that the engine room telegraph on the bridge was at "slow ahead" for one engine and at "half ahead" for the other. He had seen this when he first dived into the bridge house. "They have since been moved," he said, "I don't know by whom, but someone must have been playing around with them." He also added that the covering glass on the load meter was broken "by someone or something" after it was taken from the dredge and placed in a small surface boat.

At the time of the capsizing Constable Ivan J. Adams of the Water Police contacted Engwirda, and they used the diver's speedboat to reach the scene at about 7:00 A.M. He said the ship was "anchored" in the sand, principally by the bridge, the funnel, and the masts and gantries. "I did not observe any marks on the hull which might indicate that the ship might have grounded," he added. "Neither did I see any cracked plates or dents on the hull. I also examined the chains supporting the hopper doors. All locking pins were in place, while the ship's suction pipe was still attached. The head of the pipe was also connected and in one piece."

Constable Adams explained that the lifting wires were lying in the sand, but he could see no breaks. He added that "on the bridge I saw a series of levers with black knobs. All were in a neutral position except one. This was pulled back and I could read the inscription that said: 'Use only with key.' There were a considerable number of spare pieces of gear, steel plate, chains, nuts and bolts lying on the seabed. I could not see the anchors or cables on the bottom, but the lifeboats were still attached to their davits."

The capsizing of the dredge *Kaptajn Nielsen* has never been fully explained. The fact that the vessel's main hopper door chains were still intact exploded the theory that the disaster was caused when those doors suddenly opened, dumping half the dredge's load. Nevertheless, the majority of mariners who studied testimony at the various post-accident hearings agree there was much that could never be either proved or understood concerning this strange marine disaster.

Long after other incidents in connection with this tragedy are forgotten, the astounding feat of Seaman Eric Poulsen that terrifying night will be recalled. His remarkable swim and run along the beach to obtain aid rank high in heroism and bravery.

PIRATES, SHIPWRECKS
AND HISTORIC CHRONICLES

TO MY WIFE
ANNA-MYRLE SNOW
WITHOUT WHOM THIS
BOOK WOULD NEVER
HAVE BEEN ATTEMPTED
OR COMPLETED

Contents

Part Five: Incredible Occurrences

Part Six: Shipwrecks

Part Seven: Supernatural Tales

Preface

As I put the finishing touches on this, my ninety-seventh volume, I look out across the 7-1/4-mile-expanse of ocean that is used by ships of all sorts and realize how lucky it is that I am by the edge of the North River, where more than one thousand sailing vessels were launched. From this vantage point sparkling water, breaking waves and a delightful coast with touches of glistening sand and rocky beach create the perfect atmosphere for the completion of this volume, which combines tales of pirates, treasure, shipwrecks, lighthouses and ghosts.

Over the years I have received so many letters from young people that for this book I have chosen stories which will appeal particularly to this group as well as to readers of all ages.

Institutions that have been of great help to me include the following: Marshfield's Ventress Library, the Scituate Library, the Hingham Library, the Boston Public Library, the Boston Athenaeum, the American Antiquarian Society and the Bostonian Society. The United States Coast Guard, which I admire so much, has helped when needed.

Those individuals I shall acknowledge, in addition to those who claim anonymity, are Samuel J. Parsley, Robert Sullivan, Fred Hooper, Police Officer Magee, Mrs. Doris Prosser, Dr. Jules Friedman, Paul Cantor, Richard Nakashian, Chester Shea, Marguerite Miller of the Daggett House on Martha's

Vineyard, Councilor John W. Sears, Suzanne Gall, Dorothy Snow Bicknell, Leonard Bicknell, Laura Bicknell, Jessica Bicknell, Eunice Snow, Donald Snow, Alfred Schroeder, Melina Herron Oliver, William Pyne, Frederick G. S. Clow, Trevor Johnson, Jean Foley, Walter Spahr Ehrenfeld, James Douglass, Arthur Cunningham, Marie Hansen, Richard Carlisle, Susan Williams, Elva Ruiz, Joel O'Brien, Joseph Kolb, Charles Marks and Frederick Sanford. I am extremely grateful to my secretary, Helen Salkowski, and to John Herbert of Quincy for their assistance in preparing this book.

EDWARD ROWE SNOW
Marshfield, Massachusetts

PART ONE

Pirates

CHAPTER 1

Captain Phillips, Whose Head Was Pickled

John Phillips, whose head was brought to Boston in a pickle barrel, worked in the carpenter trade while a young man in his native England. He later resolved upon a seafaring life, shipping on a voyage to Newfoundland. The vessel was captured and the crew taken prisoner by the pirate Anstis. Evidently Phillips was soon attracted to the life of a marine highwayman: he signed pirate articles and became carpenter aboard Anstis's ship.

Phillips's initiation into the brutal side of piracy occurred when Anstis, sailing off Martinique, captured the ship *Irwin,* commanded by Captain Ross. A woman passenger aboard the *Irwin* was seized by a pirate and assaulted. Colonel William Dolly of Monserat forcibly intervened, whereupon he was terribly abused and severely wounded for his efforts to protect the unfortunate woman.

A short time later the pirates decided to try for a pardon from the English government. The members of the buccaneer band sailed to the island of Tobago. There they drew up a round robin, signing their names in a circle so that no one signature headed the list. In this petition they appealed to the King for clemency, claiming to have been forced to a life of crime by the master pirate Bartholomew Roberts. They further claimed that they loathed and despised the mere thought of piracy, and their only reason for capturing vessels was to use them as a means of escape, and to obtain a pardon.

This unusual message was sent to England aboard a merchant vessel from Jamaica. Several of the braver pirates also shipped on the merchantman, including John Phillips. On reaching England he went at once to some friends who lived in Devonshire. He was soon rudely awakened from his dream of clemency when he heard that other pirates who had returned with him had been locked in the British jail. Hurrying to Topsham, he again shipped on a voyage for Newfoundland, this time under Captain Wadham.

When he arrived safely on the American side of the Atlantic, Phillips jumped ship and, as the season was getting underway, became a Newfoundland fish splitter. At heart, however, he was still a dyed-in-the-wool pirate. Becoming better acquainted with his fellow fish splitters every day, he evaluated the character of certain of the men. He chose an auspicious moment to ask if they would care to exchange a fish-splitter's apron for the Jolly Roger. The answer was to his taste, a credit to his discernment. Sixteen of the men were in hearty accord with the suggestion.

At anchor in the harbor of Saint Peters, Newfoundland, lay a comfortable schooner belonging to William Minot of Boston. The pirates-to-be planned to seize this vessel on the night of August 29, 1723. But when the appointed hour arrived, only four of the sixteen summoned courage enough to make their appearance. Phillips was tired of fish splitting and decided to attempt the venture despite reduced numbers. The five men appropriated and sailed the schooner from the harbor without trouble.

When safely away, the pirates began to draw up articles but almost had to abandon this procedure when it was found there was no Bible on board upon which to take an oath. Finally one of the resourceful pirates found a hatchet, which was used instead of the Bible, and the ceremony continued. The articles for Phillips's newly christened ship *Revenge* included:

THE ARTICLES ON BOARD THE *REVENGE*

1. Every Man shall obey Civil Command; the Captain shall have one full share and a half in all Prizes; the Master, Carpenter, Boatswain, and Gunner shall have one Share and quarter.

2. If any Man shall offer to run away, or keep any Secret from the Company, he shall be maroon'd with one Bottle of Powder, one Bottle of Water, one small Arm and Shot.

3. If any Man shall steal any Thing in the Company, or game to the Value of a Piece of Eight, he shall be maroon'd or shot.

4. If at any Time we should meet another Marooner that Man shall sign his Articles without the Consent of our Company, shall suffer such Punishment as the Captain and Company shall think fit.

5. That Man that shall strike another whilst these Articles are in force, shall receive Moses' Law (that is, 40 Stripes lacking one) on the bare Back.

6. That Man that shall snap his Arms, or smoak Tobacco in the Hold, without a Cap to his Pipe, or carry a Candle lighted without a Lanthorn, shall suffer the same Punishment as in the former Article.

7. That Man that shall not keep his Arms clean, fit for an Engagement, or neglect his Business, shall be cut off from his Share, and suffer such other Punishment as the Captain and the Company shall think fit.

8. If any Man shall lose a Joint in Time of an Engage-

ment, he shall have 400 Pieces of Eight, if a Limb, 800.

9. If at any Time we meet with a prudent Woman, that Man that offers to meddle with her, without her Consent, shall suffer present Death.

Phillips was made captain. John Nutt became navigator, James Sparks gunner, and Thomas Fern carpenter. William White, whose career ended later in Boston harbor, became the single crew member. It was not long before he had company, for the piratical cruise gathered ships and men. Some willingly joined the pirates; others had to be forced. Among the former was John Rose Archer, who had already served in illustrious company with Blackbeard, as bloodthirsty a villain as ever hoisted the Jolly Roger. Based on his background of buccaneering bravery, Archer was made the ship's quartermaster.

September 5, 1723, was a busy day for the pirates. They captured several fishing vessels off Newfoundland and forced three men into service: Isaac Larsen, an Indian; John Parsons; and John Filmore, the great-grandfather of President Millard Fillmore.

Later in the month Captain Furber and his schooner were taken. The Massachusetts Archives reveal that the next capture was a French vessel, from which the pirates removed thirteen pipes of wine, many supplies and a large cannon. Two of the crew, Peter Taffrey and John Baptis, were forced into service.

Early the next month an important capture was made. The buccaneers overtook the brigantine *Mary,* under Captain Moor, and removed her cargo worth five hundred pounds. A few days later another brigantine fell to the pirates. This time a William Taylor joyously accepted membership in the pirate crew. According to his words, he was being taken to Virginia to be sold when "they met with these honest men and I listed to go with them." Just how honest Taylor eventually found the pirates is a question.

Ship after ship was captured as the pirates continued their profitable undertaking in the West Indies. Eventually, however, their fortunes changed and provisions ran low. When the meat rations were practically exhausted, they ran afoul of a French sloop from Martinique, mounting twelve guns. Ordinarily they would have sailed clear of this formidable opponent, but hunger made them reckless. Hoisting the black flag, Phillips ran alongside and shouted that unless immediate surrender was made, no quarter would be given. The French crew unexpectedly gave in at once. The buccaneers plundered the sloop and took four of her men, then allowed her to sail away.

By this time the bottom of the *Revenge* needed cleaning. The ship was sailed to the island of Tobago, where she was run up at high tide and careened. Bad news awaited the pirates: their old buccaneering associates had all been taken to Antigua and hanged. As the *Revenge* was having the heavy sea growth removed from her sides and bottom, the masts of a man-of-war became visible on the leeward side of the island. In hot haste the *Revenge* was launched and sailed from the harbor at the flood of the tide, leaving four Frenchmen on the beach.

For the next few days in February 1724 the pirates followed a northerly course, sailing some distance to the south of Sandy Hook. They soon fell in with Captain Laws, master of a snow bound for Barbados. Thomas Fern, James Wood, William Taylor and William Phillips (not to be confused with Captain John Phillips) were sent aboard the square-rigged ship and ordered to keep company with the *Revenge.* The two vessels pursued a southern course until Latitude 21°, whereupon Fern, disgruntled because Archer had been made quartermaster, tried to run away with the snow. Captain Phillips was on the alert, however, and gave chase.

Drawing alongside, he ordered Fern aboard the *Revenge.* For a reply Fern fired his pistol at Captain Phillips, missing him. A short skirmish ensued; Wood was killed, William Phillips badly wounded in the leg, and Taylor and Fern forced to surrender.

Something had to be done at once for William Phillips, in agony from his wound. The decision was made to amputate. The ship's carpenter, because of his experience in sawing, was chosen to perform the operation. He went below and soon appeared on deck with the largest saw he could find in his chest. Taking the painfully injured leg under his arm, he fell to work. Finally the limb dropped off the injured man's body. To seal the wound, the carpenter heated his broadax white-hot and seared the leg as best he could. The operation proved a complete success. Shortly after the operation a fishing schooner was captured. The pirate captain suggested Phillips be put aboard, but the injured man demurred, fearing he would be hanged upon reaching the mainland. He chose to convalesce with the pirates, and he lived on to be tried later as a pirate, condemned and pardoned.

Within a short time the buccaneers seized a ship from London, from which they removed cannon and powder. An expert navigator, Henry Giles, was forced from this ship to the *Revenge* with his "Books and Instruments." Since he was a man of importance and education, sailing master Nutt placed him in charge of the journal.

Soon Fern again attempted escape. This time Captain John Phillips promptly shot and killed him. Another person who tried to get away a little later was also summarily put to death. The rest of the forced men decided to be more cautious, having plans afoot, however, for eventually taking over the *Revenge*.

Two ships from Virginia were now captured, one of them in charge of another Captain John Phillips. The second ship was commanded by Captain Robert Mortimer, a young married man on his first trip as a master. While pirate Phillips was aboard Mortimer's ship, he heard of a mutiny on his own vessel. Captain Mortimer quickly seized this opportune moment to start a fight of his own. Grabbing a handspike, he hit Phillips on the head. The blow either lacked force or Phillips's head was singularly hard. He staggered back, drew his sword and ran Mortimer through. At once two of the pirate's men cut Mortimer to pieces. Mortimer's own men, frightened at the bloodshed, stood by without offering a hand to help their captain.

Two men were forced from the other ship: seaman Charles Ivemay and carpenter Edward Cheeseman, needed to replace Fern. John Filmore, while rowing Cheeseman across to the *Revenge,* found the opportunity to discuss certain plans with the carpenter, schemes that called for the eventual seizure of the *Revenge.* Cheeseman gave his heart and soul to the idea, and from that moment the perfection of details which brought final escape was effected.

Resuming the cruise, the pirates captured eleven vessels in rapid succession. William Lancy, captain of a fishing schooner, was brought aboard the *Revenge* and while there saw nine vessels overhauled and captured. One of the captains gave the pirate a merry chase but was finally taken. Captain Phillips, enraged at this lack of consideration, ordered the unlucky commander, Dependence Ellery, aboard the *Revenge.* He was prodded around the deck and made to dance and jump until he collapsed in a dead faint.

Now begins the voyage that ended in the death of Phillips. On April 14, 1724, Captain Andrew Haraden sailed from Annisquam for a trip aboard the *Squirrel,* his new fishing boat whose deck was not quite finished. Leaving Ipswich Bay, the sloop fell in with another vessel, which was actually the pirate ship *Revenge.* Off the Isles of Shoals Captain Phillips sent a shot across the sloop's bow and ran up a black flag with a skeleton on it. When Haraden saw that the situation was hopeless, he rowed to the *Revenge* and surrendered. Phillips liked the lines of the *Squirrel* and ordered all stores transferred to the trim sloop. The other fishermen were allowed to go aboard the *Revenge* and sail for home, but Haraden was forcibly detained on his own vessel, which now became the pirate flagship. Before long Cheeseman approached Haraden with ideas of escape; Haraden was very interested.

Several of the forced men believed that the best time to capture the sloop was at night. But the presence of tall, husky John Nutt proved a stumbling block. The conspirators finally decided it would be too risky to try to take him without fire-arms. Cheeseman suggested a daylight attempt, when there would be less chance for confusion, and the conspirators agreed upon this plan. High noon on April 17, 1724, was chosen as the most appropriate time. The various tools of the carpenter could be placed around the unfinished deck, on which men were working. Then, at a given signal, the attack was to be made with the tools as weapons.

The moment arrived. Cheeseman brought out his brandy bottle, took a drink and passed it to John Nutt, offering as a toast that they should all drink to their next meeting. Then Cheeseman and Nutt took a turn about the deck. Passing a broadax lying on the planks, Filmore casually picked it up. Holding it carelessly in his hand, he watched Cheeseman as the latter asked Nutt what he thought of the weather. Before Nutt could answer, Haraden winked knowingly at the other forced man, whereupon Cheeseman thrust a hand between the aston-ished Nutt's legs, grabbing the sailing master by the collar with the other hand. Striding across the deck with the struggling pirate, he attempted to throw Nutt over the side. But Nutt grabbed frantically at Cheeseman's coat sleeve, crying, "Lord, have mercy upon me! What are you trying to do, carpenter?"

Cheeseman answered that it was obvious what was happening. "Master, you are a dead man," he cried. Striking Nutt heavily on the arm, Cheeseman watched the pirate fall to his death in the sea.

Meantime there was plenty of action elsewhere on the sloop. When Filmore saw the sailing master being thrown to his death, he split the boatswain's head clear down to his neck in one mighty blow. Captain Phillips rushed on deck just in time to receive a terrific blow on the head from a mallet wielded by Cheeseman. This broke the pirate's jaw, but Phillips leaped for his assailant. Haraden then sprang at the captain. Cheeseman, seeing Gunner Sparks trying to interfere, tripped him, causing him to fall into the way of the two Frenchmen, who hurled him into the sea.

Haraden now brought his trusty broadax down on the captain's head, killing him instantly. Cheeseman started toward the hold looking for John Rose Archer, the quartermaster. Encountering him in the runway, Cheeseman hit Archer two or three times with his mallet, but as he was about to finish him off, he heard someone shouting, "Stop!" It was Harry Giles, the young seaman, who said that some of the pirates should be taken alive as evidence. Recognizing the wisdom of this, Cheeseman bound Archer and three other pirates hand and foot with ropes.

Captain Haraden was again in command of his sloop. While the *Squirrel* was running for Annisquam, the sailors cut the head from the body of Captain John Phillips and affixed it to the mast of the sloop for a time.

Sailing up the bay, Captain Haraden ordered a gun fired to announce their happy homecoming. Unfortunately the gun went off prematurely, killing the French doctor on board. It is probable that the bodies of several of the pirates who had been killed in the struggle were taken ashore at Hangman's Island, in Annisquam harbor. Tradition, always a little at fault, has it that the men were hanged at the island. But they were already dead, so it seems likely that their bodies were strung up in chains to warn other pirates. There is no evidence on this point, however. The heads of Captain John Phillips and another pirate, Burrill by name, were brought to Boston in a pickle barrel to preserve them for evidence.

The *Boston News-Letter* estimated the pirates' victims as three shallops, fifteen fishing vessels, three schooners, three brigantines, four sloops, and five ships—thirty-three vessels that Phillips had captured in less than eight months.

Captain Andrew Haraden had now the not-too-easy task of proving his own innocence. He at once went to the "Harbor," as the present Gloucester was then called. There he made oath before Esquire Epes Sargent, swearing the details of his capture by the pirates and his eventual delivery. He then returned to the sloop to await investigation. Shortly afterward, on May 3, the four real pirates and the seven forced men were all locked up in the Boston jail.

The Court of Admiralty, with its customary pomp and ceremony, was held in Boston on May 12, 1724, to try the men accused of piracy. Lieutenant Governor William Dummer, erstwhile commander of the great fort at Castle Island, presided at the court in what is now the Old State House. Skipper Haraden, who does not seem to have been brought to trial, gave important testimony as to the character of John Filmore and Edward Cheeseman, who were tried first. When Haraden told of the events of April 17, in which Filmore and Cheeseman fought so effectively against the pirates, the court was visibly affected. Dummer ordered the room cleared, and the verdict of "not guilty" came as welcome news to the two accused men.

Later that day the court sat again. This time one-legged William Phillips, navigator Henry Giles, Indian Isaac Larsen, and other pirates were brought to the bar. When it was revealed that Larsen had held Captain Phillips's arm when Haraden struck him with the adz, the court seemed favorably inclined toward the Indian. Filmore said that he had never seen Larsen guilty of piracy except when "they now and then obliged him to take a shirt or a pair of stockings when almost naked." William Phillips, who had lost a leg, claimed to have been a forced man, but the evidence seemed to prove his guilt.

William White, the only one left of the original five who captured the sloop at Newfoundland, was then brought in. Filmore, who had been at Newfoundland when the sloop was stolen, testified against him. Filmore said that White admittēd he had been drunk when he joined up. William Taylor had so often been in conference with Captain Phillips that he was adjudged guilty. John Rose Archer, whose record was very bad because of his previous service with Blackbeard, was found guilty along with William Phillips and William White. The two Frenchmen were pardoned when it was shown that they had assisted in defeating the pirates. Phillips and Taylor were also reprieved, so there were only two pirates left in government custody on the date of execution, June 2, 1724. All others had been pardoned, for one reason or another.

Cotton Mather preached his usual sermon to the condemned men on May 31, 1724. According to Mather, both pirates had requested the sermon. Afterward Mather conversed with the condemned men privately, and believed them truly repentant.

Before the hangman sprung the trap, both pirates gave substantial speeches of penitence. Said Archer:

> I greatly bewail my profanations of the Lord's Day, and my Disobedience to my Parents. And my Cursing and Swearing, and my blaspheming the Name of the glorious God. . . .
> But one Wickedness that has led me as much as any, to

all the rest, has been my brutish Drunkenness. By strong Drink I have been heated and hardened into the Crimes that are now more bitter than Death unto me.

I could wish that Masters of Vessels would not use their Men with so much Severity, as many of them do, which exposes us to great Temptations.

William White followed with his parting message. Probably Cotton Mather had helped him compose the details.

I am now, with Sorrow, reaping the Fruits of my Disobedience to my Parents, who used their Endeavours to have me instructed in my Bible, and my Catechism. . . .

But my Drunkenness has had a great Hand in bringing my Ruin upon me. I was drunk when I was enticed aboard the Pyrate.

The usual large gathering of Boston people then watched the two men climb the ladder to the scaffold. At one end of the gallows the black pirate flag had been hung, the skeleton on it dancing in the wind as the men climbed the last rungs. The local paper said that the flag gave the whole affair "the sight dismal." At the signal the two pirates were left hanging in the air. So died pirate John Rose Archer, age twenty-seven, and pirate William White, age twenty-two, between the rise and fall of the tide at the Charlestown Ferry in Boston. A few hours later their bodies were cut down, placed in an open boat and taken to Bird Island, whose low-lying flats were between Noddle's Island and Governor's Island.

Down at Bird Island, meanwhile, Marshall Edward Stanbridge busily superintended the erection of a gibbet. Measurements had been made of Archer's head and the local blacksmith had turned out a wide iron band that fit nicely. Other iron bands were made to go around Archer's chest, hips and ankles, with chains connecting the various bands to keep them from slipping. On the arrival of the bodies at the island, White was quickly buried. Archer, who had been with Blackbeard, was hung in chains as an example for all to see. The iron bands and the chains, together with the hire of an extra man to help secure the bands and chains, cost twelve pounds ten shillings.

So the body of Archer swung in the wind, its iron bands creaking rhythmically, a reminder of the awful fate awaiting pirates. Bostonians made excursions and trips out to Bird Island to see at close range the gruesome sight. One good citizen, Jeremiah Bumstead, a brazier by trade, took his wife and ten friends down the harbor six days after the execution to see the "piratte in Gibbits att Bird Island."

In later years Bird Island washed away completely. Today it is only a memory, like the pirate who hung there and the captain's pickled head.

CHAPTER 2

Marblehead's Crusoe

Every reader knows and marvels at the tale of Robinson Crusoe. Less known, yet perhaps more incredible, is the story of Philip Ashton of Marblehead, who in three years lived through more adventures on the seas than most men could experience in a lifetime.

The exploits of this young Marblehead sailor began while he was with the fishing fleet in waters off Cape Sable. At that time, 1722, it was customary for the entire fleet to stop fishing on Friday afternoon and sail into Port Roseway, near what is now Shelburne, Nova Scotia, to await the Sabbath and observe it there. As the shallop carrying Ashton entered Port Roseway on June 15, 1722, he noticed not only the usual number of fishing boats in the harbor but a brigantine, which he incorrectly assumed to be an inward-bound West Indiaman.

Shortly thereafter a boat from the brigantine came alongside Ashton's shallop. Suddenly the men in the boat jumped aboard the fishing vessel and pulled out cutlasses and pistols, soon overcoming the astonished fishermen. This maneuver was repeated until more than a dozen fishing vessels anchored in the harbor had been captured.

When the fishermen were brought aboard the brigantine, they found that it was commanded by none other than the infamous villain, Captain Edward Low.

Philip Ashton was soon sent for, and he went aft to meet the notorious pirate. Confronted by the man whose name alone was enough to strike terror in the hearts of all honest sailors, Ashton was asked to sign articles and go along on a voyage. In his own words, Philip Ashton tells us what·then occurred:

> I told him, No; I could by no means consent to go with them, I should be glad if he would give me my Liberty, and put me on board any Vessel, or set me on shoar there. For indeed my dislike of their Company and Actions, my concern for my Parents, and my fears of being found in such Bad Company, made me dread the thoughts of being carried away by them; so that I had not the least Inclination to continue with them.

When Ashton refused to join up and sign articles with Captain Low, he was roughly handled and thrown down into the hold. While there he heard the various crews of the fishing fleet being brought over to the brigantine, one by one, and realized that there was little hope of assistance from the other vessels. The next day about thirty or forty of the fishermen who had refused to join up were placed on Mr. Orn's fishing schooner, which was turned into a floating prison for the dissenters.

At noon on Sunday Quartermaster John Russel boarded the schooner and took away six of the fishermen. They were Nicholas Merritt and Lawrence Fabens, both of whom later escaped; Joseph Libbie, who finally became a pirate and was hanged at Newport; Philip Ashton; and two other men whose names are not known. The fishermen were rowed over to the pirate chieftain's flagship, where they were lined up on the quarterdeck. All of them were under twenty-one years of age.

Captain Ned Low approached them, pistol in hand. "Are any of you married men?" asked Low. The question, unexpected as it was, struck the listeners dumb for the moment. The silence infuriated the pirate, and he cocked his pistol, shoving it against the head of poor Philip Ashton. "You dog," cried Low, "why don't you answer me? I shall shoot you through the head unless you tell me now if you are married or not."

Ashton, greatly frightened, stammered that he was not married, and the rest of the group answered similarly. Low then walked away. Ashton later found out that the pirate's concern was due to Low's wife having died, leaving a small child, who even then was living in Boston.

Later in the day Low again interviewed the six men and asked them to sign papers. All refused. Still later he had each man sent for singly, whereupon he repeated the question. Each fisherman again refused. Then Philip Ashton was taken below into the steerage, where the quartermaster tried to tempt him with stories of great riches and wealth. Other pirates gathered about him and tried to be friendly, to win his confidence. They asked him to "drink with them, not doubting but that this wile would sufficiently entangle me, and so they should prevail with me to do that in my Cups, which they perceived they could not bring me to do while I was Sober; but . . . I had no Inclination to drown my Sorrows with my Senses in their Inebriating Bowls, and so refused their Drink, as well as their Proposals."

After his final refusal Ashton was taken back up on deck, where Captain Low threatened him with death unless he changed his mind. Ashton said that whatever happened he could not join the pirate band. Eventually Low signed him on as a forced man, together with all his companions.

The following Tuesday the buccaneers chose a schooner belonging to Joseph Dolliber of Marblehead as the new flagship, and all the pirates went aboard her. With the exception of the six forced men and four others who had joined from the Isles of Shoals, the prisoners were sent over to the brigantine and allowed to proceed to Boston. This was discouraging to Philip Ashton, who made one final attempt to appeal for freedom. He and Nicholas Merrit went to Low, falling on their knees before the pirate captain and asking for release. Low scornfully refused, telling them if they attempted to escape they would be shot. The brigantine soon sailed off, and the forced sailors were alone with the highwaymen of the sea.

Just as Ashton had given up all thought of deliverance, an accident occurred that gave him hope. One of the pirates had left a dog on the beach when he came back to the ship, and the dog began to howl dismally. Low, hearing the disturbance, ordered that the dog be brought out. Two Marblehead boys volunteered to row in and get him, and nineteen-year-old Philip Ashton decided this was a good chance to escape. He rushed to the side of the ship and was about to jump into the boat, but Quartermaster Russel caught hold of his shoulder, saying that two men were sufficient to bring out one dog.

The pirates watched the boat land on shore and the Marblehead men walk inland away from it. They never returned, and the pirates lost their boat as well. The dog soon wandered off and was not seen again.

Quartermaster Russel believed that Ashton had tried to join the two, knowing that they planned to escape. But the truth was that while Ashton had planned to flee, he did not know the other two had the same objective. Nevertheless, the quartermaster was so infuriated that he attempted to kill Ashton then and there.

Russel seized Philip Ashton by the shoulder, clapped his great pistol against his skull and pulled the trigger. The gun misfired. Again and again the quartermaster snapped the pistol, but each time it failed to go off. Disgusted with his firearm, Quartermaster Russel went over to the side of the ship. Standing by the rail, he reset the pistol, pulled the trigger and fired the gun successfully into the ocean. The exasperated pirate now drew his cutlass and lunged for the boy. Terrified, Ashton ran down into the hold, where he cowered in the midst of other pirates, thus escaping Russel's further wrath.

It was a hard lot that lay ahead for the Marblehead lad, and he soon learned to hide in the hold most of the time. Once a week, however, he was brought up under examination and asked to sign articles, and every time he refused. Thrashed and beaten with sword and cane after each refusal, Ashton would escape to the hold as soon as he could to nurse his cuts and bruises for another week. Probably some of the kinder-hearted rogues took care of him in their crude way, so that he was able to get something to eat every day.

Week after week passed without hope, and despair made Ashton utterly miserable. In the book he later wrote, he speaks of Low's narrow escape from an encounter with a British man-of-war in the very harbor of Saint John's, Newfoundland, mentioning the seizure of seven or eight vessels the next day. Later a captured sloop manned by impressed pirates ran away from Low and was never seen again. Nicholas Merrit, one of Ashton's Marblehead friends, was aboard this vessel. The schooner and a captured pinkie were careened at the island of Bonavista, after which seven or eight forced men from the pinkie went ashore to hunt. They never returned to the ship. With so many escaping from Low, Ashton felt that his chance would eventually come. In this he was not mistaken.

A terrible storm caught the pirates shortly afterward, and for five days and nights Ashton feared that they would all go to the bottom. Even the most foul of the buccaneers was afraid during the fearful tempest, as Ashton recorded one of the bloodthirsty ruffian's exclaiming in his particular moment of spiritual anguish, "Oh! I wish I were at Home."

At last the storm subsided and the pirates headed for the

three islands called the Triangles, located in the West Indies about forty leagues from Surinam. Captain Low decided that another careening was necessary. In heaving down the pinkie, so many hands climbed into the shrouds that it threw her open ports under water. Low and the doctor, below in the cabin, almost drowned but managed to get out in time. The vessel went over on her beam ends in forty feet of water, throwing the men into the sea. As the vessel righted itself, the men climbed back into the shrouds. The entire hull remained far under water. It had been a narrow escape for the notorious Captain Low.

In the excitement two men drowned. Ashton, who was a poor swimmer, almost perished before he was rescued. The pinkie had carried most of the provisions and the drinking water, both of which were lost, so every sailor transferred to the schooner, which at once put out to sea.

Reaching the island of Grand Grenada, eighteen leagues westward of Tobago, they went ashore for water. The French on the island, suspecting them of being in the smuggling trade, sailed out to capture Low and his men. When Low saw them coming he ordered all the pirates to their stations, and the French sloop was quickly seized and made one of the pirate fleet. The buccaneers captured seven or eight vessels in short order, then took two sloops off Santa Cruz.

Low now desired a doctor's chest. He sent four Frenchmen ashore at Saint Thomas, demanding of the residents a chest of instruments and medicines or their town would be sacked and burned. The doctor's chest arrived within twenty-four hours, and the Frenchmen who had been prisoners were allowed to sail away in one of the captured sloops.

From Santa Cruz the pirates sailed to Curaçao, where they encountered an English man-of-war and a "Guinea-Man." Low escaped by sailing over some shallows on which the man-of-war ran aground. On this occasion Ashton was aboard the schooner, under command of Quartermaster Farrington Spriggs. The two pirate vessels separated in the chase, with Spriggs heading for the island of Utilla, near Roaton. Having lost Low completely, Spriggs decided to sail up through the Gulf of Mexico to New England, where he could increase his small company and reprovision his schooner.

There were eight forced men in Spriggs's entire crew of twenty-two who secretly plotted to capture the schooner. The scheme was to get the pirates drunk under the hatches as soon as the *Happy Delivery* approached the shores of New England. The forced men would then sail into the nearest harbor and throw themselves on the mercy of the government.

It was a good plan, but the men never had a chance to try it. Sailing from Utilla they fell in with a large sloop, which bore down on them, opening fire as it approached. Spriggs did not come about, running for possible escape instead. Then pirate colors were hoisted from the sloop. At this the regular pirates aboard Spriggs's vessel broke into cheers, for it was none other than Low's famous ensign that fluttered high above the sloop's decks. Soon the two old cronies were together again, and all was well except for the forced men, whose scheming came to an end. In the five weeks that Low and Spriggs had been separated, the forced men had hoped they had seen the last of the villain. But such was not the case. To make matters worse, one of the forced men eventually informed on the others. Spriggs was in favor of shooting them down, but Low laughed it off.

On returning to the schooner, Spriggs told Ashton he deserved to be hanged from the yardarm. Ashton informed the schooner's captain that his only desire was to be free of the pirate vessel, and he intended to harm no one. The incident was soon forgotten.

Low now steered a course for Roatan harbor, in the Bay of

Honduras. The pirate chieftain went ashore to indulge in drinking and carousing for a few days while his buccaneers were occupied careening and scraping the vessels. The schooner was loaded with logwood and sent out in charge of John Blaze, with four men aboard. When Low and Spriggs, together with many of the pirate leaders, went off to another island, Ashton's hopes were raised again. He would try to escape.

Saturday, March 9, 1723, was an eventful and thrilling day for Philip Ashton. Noticing the cooper with six men getting ready to row ashore from Spriggs's vessel, he impulsively asked to be taken with them, as he had not been on land since his capture almost nine months before. Since the island was desolate and uninhabited, the cooper finally gave in to the pitiful pleadings of the lad from Marblehead. Young Philip jumped into the longboat, dressed "with only an Ozenbrigs Frock and Trousers on, and a Mill'd Cap upon my Head, having neither Shirt, Shoes, not Stockings, nor any thing else about me; whereas, had I been aware of such an Opportunity, but one quarter of an Hour before, I could have provided my self something better. However, thought I, if I can but once get footing on Terra-Firma, tho' in never so bad Circumstances, I shall call it a happy Deliverance; for I was resolved, come what would, never to come on board again."

When the longboat landed, Ashton was the most active worker of all in moving the heavy casks up on the beach. When the task was over he naturally went off by himself as if to rest, picking up stones and shells along the beach until he was quite a distance from the others. Then he walked toward the edge of the woods, whereupon the cooper called out to him, asking where he was going.

"I'm going to get some coconuts," Ashton replied. Soon he reached the forest and broke into a run, out of sight of the pirates. This daring act is so much like Stevenson's hero in

Treasure Island that it may be Ashton served as a model for that tale.

In the meantime the pirates had filled the water casks and were ready to return to the ship. Ashton huddled in the dense forest, burrowing into a thicket, while the cries sounded out around him, calling him back to the longboat. Ashton kept a discreet silence. After a long time the pirates gave up and rowed out to their ship. Philip Ashton was thus alone on a desolate, uninhabited island.

When he was sure the pirates had left, Ashton ventured from his hiding place to a spot down the beach about a mile from the watering place, where he could observe what went on aboard the pirate vessels. Five days later they sailed away, leaving him very much alone on the island.

> I began to reflect upon myself and my present Cond́i-
> tion; I was upon an island from whence I could not get off;
> I knew of no Humane Creature within many scores of
> Miles of me; I had but a Scanty Cloathing, and no possibil-
> ity of getting more; I was destitute of all Provision for my
> Support, and knew not how I should come at any; . . .

Ashton walked around the island, situated to the north of Cape Honduras in Central America, estimating it to be some thirty miles in length. There were no signs of human habitation. Later, however, Ashton located a great grove of lime trees and near them some broken fragments of earthen pots, from which he concluded Indians had formerly lived on the island.

Wild figs, grapes and coconuts were plentiful, but Ashton found no way of opening the coconut husks. Then he discovered an oval-shape fruit, larger than an orange, which was red inside and contained two or three stones slightly smaller than a walnut. Fearing he might be poisoned, Ashton kept away from them until one day he chanced upon a group of wild hogs devouring the fruit. This encouraged him to sample the fruit, which he found delicious. He called them "Mammees Supporters"; today they are known as papayas. Ashton discovered sundry other fruits and herbs, although he avoided the "Mangeneil Apple," which he claimed would have killed him.

Deer, wild hogs, lizards, ducks, "Teil," curlews, "Galdings," snakes, pelicans, boobies, pigeons and parrots, with tortoises along the beaches, made up the wildlife on the island of Roatan. Ashton could not take advantage of the situation, however, for he had no knife or weapon of any kind, and was without means of making a fire. But he did discover hundreds of tortoise eggs in nests on the beach, and grew very fond of this change in his fruit-and-vegetable diet. He became quite a naturalist in observing the habits of the tortoise, noticing that the creatures lay their eggs in the sand above the high-water mark, depositing them in a hollow twelve to eighteen inches deep. Then the tortoise fills the hole, and smooths over the sand. The eggs, Ashton found, usually hatch in eighteen to twenty days, after which the young turtles make a rush for the water.

The lizards were giants, as big around as "a Man's wast," and about twelve to fourteen feet long. Ashton's first encounter was a terrible experience, for he mistook it for a log, whereupon it opened its mouth wide enough "to have thrown a Hat into it, and blew out its Breath at me." There were smaller serpents on the island, some of them poisonous, especially a snake called the "Barber's Pole, being streaked White and Yellow. But I met with no Rattle-Snakes there, unless the Pirates," concluded Ashton.

The mosquitoes and flies bothered Ashton greatly, in particular the small black flies. He found that a certain key located off the island was free from all flies and insects. Being a poor swimmer, he constructed a bamboo life preserver to ensure his arriving safely at the island. With his frock and trousers bound to his head, he swam across, donning his clothes on reaching the island. Unfortunately he never was able to bring out enough wood or branches to construct a hut there, or he might have made the low, treeless key his permanent abode. His new home he called Day Island, his older residence Night Island.

One time, just as he left the deep water while swimming to Day Island, he was severely struck from behind. To his astonishment the culprit was a huge shovel-nosed shark, grounded in the shallow water and thus not able to seize him. Ashton became a more and more experienced swimmer, but he never forgot that narrow escape from death.

The greatest trial Ashton had to endure was the lack of shoes. His bare feet soon were masses of ugly bruises and cuts from the sticks and stones away from the beach and the sharp shell fragments on the shore. Although he walked along as tenderly as he could, he would frequently step on a sharp rock or shell, which would "run into the Old Wounds & the Anguish of it would strike me down as suddenly as if I had been shot thro', & oblige me to set down and Weep by the hour together at the extremity of my Pain."

At one time he fell ill and was attacked by one of the wild boars. Managing to climb partway up a tree, Ashton felt the tusks of the boar as they ripped through his clothing and tore away a substantial section of the cloth. The boar then left the scene. This was the only time a wild beast bothered him in any way, but it almost proved fatal.

Growing worse instead of better, Ashton despaired of life itself. In his sickness and unhappiness, he longed for the sight of his parents.

The rains began during October and continued for five months. Throughout this time the air was raw and cold, similar to a New England northeasterly storm. During these months he wished for fire but was never able to produce it while alone on the island.

An amazing incident took place in November 1723, when Ashton sighted a craft approaching him in the distance. As it drew closer he could see it was a canoe, with one man paddling. Ashton, very feeble at the time, made no effort to conceal himself. The canoeist paddled close to shore and observed Ashton at the edge of the beach. Shouting to the Marblehead sailor, the canoeist asked who he was and what he was doing. After Ashton told his story, the stranger, whose name Ashton never found out, came ashore and shook hands with the sick islander.

It was a happy occasion for poor Philip Ashton when he could actually see and talk with another human being. The man, who was English, had been living with the Spaniards for the last twenty-two years, but for some undisclosed reason they decided to burn him alive and he fled to Roatan Island.

Building a fire—he had tongs and a flint—the Englishman told the sick Marbleheader that he would paddle out and hunt venison for him, planning to return in a few days. He gave Ashton his knife, the tongs and flint, five pounds of pork and a bottle of powder before departing three days later.

Ashton never saw him again. Within an hour after the canoe disappeared in the distance, a terrific storm hit the island, probably drowning the Englishman at sea. A canoe drifted ashore some time later, but after careful examination Ashton decided it was not that of the Britisher.

With the aid of the tools and implements his friend had given him, Philip Ashton was soon eating a more balanced diet, and the fire kept him comfortable during the bad weather. Slowly regaining his strength, he would walk along the beach, watching the crabs in the shallow water. Ashton finally developed a manner of catching them at night, by lighting a torch and wading waist deep with it in the water. The crabs, attracted by the light, would hasten to it, whereupon Ashton would spear them with a sharpened stick he carried in his other hand.

Growing stronger daily, Ashton made plans that involved the canoe he had found on the beach. He then thought himself "Admiral of the Neighbouring Seas," and decided to make a tour of some of the more distant islands. Storing up a supply of grapes, figs, tortoise and other eatables, with his precious flint box safely packed away, he set out for the island of Bonaca, some six leagues westward.

Approaching the distant land, Ashton noticed a sloop off the eastern shore. He pulled his craft up on the beach at the western end of Bonaca. He walked overland to the other side of the island but could not make out the sloop. Tired from his journey, he sat down at the foot of a large tree near the shore and went to sleep.

Suddenly awakened by gunfire, he jumped to his feet to find nine large canoes, filled with Spaniards, coming up on the beach in front of him, with several of the men discharging their guns at him. He ran for the nearest thicket, whereupon they all landed and went after him. But he was adept at concealing himself by this time. After searching for several hours, the Spanish sailors paddled away from the vicinity and Ashton went down to the shore. He noticed the tree where he had fallen asleep, and saw several bullet holes uncomfortably near where his head had been. It took him three days to return to his canoe, for his rush into the thicket had opened up old wounds. He found the canoe undisturbed and was soon paddling away from the island. His experiences while there made him eager to return to Roatan, which he reached without incident.

Seven long months passed. Finally, in June 1724, when he was out on his Day Island off the shore, two large canoes approached. The men aboard noticed the smoke from Ashton's fire. Ashton at once fled to the Night Island in his canoe.

Glancing back, he saw that the canoes were slowly following ashore, indicating that they were as afraid of Ashton as he was of them.

Observing their extreme caution, Ashton decided they could not be pirates. He went openly down to the shore to find out what he could. The visitors leaned back on their oars and paddles and asked Ashton who he was.

I told them I was an English Man, and had Run away from the Pirates. Upon this they drew something nearer and enquired who was there besides my self; I assured them I was alone. . . . They told me they were Bay-men, come from the Bay [Honduras]. This was comfortable News to me; so I bid them pull ashoar, there was no danger.

They first sent one man ashore, whom Ashton went down to meet. When the visitor saw such a "Poor, Ragged, Lean, Wan, Forlorn, Wild, Miserable, Object so near him" he started back, frightened from the shock. On recovering, he shook hands with Ashton, who embraced him with joy. Then the sailor picked poor Ashton up in his arms and carried him down to the canoes, where the entire company soon surrounded him in wonderment.

When Ashton told them he had been living on the island for sixteen months, the group was amazed. After they gave him a small amount of rum, he fell down insensible, overcome by the effects of the drink to which he was unaccustomed. But he revived slowly and later was as well as could be expected.

The Bay men told him that they had fled from the Spaniards, who, they feared, were about to assault them. They soon moved everything ashore, and within a short time had erected a substantial dwelling a little distance away on one of the windswept keys. They named this new home the Castle of Comfort. Ashton recovered his strength and spirits aided by the presence of so many human beings around him, and was soon joining in hunting expeditions. He made a good friend of an old man the Bay men called Father Hope, who told him of his many experiences, finally revealing that he had buried a small treasure chest in the woods.

Six months later pirates appeared. Ashton had gone over to Bonaca to hunt with three other men. Returning one night to Roatan Island, they were surprised at the sound of heavy firing. Coming into the moonlit harbor, they noticed that a large vessel was besieging the "Castle of Comfort." Taking down their sail as rapidly as possible, the four islanders rowed out of the harbor. Unfortunately, they had been detected. Soon a canoe with eight or ten men was chasing them. Drawing closer to the fleeing men, the invaders discharged a swivel gun mounted in the bow of the canoe. The shot landed in the water ahead.

The attacking party were actually pirates from Spriggs's vessel, the same from which Ashton had escaped. Reaching shore before the buccaneers could catch them, the islanders fled into the woods. The disappointed pirates landed on the beach, taking the canoe that the men had left on the shore, and then departed from the island. Ashton described what happened when his friends surrendered:

Accordingly they took all the Men ashoar, and with them an Indian Woman and Child; those of them that were ashoar abused the Woman shamefully. They killed one Man after they were come ashoar, and threw him into one of the Baymens Canoes, where their Tar was, and set Fire to it, and burnt him in it. Then they carried our People on Board their Vessels, where they were barbarously treated.

Learning of treasure in the woods that had been hidden by old Father Hope, the pirates beat Hope unmercifully until he revealed the location. They found the treasure and took it away with them. Before leaving, the pirates gave the Bay men a craft of about five tons in which to sail to the Bay, but made them promise not to communicate with Ashton or his group. Then the pirates sailed away for good.

Father Hope decided a bad promise was better broken than kept, so came at once to the hiding place of Ashton and his friends. A conference was held on plans for the future. All except Ashton, John Symonds and a slave belonging to Symonds wished to leave at once for the Bay. Ashton at first was tempted to go, but decided that the chances for a ship were better at the island. Farewells were made, and the Bay men left in their small craft.

The season was now approaching for the Jamaica traders to sail in the vicinity. Because Bonaca was a favorite watering place for the traders, the three men went there. On the fifth day a great storm came up, which blew hard for three days. When the worst of the gale had passed, Ashton noticed a large fleet of vessels standing for the island's harbor. The larger vessels anchored off, but a brigantine came in over the shoals, making for the watering place. Three Englishmen, as Ashton could tell by their dress, rowed a longboat to shore. Ashton ran down to the beach.

Seeing the queer apparition, the men stopped rowing and asked Ashton who he was. He joyfully answered, "An Englishman run away from pirates!" They were satisfied and came to the beach. Ashton soon found that the ships were the British man-of-war *Diamond,* with a fleet of traders in convoy, bound to Jamaica, and that they were ashore to get fresh water because many sailors were very sick aboard ship. After a short time Mr. Symonds showed himself. He had been careful to keep out of sight for fear of alarming the sailors.

The brigantine proved to be from Salem, Massachusetts, less than three miles from Ashton's home. The master of the brig, Captain Dove, was shorthanded and signed Ashton on at once. It was a sad farewell with Symonds a few days later, but as Ashton said, "I was forced to go thro' for the Joy of getting Home."

One can imagine the thoughts that passed through Ashton's mind on the sail up through the Gulf of Florida, and finally the thrill when the brigantine first came abeam of Halfway Rock and headed for the passageway between Baker's Island and the Miseries in Boston Bay. He had been away from home two years, ten months and fifteen days. As soon as the ship landed, he journeyed at once to his home in Marblehead. His family, which had long ago given him up for lost, joyously greeted him.

Thus ends the remarkable story of Philip Ashton. When he recovered his health and strength, Ashton related his experiences to the Reverend John Barnard, who had preached a timely sermon in honor of the boy's return, choosing as his text "God's Ability to Save His People from All Danger."

CHAPTER 3

Edward Teach, Alias Blackbeard

Edward Teach, alias Blackbeard, was born in Bristol, England, although the exact location of his birthplace is unknown. Going to sea at an early age, Teach did not attract attention until 1716, when he was serving under pirate Benjamin Thornigold. Early the next year Captain Thornigold, with Teach aboard, sailed from New Providence in the West Indies for the American mainland, capturing several vessels in rapid succession, including a Havana sloop with 120 barrels of flour and a ship loaded with wine from Bermuda. Next a craft from Madeira, loaded with a rich cargo of silks and bullion, was intercepted and robbed, after which the vessel was allowed to proceed to her South Carolina destination.

Their next capture was a large French guineaman bound for Martinique. By this time Edward Teach had shown such energy and leadership that he asked Captain Thornigold if he could take charge of the latest capture. Thornigold agreed, and Captain Edward Teach began a piratical career of his own. Because of the King's proclamation offering pardon to all pirates who would reform, Captain Thornigold soon returned to New Providence, where he surrendered to the mercy of the government there.

Teach soon had forty sizable guns, most from recent captures, mounted on board his vessel. He named the craft the *Queen Anne's Revenge.* Near the island of Saint Vincent he fell in with the *Great Allan,* commanded by Captain Christopher Taylor. A thorough job of pilfering was done on this fine vessel, with all valuable supplies removed to the pirate sloop. The crew members of the *Great Allan* were put ashore at Saint Vincent and the ship set afire.

An event now occurred which put Teach on a special pedestal in the annals of piracy. Falling in with the British man-of-war *Scarborough,* of thirty guns, Blackbeard successfully fought the English warship for several hours while blood flowed freely on the decks of both ships. The Britisher withdrew and ran for the nearest harbor in Barbados. Pleased with his defeat of the English warship, Captain Teach sailed triumphantly for Spanish America, with his fame as a bold and dangerous pirate spreading rapidly around the blue waters of the Atlantic Ocean.

Shortly afterward he fell in with a Major Stede Bonnet, an interesting pirate who had formerly been a gentleman of good reputation and estate on the island of Barbados. This man had taken up piracy for excitement and adventure. Unfortunately for Bonnet, however, he knew nothing of navigation, so Blackbeard tactfully suggested that the major come aboard the *Queen Anne's Revenge* to serve as Teach's lieutenant, while Teach would send an experienced master aboard Bonnet's own sloop, the *Revenge.*

"As you have not been used to the fatigues and cares of such a post," said Teach to Bonnet, "it would be better for you to decline it and live easy, at your pleasure, in such a ship as mine, where you will not be obliged to perform duty, but follow your own inclinations." Major Bonnet quickly saw the wisdom of Teach's statement and exchanged places with pirate Richards, who took charge of the Bonnet sloop.

A short time later the pirates were loading fresh water at Turneffe, near the Bay of Honduras, when they saw a sloop enter the inlet. Captain Richards, hoisting the black flag of piracy, slipped his cable and ran out to encounter the stranger. The sloop was the *Adventure,* commanded by Captain David Harriot, who observed the black pirate flag on Richard's mast and ordered his own sails struck at once, finally coming to under the stern of the *Queen Anne's Revenge.* Harriot and his crew were quickly transferred to the larger vessel. Israel Hands, whose name Robert Louis Stevenson borrowed for one of his pirates in *Treasure Island,* was given command of the *Adventure.*

On April 9, 1717, the pirate fleet weighed anchor and left Turneffe for the Bay of Honduras. Here they found a ship and four sloops. The ship was the *Protestant Caesar,* out of Boston, commanded by Captain Wyar. When Teach hoisted his pirate flag and fired his gun, Captain Wyar and every member of his crew fled ashore in their boat. The four sloops were quickly captured, whereupon the *Caesar* was ransacked and set afire, along with one of the sloops. Teach explained that the two vessels were destroyed because they came from Boston, where the inhabitants had had the unmitigated nerve to hang certain captured pirates.

Some time later the sea rovers, cruising in waters around Grand Cayman, about sixty miles westward of Jamaica, seized a small craft occupied in hunting turtles, which abounded in the waters nearby. Working northward toward the Carolinas on the Atlantic coast, they engaged and captured three more vessels. Soon the buccaneers sighted the shores of the North American mainland.

Off the bar at Charles-Town, or Charleston as it is known today, they waited several days until a ship came out. It was a vessel bound for London, commanded by Captain Robert

Clark. The pirates took it in short order. The following day four more captures were made: a ship, a brigantine and two pinkies. All the prisoners were herded aboard the pirate vessels. This activity threw terror into the hearts of the inhabitants of Charleston.

At this time there were eight sails in Charleston harbor, none of which dared go out and risk capture by Blackbeard. Word also reached other ports that the notorious Edward Teach was near Charleston harbor, so incoming commerce as well was suspended. It was a particularly trying period for the colonists of South Carolina, who had just finished a grueling war with the Tuscarora Indians.

Every ship and every man taken by Teach had been detained off the bar. Now Blackbeard showed not only his colossal nerve but his contempt for Americans in general. He sent his representative, Captain Richards, right into the harbor and ashore in the center of town, with a message demanding a chest of medicine for the pirate fleet. Teach could afford to be insolent, for aboard his ship as a prisoner was Samuel Bragg, one of the governor's councilmen. Richards told the people of Charleston that unless they sent the chest of medicine out to the fleet, all the prisoners would be murdered and every ship set afire. Richards and the other two pirates strutted through the streets of Charleston, appearing wherever and whenever they wished.

The governor soon reached a decision with his councilmen. Since there was nothing else they could do but comply with Blackbeard's wishes, the citizens of Charleston sent the pirate fleet an expensive chest of medicine worth at least three hundred pounds. When Teach received the chest, he kept his word and freed every prisoner after he had robbed them of their wealth, which totaled 1500 pounds in gold and silver.

North Carolina was now the destination of the pirate fleet, which consisted of Teach's "man-of-war," two "privateers" and a small sloop serving as a tender. The pirate captain soon broke up his company, cheating and marooning those for whom he did not care and dividing the spoils with his friends.

About this time Teach decided to take advantage of the proclamation of His Majesty granting a "gracious pardon to those guilty of acts of piracy who would surrender themselves to the authorities on or before a certain date." He visited the governor to obtain a certificate of his desire to retire from the pirating profession. Then followed a shameful act by Governor Charles Eden, who ordered a court of Vice-Admiralty held at Bath-Town for the purpose of declaring Teach an honest privateer. This farce of justice was carried through according to law, thus enabling Blackbeard to lay claim to a vessel he had captured from the Spanish some time before, although England and Spain were not at war when the capture was made.

Before Captain Teach left Bath-Town he fell in love with a girl of fifteen. He asked Governor Eden to officiate at the marriage, although the pirate's marital life was a trifle overcrowded: he had thirteen wives. The governor readily performed the ceremony, after which Blackbeard moved for a few days to the plantation of his new wife's family. The girl's happiness was short-lived, for Blackbeard invited his ruffian friends out to the plantation, where they all caroused, gambled and drank night after night. It was not long before the poor girl was totally miserable. Much to her relief, Teach sailed away shortly afterward. Tradition has it that the pirates went far to the north on this particular voyage, running in at the Isles of Shoals off the New Hampshire coast.

According to legend, Blackbeard often went ashore at the Isles of Shoals, having as his special abode Smuttynose Island. After a trip to England he returned to the islands with a woman whom he took ashore. A considerable portion of Blackbeard's silver treasure was buried at this time. Telling the girl to guard the treasure until his return, Teach sailed away with his pirate band but never came back, continuing his career elsewhere. There she lived for many years and finally died on this lonely island. It was said her ghost haunted the Isles of Shoals for almost a century. Regardless of the truth of the story, there is no question that Samuel Haley, in building a wall many years later, uncovered four bars of solid silver worth a fortune. Haley built a breakwater between his property and the adjoining island at Malaga after the discovery of the fortune, and many believe that part of the money he used was from Blackbeard's treasure.

Teach sailed for Bermuda in June 1718. Falling in with three English vessels, he took from them only such food and provisions as he needed. Shortly afterward he came upon two French sloops bound for Martinique. He put both French crews aboard one vessel, which he permitted to go free. Teach sailed the second ship to North Carolina, where he and the governor shared the spoils. Governor Charles Eden demanded that everything should be done legally, and so he had Teach swear that he found the French ship adrift at sea. The governor then convened a court that declared the vessel condemned. This action allowed Governor Eden to have sixty hogsheads of sugar as his share; the governor's secretary, Mr. Knight, received twenty barrels for his efforts. The pirates were permitted to have the rest of the cargo, but the ship remained in the harbor, causing Teach a great deal of worry. He was afraid that other vessels might recognize her, so he told the governor the ship was leaking and might sink, blocking the inlet. Thereupon Governor Eden ordered Teach to sail her out, giving Blackbeard the opportunity to burn her to the water's edge and sink the vessel in deep water.

Records of some of the strange incidents aboard Blackbeard's ship have been preserved. One night Teach sat drinking in the cabin with Israel Hands and another man. Suddenly he drew out two pistols and cocked them under the table. The other pirate observed what was going on and quickly left the cabin, but Hands did not notice Teach's action. Blackbeard suddenly blew out the candle, crossed his hands under the table, and fired. Israel Hands received the full force of one of the pistols in his knee, leaving him lame for the rest of his life. Some time later other members of the crew asked Blackbeard why he had injured one of his good friends. "If I do not now and then kill one of you, you'll forget who I am," was the astonishing reply.

Teach's beard was the talk of two continents. Jet black, it completely covered his face, even growing around his eyes, giving him a fierce appearance that he made the most of. He would twist the ends into small pigtails, fastening them with hair ribbons and turning them about his ears. When going into battle he purposely tried to create an effect to overwhelm his adversaries with fear, wearing three braces of pistols hanging in holsters from his shoulders. Inserting hemp cord under his hat, Blackbeard would set the hemp ends afire to burn like punk, making his eyes look fierce and wild. His whole appearance suggested the Devil himself.

There was one man who had heard of the notorious buccaneer Edward Teach and had determined to end the career of this monster who preyed on shipping up and down the coast. He was Lieutenant Robert Maynard of the British man-of-war *Pearl*. Maynard was thoroughly exasperated by the fear Blackbeard created among some of the inhabitants of North Carolina and the tolerance with which he was treated by others.

A group of planters and traders of the North Carolina coast, also deciding that they had had enough of the deprivations of Blackbeard, met together secretly to plan a campaign of retaliation. Knowing that their governor was hand in hand with Teach, they expected no help from him and so decided to send a delegation of protest direct to Virginia.

Governor Alexander Spotswood of Virginia received the

North Carolina planters with courtesy and kindness. He agreed that something must be done, and that it was useless to consult Governor Eden of North Carolina. It was arranged that two small sloops should be hired, capable of running over the shoals where buccaneer Teach was lurking. It was also agreed that they should be manned by two crews chosen from the man-of-war vessels *Pearl* and *Lime,* then at anchor in the James River. The command of the expedition was given to pirate-hating Robert Maynard.

As the two sloops were made fit for sea, Governor Spotswood called an assembly, which agreed with him on the actions to be taken. Of course, the Virginia governor must have realized that he had not the slightest jurisdiction over North Carolina, which he mentioned in his proclamation. But he probably decided that the legal sidestep was necessary because of the gravity of the situation. And he was right.

Lieutenant Maynard lost no time getting the expedition ready for sea. Sailing from Kicquetan, on the James River, the two vessels had reached the mouth of Ocracoke Inlet when the spars and masts of Teach's vessel were sighted. Although the proclamation had not been officially issued at the time Maynard arrived off the inlet, Mr. Knight of North Carolina, who had spies in Virginia, had already written to Blackbeard, warning him of trouble brewing. When Blackbeard saw the sloops approaching, he stripped his vessel for action, and awaited his adversaries.

By the time Maynard reached the vicinity of the pirate stronghold, darkness was falling. Maynard wisely anchored for the night.

The channel was intricate, with many shoals. When morning came Maynard sent a boat ahead to sound, and followed slowly behind. Despite this precaution, the sloops grounded on several sandy spots. Maynard ordered all ballast thrown overboard.

Even the water barrels were emptied, for Maynard was determined to capture Blackbeard or die in the attempt.

Finally Blackbeard fired a shot in the direction of the two sloops, whereupon Maynard hoisted the King's colors and stood directly for Captain Teach's vessel. The pirate chieftain cut his cable, planning to make a running fight of it. The sloops were without cannon, while Teach could use his, giving the pirates a definite advantage at first. Maynard was not deterred in the least by this, proceeding with his plans as if all were in his favor. Finally the two opposing forces were close enough for hailing distance.

"Damn you for villains, who are you?" asked the exasperated pirate captain. "And from whence came you?"

"You may see by our colors we are no pirates," responded the resolute Maynard, who now felt fairly certain of his objective.

Blackbeard then asked Maynard to send his boat aboard, so he could find out who he was. But Maynard was not to be tricked. "I cannot spare my boat, but I will come aboard of you as soon as I can with my sloop," replied the British lieutenant.

This so upset Blackbeard that he went below to regain his composure. Returning to the deck, he glowered across at Maynard. "Damnation seize my soul if I give you quarter or take any from you," the thoroughly angered buccaneer declared.

"I do not expect quarter from you, nor shall I give any," replied Maynard. It is clear why Maynard was called a brave man. He was about to tackle one of the hardest fighting pirates the world has ever known, and had nothing but small arms while buccaneer Teach was armed with many cannon.

Blackbeard's sloop, which had run aground, was soon floated off in the incoming tide, but the wind died down completely. Afraid that his prey would escape, Maynard ordered his men to the sweeps, and in this manner he rapidly gained on the becalmed pirates. Suddenly Captain Teach let go with a broadside, which did terrific slaughter to the poor men at the sweeps who were exposed as they were rowing. When the smoke of the discharge had cleared, it was discovered that no less than twenty-nine were either killed or wounded in Maynard's two sloops.

It was a serious blow to the English officer's plans. Many another equally brave leader would have given up then and there. Maynard, however, was determined to capture or kill the great Blackbeard and forever rid the seas of his presence. The British lieutenant ordered all hands below, remaining on deck alone with the man at the helm, whom he told to crouch down as far as possible. The other sloop was out of the contest, temporarily disabled by the broadside. The wind now freshened a trifle, allowing Maynard's sloop to draw closer to the pirates. But it was a difficult course, the sloop grounding and sliding off time and again.

Maynard ordered two ladders placed in the hatchway so that the men could scramble from the hold on signal. Closer and closer the sloop came to the pirates, who were awaiting them with hand grenades. When within throwing distance, the pirates lighted the short fuses on the grenades and tossed them over to the deck of the sloop. With most of the sailors below, the grenades exploded harmlessly.

When the smoke had partially cleared, Blackbeard looked over at the sloop. "They are all knocked on the head except three or four," he exclaimed. "Let's jump aboard and cut them to pieces."

As the two ships came together, Blackbeard and fourteen of the pirates jumped across to Maynard's vessel. Then the men belowdecks raced up the ladders and the bloody conflict began. The tides of victory surged back and forth, with sabers gleaming and flashing in the sun and the fatal charges from pistols echoing across the water. The two forces fought on until almost every man was bathed in blood.

Edward Teach, alias Blackbeard, was in his last fight, although he probably did not realize it. Anxious to come to blows with the British upstart who had threatened his piratical kingdom, he gradually worked his way aft until he could see Lieutenant Maynard. The brave British officer had also noticed the fearsome spectacle that he identified as Blackbeard, and was advancing to meet him. Having waited for such a long time to come to grips with this hated outlaw, who represented everything loathsome connected with the ocean, Maynard was not frightened by the truly dreadful apparition that came at him from the thinning smoke of gunshot and hand grenade.

Maynard and Blackbeard fired at each other simultaneously. Blackbeard missed while Maynard wounded his adversary in the body. Despite this, the huge, lumbering form kept moving steadily forward, suddenly striking with a terrific sweep of his cutlass, smashing into Maynard's sword with such force that it broke the weapon at the hilt. Regaining his balance for a fresh lunge to finish off the lieutenant, Blackbeard drew back his cutlass. As he started his second sweeping parabola, he was given a terrific blow in the throat by a British marine. This telling wound deflected his own blow so that it struck Maynard's knuckles instead of killing him.

The odds of the battle seemed to change time after time. Finally, when Blackbeard had suffered twenty saber thrusts and five pistol wounds, he was seen to waver. Just as he began to cock his last pistol, having fired three others previously, he was seized with a spasm. Tottering for a brief moment in helplessness, Blackbeard fell dead at the very feet of the man who had sworn to take him, Lieutenant Robert Maynard. By this time only a few of the buccaneers were left alive. When they saw that their leader was dead, they quickly jumped over the side into the water, crying for quarter. Maynard told them they could have mercy, but did not guarantee them from hanging later on.

Back on the pirate ship the sailors from Maynard's other sloop had finally gone into action. The outlaws aboard Teach's vessel, who had seen Blackbeard go down to death and defeat, also asked for mercy.

It had been a glorious but fearful day for the British officers and sailors. Lieutenant Maynard deserved all the credit for the victory, for he had pushed ahead in the face of what seemed hopeless defeat to win one of the greatest encounters ever staged with pirates along the Atlantic coast. His subsequent conduct in continuing the fight after twenty-nine of his small force had been put out of action showed the highest bravery.

Blackbeard's plans miscarried aboard his own vessel. Had not Teach believed victory was certain when he boarded the Maynard sloop, the pirate vessel would have been blown up, for Blackbeard left explicit orders to set off the gunpowder should defeat seem imminent. Apparently victory changed to disaster so rapidly and unexpectedly that the pirate charged with blowing up the ship if defeat threatened could not reach the powder magazine in time. Thus the outlaw vessel, with all its incriminating documents, was left secure for Maynard to go aboard and salvage. Among the documents Maynard found were many letters addressed to Teach from leading citizens in various colonies along the Atlantic coast.

After all had been secured, Maynard ordered Blackbeard's head severed from his neck and suspended from the bowsprit of the victorious sloop. In this manner Maynard sailed into Bath-Town, where he and his ship excited the awe and amazement of the entire populace. Sending his wounded men ashore for treatment, Maynard left at once for the governor's storehouse. Armed with the incriminating letters between Secretary Knight of Bath-Town and pirate Teach, involving twenty barrels of sugar for Knight and sixty for Governor Eden, Maynard boldly seized the eighty barrels piled up in the warehouse and ordered them taken away. Secretary Knight was so frightened that he actually fell sick with fear, literally scared to death by the consequences of his act and its discovery. He died a few days later.

With the ferocious head of the infamous Blackbeard still dangling from the end of the bowsprit, Maynard sailed out of Bath-Town and reached the James River, where the inspiring news of his daring exploit had preceded him. The sale of the pirate sloop and of certain pirate effects and supplies located ashore came to 2500 pounds, a tidy sum, in addition to the rewards paid for the apprehension of the pirates. All of this small fortune, the equivalent of well over $20,000 today, was given to the survivors of the battle aboard the *Pearl.*

The result of the trial held later in Virginia was a forgone conclusion, with two exceptions. Israel Hands, ashore at the time of capture, was later apprehended and brought to the bar, where he was convicted and sentenced to be hanged. Told of the extension of King George's proclamation, this condemned pirate in the shadow of the gallows had the cleverness to announce that he would agree to the King's offer and turn honest. The astonished justices in turn were forced to accept his statement as sincere, and pardoned him on the spot. Some years later pirate biographer Johnson heard that Hands had turned up in London, where he practiced for many years as a professional beggar.

Another pirate, Samuel Odell, was discovered to have been removed from a trading sloop the very night before the engagement. Having received no less than seventy wounds in the encounter, Odell was acquitted, and gratefully left the courtroom. He later recovered completely from his many injuries.

Nine of the pirates had been killed in the battle, with the two acquitted making eleven who were not hanged. All the other pirates, fourteen in number, were hanged with proper ceremony in the royal colony of Virginia. But the body of Captain Edward Teach, alias Blackbeard, did not grace any Virginia gibbet. This most ferocious pirate ended his career as he probably wished it would end, fighting a worthy opponent in the throes of a wild and thrilling conflict at sea.

PART TWO

Lighthouses

CHAPTER 1

The Flying Santa

The idea of a Flying Santa originated in 1927 with the late Captain Bill Wincapaw, who turned distribution of yuletide packages over to me in 1936. Since that time I have flown every year but one, 1942, when I was serving with the Air Corps. The Santa flights are not sponsored in any way, but voluntary contributions have helped considerably. Each year more than 90 percent of the flight cost is borne by me, and I have been more than repaid by the pleasure of seeing the waving lighthouse keepers and their families and by the letters they later send to me. My wife, Anna-Myrle, has gone on a majority of these flights, and our daughter, Dorothy, went each year until she was married.

The bundles contain balloons from Tillotson Rubber Company, Sevigny candy and lollipops, Gillette razors and blades, gum, pens and pencils, dolls, pocket edition books and a copy of my latest book. One year a friend gave doll clothes she had made, another sent socks and potholders, while others have sent money for cigarettes and children's toys. On occasion Girl Scout troops and women's church groups have contributed.

In the past we have at times invited our neighbors and friends to help wrap the bundles. After clearing the Ping-Pong table, we assign the various jobs: cutting twine and tying a bowline on the end, opening newspapers for preliminary wrap-

505

ping, arranging materials in an assembly line, checking the master list to see that everything is gathered, then the final packing.

Each gift is wrapped in newspapers. Excelsior is placed in a grocery bag before the gifts are put in, with more excelsior on top to form a cushion. Heavy wrapping paper next encases the gifts, with additional excelsior and then twine securely around the bundle. Finally there is a neat row of bundles ready to pack into the car and later into the plane.

More and more lighthouse keepers ask me to visit them. We have no regular route and have not tried to visit every light every year. But we have gone from the French possession of Saint Pierre and Miquelon, Sable Island off Nova Scotia and the Maine lighthouses down to Saint Augustine, Florida, and Bermuda. On one occasion we dropped a package at New York's Fire Island Light in the morning, then crossed the country to drop bundles at various light stations in California that evening. A card of acknowledgment from Fire Island Light, Bay Shore, Long Island, New York, said:

12-17-53

Dear Flying Santa,
We have received your package. Many thanks, and a Merry Christmas to you and Happy Landings.

The Mahlers and Hodges

The next card we received was from California:

Point Vincente Light Station
Palos Verdes Estates, Calif.
December 17, 1953

Dear Mr. Santa Snow:
We received the packages and thanks a lot for the

same. May the good Lord give you as much pleasure in delivering as we get in receiving. Once again we all thank both of you for your kindness. God Bless You.

Joseph Mary

In years past we have had a window in the airplane that could be opened to drop one, two or three packages at a lighthouse. Coming in low over the station, I let the package go just before the light flashes by, and the angle of approach allows the bundle to hit the target nineteen out of twenty times. Since airplane rules and regulations have become so strict, we have been forced to vary this in recent years.

Flying alone in the plane, chart before us to guide our approach and packages around us, excitement fills the cabin. Far in the distance we see a tiny shaft of white. For example, on one occasion we picked up the Isles of Shoals Light from a point over Gloucester, climbed for five minutes and started on our long gliding approach. First we buzzed the tower to alert the keeper, then came back to drop our bundle. For that brief moment the plane, the lighthouse and the package were all that really mattered. Then on a tight turn we came back over the tower to see legs running as fast as they could to retrieve the bundle and hold it up with a gesture of thanks.

One Sunday in 1940 I dropped Keeper Marden a package in Marblehead. He was in church, and his neighbors saw a car stop near where the bundle had hit. A man jumped out, swooped up the parcel and drove away rapidly. The next year I determined that the incident should not be repeated. Coming in less than one hundred feet in the air, I dropped the package at exactly the right moment and watched it thud on top of his roof and roll off to the ground. Keeper Marden, equal to the occasion, wrote to me the following day: "I received your package which arrived in good order, landing on the roof. Thank God it wasn't a bomb."

Captain Veidler was keeper at Nauset Beach Light, Cape Cod, during the 1940s. In 1943 he prepared an unusual greeting for me when I flew over Nauset Light with his Christmas parcel. As we banked over the lighthouse, I noticed that a welcome had been spelled out in the area just behind the building. The greeting, SANTA HELLO, was formed with scrub pine branches. Keeper Veidler, his son and his wife had worked all morning arranging the boughs so that we could read the words from the air.

Keeper Bakken and his wife put up their Christmas tree and waited to decorate it until the Santa package arrived at their station at Cape Porpoise Light on Goat Island, Maine. As soon as the plane zoomed in, dropped the gifts and left, the three children and the keeper rushed out to retrieve it. They put the wrapped gifts around the tree and perched the toy airplane at the very top. On Christmas morning the children were up early to open their gifts from the Flying Santa.

Many years ago I received a letter from five-year-old Seamond Ponsart of Cuttyhunk in the Elizabeth Islands. Seamond wanted the Flying Santa to drop her a doll. Santa complied, but Cuttyhunk Island is covered with huge boulders, and the doll smashed. As a result the broken-hearted little girl cried herself to sleep that night. The following year Keeper Ponsart moved his family to West Chop Light on Martha's Vineyard. I decided to deliver my gifts at that time by helicopter and was able to present her the doll in person. The trip was successful, and Seamond went to bed happy that night. Each year I receive a gift or a card from Seamond, who has been married and is now a member of the Coast Guard in New Orleans. I kept the first thank-you card sent by her parents long ago:

We have received your package and thank you very much. Seamond likes her doll and went to bed with it very much pleased with her Santa. . . . She was also pleased with the other things in the package and also the rest of us. Come and visit when you can. . . . West Chop Light

—O. J. Ponsart, Keeper

Some years ago we were out over Boon Island. Swooping in low, the red twin-engined plane was barely fifty feet over the rocky ledges when I released the first aerial Christmas bomb, followed a moment later by another. The first landed successfully. But the second, to our surprise and horror, did something no package before or since has ever done: it became caught in the tail's elevator horn and completely locked the tail mechanism. Portsmouth, New Hampshire, was the nearest airport, and we landed there safely. Jumping to the runway, I walked back to the tail assembly while everyone at the airport ran out to see what had happened. The discovery of a Christmas package wedged in the tail made us realize what a narrow escape we had had.

On another occasion I threw a package out at far-flung Graves Light. We watched hopefully as the bundle dropped away from the plane, spinning down lower and lower, until finally it struck the riprap ledge near the tower and plopped into the sea. I had failed.

While we were making our cloverleaf turn, Keeper Reamy, who had watched from inside the tower as the parcel hit the ledge and then the water, was descending the metal stairs and could neither hear nor see us as we returned.

Back over the tower one minute later, I dropped a second bundle and watched it lodge safely in a cleft of the rocks. However, the keeper, unaware of what had happened, never did find it. Instead, he launched his dory into the teeth of a twenty-mile-an-hour gale and rowed desperately for forty minutes before retrieving the first package.

It was not until the following spring that I was able to journey by boat out to Graves Light, and we had quite a chat
concerning the packages.

"Yes," admonished Reamy, "you made me row almost a
mile to recover your bundle. A poor shot, I'd call it."

I explained that I had returned with another bundle, which
I had dropped successfully. But he refused to believe me.

"Well," I cried, "let's go down and look."

The storms and waves had swept the ledge scores of times
since I had dropped the parcel, but when I found the weather-
beaten package, the articles could still be identified. The pen
and pencil set had rusted, the cigars and cigarettes were soggy,
the book pages were stuck together, the candy was ruined.
Everything was completely spoiled, with one exception: the
Gillette razor blades. The keeper carried these away in triumph
and used them that very night.

Then there is the remarkable tale of the Flying Santa bundle
dropped at Whaleback Light many years ago. I watched it
become one of my more outstanding failures as it hit the sea at
least forty feet from the lighthouse. After releasing another, we
flew on our way.

That was December 18. On January 5, Colonel Eugene S.
Clark, eminent marine expert of Sandwich, Massachusetts, was
hiking along the Cape Cod beach after a storm. He saw something wrapped in brownish paper floating toward the shore.
Retrieving the bundle, he found that it was the package I had
dropped almost three weeks before at Whaleback Ledge. The
bundle had floated across Massachusetts Bay to land in front
of him on the Cape Cod beach, ninety miles in a direct line. The
last I knew, he still had my book he found in the package,
Storms and Shipwrecks of New England, now out of print.

Some years ago I released a package at Eastern Point Light,
Gloucester. The keeper was watching the plane maneuver as I

dropped the bundle but, because of our speed, it was hard to follow closely. The package landed safely, lodged in a rocky cleft, and on we flew. The following summer we visited the keeper, who refused to believe I had dropped anything for him as he had never found it.

The next year I made it a point to direct the bundles in plain view of the keeper. I telephoned to make certain he had received the three I dropped him. That August, twenty months after I dropped the package he said I had not left for him, my phone rang.

"Well, Mr. Snow," said the keeper of Eastern Point Light, "I've just been given the long-missing package. Some boys found it down near the rocks in a little cavity. It was wedged there securely. I must apologize for doubting you in the first place."

At times requests come for the Flying Santa. The Stockbridges of Burnt Island Light in Boothbay harbor, Maine, wrote: "This is our last Christmas at the Lighthouse, and we would so much like to see the Flying Santa for the last time. Happy landings and good luck and do save time to be at your own home during the holiday."

> Ram Island Light
> Boothbay harbor, Maine

Dear Mr. Edward Rowe Snow:

> All of us will be watching for your plane, my husband Keeper Wendell J. Reece, my uncle Henry F. Knightley, my German Shepherd Rocky IV, my three little kittens and myself.

> Mrs. Tessie M. Reece

A special package was made for the Reeces, including dog biscuits. A telephone call that night assured us that the bundle had landed safely and that Rocky IV was already enjoying his present.

Two interesting incidents connected with the Santa bombing occurred at Ipswich Light years ago. One package landed inside the open door of the keeper's garage and was there waiting for him when he returned home. On another occasion the keeper was working in the cellar of his house. He had invited a group of children to a party to be held directly after the dropping of the bundle. The hour approached when the plane should make its appearance, so the keeper called out to his wife, "Has Santa arrived yet, dear?"

Before the lady could reply there was a terrific crash upstairs, and the bundle came hurtling along the upper hall after its surprising entrance through the skylight. His wife was equal to the occasion, and quickly answered without a tremor in her voice: "Yes, dear. We can start the party now."

We often visited Keeper Hopkins and his wife and son at their Ten Pound Island home, and found them a happy family. One Christmas week when I was about to take off from the East Boston Airport on the annual Christmas flight over the lighthouses, Mrs. Hopkins heard about it over the radio.

"Let's do something special for Ed Snow when he comes over," she suggested to her husband.

"What can we do?" he asked, and went back to reading a magazine story.

Mrs. Hopkins disappeared down the cellar stairs, coming up a short time later with her arms full of old newspapers. These she spread on the lawn beside the house to form the words MERRY CHRISTMAS. Then she nailed the papers to the ground so that the wind would not rearrange them.

An hour later I circled the island and was thrilled to read her greeting spelled out in the grass. A picture was taken, and when we returned to Boston later that day, it was processed by the

Associated Press. On the front pages of some of the late afternoon papers was that view of the greeting to the Flying Santa. Keeper Hopkins's son, returning home from school, purchased a copy of one of the Boston papers. He rowed out to the island and entered the kitchen, where his father was still sitting in his favorite chair, deep in a magazine. The son handed Hopkins the paper, holding it open to the four-column aerial picture of his own lighthouse and home, with the words MERRY CHRISTMAS in the grass.

His good wife continued to tell her story for many years, how she put one over on her husband by arranging the welcome for the Flying Santa.

One year at North Light, Block Island, Keeper John Lee had been shopping in Providence the week before Christmas and had purchased my latest book. In a day or two the same volume arrived as a present from a relative. Then when I flew over and dropped my package, another identical book was enclosed. In the letter of acknowledgment I received from John Lee, he told me what had happened. I mailed him another of my books with a different title.

The largest number of books I ever gave during the Flying Santa trips was four hundred pocket edition volumes, which I left at far-flung Sable Island in 1954. The bundles and books were fully appreciated by the children and grown-ups on this strange sand island of shipwrecks and wild horses.

At Baker's Island one year they had a HELLO SANTA greeting for us made out of driftwood, which the keeper collected on the beach and laid out to form letters in the snow near the lighthouse.

At Minot's Light, before the beacon was made automatic, we had to tie two or even three packages together with rope twenty feet long, arranged in a sort of meshing, so that when I released them they floated down and spread out to catch on one of the upper platforms of the tower. Nevertheless, as often as not they came down in the sea.

When two packages landed in the water on a blustery day at Ten Pound Island, Gloucester harbor, we thought they were lost. We did not know that the dog on the island, a retriever, swam out and brought the bundles ashore in good condition.

At Chatham Light an unusual incident took place. The keeper's card explains:

> We have received your package. Appreciated by all hands, excluding the broken windshield.
> > Mahlon A. Chase BMC OIC
> > Coast Guard Station
> > Chatham, Mass.

It seems that my aim was too good and the bundle went through the windshield of the car.

Here are a few more replies to the Flying Santa:

> As you well know the life of a light keeper at its very best is very lonely, and it gives one a good feeling to think that someone of your status would remember us on Christmas Day. I have been in the Coast Guard 21 years. . . . Again thank you very much.
> > Lyman D. Beach, BMC, USCG
> > Light Station, Mount Desert Rock

> Recovered 3 packages, one was water soaked and spoiled, one was wet and somewhat broken, and one was dry and in good condition. Thanks heaps. Good Luck.
> > Ram Island Light
> > Boothbay harbor, Maine

You will never know how much your thoughts made happier a routine lonely holiday away from home. This is about the only day that will get to a man out here on these stations. So well do I know as I spent 2 of them on lights on the west coast. With kind thoughts from people like you it still seems worthwhile. It was wonderful.

Robert L. Zoner OIC
Officer in Charge
Seguin Light Station
USCG

Just took over this duty. Was surprised and pleased to find the package. Thank you.

T. H. Brown, BMC, USCG
Race Point Light

One Coastguardsman, R. E. Morong, wrote thanking the Flying Santa and said that he could remember when he was a "lad of eleven when my Dad was stationed at Race Point Light Station, the fun we had looking for the packages that you dropped from the plane. It was a big event in our life."

In 1969 we stopped at the Rockland Airport, where several members of the Coast Guard and their families greeted us. Kenneth Black, at the time commanding officer of the Rockland Coast Guard Station, surprised the Flying Santa with a lamp presented on behalf of the members of the station. We distributed packages to the personnel along with balloons, candy, razors and books to the families there.

In the plane coming in from Rockland's Owl's Head, we can make out the almost perfect lighthouse setting of Curtis Island off Camden, Maine. Circling this beautiful isle makes me think of the thousands of people who have watched the movies we have made year after year from the plane.

Two years ago I did something I always wanted to attempt. Going on the Flying Santa trip by helicopter, I was able to stop at the lighthouses and meet the families of the Coast Guardsmen tending the lights. Several of the score of places where I landed are the Isles of Shoals, Seguin, Gloucester's Eastern Point and Cape Porpoise Light.

This reply card is typical of the many sent to us over the years:

> We have received your package. Thank you so much. We have a little boy who will be a year old tomorrow. He'll just love the balloons and punch ball. We've only been here two weeks, so you've certainly brightened our Christmas.
>
> Mr. and Mrs. C. E. Trebilcock
Wood Island Light Station
Biddeford Pool, Maine

CHAPTER 2

An American Army of Two

Attached to the old Scituate Lighthouse is a tablet bearing the words:

SCITUATE LIGHT HOUSE / BUILT 1810 / LIGHTED 1811
SIMEON BATES, REUBEN BATES, JAMES YOUNG BATES,
KEEPERS
REBECCA AND ABIGAIL BATES, DAUGHTERS OF SIMEON,
CALLED
"THE AMERICAN ARMY OF TWO"
PLACED BY THE BATES ASSOCIATION INC. 1928

It is unfortunate that a controversy still rages about the names of the two little heroines and what they did. Some claim that the whole story is a fabrication, but evidence indicates otherwise.

The usually accepted version of this interesting tale is that Reuben Bates,* the keeper at Scituate Light during the War of 1812, had two young daughters, Rebecca and Abigail, who were anxious and willing to help their country against the British. In the spring of 1814 the English man-of-war *Bulwark* lay at anchor off Scituate harbor. Keeper Bates feared that his light-

---

*As the years have gone by, the names of Reuben and Simeon have become inter-changed, and there is no way of settling the matter at this late moment.

517

house would meet a fate similar to that experienced by Boston Light during the Revolution, when the upper works of America's oldest beacon were blown to pieces. But the British did not molest Scituate Light. On June 11, 1814, however, when the citizens of Scituate refused to furnish fresh meat and vegetables to the men on the *Bulwark,* two English barges were sent into the harbor itself, where the British marines set fires that destroyed many American boats and schooners.

Later in the summer a regiment from Boston under the command of Colonel John Barstow arrived in the vicinity, and the *Bulwark* soon left Scituate harbor. As the summer weeks passed without incident, discipline among the American soldiers was relaxed, so that the guards were visiting the village and combining pleasant diversions with their daily tasks.

One day early in September the British man-of-war *La Hogue* appeared off the coast when there were no guards at Scituate Lighthouse. Only the eldest daughter of Keeper Reuben Bates, fourteen-year-old Rebecca, her younger sister Abigail and a younger brother were at the light. Rebecca, high in the tower when she sighted the *La Hogue,* sent her brother off to the village to warn the people. Then she went down on the beach to plan what could be done. She watched the powerful warship tack and stand off to sea, then tack again and make for the harbor. The tide turned and began to come into the bay. It was a fine day, and a gentle breeze slightly ruffled the water as the *La Hogue* sailed nearer and nearer.

When high water came at two that afternoon, the man-of-war let go her bowers, swung her yards around and lay quiet in the afternoon sun less than half a mile from the First Cliff.

Climbing the light so that she might have a better vantage point, the terrified girl, alone with her sister at Cedar Point, observed that the British were launching boat after boat into the sea. The town was to be burned, she thought, just as the City of Washington had been destroyed.

In the village there was confusion and uproar when the boy arrived with the news. Forgetting the lighthouse, the villagers and soldiers planned to defend the shore near the town against the invaders, using the fish houses for a fort.

Then began the approach. Five large whale boats, loaded with marines and manned by British sailors, started for the beach. It was a splendid but fearful sight, the marines with their bright red coats and their guns held upright, bayonets glistening in the sun. The oars in the whaleboat moved with orderly precision as the Britishers neared the point of land where the girls were watching.

All at once Rebecca remembered that in the lighthouse residence, attached to the tower itself, were a drum and fife that belonged to the missing guardsmen who had amused themselves during their leisure by teaching the girls to play. Rebecca flew down the steps of the tower, handed her sister the drum and picked up the fife. The girls stole out of the building and hid behind the lighthouse. Then, as the steady, measured strokes of the British sailors could be heard nearing the spit of land where the lighthouse stands, Rebecca began to play the fife and her sister to beat the drum. Louder and louder came their efforts, until the British oarsmen passing the lighthouse stopped their labors. Could the Americans be massing to overcome them?

The officers in the whaleboats were in a quandary. As they were debating what to do, the ship's commander aboard the *La Hogue,* hearing the drum and fife, ran up a flag signifying danger and ordered a gun to be fired. This was the signal agreed upon for a return to the *La Hogue,* so the expedition was turned into a retreat. Cheers could be heard coming from the townspeople of Scituate as the girls, triumphant but exhausted from their efforts, sat down to rest. What a proud moment it must have been for the young girls when they realized that their ruse had saved the town of Scituate!

As darkness fell over the bay, a gun flash was seen from the British warship. A single shot, aimed at the lighthouse tower, described its parabola from the deck of the *La Hogue* but screamed into the water more than fifty yards short of the mark. It was merely a parting gesture, however, for the *La Hogue* then hoisted sail and was soon hull down bound northward. In a short time the townspeople reached Cedar Point, and the girls who comprised the American Army of Two were soon made to feel their importance.

More than half a century later Rebecca and Abigail both signed the statements below. Through the courtesy of Helen Ingersol Tetlow we publish Miss Abigail Bates's own statement:

> Abbie the Drummer one
> of the American Army of
> two in the War of 1812
> > Miss Abbie Bates
> > aged 81
> > Mass.

Miss Rebecca Bates made the following statement:

Born 1793   1878
Rebecca Bates, aged 84 years, one of the American Army of two in the war of 1812 who with her sister aged 15 saved two large vessels laden with flour from being taken by the British with fife and drum.

In 1874 the *Saint Nicholas Magazine* published an article by Charles Barnard describing the incident. He claimed that Abigail had not helped in the Britishers' repulse, but gave the honor to a Miss Sarah Winsor, who, Barnard relates, was visiting Rebecca at the time. There is no controversy about Rebecca Bates's part in the story.

Regardless of which two girls were responsible for saving Scituate from the enemy during the War of 1812, it was a heroic incident at Scituate Lighthouse that summer of 1814. In the words of Lilla A. Ham:

Thus Rebecca and Abigail, loyal and true,
Once composed the American Army of Two.

PART THREE

Treasure

CHAPTER 1

Marshfield Mansion Gold

The thought of finding treasure appeals to almost every adventuresome person. For most of us who actually search for it, however, our efforts usually end in disappointment. Nevertheless, on at least some occasions the seeker is handsomely rewarded.

One of the rarest treasure stories, based in my hometown of Marshfield, involves an organ, a dream, a spinster and a chimney. This peculiar tale begins in the year 1789. Its principal character is Stuart Alton.

At the age of twenty-one Stuart was taken into a substantial banking business his father had founded, and for the next few years he prospered along with the rise of the town. Stuart married a local girl, and the couple had three children.

By 1807 Stuart had become interested in playing the harpsichord. The following year he journeyed to a nearby city, where he discovered a beautiful organ prominently displayed in a music store. This organ, built by the firm of Astor and Broadwood, had been constructed by George Astor himself, the brother of John Jacob Astor, and became a favorite of almost everyone who played it.

Stuart Alton not only fell in love with the organ but desired it for his own. He was only a fair player, but his interest in the organ made him anxious to improve his musical ability. He began visiting the nearby city and studying the organ with one of the leading players of the day.

Finally, in 1810, his teacher told him that he had improved sufficiently to allow him to go ahead and purchase an organ. Alton was a happy man when he found that an Astor and Broadwood organ was still on sale in the music store. Three weeks later his instrument arrived at his home, and night after night he would play the songs and hymns of the period. Once a month regularly he went to the city to take a music lesson, until finally his teacher declared that he had become an accomplished musician.

The War of 1812 brought family tragedy. Stuart's wife, returning by sea to town after visiting her son aboard the Frigate *Constitution,* was lost with all others aboard a small coastal packet. The shock was too great for Stuart. He closed the organ and decided never to play it again. To take his mind from his grief, his doctor recommended that Alton take up fishing. The banker would often row out a mile from shore, when the waves were not too high, to fish for hours at a time. One day two British sloops came in from the ocean and captured Stuart. Taken aboard one of the sloops as a prisoner, he was interrogated for over a week, then released near Pemaquid Point, Maine, whence he returned to his home.

The humiliation of his capture, together with the recent loss of his wife, led Stuart to decide to move away from the seashore and settle nearer the center of town. He purchased an attractive plot of land and renovated the fine old mansion on it. The house contained a remarkable fireplace almost large enough for a man to walk in upright. The left side was arranged as an oven.

Stuart was seriously considering playing the organ again, waiting only for the right time and opportunity. And so, across from the fireplace, in order that he might play by the firelight, he placed his organ.

In 1832, when Stuart Alton retired from business, he was

considered a fairly wealthy man. On November 1 he wrote to his children, asking that they humor an old man's wish and visit him during the coming holiday season.

All three children came with their own children, and for the next few days the house resounded with gaiety and laughter. Then, on the final night of their visit, Stuart had them all sit around the fire. He went over to the organ and began playing. Everyone expressed pleasure that Alton had decided to play again, and the former banker was a happy man when he bade them farewell the next morning. The family visits became annual affairs.

As for his organ, Alton decided that once more he could journey to the city and resume his lessons. He was forming an unusual plan in his mind. This time he went to another teacher, a musical expert on composition. Before long Stuart Alton began composing his own pieces. Those who passed his window in the summertime could hear the strains of the unusual organ melodies he was creating.

In 1851 Stuart suffered a bad fall and was unable to leave the house. Nevertheless, when winter came, he sent out his invitations to his family as usual and everyone came, transforming the house once more by the activity and gaiety. Again came the final night of the visit, with all Stuart Alton's descendants gathered in the living room, where the great logs were sparkling and blazing merrily.

Later, as the fire began to die away, old Stuart Alton hobbled across to his beloved organ. All eyes were upon him as he began his first selection. Soon his listeners noticed a strange undertone in the playing that made them uneasy. Then suddenly, without warning, the organ stopped.

By this time the light from the dying fire barely illuminated the bent form of the aged man, but they could see him faintly as he grasped the organ seat in an attempt to stand erect.

"Children," he began, "I've been practicing in my feeble way on a musical composition that I trust will interest you all. It was written in an attempt to place a special significance on what is to follow. At its conclusion I'm going to reveal something of extreme interest to every one of you, and I shall not repeat it."

Stuart Alton again sat down at the organ. He began playing. Indeed it was an unusual composition to which the entranced group listened, and as the old man worked his aged fingers up and down the keyboard there seemed to be a hidden message for each of them in his inspired playing.

At the height of his composition, as he played on with intense concentration, the others noticed that his face began to glow and his breathing became labored. They could see that it was harder and harder for him to continue.

Suddenly, at the very climax of his playing, the old man gasped, grabbed at his chest and then slumped down between the organ and the seat. His children and grandchildren rushed to him and carried him to a sofa. But it was too late, for even as they gathered around him they realized that he had suffered a shock and was dying.

"Come," he muttered feebly, "I *must* finish. . . ."

But Stuart Alton was dead.

Three days later his funeral was held in the same living room, and all who had known him attended. The minister spoke highly of Alton, and mentioned the two episodes in his life that had affected him so deeply. Then his final remains were buried in the village cemetery, and his family gathered at the local bank to hear the reading of his will.

Everyone present was surprised and disappointed, for the will merely mentioned the house, the organ and the chimney, and what was to be found therein. There was no mention of any substantial amount of money, except for scarcely more than $1200 at the bank, in an account that had seen heavy withdrawals during the last few years. And the bank's cashier declared that the withdrawals had always been in the form of ten- and twenty-dollar gold pieces.

Where then, Stuart Alton's heirs asked, could the money have gone? Two inspired members of the family decided to take the organ apart, but they got nothing for their pains except the task of reassembling it again. Then the chimney was discussed. It was carefully examined, almost brick by brick, but no hidden vaults or recesses were revealed. Finally the family members swallowed their disappointment and returned to their respective homes.

Several months later business reverses left one of the children temporarily short of money, and he sold his own home and moved into Stuart's spacious residence, where he stayed for the remainder of his life. In turn his son and daughter took over the house when the father died. The son passed away in 1896, leaving the girl, Lucy Alton, alone in the great mansion. She had become a schoolteacher, and a good one, but her pupils wondered why she lived in the great house all alone except for two cats.

Strangely enough, Lucy Alton was not in the least lonely, for the woman was fascinated by the ancient mansion. Her father had often told her of the unusual episode of her grandfather's death, and how he had been playing the organ when he died.

From the time she was a child, the organ and the fireplace had always seemed to cast a spell over her, and at an early age she learned to play the instrument. As the years went by she studied her grandfather's career, having preserved all of his letters and musical compositions that she could find. Eventually she was able to play all his compositions, especially the weird piece with the unusual ending.

When Lucy Alton retired from teaching she concentrated on the disappearance of her grandfather's wealth but came to no definite conclusion concerning it. Not one of the letters gave her the slightest clue as to the whereabouts of all those gold pieces he had taken from the bank.

Lucy Alton was the very last of the Alton line, for the War Between the States and the Spanish–American War had wiped out the remaining male members of the family. By the time of her amazing dream, which is here related, not a single relative remained alive.

One Sunday evening, as was her custom, she opened the organ. Before her she placed her grandfather's famous composition, which she played slowly and with great feeling.

At the end of the work she closed the organ, put out her cats and retired upstairs to bed. The lingering strains of the music were uppermost in her mind as she fell asleep.

In her dream a vision appeared. It was her grandfather, whom she had never seen, seated at the organ and playing the very piece she had completed a short time before. She felt herself urging him to continue his playing, to finish his composition. And that was just what the vision did. He played his musical effort through to the end, stood up and walked over to the huge fireplace. Picking up a poker, he entered the fireplace, walking to the left side, where he tapped significantly against the bricks at the back.

Then the dream faded, and Lucy sat upright in bed. Could there possibly be some unusual significance to the dream? She lay back and pulled the covers over her shivering form. Just as she was about to forget the whole episode, she heard a sound that made the blood surge violently through her veins.

Downstairs someone seemed to be actually playing the organ. Terrified, but filled with a determination to find out if someone was really at the organ, Lucy threw on her wrapper and went to the top of the stairs. The playing had stopped.

Crawling back into bed, she made a solemn resolve that she would investigate the chimney the very next morning.

Awakening early, she dressed hurriedly and traveled to the

home of the handyman of the neighborhood. After binding him to secrecy, she asked him to accompany her back to the house, and the two went into the chimney.

There Lucy told the handyman, whose name was Jim, just what her dream was about. Jim smiled tolerantly, thought to himself about the peculiarities of spinsters in general, and agreed to carry out her wish: to break through the back wall of the chimney.

He became much more interested when he noticed something that no one had ever apparently seen before. A certain brick, shoulder high, appeared to have been reinforced at one time, as if it had been removed and then cemented back into place. For tools he had only several long, thin screwdrivers and a hammer, but he had the brick loose in a little more than an hour.

Pulling it out, he examined it carefully. The brick showed evidence of mortar applied at two different periods. Then Jim flashed a light through the hole where the brick had been. There was a small area, less than three inches across, between the row of visible bricks and another row of bricks immediately in back.

Lucy was an excited observer as Jim removed the brick and found the space between the two brick walls. But she was not going to get her hopes up too high.

"What do you find in the hole?" she asked Jim.

"It's too small to see anything. Shall I take out some more bricks?"

"Of course, let's settle this once and for all."

By noon only three tiers of bricks had been removed from the chimney wall, but they were too excited to stop for lunch. At one-thirty in the afternoon Jim had made a hole large enough to reach down as far as a foot above the ground.

"Go ahead, Jim," urged Lucy, "try to find something, anything. I am getting very nervous in spite of myself."

So Jim stood up, rested a moment and then rolled his sleeve above the elbow. Thrusting his long, bare arm inside the wall, he groped lower and lower. Then there was a faint tinkle as Jim's arm started to withdraw.

"Darn it!" he cried. "I dropped it."

"Dropped what?" shouted Lucy.

"I'm not sure," he admitted, "but it felt like money!"

"For heaven's sake, try again, Jim, try again!"

This time Jim decided to pick up just one piece instead of a handful, and thrust his arm in again. His second try was successful, and the two excited people stared, fascinated, at the twenty-dollar gold piece he held up.

"Jim, we've found the treasure!"

"I guess you're right, Miss Lucy, I guess you're right."

At three o'clock that same afternoon two bank representatives were gazing in wonderment at the golden pile of ten- and twenty-dollar gold pieces that threatened to overflow the living room table where they had been placed. That night the money was counted, put in canvas bags and stored in the local bank. Lucy Alton, even after paying Jim $1000 for his efforts, was $36,600 richer than she had been the day before. And as she was the sole remaining survivor of the Altons, every cent was hers.

It seems that Stuart Alton had used the chimney as a receptacle for the gold pieces just as we use razor blade receptacles today. And that was the surprise he had planned for his family on the night of his death. No one had been clever enough to notice the brick that showed evidences of having been removed —no one except handyman Jim.

As for the dream, Lucy claimed that it happened just as she said it did. However, she did offer a reasonable explanation for the organ playing after her first dream. She believed she fell asleep after sitting up in bed and dreamed a second dream, in which she heard the playing again. In any case, she was grateful for the second dream, for otherwise, she always contended, she would never have attached any particular significance to the first.

CHAPTER 2

The Code to the Treasure

My first knowledge that there ever was a King of Calf Island came from a man whose name was King—Joe King. He conducted a business on Commercial Wharf, Boston, and I learned about him while I was collecting information concerning Apple Island, Boston harbor. I had been told that Mr. King lived for several years at Apple Island, where he often searched for the treasure supposed to have been buried there a century before.

In 1934 I interviewed him on Commercial Wharf about the Apple Island treasure, but he never acknowledged having found any money. However, before the interview ended, he had told me about certain mysterious events that had taken place in Boston's outer bay, several miles from Apple Island, where he had lived for a few summers.

Mr. King told me that out on the Brewster Islands a man known as the King of Calf Island was said to have buried something of importance, either in the foundation of a fisherman's house or in the ruins of another building. He was not sure, but it may have been pirate treasure or a clue that might lead to treasure of some sort. The story fascinated me, of course, and I determined to find out more about it as soon as possible.

The following year I decided to put into book form the information I was collecting about all the islands and lighthouses in Boston harbor. While gathering information and stories about the outer bay, I landed by canoe with Mrs. Snow at

Great Brewster Island. This high, drumlin-type island, with two hills and a flat valley between, is surrounded in large part by a government-built seawall.

The higher of the two hills, at the northern end of the island, is 104 feet, with steep cliffs on its eastern, northern and western sides; on the south it slopes gently toward the flat, level area in the middle of the island. The other hill is smaller, with cliffs on the southern and eastern sides.

From the southern tip of the island stretches an unusual bar that winds in a mighty S-shaped curve for almost two miles, ending at a channel called the Narrows, just across from Fort Warren. At the extreme tip of the bar, which is known as the Brewster Spit, there stood a lighthouse from 1856 until June 7, 1929, when it burned down. The lighthouse, called the Narrows Light, was known locally as Bug Light because of the seven spindly iron legs on which it stood. Today the spindly legs remain, but the burned lighthouse was replaced by an automatic beacon, and now no lighthouse keeper lives there.

At low tide it used to be possible to walk along Great Brewster Spit from Great Brewster to Bug Light and back in plenty of time to avoid getting your feet wet. Dredging by man has eliminated this delightful activity. Another bar goes out to Boston Light, half a mile southeast of Great Brewster. And a submerged bar, bare only once or twice a year, runs out from the northern tip of Great Brewster over to Middle Brewster Island. Usually at low water it is knee to waist deep. The bar is covered with barnacled rocks and heavy streamers of rockweed and seaweed.

After landing on the beach at Great Brewster, Mrs. Snow and I pulled the canoe high above the reach of the incoming tide. Then we hiked up the slope of the larger hill, where in a little cluster of houses we noticed smoke coming from one of the chimneys. It was here that we first met the island caretaker,

John J. Nuskey. He greeted us cordially, and soon we had
learned his history.

Caretaker Nuskey was then fifty-nine years of age, a lobster
fisherman by trade. He received $10 a month from the govern-
ment to watch over the island where he lived. Having lost the
lower part of his right leg many years before, he was known
around the island as "Peg-Leg Nuskey," and walked around the
island with the aid of a cane.

Pulling out notebook and pencil, I commenced my questions
about the mysterious doings mentioned by Joe King. Nuskey
fortified himself by taking a sizable chaw of tobacco from his
pocket and then was ready for me.

"Mr. Nuskey," I began, "have you ever heard of any unusual
or mysterious happenings on this island which might be of
interest for the book I'm writing?"

John Nuskey thought carefully for almost a full minute,
chewing away at the tobacco he had crammed into his square
jaws, as if debating how much he should tell us and how much
he had better refrain from mentioning. Then we could see him
make up his mind. Spitting a copious amount of tobacco juice,
Nuskey cleared his throat. "Well, Mr. Snow, it's a sort of
yes-and-no story. I promised some years back I wouldn't tell
too much of it, but it's been so long, and nothing has ever been
done, that you might as well have most of the story now.

"Back in the second year I came here, 1926, there was something unusual. I've been a fisherman around here all my life
almost, and got this job in 1925, but I never saw, either before
or since, a man with steel rods sinking 'em all over the island,
wherever he thought there might have been a house.

"This fellow, named Redwell or something like that, came
down here from Canada. He had permission and everything,
that part was in order, but he spent two whole weeks sinking
those long, thin rods down through the ground around old

cellar holes and buildings. Before he finished we were all pretty curious about it.

"Finally, I guess his vacation time was up, and he got one of us to take him into Boston. I went with him, and in the boat he wrote out something which he gave me concerning what he was doing. I have it around somewhere. The poor fellow had come all the way from Canada for nothing, I guess. Perhaps one day I'll find the paper, but I haven't seen it for years."

I questioned him further, but he was rather vague about certain points I brought up. He did promise to ask his fishing mate, whose name, for reasons obvious later, I shall refrain from mentioning.

I subsequently found out that the Government had taken over the island in 1898, when the Army planned to erect fortifications here. They abandoned their plans, and it was not until World War II that the plans were carried out.

Meanwhile, as we saw during our visit in 1935, a dozen or so families had built summer cottages on the island, paying the Government a nominal fee for this privilege. Among the families then on the island was that of Mrs. Gertrude Crowley, who lived here with her two children. Later I learned that Mrs. Crowley's grandfather was James Turner, otherwise known as the King of Calf Island, the man for whom I searched.

For the next few years we made summertime calls in our canoe at Great Brewster Island, and John Nuskey was always a pleasant host. We would pull our canoe above the tide, make a little fire and enjoy a meal. Usually before the meal ended Caretaker Nuskey, supporting himself with his cane, would come limping down the hill to greet us, his peg leg making cuplike depressions in the sand.

He pointed out many things, including the deep Worthylake well, located halfway up the big hill and dug some time before 1695 by the father of the first keeper of Boston Light. We would often climb the hill to drink the water there. And, as it happened, it was the last place we ever saw John Nuskey alive.

Then came the month of September 1940. I was teaching school in Winthrop at the time, and my wife and I always tried to plan a long canoe trip just before the beginning of my educational duties. On September 5, an hour before sunrise, we were down on the Winthrop shore with our notebooks, food and cameras. I carried the canoe to the water's edge and loaded it. Soon we were paddling away for our last day of adventure before the start of school.

Sunrise caught us as we rounded George's Island. After visiting several other locations, we reached Great Brewster Spit, at Bug Light. We took a swim and then paddled along on the northern side of the spit, finally arriving at a formidable ledge known as the Black Rocks, located close by the spit. Paddling toward the ledge, we decided to get out there and rest our weary limbs, for we had already covered a considerable distance. I steadied the canoe while Anna-Myrle stepped out across the bow onto the barnacle-covered ledge. Then she stood up, her white bathing suit glistening in the morning sun.

Suddenly, without the slightest warning, there was a cry from the other side of the rocks.

"Say, what are you?" came an astonished voice. "Are you one of those things called mermaids?"

The voice was that of John Nuskey, who was in his lobster boat hauling traps in the deep water on the other side of the ledge. As he explained later, he had seen Anna-Myrle's head and shoulders appear above the rocks. Wearing the white bathing suit, she must have presented quite a picture to Nuskey, who up to that moment had seen neither the canoe nor its occupants, for our approach had been shielded by the Black Rocks. We had not seen Nuskey either, until startled by his amazed shout when he noticed Anna-Myrle's form as it appeared to rise out of the sea.

My wife and I returned to the canoe, paddled around the Black Rocks and brought the canoe up to the lobster boat, holding onto the gunwale with our hands.

"Say," Nuskey began, "it's strange that I should have seen you appear that way just now, for I've been looking out for you for two weeks. When you get a chance, come over to the island and meet me up by the well. I'll be finished hauling soon. I've got something to show you."

We agreed that after we visited Graves Light and Boston Light we would return to Great Brewster Island for a rest and some food.

It was shortly after two o'clock that our canoe grounded on the shale at Great Brewster. We had made our circuit of the harbor and were very tired and hungry. I pulled the craft up above the reach of the tide, and Anna-Myrle began preparations for cooking bacon and eggs for our late lunch. But I had been wondering what Nuskey was going to show me, and soon clambered up the bank and reached the well. He was there waiting for me, smiling broadly.

"I've been watching you for the past hour," he admitted. "Boy, you must be tired. You know, I'd never trust myself in one of those canoes. They look too dangerous." We both took a deep drink of water from the Worthylake well, and then he turned to me.

"That gave me quite a start this morning, when your wife appeared that way. It sort of made me wonder whether I shouldn't tell you the whole story." He paused, then went on. "Well, in the first place, I found the paper. The man's name wasn't Redwell, as I said, but Tom Redwick, and here it is on the paper." Nuskey handed me a grimy piece of yellow paper, on which the following statement was written:

Write Thomas Redwick, General Delivery Kingston, Ontario, if you find old book on Brewster Island, cover of skin, message inside. In old sail in foundation fisherman home. Good reward I promise.

Thomas Redwick

John Nuskey went on with his explanation. "Of course Redwick was the Canadian stranger, and I found out later that his grandfather was a relative of Captain Turner, the old Bug Light keeper who became King of Calf Island. I found the paper a couple of weeks ago." Nuskey took another deep drink of water, then continued with his story.

"My fishing mate and I always wondered what it could be. We were never going to tell anyone, but we're not getting along too well lately, for he seems to be getting ugly, dang him. Perhaps you'll be able to figure out something that we couldn't. Go to it."

Excited beyond belief at the actual evidence of a message that told of something buried in the outer harbor, I examined the paper carefully. Then the words Brewster Island caught my eye. There were four Brewster Islands, and why not look on one of the others? Boston Light at Little Brewster would be too small and open to attempt any hiding there, while Outer Brewster was separated by a deep channel from Middle Brewster, connected by bar to Great Brewster. Yes, as I suggested to John Nuskey, it was perhaps likely that Middle Brewster was the island to visit. He seemed to agree with the possibility.

An hour later, after a delicious lunch, my wife and I climbed the bank together. This time I had my camera, and we found Nuskey down by the well again. We talked for perhaps ten minutes.

"You know," he said, "I've been thinking over what you

said. I may go over to Middle Brewster and look around myself." Shortly afterward I asked him to stand down near the
well, and I took several pictures of him there. Those photographs were the last ever taken of Caretaker Nuskey.

On September 9, 1940, an overturned skiff floated ashore on
the jagged rocks of Middle Brewster Island. It belonged to
Caretaker Nuskey, but there was no sign of the sixty-four-year-
old fisherman, who had then been missing since the afternoon
of September 5. His cane, without which he could not walk, was
lying near his house on Great Brewster.

At three o'clock in the afternoon of Monday, September 16, Patrolman James A. Melvin of the Hull Police Department was notified by a resident of the vicinity that there was
a body on Nantasket Beach, some three hundred yards north
of where the old schooner *Nancy* had come ashore in 1927.
Patrolman Melvin went to the scene, where he found the lifeless
remains of Peg-Leg Nuskey.

Later, when Mrs. Snow and I read of the strange death of our
friend, it gave us a weird sensation, for we realized that we
might have been the last ones to see him alive. John Nuskey,
had he desired to reach Middle Brewster Island, could not have
hiked across because of his peg leg, but would have rowed over
in his skiff. It was entirely possible that he had journeyed across
to Middle Brewster that very afternoon of our visit, and there
met his death in a manner we shall never know. He may well
have died in pursuit of the treasure of Captain Turner, keeper
of Bug Light and King of Calf Island.

I recalled an interview I had conducted some years before on
Deer Island, Boston harbor, with Wesley Pingree, former
keeper of Deer Island Light. His father, Henry Pingree, was
erstwhile keeper of Boston Light. I went through my papers
and found the record of our conversation, which follows:

"If you want a colorful figure for the outer bay, it was Captain Turner, without question. A giant in size, he had a long, flowing beard. He fled down here from the Great Lakes around 1845 and settled on Calf Island. When the Government finished Bug Light in 1856, James Turner was given the position as keeper. He remained there over thirty years.

"I'll never forget when I first heard about Captain Turner. I was just a lad at the time, and probably a little fresh. I wanted to hike across the bars from Boston Light down to Bug Light and visit him. Then, when I got there, I stayed too long, and he realized he'd have to row or sail me back home, for the spit was covered with water.

"He sailed back to Boston Light with me, but before doing so he went over to Fort Warren for the mail. I made such a fuss at his not taking me right back to Boston Light that he decided to teach me a lesson. Just off the Boston Light wharf he reached over, grabbed me by the scruff of the neck and, before I realized what was happening, tossed me into the sea. He knew I could swim, all right, but he never turned around once to see if I got ashore alive! He sailed away to Bug Light, probably rather pleased with himself for teaching me a lesson.

"Father watched me as I crawled up on shore like a wet kitten. Although he was smiling, he warned me to be careful in the future. He told me that I'd had it coming, probably, but that I should be cautious of what I did in the future in the presence of Captain Turner. He explained that Captain Turner had lost his temper once on the Great Lakes, killing a man with a barrel stave there. Rest assured, I never bothered Turner again. They always said he was a pirate, and had brought treasure with him when he landed in Massachusetts. He came to Chatham first, they say, for he was afraid the Boston police were looking for him. But we really never knew."

Two other clues helped me to build a better picture of the King of Calf Island. Landing at Calf Island one day, I met an old man, Mr. Augustus Reekast, who dated everything from the Chelsea Fire of 1908.

He told me he had something to show me—pictures of the island the way it formerly was—and the next time I met him he gave me a folded magazine story to read about the outer harbor islands, an article that included a picture labeled "The King of Calf Island." I had never expected to see a sketch of Captain Turner, and was tremendously pleased.

The article was written by William H. Rideing and had been published in *Harper's* in August 1884. Evidently Mr. Rideing found Turner just as interesting as I later discovered him to be:

> The occupants of the other islands are lobster-men, chief among them being old Turner, who from time immemorial has hauled his pots in the waters surrounding the Brewsters. . . . I do not imagine that old Turner ever smiles; his deep-lined visage is puckered with seriousness, and though he is not talkative, an unexplained pathos speaks out from his eyes, which are screened from the forehead by a bristling pair of brows. He has been so saturated with salt water for nearly fourscore years that he has a half-pickled appearance, and his beard and the curly locks which still flourish, though bleached by age and exposure, are always wet with brine.

The second clue I uncovered at the Hull Town Hall, where an examination of the vital statistics showed that Captain James John Turner was born February 12, 1803, and died in Hull on March 12, 1888, at the age of eighty-five years and one month. Although the details concerning his father were missing, Turner came from Brighton, England, where his mother's maiden name had been Hannah Cronan. Captain Turner was buried at Mount Auburn Cemetery in Cambridge, Massachusetts.

I also discovered that either Turner or a friend had cut the date of his birthday on a Calf Island ledge, back in 1851. Later I found out that Turner enjoyed hiking around the outer harbor islands, as he was often seen by the keeper of Boston Light, his huge form moving rapidly along the low-tide gravel bars of the outer bay.

Night after night I worried over a nautical chart, wondering if Turner could have hiked across to Middle Brewster. I thought that it was at best an outside chance. On the other hand, the message did not specify which Brewster Island was meant.

World War II intervened and I went overseas, returning later as a casualty. After I had reached home, I was going through my belongings in the attic one day when I came across the chart over which I had pondered so often.

At the end of the war I made up a party and went out to Great Brewster Island with Captain William Van Leer, aboard his vessel the *Charlesbank*. When I suggested a hike across to Middle Brewster, only a few others besides Mrs. Snow decided to make the venture.

It was not an easy day to make our crossing. To begin with, there was neither a new-moon tide nor a full-moon tide, both of which bring unusually low water. In addition, the waves that day were rather rough. But an hour before low water we started across in pairs to support each other and prevent slipping, and soon were more than halfway across. From then on it was deeper water and we were up to our waists, sliding and scraping along over the barnacle-covered rocks and through the heavy kelp and rockweed. No one who has made that crossing ever forgets it. Time after time the boisterous waves battered us off our feet. When we arrived at Middle Brewster Island, our ankles and legs were cut and bleeding from scores of encounters with barnacles.

The others decided to hike around the outer circumference of the island and explore the cliffs and semicaves there. But my objective was the cliffs toward the center of the island, where the Richard S. Whitney property was located.

The Whitney's residence proved to be the only building old enough to have been visited over a century before by Captain Turner. When I had phoned Mrs. Whitney to get permission for my trip, she had said that the building was purchased from an old fisherman on the island and that her husband had rebuilt the house, modernizing it at the time. Then he had erected a giant flagpole on the ledge above the house. I asked Mrs. Whitney about the cellar, and she said that although in the middle of the living room there was a trapdoor that led down into the cellar, they had rarely opened it, and not one of the family had ever examined the basement. Of course, there was no known reason for their going down into the cellar.

I went up to the Whitney house and surveyed the ruins. The giant flagpole had fallen across the backwall at the top of the island. I read the inscription on it: ERECTED BY RICHARD S. WHITNEY 1902. Down below, the ruins of the Whitney home stood, the western ell smashed in, every window missing, the roof stripped of shingles. The years had taken their inevitable toll with a vengeance.

Gingerly I made my way across the kitchen floor to the living room, where the three-foot-square trapdoor awaited me. Surrounded by the ruins of what had once been exquisite furniture, the wooden square proved a formidable barrier to my plan of entering the cellar. After fifteen minutes of pounding and prying, I forced a corner up, and the rest was easy.

A pit of blackness awaited below, smelling musty and unused. I lowered myself into the pit, and as soon as my eyes were accustomed to the darkness, I began exploring the area. Then a rat, disturbed from its nest, scampered across my body, and I was not too anxious to keep on with my explorations. After resting a moment to recover my nerve, I continued. It must have been another half hour before I came across what appeared to be a collection of old rags, piled up in a heap in the southeastern corner of the cellar. I kicked at them, and seemed to hit something fairly solid. Could it be another rat? I kicked again, rather cautiously, for in my bathing trunks and sneakers I could not offer much opposition to an outraged rodent.

At my second kick the mass went to pieces, leaving a dismembered book, which I gazed at in complete astonishment. My last kick had broken the binding of the volume, separating it into two sections.

What a disappointment! Merely an old book, I thought, discarded years ago by the fisherman, not important enough to take away with him. But wait, could it possibly be that unknown object for which so many had looked? Could that book contain a secret treasure map or document?

Picking up the two sections of the volume I had kicked apart, I wrapped the pages in several rags, which actually were crumbling folds of canvas. Climbing up through the trapdoor, I replaced the wooden square in the floor and made my way down to where the others were waiting. They saw the canvas-wrapped bundle.

"What do you have there?" they asked.

"Oh, just an old book I found in a cellar," I replied.

No one appeared to show unusual interest. Unfortunately for our plans, I had taken too long down in the cellar, for the tide had gone out and was then almost two hours in. We all made our way down over the rocks to the tidal bar, joined hands again for safety and started back. In several places the tide was neck deep and I held the canvas-wrapped book high in the air. When we gained the shallow water at Great Brewster Island, the volume was still untouched by the sea.

That night I carefully examined what I had found in the old cellar. It was a volume 7 by 9 1/2 inches in size, 1 1/4 inches thick. The outer covering was of skin, said by some to be human. Inside the cardboard-reinforced cover was a statement pasted against the heavy paper. It was signed by one of the consuls on the island of Malta:

Malta/20 November 1839

I hereby certify that to my personal knowledge this volume belonged to the library of the Knights of St. John of Malta of the order of Jerusalem.

Witness my hand on this day and year above written——

Robt Ligetz

On the front flyleaf was written a single word, *Vertiz.* On the title page of the volume was the following, written in Italian:

L'AMBASCIADORE POLITICO CRISTIAN OPERA
DI
CARLO MARIA CARAFA
PRINCIPE DI BVTERA, & C.

Written by hand on the outer skin of the volume, evidently by a scribe in the Malta library, was the following title and numbers:

POLITICO CRISTIANO
352

The volume was printed August 1, 1690, on a private printing press in Mazzarini, Sicily, and was extremely rare. No other known copy in North America was as old as mine. Bookworms and rats had eaten into almost half the more than two hundred pages. All through the volume various pages had been corrected by pen.

After examining the volume from cover to cover, I discovered a secret compartment between the recesses of a double page, but there was nothing inside, much to my disappointment.

Later I telephoned Mrs. Whitney and told her about the book, but she said that never had either she or her husband owned such a volume, and by the laws of treasure-trove the book was mine to keep.

I showed the volume to several friends.* One of them, Robert M. Evans, who read Italian readily, pronounced it rather uninteresting except for those portions especially concerned with procedure in the papal courts.

Later I took the volume to the Rare Book Department of the Boston Public Library, where I showed it to my friend, Miss Harriet Swift. She had often helped me while I was gathering material for my first book, published in 1935, and I knew that she would be interested in what I had discovered.

Returning a week later, I found that she had identified the book as a rare one. But when I mentioned my hope that there might be a clue regarding buried treasure, she smiled tolerantly.

However, a few days later my telephone rang. It was Miss Swift, and from her manner she was a little excited. "Come in here just as soon as you can, Mr. Snow, for I've something to show you."

An hour later I was in the Rare Book Department, where Miss Swift greeted me.

"I know that it's foolish to get excited, but I may have

*In 1971 the author and his wife were bound and gagged in their home while the Italian book and other items were stolen. None of the items was ever recovered.

something for you," she said as she opened my old book at pages 100 and 101. "Look carefully," she went on, trying to conceal her excitement.

I glanced carefully at the open volume but saw nothing unusual.

"Hold up page 101 so that the light shines through," she suggested.

I did so, and except for a few words that had been rewritten, there was nothing to notice. There were about 270 words printed in Italian, but nothing of importance, or so it seemed to me. Concealing my disappointment, for I had come all the way from Winthrop evidently for nothing, I continued to study page 101.

"Well," said Miss Swift, "what can you tell me?"

"Except for a few smudges and a little rewriting of the letters, there's nothing unusual," was my answer.

"Nothing unusual?" Miss Swift smiled. "That page actually contains a crude attempt at a coded message. Study it and you may have your answer as to why the book was hidden. For example, glance at the eleventh line up from the bottom of the page."

I did so, and found that the line had been corrected in pen, probably centuries ago. I studied it carefully, trying to read it aloud in my best Italian pronunciation. *"Appostolica. Sceso di poi l'Ambasciadore dal palchetto."*

"Never mind what it says," Miss Swift broke in. "The line itself isn't important. I was first drawn to it by the unusual corrections in ink. You see, *Sceso di poi* was evidently written in as a correction by the printer or proofreader after the volume was finished and bound. That of course is interesting, but not as important as the next word. Look carefully at the next word, *l'Ambasciadore.* Do you see anything unusual about the *o* and the *r*?"

Suddenly I realized what she meant. Over each of the two letters was a small hole or pinprick in the page itself. Miss Swift had discovered the secret of the book, and there was probably a hidden message pinpricked into the paper of page 101, each tiny hole placed exactly over a certain letter. There were about forty-five pinpricks.

Whoever had done the work had not been careful, for the holes had gone through the back of the paper and through the next page. But as page 101 was the only page where the holes hit exactly over letters, we knew that neither on page 102, 103 or 104 could there be a message.

"Now go home and see what you can discover, young man," Miss Swift suggested.

Gratefully acknowledging my thanks, I returned home and stayed up half the night trying to arrange the pinpricks so that they meant something.

After arranging and rearranging the words that contained pinpricks on them, I worked out a system that eventually allowed me to solve the code.

For the benefit of those who prefer to forgo the work of translating essentially what is on page 101, Robert M. Evans translated it as follows: "Page 101 consists of a series of rather involved directions covering the somewhat stilted protocol to be observed at the Papal Court upon the occasion of an Ambassador to His Holiness presenting his credentials and delivering to his Secretary of State the message entrusted to him by the King who sent him."

Thus I came to feel that there was nothing of importance in the translation of the pages that had the pinpricks, and that any possible solution lay in the arrangement of the pinpricked letters or words. For the purpose of simplification, from the approximately 270 words on page 101 in the Italian volume, I list below only those necessary for the eventual solution, the words that were overscored with pinpricks, with small black dots for identification:

brevemente	Ambasciata	baciata	rispondera
brevita	nuova	ceremonie	apparacchiato
salutera	chinando	occorrera	dovranno
ambi	genuilettre	ossequio	parimente
genuflessione	Santita	l'Ambasciadore	tornera
si	Maestro	ceremonie	Ambasciadore
tra	Nipote	segretario	stato
se	eccedere	numero	andare
genuflessione	del	soglio	

Actually, the secret code was not really a code at all, merely the simplest form of deception, a form Edgar Allan Poe or A. Conan Doyle probably would have scorned, so simple that it may fool the average reader even now. So in all fairness I suggest that you do not read ahead for the solution until you have made at least a slight effort to solve the puzzle yourself; you already possess every clue necessary to solve the message.

The solution of the message that led to finding the treasure at Cape Cod follows:

Placing the pinpricked letters of each line side by side we get the following result:

RABR
ETUOMAHT
AHCDN
ALSI
GNORT

SSEER
TTSA
EEUD
SIDLOG

An effort to solve the message by putting down the first letter in each line gets the reader nowhere. Another possibility is to arrange all the characters side by side, as follows: RA-BRETUOMAHTAHCDNALSIGNORTSSEERTTSAEEUDSIDLOG

The solution still eludes us. Even by alternating the letters, first taking every other letter and every other third letter, the results are neither satisfying nor instructive.

Finally, after many hours of experimentation, you may try writing the letters backwards: GOLDISDUEEASTTREESSTRONG-ISLANDCHATHAMOUTERBAR

Introducing the spaces at the proper intervals, you can read:

GOLD IS DUE EAST TREES STRONG ISLAND
CHATHAM OUTER BAR

The next step after finding the directions on page 101 of the Italian book was to act on the information. The discovery of the book and its code had been announced in the local papers, and Mrs. Gertrude Crowley of Winthrop, granddaughter of the bearded Captain Turner of Calf Island and Bug Light fame, volunteered the information that her family had always heard Captain Turner had buried not one but two boxes of treasure, both down on Cape Cod, before he ever came to Boston Harbor.

It seemed to me that the best method of looking for the treasure was by metal detector. I sent for one from Palo Alto, California. We tested it and it appeared to be satisfactory, reacting to metal from four to five feet down. The following week I reached Chatham and went to work, lining up the old trees on Strong Island with the outer bar due east. It was very disappointing. Every fragment of old shipwreck or ship timber in the vicinity had its own metal spikes or strapping of iron, and the chains and metal of various sorts in the vicinity made the hunt harder and harder.

My visits continued day after day, weekend after weekend. Although I found an amazing amount of almost every sort of iron or brass and copper fragments, there was nothing resembling gold.

One night I went to see Good Walter Eldridge, and after that he rowed over to visit me from time to time. His eyes would glisten with excitement as he watched me work. He would not offer to help but would always be encouraging. And when he went away he would say: "Well, I've got to go out to *my* treasure ship soon, and see if she's coming out of the sand down there on the bottom." But when Good Walter would return and I'd ask him about it, he'd say, "No, I haven't gone out yet."

October came, and with it the last Cape Cod summer visitors vanished, the people Captain Nickerson calls the "health eaters."

It was a Friday afternoon when the metal detector paid for its cost. I had already hit six "duds" that morning, and after lining up Chatham Light radio mast with a point of land nearby for my bearings, I set out again, slowly and painstakingly walking between the long wooden handles of the detector. My earphones on, I watched the M-Scope indicator as the needle rose and fell.

The sun was still hot and strong, and I was just about to stop and take a drink of water when the needle gave a little jump. The hum of the phones increased correspondingly. It did not seem too important at the time, for on several other occasions the recording had actually been much higher.

I recrossed the area from side to side, and the phones

hummed encouragingly at each crossing. Finally I had centered the area of activity to a spot a yard in diameter, and it was there that I prepared to dig. Setting down the indicator, I returned to the boat for my spade, and was soon hard at work.

Throwing up spadeful after spadeful of sand, I dug until I was two feet below the surface. The sand kept sliding back in, and so I widened the pit I was making. Soon my waist was almost even with the top of the pit, but I had found nothing. Whatever metal had caused the M-Scope reaction was still undiscovered.

Resting briefly, I wiped the perspiration from my brow. Eventually I was ready for another try, but I needed a little reassurance that the metal was still there. Surely enough, when I tried out the M-Scope, the needle rose higher than ever.

Still, it would do that if I were getting closer to any object, be it iron, brass, copper, pieces of eight or doubloons. Finally I was down so far that I knew I would have to strike something soon. Measuring from the surface, I had almost reached the downward limits of the detector's power. Desperately I plunged the spade into the center of the pit—and struck a hard object six inches down. It felt like wood, but it seemed to yield.

I dropped to my knees and scraped feverishly at the sand with my bare hands, until I reached what my spade had encountered: a piece of rotten wood. Tossing it aside, I came across another and still another fragment of decayed wood. Then there was an entire area spotted with minute, rotted fragments of some type of wooden container.

Grabbing the spade again, I dug in four or five times and then threw the combined mass of sand and rotted wood out of the pit. Holding the spade for another plunge, I pressed it firmly with my left foot, but the spade went down just a few inches, clinking to a stop against a hard, metallic-like object that did not yield to pressure.

Could it be the object for which I searched, or was it merely another spike attached to an ancient, forgotten shipwreck?

There was only one way of finding out, and again I dropped to my knees and began pawing away the sand, digging and scraping until my fingers were almost bleeding. Then my fingernails clawed across the top of a small chest.

At the possibility of actually finding treasure, I fought a losing battle with myself—a vain struggle to keep nerves and blood pressure at normal level. I was excited and tense despite all my efforts to be calm.

Impatiently scattering the broken bits of wood out of the way, my probing fingers were soon surrounding the upper section of the box, which was about eight inches wide and six inches square. Tugging and pulling, I finally released it from the sand that had held it for over a century. The lid would not open, so I pried it up with the spade point.

I was not disappointed. There, revealed to my fascinated, unbelieving eyes, was a collection of silver and gold coins, covered with rust, sand and ancient bits of paper. I sank exhausted against the side of the pit.

I had reached my objective! *I had found treasure!*

Two days later, when the excitement had died down a trifle, an appraisal of my collection was attempted. The most costly piece of all, strangely enough, was not a Spanish doubloon nor a Portuguese moidore, but an old silver piece of eight, misshapen and apparently of low value. Robert I. Nesmith, famed collector and writer on Spanish and South American coins, gave me a surprisingly large amount for the piece of eight, which he identified as one of unusual rarity. In all, the 316 coins I found in the treasure box were worth almost $1800, not a large sum by today's values, but neither a small one.

Whenever my thoughts go back to the King of Calf Island and his treasure, I still have a strange feeling about the entire affair. There are so many questions that were not answered, chief among them the following:

Why and how did Caretaker Nuskey meet his death?

Why did James Turner hide his rare volume in a Middle Brewster Island cellar?

Where did Turner get the rare volume in the first place?

Why did Turner bury the treasure so far from his home at Calf Island?

These four questions hold the key to the unsolved part of this strange mystery, but it is my belief that the answers will never be found.

CHAPTER 3

Treasures of Martha's Vineyard

There are many stories of treasure connected with the delightful island of Martha's Vineyard. Each of the tales that I have enjoyed most has an unusual distinguishing feature—a French galleon, a blue rock, a secret staircase. However, just because a story is enjoyable does not mean that it is true. Of the three mentioned above, it is probable that the French treasure tale is valid.

During the Revolution a French galleon was wrecked on the south side of the Vineyard. The ship was carrying a large sum of money, part of the payroll for the French troops then in America. Her officers, believing it impossible to transport the money to the troops, buried it with the intention of later returning and delivering it to the proper authorities. For some reason they never came back.

The money remained in its underground resting place until many years later when, according to tradition, a horseman riding along a path that followed the shore of one of the Great Ponds discovered it when his horse broke through the marsh and stuck a foot into the chest. The finder, being a man of unusual uprightness, informed the authorities of his discovery. The Federal Government took charge of the matter and claimed the money, but a substantial reward was given to the finder. In 1946, when I gave Joseph C. Allen, Martha's Vineyard historian, a helicopter ride to Gay Head Light, he told me that one of the great fortunes on the island was based on the reward given for the recovery of the money.

Then there is the story of the Blue Rock of Chappaquiddick. This enormous boulder of blue stone is located near the shore not too far from where Cape Poge Light now stands. One day at dusk a local farmer was searching for a cow when he heard the sound of oars and voices. As pirates and other people of questionable character often sailed in close to Chappaquiddick, the farmer hid in the woods and waited to see who was approaching.

A short time later a group of men landed on the beach. Pulling their craft above the water, they lifted from it a heavy chest, which they proceeded to carry to the Blue Rock. One man, who appeared to be the leader of the group, directed the others to dig a hole near the boulder. This done, they lowered the chest into the hole.

Suddenly the leader turned on the two nearest men, shot them dead and ordered their bodies thrown into the hole with the chest. The others then quickly filled the hole with dirt and hurriedly departed the island.

The farmer who had witnessed this nefarious activity decided it would be safer to wait until morning to investigate the site. But when he came back at dawn he could find no trace of either the chest or the bodies of the two murdered men. He tried to locate the buried chest time and again, always without success. To this day the story remains a mystery.

The tale of the treasure of the secret staircase is another that has never been proven. The staircase itself does actually exist. It is in the famous Daggett House, a snug little pre-Revolutionary inn on a waterfront street, where seafaring men gathered for many years. The building was the first tavern on Martha's Vineyard.

The secret staircase, which goes off from the dining room of the inn to the floor above, has a door that is so completely concealed behind a cupboard-like arrangement that the average person would never even dream of its existence.

I have talked with Marguerite Miller, manager of the Daggett House, and with Fred H. Chirgwin about this unusual set of steps. I have also walked up and down them, observing the dents in two of the stairs. According to tradition, the dents are the result of the steps being forcibly hit with heavy bags or chests of treasure as they were carried up or down the stairs.

Irrefutably the dents are there. Whether or not they were made by pirate treasure bags is a mystery never to be solved. Marguerite Miller told me of an article published by the Dukes County Historical Society, suggesting that the staircase was secreted behind the panel to enable sailors to hide from the impress gangs that were on the island. However, I believe that the steps were built to accommodate the smuggling or piratical activities of some citizen or citizens of Martha's Vineyard prone to work of that nature. Undoubtedly, a staircase concealed so carefully was constructed for a purpose that also had to be concealed, and I do not doubt that smugglers or pirates trod it at regular intervals. It is quite possible that the dents were created by a chance encounter with some of their bags or chests of loot. I do have reservations, however, about the particular pirate story connected with the secret staircase.

Late in 1846 the brig *Splendid* cleared from the port of Salem, Massachusetts. Her master, Captain Harding, was sailing with an assorted cargo around the Cape of Good Hope, bound for the East Indies. Hidden away in a large iron-bound oak chest in the captain's cabin were $60,000 packed in sixty canvas bags, each bag containing $1000 and weighing fifty-six pounds. This hoard was in addition to the substantial sum necessary to have aboard ship in those days to conduct regular commercial business in distant ports.

The silver had been brought aboard when no one was around. The captain and the mate, Howard Walker, planned to add to their combined fortunes as a result of the trip. Captain Harding had locked the chest and hidden the key in a secret compartment in the cabin, but Walker soon found out where it was by cautiously observing the master. Walker, a former pirate, had brought aboard a private collection of drugs that he planned to use to his advantage at the first opportunity.

Walker managed, without having suspicion fall on himself, to drug the captain, who died soon afterward. He then took control of the ship and the money. Eventually he arrived with his hoard on Martha's Vineyard.

It is here that the secret staircase enters the story. According to the tale, Pirate Walker concealed his treasure temporarily in the room at the top of the secret staircase in the Daggett House while making arrangements for a permanent home across on the mainland at Falmouth, Cape Cod.

It was not long before Walker decided he was ready to leave Martha's Vineyard. Obtaining the help of several local fishermen—for a good price, of course—one dark night Walker hauled his treasure down the secret staircase, out of the Daggett House and into the waiting craft. A course was set for Falmouth. By two o'clock the hustling men had anchored the vessel, gone ashore with the treasure and dug out a shallow pit near the sandy beach. Tradition tells us that when the sun rose all the money had been buried, and Captain Walker hastily placed a bright red scarf around the base of the nearest tree in order to identify the hiding place.

Walker then went into the village to conduct some business relating to the property he wished to buy. He had not been there very long when he heard from an excited merchant of a buried treasure just found near the beach. His informant told Walker that a fisherman, returning from his daily trip, had pulled his dory up on the shore and started for his home. Noticing a red scarf tied to a tree, he became curious and searched the area. He soon spotted freshly spaded earth nearby. On investigating further, he uncovered a treasure hoard. Rushing into town, he told the authorities. They commandeered a wagon and team, returned to the spot, loaded the treasure aboard and brought it to the local bank, where it was safely locked away.

Walker was in a state of shock and rage, but he could do nothing without giving himself away. It was only a matter of time, however, before investigations led to his arrest and conviction for robbery and piracy on the high seas.

That is the account of the treasure of the secret staircase. Whether or not it is true in any or all details is a question. However, I would suggest that anyone intelligent enough to steal such a sum of money in such a devilishly clever manner and manage to move it all the way from a ship at sea to Martha's Vineyard, and then conceal it in a room at the top of a secret staircase, would not be foolish enough to identify its final hiding place with a brilliant red scarf.

PART FOUR

Historical Anecdotes

~~~~~~~~~

CHAPTER 1

America's First Thanksgiving—
at Clarke's Island

Few of us realize the unusual chain of events that led the Pilgrims to decide eventually on Plymouth harbor for a settlement.

The *Mayflower* arrived at Cape-End harbor, or Provincetown harbor as it is called today, on November 11, 1620. The women went ashore to do a great washing, while the men made plans to explore the area.

Many historians claim that the Pilgrims intended to settle in Virginia but changed their minds while at Provincetown harbor and decided on Massachusetts. I have always believed they had the idea of a New England settlement from the beginning, merely talking about Virginia while planning otherwise. The reason is that while New England was a wilderness, there would be neither an established Anglican Church nor an established government, both of which then existed in Virginia.

In any case, the men brought ashore at Provincetown a long-boat, called a shallop, and began to repair it for a voyage of exploration. Meanwhile a party of sixteen set off hiking and exploring. They eventually returned with corn stored by the Indians, which they had found on the way.

At last the shallop was ready. Thirty-three men went aboard

under the command of Captain Jones of the *Mayflower,* who had been named chief of the expedition because of his "kindnes & forwardnes."

The shallop reached Corn Hill, where they had earlier found corn on their first hike. With the aid of cutlasses and swords, they broke through the snow and frozen ground to gather a great abundance of corn, which they brought back on the shallop to Provincetown.

The corn so pleased those on board the *Mayflower* that there were many who now suggested settling at Corn Hill. Mate Robert Coffin, however, told the others about Thievish harbor, which was more suitable than Corn Hill for a settlement.

The morning of December 6, 1620, found eighteen men aboard the shallop, intending to sail up the coast until they entered Thievish harbor and then to go ashore. Among the eighteen were ten Pilgrims who had volunteered to make the trip with the crew, including Robert Coffin, William Bradford, Myles Standish, Stephen Hopkins and John Carver, who later became the first governor of the Plymouth colony. Stephen Hopkins had taken along his servant, Edward Dotey.

It was a bitter cold day, typical of December, with a hard wind whipping across Massachusetts Bay. The spray from the waves froze on their clothes, which turned to "coates of iron." Several of the men became sick "unto death" from seasickness, while others fainted from the cold. They went ashore that night somewhere along Wellfleet Bay and discovered where Indians had been cutting up a huge black fish. While camping that night on shore, they were attacked by Indians, but fortunately they were able to fight off the intruders.

The next morning another high wind hit the coast, but the Pilgrims pushed off from shore. Soon it was snowing hard, and by midafternoon an easterly gale began lashing the area. At the mercy of wind, waves and snow, which obliterated all coastline, the Pilgrims were in desperate straits. Suddenly a great billow smashed into the shallop. The strain on the rudder proved too much, and it snapped off. The men were now unable to keep the craft before the wind, although two oars made it possible to hold a course of sorts.

They were approaching land. With darkness settling over the ocean, it was agreed that they should put up more sail and take a chance on getting into harbor before nightfall. Suddenly another towering wave smashed the shallop. The mast broke into three pieces and toppled overboard with the sail, in what was described as a "very grown sea." Working with great speed and diligence, the men cut away the fragments of mast and sail and thus avoided capsizing.

Then probably off the Gurnet, they realized their situation was not one to be envied. Relentlessly the wind, waves and incoming tide swept them along in the pitch blackness of the night. The roar of mighty breakers indicated land ahead. All aboard could see through the darkness the white surf rolling shoreward on a rocky beach. Mate Robert Coffin, who had been reassuring the others that he believed he knew where he was, now abandoned all hope.

Just as the shallop was about to be swamped by a giant comber, one of the sailors took momentary charge of the situation. Grasping his steering oar firmly, he shouted at his fellow seamen: "If you are men, about with the shallop, or we are all cast away!"

The others steadied their oars. Rowing with superhuman effort for about five minutes, they rounded a point of land I like to believe was Saquish, finally finding themselves in the lee of a large promontory. In the blackness of the night they decided to stay aboard the shallop rather than go ashore and face a possible attack by more Indians, which the Pilgrims called a "huggery."

Soon the wind shifted to northwest, and it became much colder. John Clarke, acting first officer, announced that he was going ashore anyway. He and several others soon landed from the rough surf. They lighted a fire, and one by one the others joined them and warmed themselves. When morning came they found that they were actually on an island (later named Clarke's Island for John Clarke) in Plymouth harbor. Exploring, the Pilgrims discovered a huge rock, which still stands on the island, and climbed to the top.

As it was then Saturday, they agreed to rest there, dry out their gear and conduct a service of thanksgiving on the rock, in which they would give the Lord "thanks for His mercies, in their manifould deliverances."

I like to think of this thanksgiving service at the giant rock as the first real Pilgrim Thanksgiving. I often visit the giant boulder, which still remains unchanged and unmoved, not like its sad companion, the famous Plymouth Rock, which has traveled many hundreds of feet and has lost many hundreds of pounds from its original weight.

Early on Monday morning, December 17, 1620, the Pilgrims sailed back to Provincetown in their repaired shallop and reported to the rest of the company that Plymouth harbor was their choice as the location for a settlement. And so it was that a party went ashore from the *Mayflower* on December 18, 1620, landing not very close to the large boulder on shore we have come to call Plymouth Rock.

CHAPTER 2

America's First Flyer

The name of John Childs should go down in history as the first successful American flyer or glider. There are two completely different accounts as to where John Childs was born: one indicates the North End of Boston in the vicinity of Unity Street, the other claims Europe as his place of birth but that he arrived in Boston early in life.

When Childs was quite young he became interested in the way birds fly. He would go down to the waterfront and observe in detail the flight of seagulls, ducks, sparrows and pigeons. He especially watched the actions of seagulls, studying them closely as they perched on the wharves, always facing the wind so that they would be able to fly successfully at almost any time.

As Childs grew into maturity, he developed many sound theories he was able to test later. He studied wind action and realized early that a good time to fly a kite was also a good opportunity to copy the birds and soar away into the sky, providing that his "wings" were of sufficient length and area.

In considering the possibility of a man flying compared to the ability of a bird, Childs decided greater areas of sail must be used for man to compensate for the difference in type of human weight to that of birds. Giovanni Borelli in 1680 proved that man's muscles were far too heavy and could not be compared to those of a bird. Childs offset this by making wings that were

567

larger and longer in proportion to a human than the proportion of a bird's wings to its body. Probably Childs did not know that Leonardo da Vinci had drawn practical plans for flying. Otto Lilienthal used these plans successfully long after da Vinci and Childs were both dead.

It is possible that John Childs had heard of the tower jumping of the Marquis de Bacqueville. In 1742, just twelve years before Childs became active in the area around the Old North Church, the Marquis attached long wings to his body and leaped from his mansion near Paris to soar gracefully out over the Seine River. Unfortunately he landed ignominiously on a washerwoman's clothes barge anchored in the stream. Childs was an exception to most people attempting such a flight in that he never injured himself.

Gladstone Earl Millett of the Old North Church relates that Childs made his first descent without too much fanfare, landing successfully in a nearby field. On his second attempt he was greeted by scores of workmen and other Boston residents who had learned of his flight with admiration and wished to observe his next effort.

This time he took off from the Old North Church belfry, stretching wide his arms with their winged attachments to their fullest extent. A short time later Childs landed one hundred yards away in a field identified as in the vicinity of Henchman's Lane.

Finally the town fathers announced that since there was too much watching and not enough working because of the excitement of the flight, in the future no aviation of any sort would be allowed in Boston.

Hurrying to beat the date the edict would become law, Childs advertised that he would make the ultimate flight from the Old North Church. Not only would he fly, but he would be armed with two pistols which he planned to discharge on his way through the air from the belfry to the ground.

The appointed day, September 13, 1757, practically became a holiday, with hundreds of people from all walks of life assembled in the area where they believed Childs would make his descent. No one worked, it is said, within half a mile of the church.

Then came the moment when America's first flyer raised his wing-strapped arms, perched himself high on the edge of the belfry, watched his wings carefully as he unfolded them and leaped out into space. In the air on his way down he removed his two pistols from his clothing and fired first one, then the other, if we are to believe the records of the period.

Landing successfully once again, he accepted the applause of the thousands of onlookers in the North End. That was his last flight in Boston, for he vanished from the scene in similar fashion to the notorious Captain Gruchy, to whom a memorial still stands in the Old North Church auditorium.

The law against flying in Boston never has been repealed, and perhaps the residents of South Boston, East Boston and Winthrop may have some satisfaction in knowing that as far back as 1757 it became illegal to fly over Boston.

In 1923 the Colonial Dames erected a memorial to John Childs, and it stands today in the garden of the Old North Church. The Dames chose that year to erect the tablet because it was in May 1923 that the first nonstop cross-country airplane flight occurred, with John Macready and Oakley Kelly as the aviators.

The *Boston News-Letter* for September 8 to September 15, 1757, mentions John Childs and his daring feat. But did Childs really fire the pistols in midair as has been reported?

Here are the exact words of the *Boston News-Letter* article:

Tuefday in the Afternoon John Childs, who had given public Notice of his Intention to fly from the Steeple of Dr.

Cutler's Church, perform'd it to the Satisfaction of a great Number of Spectators; and Yefterday in the Afternoon he again performed it twice; the laft Time he fet off with two piftols loaded, one of which he difcharged in his defcent, the other miffing fire, he cock'd and fnap'd again before he reached the Place prepared to receive him. It is fuppos'd from the Steeple to the Place where the Rope was Fix'd was about 700 Feet upon a Slope, and that he was about 16 or 18 Seconds performing it each Time. As thefe Performances led many People from their Bufinefs, he is forbid flying any more in the Town.

CHAPTER 3

A Pig of Importance

Out of unimportant incidents come matters of great significance at times. Such was the case of the "sow business" in 1642, when controversy in the courts between the magistrates and the deputies cost a great deal in time, tempers and money. The dispute over the hog, trivial in itself, was responsible for the bicameral system of our government. After this court case was finally settled, the magistrates met by themselves as our senate does while the deputies constituted an independent house, thus establishing the two bodies in our legislature—the Senate and the House of Representatives. This system of government has lasted for more than three hundred years, and all because of a hog!

In 1636, when Sir Henry Vane* was governor of the Massachusetts Bay Colony, there came to Boston a traveling salesman, also called a drummer, who represented an English business house. His name was George Story, and he lodged at the home of a Mrs. Sherman. Story had samples from which to take orders. He hoped to get many orders in Boston, send them home to England and make a comfortable commission on his sales.

*Sir Henry Vane, whose statue is at the Boston Public Library, was later executed by having his head cut off in the Tower of London.

But Drummer Story was not welcomed in Boston. The Bostonians preferred to keep all business and all commissions among themselves instead of sending off to England. The merchants and magistrates of the area made it very unpleasant for George Story. They considered him most undesirable. There was a law against objectionable or obnoxious persons staying more than three weeks in town. When George Story overstayed this limit, he was brought before the governor upon the complaint of Captain Robert Keayne.

Captain Keayne was a prosperous merchant, a rich landowner and the first leader of the famous "Ancient and Honorable Artillery Company." He lived at what is now the corner of State and Washington streets. Like many highly connected men, he was often the object of ill will among the less wealthy, and at the time of this incident was under suspicion of extortion. In other words, he was also not universally popular.

George Story did not enjoy his encounter with the governor and determined to get even with Captain Keayne, the man who had caused his public discomfort. He decided he would wait until the perfect opportunity, which came in the form of a pig.

This pig belonged to Mrs. Sherman, at whose house Story boarded, and like most of its kind was of a roving disposition, very irresponsible, with the troublesome habit of running away whenever possible.

One day Captain Keayne saw this pig wandering along what is now State Street. He captured the pig and had it "cried"* through town. When no one claimed it, he put it into his own pigpen and gave notice that the owner could have the pig by proving its identity.

For some reason Mrs. Sherman never attempted to prove it

---

*The official town crier would make announcements through a small megaphone from various locations in Boston.

was her property or tried to identify it. When nearly a year had passed, Captain Keayne thought he had kept the pig long enough. As undisputed possession was ownership, he counted the pig as his and killed it for winter food.

That action was watchful George Story's opportunity for revenge. He knew of the whereabouts of Mrs. Sherman's pig even if she did not. As soon as the pig was killed, he induced Mrs. Sherman to believe that Captain Keayne had defrauded her of the pig by slaughtering it.

This was more than Captain Keayne, a magistrate of Boston, could stand. He objected to the accusations of Mrs. Sherman's friends that he was a pig murderer. He brought suit against both Mrs. Sherman and George Story for slander and defamation of character. The magistrates believed his story and fined Mrs. Sherman twenty pounds for damages.

George Story, realizing that events had not turned out exactly as he had planned but seeing an even greater opportunity for blackening Keayne's character, went about town telling Mrs. Sherman's sad tale, saying that it was outrageous that a poor woman be fined twenty pounds just because she had tried to obtain her just rights. Then he persuaded Mrs. Sherman to appeal to the General Court for justice and protection.

The General Court, the lawmaking and governing body of the Massachusetts Bay Colony, was the highest court of appeal, whose decisions were final. It was composed of nine magistrates, elected by the freemen, and thirty deputies, elected by the different towns. They all sat together—magistrates and deputies—in the General Court, and acted as a single voting and lawmaking body. The governor could not veto any decision.

Governor John Winthrop in his journal begins his account of the "sow business" with these words: "At the same general court there fell out a great business upon a very small occasion."

When Mrs. Sherman's appeal for justice because of the killing of her pig came to a vote, the Great and General Court was divided. Thanks to George Story's work among the people, the sympathies of the deputies were with Mrs. Sherman. But the magistrates were on the side of Captain Keayne. John Winthrop gives details of the voting:

> . . . the best part of seven days were spent in examining of witnesses and debating of the cause; and *yet it was not determined,* for their being nine magistrates and thirty deputies, no sentence could by law pass without the greater number of both, which neither plaintiff nor defendant had, for there were for the plaintiff two magistrates and fifteen deputies, and for the defendant seven magistrates and eight deputies, the other seven deputies stood doubtful.

Eventually it was decided by the court that the matter would be settled by Captain Keayne paying back the three pounds he had collected of the twenty-pound fine levied against Mrs. Sherman.

The actual importance of this dispute, which went on for years, is that it caused the wiser heads in the colony to see the impossibility of an elective assembly acting as a judicial tribunal. The deputies would most likely decide as the people who elected them desired, not necessarily as the real justice in the case demanded.

At last a compromise was arranged. The magistrates were to sit by themselves, the deputies by themselves. Each group would conduct its business separately, with new acts *approved by both* to become law.

This was the origin of the Massachusetts State Legislature.

The magistrates or assistants are the Senate, and the deputies are the House of Representatives, or the Assembly as it is sometimes called. And so the Great and General Court of Massachusetts was created in its present bicameral form because of a pig!

CHAPTER 4

America's First Aerial Photograph

An article in the August 1958 issue of *Flying,* entitled "Flashlight Lawrence," included a statement that Lawrence, "the first aerial photographer" of America, used balloons, kites and ingenuity when he took pictures from the air over the ruins of San Francisco after the earthquake of 1906.

The photographer may have operated as claimed, but one thing is certain: Flashlight Lawrence was *not* America's first aerial photographer. That honor rightfully belongs to James Wallace Black, a Bostonian. The article in *Flying* incorrectly asserts that the San Francisco pictures, made in April 1906, were the first air photos taken in this country. Actually, almost forty-six years before, on October 13, 1860, James Wallace Black took the first successful aerial picture in America from a captive balloon over Boston Common.

Black, whose earlier photographs of the construction of the present Minot's Light were masterpieces, had a studio in Boston at 173 Tremont Street, where he not only photographed the leading citizens of the day but also taught the science of photography to Oliver Wendell Holmes and many others.

Photography in the 1850s and 1860s was a very risky business, with perfect sunny weather necessary for outdoor pictures. Aer-

576

ial photography was undreamed of until Black and a Providence friend, Samuel A. King, decided to attempt to make a picture of the Rhode Island capital from a tethered balloon high over the city.

The majestic *Queen of the Air* was the balloon they used. Although at first the day was bright and clear, wind clouds soon appeared in the distance. Black, working against time while high in the air, made a hasty attempt with the wet plates then in use, and a fair picture resulted. For a brief period of time the impression remained on the sensitized glass. But before permanence could be achieved, the storm clouds hit the balloon and the fixing material spilled and could not be applied. No more pictures could be attempted, for although the wind later diminished in strength, the clouds hid the sun for the remainder of the day. The first attempt at aerial photography had failed.

After careful organization of each minute detail of their plans, Black had the balloon brought to Boston, choosing Saturday, October 13, 1860, for the initial air photograph attempt over that city.

The project called for the balloon to take off from the usual location on Boston Common near the baseball diamond. The *Queen of the Air* soon soared aloft until it reached a position over what is now known as the Soldiers and Sailors Monument on the rise in ground then called Flagpole Hill.

When the balloon was tethered, it was arranged that a certain amount of its hydrogen gas would be released the instant a picture was made. Then, suspended about twelve hundred feet in the air, Photographer Black ordered the curtains lowered around the basket to simulate a dark room so that he could prepare his wet plates. Pictures had to be taken almost at once after the glass plates were treated with emulsion.

Immediately after the picture was exposed, he carefully treated the wet plate with the hydrogen, which blackened the picture to the degree desired. Then, when the sensitized glass was perfectly developed, he applied the fixing solution to make it permanent. His negative was completed as soon as it was dry.

During the next ninety minutes Black prepared, exposed, developed and fixed eight negatives in all. For many years it was believed that only one was a complete success. However, this was not so. Of the six that came out, some were blurred from the swaying of the balloon and two turned entirely black and were ruined because of an excess of hydrogen.

With eight negatives finished, James Black and his friend, Samuel King from Providence, untethered the balloon and for several hours enjoyed looking at the surrounding country as they drifted along. Riding the prevailing winds, they finally brought their trip to a close thirty miles away from the city, less than a mile from the sea and within a short distance of what is now Torrey Little's auction barn in Marshfield.

On his return to the city, Black made up prints from his favorite aerial negative of the Port of the Puritans. He found that the outer limits of the picture included the Old South Meeting House on the left, Boston harbor at the top, Summer Street at the right and Winter Street at the bottom of the photograph.

When I first saw this picture at the Old State House about half a century ago, I was intrigued. Several years later I was really fascinated when I located in a camera store* a sketch from the air on a glass slide of the area that apparently had been photographed by James Wallace Black that October day in 1860.

At first I thought that the original Black photograph had been copied by the artist who made the sketch or drawing.

*The store was Handy's on Bromfield Street, where they had hundreds of glass negatives and slides. Alton Hall Blackington had introduced me to the marvels of this institution.

However, a careful study of the artist's efforts revealed that there were areas in the sketch outside the known original limits of the Black photograph. It seemed to me that the artist could not have indicated the correct size and shape of the various buildings from the ground as they might have appeared from the sky, so the great question in my mind was how the artist could draw the sketch that had a larger area than Black's 1860 photograph.

I received a clue from Robert Taft's volume *Photography and the American Scene,* which eventually led to my discovery of another of Black's aerial photographs. I found that by putting the two pictures side by side, overlapping the new one slightly on the original, there is a much larger area and a better knowledge of the appearance of Boston at that time.

These two photographs are included in this book. They are oval in shape, as were many photos in those days.

The right-hand portion is the known photo; the left was taken almost immediately before or afterward, answering the question of how the artist sketched the area that was larger than the limits of the known picture.

In the foreground of the left photograph is the prominent Park Street Church, the Granary Burying Ground, a portion of the Boston Athenaeum where it joins the burying ground (in an arch, part of which is actually over the cemetery), the Tremont House, the Parker House, King's Chapel and cemetery, the Old City Hall and the Boston Museum.

Next is the Old State House, scene of the Boston Massacre. In the distance is the Custom House before the tower was added. To the left of the Old State House is Faneuil Hall and the Quincy Market. Following along Washington Street, the Old South Church can be seen.

Moving to the right of the double photo, Washington Street leads close to the Summer Street Church, which occupies a prominent position. This church was destroyed in the Great Fire of 1872.

Winthrop Square is easily discernible, with the scene of the Boston Tea Party at Griffin's Wharf outlined against several ships in the Rowe's Wharf area.

PART FIVE

Incredible Occurrences

CHAPTER 1

Latter-Day Jonahs

Many otherwise devoutly religious individuals have expressed doubt about the accuracy of the biblical account of Jonah and the whale. In similar vein, at least two 19th-century sailors are known to have survived after being swallowed by whales.

Peleg Nye, a Cape Cod whaler, used to recount his adventure to youngsters who visited his Hyannisport home during the 1860s. One of those children, Edward A. F. Gore, later of West Medford, told me the story in 1907 when I sat on his knee on our spacious piazza in Winthrop.

In March 1863 Nye fired his bomb lance into a sperm whale, and everyone aboard the longboat assumed that the whale had been killed. Nye prodded the huge mammal with a hand lance, and suddenly the whale slapped its tail and crashed its lower jaw into Nye's boat. Nye fell forward directly into the whale's mouth.

Scrambling to escape, Nye found himself trapped as the whale closed its great jaws. A sperm whale has teeth only in its lower jaw, teeth that fit into upper-jaw sockets. Nye was caught by the whale's jaws just below his knees, but the space between the whale's teeth and sockets was large enough to prevent his legs from being crushed.

The whale soon sounded. Nye believed the huge beast reached the bottom of the ocean with him before everything went black. Then Nye breathed in some seawater and lost consciousness.

Luckily, at approximately the same time, the whale gave up the struggle and floated to the surface, dead. Just before the mammal appeared, Nye's body came to the surface and was taken aboard the whaler. It was a long time before he could be revived, but he finally came to and recovered completely before reaching home. Living to the age of seventy-nine, Peleg Nye was known as the Jonah of Cape Cod.

An even more remarkable incident took place about twenty-eight years later—so remarkable, in fact, that the scientific editor of a Paris journal debated for 4 1/2 years whether to publish the facts in his possession.

Every facet was carefully checked and rechecked. Finally convinced of the truth of the story, editor Henri de Parville authorized its publication in the *Journal des Debats* on March 14, 1896.

On the afternoon of August 25, 1891, the whaling vessel *Star of the East* had come upon a great school of sperm whales. One of the whales, which had been wounded by a bomb lance thrown from a whaleboat, seized the boat in its jaws and crushed it in two.

The sailors leaped in all directions to escape. Steersman James Bartley jumped with the others, but just as he leaped the whale made a quick turn in the water, opened its mouth and caught the falling seaman. The other sailors saw the jaws close over Bartley. Giving him up for lost, they made their way back to the *Star of the East.*

Later in the day a dead whale came to the surface of the ocean. For two days the men worked at removing its blubber. When they finished, it occurred to one of the sailors that the whale they had been working on might possibly be the one that had swallowed Bartley.

After much discussion, the other whalers finally agreed to open the stomach and intestines of the immense animal. As they cut open the stomach, to their amazement and horror they saw the outline of a man through the membranes. Carefully slicing away the muscles, they uncovered the missing sailor, unconscious but still alive.

Moving Bartley with care, the sailors placed him on the deck, rubbed his limbs and forced brandy down his throat. His entire body had turned purple, and he was smeared with the whale's blood. Working on him in relays, the men soon had Bartley washed and his circulation restored. Then he regained partial consciousness. It was his hallucination that he was being consumed in a fiery furnace. Although the average temperature of a whale is 104°, this does not account for the terrible sensation the sailor experienced. Possibly it was caused by the constant pressure of the whale's body against his own.

The return voyage to England nearly restored his health. After he had a complete rest, he made this statement about his experience:

I remember very well from the moment that I jumped from the boat and felt my feet strike some soft substance. I looked up and saw a big-ribbed canopy of light pink and white descending over me, and the next moment I felt myself drawn downward, feet first, and I realized that I was being swallowed by a whale. I was drawn lower and lower; a wall of flesh surrounded me and hemmed me in on every side, yet the pressure was not painful, and the flesh easily gave way like soft india-rubber before my slightest movement.

Suddenly I found myself in a sack much larger than my body, but completely dark. I felt about me; and my hand came in contact with several fishes, some of which seemed to be still alive, for they squirmed in my fingers, and slipped back to my feet. Soon I felt a great pain in my head, and my breathing became more and more difficult. At the same time I felt a terrible heat; it seemed to consume me, growing hotter and hotter. My eyes became coals of fire in my head, and I believed every moment that I was condemned to perish in the belly of a whale. It tormented me beyond all endurance, while at the same time the awful silence of the terrible prison weighed me down. I tried to rise, to move my arms and legs, to cry out. All action was now impossible, but my brain seemed abnormally clear; and with a full comprehension of my awful fate, I finally lost all consciousness.

So improbable did the story seem that the captain and the entire crew of the *Star of the East* thought it necessary to give testimony of the incident under oath.

Bartley was about thirty-five years of age, strong in build and constitution. The only lasting effect of his terrible experience seems to have been a recurring nightmare in which he relived his sensations in the whale's stomach.

It might be well to review what the Bible says about Jonah. It is not claimed that Jonah was in full possession of his faculties for the three days he was in the whale. We know that he prayed, and then he probably lost consciousness, just as James Bartley did centuries later. To Jonah and his associates, a miracle had occurred:

And the Lord spake unto the fish, and it vomited out Jonah upon the dry land.

So we have the names of three men who have been in the jaws of a whale: Jonah, the son of Amittai; Peleg Nye of Cape Cod; and James Bartley of England.

~~~~~~~~

CHAPTER 2

Rip van Winkle of the Blue Hills

From twenty miles out to sea, sailors in Boston Bay often sight the Blue Hills of Milton. For centuries the Indians of the area gathered in the hillside vicinity. Massachusetts Mount, as Captain John Smith called it, is said in folklore to have been one of the dead ice monsters that crawled down from the north with "stones on its back." Legend insists that all of these creatures were stopped when they reached the hollows dug by the sun god, the hollows that have become the beautiful New England lakes. There the gods pelted them with heated spears, melting the ice and leaving behind the glacial remains.

Big Blue, as it is called today, now boasts the Harvard Observatory at its peak. Three centuries ago it was relatively unpopulated, although at its base lived the Aberginians, a tribe said to be distantly related to the Indians on the Isle of Manhattan.

The chief of the Aberginians was Wabanowi, who "thought more of himself than all the rest of the people did." He doubled in brass as a medicine man, and he was a poor one. Before long, as his prophesies never came true, he was called "Headman Stick-in-the-Mud." The chief's daughter, Heart Stealer, was as beautiful as her father was stupid. The chief made it a point to nag her and to forbid her every wish, as he thought chieftains should do.

587

Then came the day when Fighting Bear, chief of the Narragansetts, visited Big Blue Hill and fell in love with the girl. He gave a long speech to Wabanowi, likening himself to the sun, the storm, the ocean and to all the strong animals he could recall. He compared Heart Stealer to a deer, a singing bird, a zephyr, the waves of the sea and flowers of the field.

Then, getting down to business, Fighting Bear asked for her hand in marriage. He went on with his speech, talking of the prophecy that a great race with "sick faces, hair on its teeth, thickly clad in summer and speaking with a harsh tongue" was soon going to drive the red man from the New England area. By this time, of course, the Indians knew that the whites had been living on the fringe of the great ocean not too far from Big Blue, but they had not caused trouble.

Stick-in-the-Mud, who considered himself the only prophet of the area, was outraged. Springing to his feet, he cried out: "Who has foretold this? I didn't. There is only one prophet in this district. I am the one. It isn't for green youngsters, Narragansetts at that, to meddle with this second-sight business. Understand? Moreover, my arm is so strong it needs no help to exterminate an enemy. I can beat him with my left hand tied behind me. Had Fighting Bear merely asked for my daughter, I would have given her up without a struggle. If somebody doesn't take her soon, I shall lose my reason. But Fighting Bear has added insult to oratory, and if he doesn't leave soon, he'll never get there at all."

Thus speaking, Stick-in-the-Mud wrapped his furs around himself so that only his nose showed.

Fighting Bear folded his arms, and with a scowl stated that his time would come. He then strode into the forest.

One evening not too long after this a heavy smoke developed over the Blue Hills, and shadowy forms were noticed flitting in and out of the smoke. All of the Indians now began to wonder what was going to happen.

Stick-in-the-Mud, who had been dozing as the smoke developed, awakened to find the spirit of a woman standing in the entrance to his wigwam. She beckoned for him to follow her. He did so at once, hoping to discover some secret that would be more useful to him than what he considered his fortune-telling matches, which usually ended in failure.

She quickly led him up a path of the Big Blue Hill. Finally they reached an outcropping of rock, and there was a cavern the Indian had never noticed before, although he had walked in the area on many occasions. The cavern glowed with a weird light, and Stick-in-the-Mud noticed that it was bedded with soft moss. Without knowing why, he sank on the bed of moss and watched, entranced, as the spirit began moving her arms in a slow, rotating motion. Soon he was sound asleep.

When on the next day his followers could not find him, they began searching the woods of the Blue Hill area but were unsuccessful. When the days turned into weeks and then months, his followers decided that he was not coming back, and elected another to take his place.

Down in Rhode Island, Fighting Bear heard that his tormentor had disappeared. He returned to the Blue Hills, where he again claimed Heart Stealer as his future bride. This time there was no one to object, and he took her back to the Providence area, where they were married.

As Charles M. Skinner tells us, now came the "men of sick and hairy faces, white men" who desired the earth and took it, making it no longer a place pleasant to live on. When war broke out, Fighting Bear and the other Indians fought valiantly but lost, and decided to keep the peace in the future.

Stick-in-the-Mud, back at the cave in the Blue Hills, awakened one day to find the cavern illuminated again, with the spirit that had taken him there standing over him. Noticing that he had awakened, she spoke: "Wabanowi, I caused you to sleep that you might be spared the pain of seeing your people forsake their home for other lands. The men with pale faces and black hearts are here. Had you been here you would have stirred them to break the peace and all would have perished. They have kept the truce. Now I set you free. Go into the Narragansett country and live with your daughter, who married Fighting Bear. Do not disturb their happiness."

The rock then swung open, and this Indian Rip van Winkle staggered out into the brilliant sunshine. His fourteen years of sleep had left him pained with rheumatism and covered with moth-eaten whiskers, which made the dogs in the area bark at him.

Stick-in-the-Mud looked down into the Neponset Valley, but all his followers had gone. Where his village had been were log houses and huts, and barnyard sounds could be heard. After gaining a little confidence, he descended from Big Blue and reached the Neponset River, where he shaved himself as best he could with a shell. An hour later he was on the road to Providence, arriving there the next morning.

He found the home of his daughter and Fighting Bear. Several of his grandchildren who were running around soon began playing games with him, in the most popular of which he served as a horse for the youngsters.

As the long Rip van Winkle-like slumber had rested him, Stick-in-the-Mud lived many years afterward. There are those who claim that he comes back once every summer to the Blue Hills area.

Every September, on the day nearest to a full moon, he appears at Big Blue and looks off at the sunset. You may see him then, or you may see him half an hour later skimming the surface of the Neponset River in his shadow canoe. Having thus visited the scenes of his youth, he retires for another year.

CHAPTER 3

Billy McLeod's Baby Seal

On Grape Island in Boston harbor lived Captain Billy McLeod and his wife as caretakers for thirty-four years. He had many, many stories to tell. One of the best concerns the tiny baby seal he found while he was strolling along the beach. Evidently the mother of the seal had been killed by one of the large boats in the area, leaving the seal to make its solitary way to Grape Island. Billy and his wife took care of the seal, feeding it carefully and nursing it along until it became quite frisky and was very attached to the couple.

In a short time the seal was performing feats of unusual agility. In the morning it would flip its way down to the shore, swim around for a time, then return to the house. When Captain Billy went out in his dory, the seal followed behind, always coming back with him.

Occasionally Captain Billy went to Boston, leaving his pet seal behind. When it was time for the captain to return, the seal swam out to meet him, was helped into the boat and rode back with him. Sometimes the seal reached the house before the captain, and there he knocked three times with his flipper as a signal that he wanted to enter. Once inside, he made a beeline for the stove, behind which a box had been installed. There he remained until suppertime. After supper Captain Billy put a little rug in the box, whereupon the little seal yawned in a knowing manner and curled up on the rug for the night.

The little seal finally died from eating green paint. Many children who had visited the pet mourned his death. Captain Billy said that although he had owned many pets since then, there never was an animal as affectionate as his little seal.

CHAPTER 4

Alice on the Bark *Russell*

One wintry night in 1907, when the snow was swirling around our Winthrop, Massachusetts, home and great icy flakes were beginning to bounce against the windowpanes, I watched and listened as Grandmother Caroline played the guitar to accompany Mother's zither.* As usual, I was fascinated at the speed with which Mother's hands flew over the zither strings.

As they often did during the long winter nights, Mother and Grandmother had promised to play some tunes after the dishes were done, for there was no television or radio in those days. Mother had interspersed the songs with stories of her unusual experiences on Robinson Crusoe's island and out on the high seas aboard the bark *Russell,* of which her father and my grandfather were captain.

For Mother, then Alice Rowe, her sea experiences began in 1869, at the age of eleven months, when she made her first trip on the *Village Belle,* captained by Grandfather Rowe. Eventually she learned to walk on that schooner. Later, when she went ashore, she found that she could not keep her balance because the land did not roll with the motion of a ship. Grandmother told me how she had to teach Alice to walk all over again.

*The zither was given to my mother in Chile, and she was taught to play it by a Dr. Harvey, an officer of a British frigate.

In the first five years of her life, Mother's parents were her only companions at sea, and they were her teachers as well. Grandmother Caroline instructed her in the usual school lessons and in guitar music and sewing. Grandfather Joshua Nickerson Rowe taught her how to box the compass, steer the ship and even "take the sun."*

When Mother and my grandfather would pace the deck every day for exercise, he told story after story of his career on the *Crystal Palace,* of unusual shipwrecks, pirate adventures and his Civil War service at sea. Often he would sketch pictures to illustrate his stories; thus Mother learned to make illustrations for the stories she wrote in letters to her cousins in Maine.

When Alice was fourteen she went on the English sailing bark *Russell* for 4 1/2 years, during which time she kept a diary or "log," as she called it. She told of the young stowaway Harry Kidd who became her companion as well as the cabin boy on the ship. She described the terrible feeling of watching in a wild storm as a vessel that had passed them was wrecked while the *Russell* was saved from striking the very same rocks only because the force of the wind brought the bark's fore lower topmast with its straining sail crashing to the deck, stopping their headway. One entry included her excitement when a whale came so close that when the ship rolled, she leaned over the rail and dropped a stick on the huge mammal's back.

Another entry told of the wonderful experience of passing through the Sargasso Sea. Her account of sailing around Cape Horn in a rough passage and finally seeing the Andes Mountains was most interesting.

While the bark *Russell* was in the harbor of Valparaiso, Chile, for repairs, her father called Alice and her mother into

*Using the quadrant to assist in finding the position of the ship.

the chart room and asked, "Where do you think we are going, young lady?"

She guessed wrong several times and finally gave up. Grandfather Rowe smiled and pointed to the chart of the South Pacific Ocean. "We are going," he said, "to Robinson Crusoe's island."

His statement astounded everyone.

Alice asked, "Father, did Robinson Crusoe really live near here, and isn't it a made-up yarn anyway, like *Little Red Riding Hood*?"

"No, it is not," replied Captain Rowe. "His real name was Alexander Selkirk, and he lived on the island of Juan Fernández, 360 or more miles west of this city. I have promised to take a freight of two masts to the island for a small ship they are building there."

After a three-day sail with a fair wind all the way, those aboard the bark *Russell* saw a great purple cloud on the horizon, which gradually changed to what appeared to be a huge pile of rocks. As they sailed nearer it proved to be a towering mountain peak called the Anvil,* 3,040 feet high. The island spread along the horizon for about fifteen miles.

When the ship reached the anchorage, a boat came out to the *Russell* carrying Count de Rodt, governor of the island, who brought fresh vegetables and goat's meat as a gift. Captain Rowe showed him around the ship, after which Alice and her father and mother were invited to go ashore with the governor and explore the island.

On one of their trips around the island they went to see the cave that Alexander Selkirk had lived in for the four years he was alone on the island. In a small boat they skirted the foot of the tall cliffs, sheer rock walls towering over 1000 feet. Sud-

*The Spanish name is El Yunque. Convicts were given their freedom if they climbed it. Few succeeded, most falling to their death.

denly they sighted a tiny beach. Captain Rowe guided the craft
in on a big rolling wave, the boat rushing up on the beach at
a dizzying rate. After climbing out of the boat they walked
along the shore and up a path that led through a natural tunnel
in the cliff until they reached the famous cave of Alexander
Selkirk.

The room inside had been dug from solid earth. Shelves
scooped around the sides held dishes and other household articles, while a hammock slung from side to side made the cave
look homelike.

Several days later they made a trip to the great lookout where
a tablet had been erected to Selkirk's memory. It was truly a
perilous journey. After making their way through a wooded
area with many burrs that stuck to them, climbing over huge
rocks, inching over a narrow ridge with yawning gorges on each
side, they finally reached the top. Alice lay down to rest. Suddenly she heard her father's voice: "I am monarch of all I
survey! My right there is none to dispute; from the center all
around to the sea, I'm lord of the fowl and the brute!" From
the topmost point he recited William Cowper's poem, "Alexander Selkirk's Soliloquy." Then Captain Rowe read aloud the
tablet, which stated that Selkirk was landed at Juan Fernández
from the *Cinque Ports Galley* in 1704, and after four years and
four months of solitude he was taken off by sailors of the
privateer *Duke* on February 12, 1708.

Captain Rowe decided to try to find a shorter path to return
to the governor's home. Plunging into a forest with beautiful
ferns and moss clinging to the trees and rocks, they eventually
found a brook running toward the sea and followed it for a time,
until it plunged over a fifty-foot precipice. After scouting
around they located a tree they thought might bend, as it was
fairly slender and yet strong. Pushing, shoving, rocking it back
and forth, they managed to bend it down until two of the

younger and more adventurous members of the party scrambled over and forced the top of the tree to the bottom of the cliff, where they held it. Everyone crawled down the trunk except the dog Jess. It seemed she would stand there barking and wagging her tail forever, but Jess suddenly decided to take a chance and started coming down the bare, steep cliff. When she reached the bottom her paws were torn and bleeding. Meanwhile the governor had sent a rescue party for them. My mother always told this story very dramatically and closed it with the question, "Did we climb up that tree or down it?"

Another adventure began when the party from the *Russell* were rowing along at low tide near the foot of the cliff and saw a black space with a deep opening. Alice wrote of her experiences that day:

"Now," Father ordered, "do just as I say. Pull hard at the oars and duck down your heads. I'll steer."

We did as he commanded, and in we shot, finding ourselves in a beautiful cavern! The flickering light was dancing over the interior with a blue tint, caused from the sunlight striking down through the azure depths of the water and reflecting up into the cave. It seemed like fairyland.

The roof was high inside, like a church, and hung down in pinnacles of rock. It extended in about a ship's length, and we could hear the waves breaking on a little beach. The water was the most brilliant blue I ever saw, and was filled with bright yellow fish. . . .

Our boat was soon made fast, bow and stern, to some jagged rocks, then out with our lines, and what sport we had. The fish were not a bit afraid of us or our lines.

I became so excited catching them so rapidly that I made my line shorter and shorter, and still on they came, until finally I was just holding the baited hook in the water, and they bit as fast as they could!

Then I proudly said: "Watch me! I am catching fish by just holding the hook in the water, without any line!"

I had hardly finished saying this when the boatman shouted in a voice of terror: "Look out, Miss Alice!"

I jumped and snatched my hand out of the water, and as I did so a pair of jaws came together with a snap!

"Well, young lady," said Father, "you just escaped having your hand bitten off. In the future never fish without a fishline! That was a water snake or a young sea serpent about five feet long. I guess we had better get out of here as fast as we can if we have stirred up a nest of those creatures."

We cast off our mooring lines and started for the mouth of the cave. There we found we were in a trap, as the tide had come in while we were fishing and the entrance was too small for the boat to go through.

But we had Father who always found a way to do what seemed impossible. . . . As the boat was higher than the overhanging rock, one side had to be tipped under the edge and pushed along while we all lay flat on the slimy fish. First one side of the boat, then the other, was tipped, and while we were tipping it we kept thinking, or I did, that if we upset we would be thrown in among all those water snakes with jaws full of big sharp teeth like a wolf's! . . . It was luck that we tried to get out of the cave before the tide was any higher, for we just managed it and that was all . . . What a supper the cook gave us that evening! Those yellow-tailed fish were delicious fried in salt pork and eaten with island vegetables. I was pretty glad to be eating cave fish instead of cave fish eating me!

*　　*　　*

Another exciting incident aboard the *Russell* was the shooting of a sea lion, which was brought aboard when it was supposedly dead. As it lay on the deck with everyone gazing in wonder at the huge creature, it rose up on its tail and roared, chasing first one person and then another. Finally Harry, the cabin boy, grabbed a sledgehammer and took it up into the rigging. After tempting the beast to come toward him, Harry waited until the animal was directly below and then, with a mighty blow, struck the sea lion on the head. This time the creature was really dead, to the relief of the captain and crew. If you know how an inchworm moves, you can imagine the sea lion walking, only instead of taking an inch at a time he took eight feet.

On the final trip of the *Russell* with Captain Rowe in charge, the bark was to sail for England with a load of manganese ore. They stopped in Chile on their way and had another adventure in which the dog Jess was the hero. Alice and her mother were wandering along a brook some distance from the rest of the party when Jess began to whimper and whine. She crouched down near Mrs. Rowe while looking intently at a large bush farther up the stream. When the bush started to move and Jess trembled even more, Alice's mother said she believed that the dog could smell some wild beast. Having heard that when in such a predicament one should never turn his back and run, she and Alice walked backward with one of them always staring at the bush until there was a turn in the brook and the bush was out of sight. Then, dropping the flowers and ferns they had been collecting, they raced to the shore, where they found the captain talking to a native fisherman. They blurted out their story and were told that the dog had saved their lives, as there were lions in the vicinity. Later, after two children had been carried off by lions, a big hunt was organized to make it safe for the people. Alice vowed never to wander in the woods again.

CHAPTER 5

Treacherous Harbor Ice

I was born in Winthrop, Massachusetts, which is almost entirely surrounded by water. On two occasions I nearly lost my life when the harbor froze over and then started to melt.

The first experience occurred when I was about ten years old. Winthrop had run out of coal, and the emergency supplies that had been trucked in were being sold to those who could transport the 100-pound bags from the Town Hall to their homes. It was my job to fetch the heavy coal bags the 2 1/2 miles to our residence high on Cottage Hill. Weary after walking all the way over to the center, I decided to take a shortcut across the ice of the inner harbor on my way home.

I thoroughly enjoyed this part of the trip until I reached some rubbery ice and fell through with my sled and the coal. With great effort I managed to climb out, and even salvaged my sled with the coal just as I was about to give up. I trudged over the ice more warily the rest of the way and then, after climbing the hill to our house, told my adventure to my family. I have always wondered whether the joy expressed upon my safe return was over the saving of the boy or the coal.

On January 2, 1918, I spent the morning hiking around on the ice of Boston harbor. Toward afternoon, because of the rising temperature, I came to some rubber ice and suddenly found myself up to my armpits in the frigid water, which was far over my head in depth. There was no one around for miles. It was then about three o'clock in the afternoon and the temperature was below zero. I could feel my rubber boots rapidly filling with water.

The rubber ice kept breaking as I fought to crawl up on it. After resting a moment by hanging onto the edge, I began a furious battle to escape. Kicking my water-filled boots in the best trudgen stroke I could muster, I clutched at the edge, gaining ever so little at times and then falling back as the ice gave way under my weight.

Again and again I fought for freedom, but each time my efforts seemed to be successful the ice would break and I would find myself back in the water up to my armpits. The air trapped in my pea jacket somehow prevented me from sinking below my shoulders.

With my sixth try came the realization that I was making some progress. Although the lower part of my body still broke through the ice, I was able to work my shoulders farther out of the water. Gradually I was able to raise my body until my waist reached the edge of the broken surface. Anxious not to lose this hard-won advantage, I continued kicking frantically, at the same time taking care not to batter the ice with my legs. Meanwhile my fingers clawed deeper into the frozen surface and I achieved another slight gain.

A moment later I worked myself out on the ice as far as my waist, and then did a quick turn of the body, rolling the remainder of my torso free of the hole. In order to keep my weight distributed as much as possible, I made three more rolls away from the spot that had trapped me. Then I stopped. I lay there breathless, just a few feet away from the narrow thirty-foot-long stretch of water I had opened, hoping I had won the fight.

I began the long, tedious trip to the safety of Apple Island. Not daring to stand erect, I rolled over and over, making probably seventy-five revolutions in all. In this awkward fashion I reached Apple Island, only to realize that trouble still lay ahead. I had half a quart or so of water in each rubber boot and knew that even if I could pull the boots off I could not get them back on again without help. I was about two miles from home and the icy weather, still far below zero, was getting colder. This was the time to prove how good a runner I was. Racing down the hill on the Cottage Park side of Apple Island, I started with great lumbering strides to cover the distance to my home.

The ice was good and solid the whole distance to the area near the Winthrop Yacht Club where I had scrambled down on the frozen harbor hours before. When I reached the mainland the sun was setting. Four minutes later I was safe at home.

I learned two things from these experiences: how treacherous harbor ice can be, and never to travel across its surface without taking special precautions. In 1936 seven boys acquired the same knowledge in an even more frightening and dangerous way.

On the afternoon of Sunday, February 9, 1936, seven boys, all from Rhode Island, on leave from their Civilian Conservation Corps camp at East Brewster on Cape Cod, started out to walk across the ice to Wellfleet, despite the warnings of their friends that the warming trend would break up the ice field.

They were later sighted three miles out by Hudson Ellis, who watched them through a telescope from his Cape Cod home. To his horror, he saw the ice on which they were walking break away from the main field. The boys continued to walk, however, unaware that they were marooned. In fact, as the youths later explained, darkness was falling before they discovered their plight.

Ellis immediately notified Lieutenant Julian Kavier, in charge of the CCC camp, who in turn summoned the Coast Guard.

A Coast Guard plane from Salem, piloted by Lieutenant True G. Miller, was sent out at once. Also dispatched were three Army bombers from winter maneuver base at Concord, New Hampshire. They were joined by a private plane from Boston, piloted by Captain William Wincapaw, for whom I took over as the Flying Santa at Christmas that same year.

Major Giles, pilot of one of the Army bombers, spotted the seven lads on two drifting ice cakes seven miles out in Cape Cod Bay. Notified of their location, the other planes dropped food and blankets to the marooned group.

Finally, after having been adrift for twenty-two hours, the boys were brought aboard the cutter *Harriet Lane* through the heroic efforts of Coast Guardsmen who braved death by pushing and rowing lifeboats through the ice field.

Two youths were rescued from a small ice cake, the other five from the main cake. All suffered from exposure, having been tossed about all night at the mercy of ice, sea and wind. One, John E. Fitzsimmons, Jr., nineteen, of Portsmouth, had both his feet frozen and needed medical treatment. The others rescued were Manuel J. Botello, nineteen, Albert M. V. Papa, eighteen, and Tony Ray, eighteen, all of West Warwick; Nicholas S. Scungio, eighteen, and Norman R. Beaulier, eighteen, both of Pawtucket; and Thomas G. Malone, nineteen, of Portsmouth.

Unable to make the East Brewster shore because of a solid blockade of ice, seven feet thick in places, the *Harriet Lane,* accompanied by the faster Coast Guard patrol boat *Argo*, ready to take off any of the young men if a medical crisis arose, headed for Provincetown on a three-hour run. Aboard were seven boys who, like myself, had learned the hard way the treacherous nature of a walk on the ice.

CHAPTER 6

The *Britannia* Sails on Time

New England is known for its variable weather and cold winters. In the old days the harbor froze over more often and more solidly than it does now. Whatever the reason—propeller-driven motors, pollution, more marine traffic or warmer weather in recent years—the water of the inner harbor does not freeze solidly as far as the docks at the present time.

Perhaps the most interesting ice episode in the entire history of Boston Bay concerns the Cunard liner *Britannia*. One day late in January 1844 the liner arrived safely at her pier in East Boston, and that very night the harbor began to freeze. With the steamer scheduled to leave soon after February 1, it became embarrassing to the merchants and residents of the city when the ice grew thicker and thicker. Because of maritime rivalry, the people of New York would never let the Bostonians live it down should the *Britannia* be prevented from sailing because of the ice.

On January 30 Mayor Brimmer presided at a meeting to decide what could be done. Matthew Hunt was appointed to cut a channel to liberate the *Britannia*. After working all through the bitterness of a blustery winter's day, Hunt found that the ice was freezing faster than he could cut it. He notified the committee that he could not fulfill the contract.

John Hill and Gage, Hittinger & Company then agreed to cut

604

the channel. Professional icemen with much experience on the ponds and lakes of Massachusetts, they recruited a large force of expert ice cutters, who soon assembled to begin the work.

Thousands of eager citizens in holiday mood went out to watch the ice cutting on February 1 and to visit the tents and booths set up by enterprising individuals. Boat Keeper Berry, one of the Boston harbor pilots, walked up to the town from Gallop's Island. Men with ladders charged a cent each for eager harbor explorers to reach the ice from the sidewalk level of the city. The men had cut holes around the public landing stairs to prevent citizens from getting on the ice in their own way without paying for the privilege.

The *Boston Journal* of February 1, 1844, reported the method of cutting the ice:

A channel of about sixty feet in width is first marked out, which is then divided into blocks of about thirty feet square. The sections marked are then *ploughed,* by which the ice is nearly cut down to the water. The plough used for this purpose is formed of seven different ploughshares, perfectly flat, and very sharp, which are arranged in a row, nearly similar to what is called a cultivator. After ploughing, the ice is sawed, so as to detach the cakes entirely from each other, after which two grapnels are attached to the cakes and they are hauled under the stationary ice by a gang of about one hundred and fifty men, some fifteen or twenty men standing on the cake in order to sink it sufficiently to make it pass under.

The blocks of ice on one side only are thus disposed of, thus forming a channel of thirty feet in width. The blocks on the other side are to be detached after this channel has been finished, and will float out to sea with the ebb tide.

The work was kept up hour after hour, and even an injury to contractor John Hill, hurt jumping from a cake of ice, did not delay proceedings. By late the next afternoon the work was completed, and the *Britannia* was assured of being able to sail the following day.

On the morning of February 3 the adventuresome inhabitants of Boston made their way to the waterfront, where they went down on the harbor ice to watch a spectacular event: the sailing of the Cunarder *Britannia.* Several hundred people viewed her moving away from the pier. Backing into the slot in the ice cut for the purpose, the *Britannia* turned her paddle wheels until the prow faced the open channel. Slowly moving her engines, the beautiful vessel sailed out through the artificial channel while at least two hundred cheering enthusiasts walked alongside all the way to Castle Island, where they gave the *Britannia* a noisy and colorful farewell.

PART SIX

Shipwrecks

CHAPTER 1

The *Home,*
Lost Off Ocracoke

The story of the *Home* is the type of steamer disaster that holds public attention for many years. When a ship goes down with her crew, it is surely considered an unfortunate event. But when a passenger craft goes down carrying great numbers of men, women and children from all walks of life, the awesome dangers of the sea are brought home to everyone who learns of the catastrophe.

The paddle-wheeler *Home* was launched in April 1836 from Brown and Bell's yard in New York. Her owner, James B. Allaire of New York, was proud of the fact that the *Home* was among the fastest craft of her day. Unfortunately her 22-foot beam proved wholly inadequate for her 220-foot length.

All went well on the *Home*'s maiden voyage from New York to Charleston, South Carolina. On her second trip the *Home* broke the speed record between the two ports, negotiating those stormy coastal waters in an amazing sixty-four hours.

Following this swift journey there was talk that after a few more trips the *Home* would be groomed for a spectacular ocean crossing. The merits of the vessel were so widely discussed that whispers of doubt as to her safety were dismissed with a tolerant but contemptuous smile by her owner, Mr. Allaire.

On the afternoon of Saturday, October 7, 1837, the *Home* was scheduled to sail from New York to Charleston. Excitement over the voyage reached a feverish pitch. Many who had not planned to make the trip were carried away by the enthusiasm of the crowd and boarded the vessel in New York. Possibly fifteen persons sailed on the *Home* who failed to give their names to anyone ashore. Because of this, the total number of persons on board the *Home* was never definitely known. It is certain, however, that there were forty-five in the crew and ninety identified passengers, of whom about forty were women and children. James B. Allaire, the owner's nephew, was among the passengers, for his uncle had certain theories about the performance of his vessel that he wished to have tested on the high seas.

At exactly five o'clock the crew removed the gangway. Farewells rang through the air as the paddle wheels began pushing the *Home* seaward. Passing through the Narrows, the steamer was proceeding at better than twelve knots. When she reached the new Captain Gedney Channel, the pilot was confused by what was then known as the Romer Buoy, and the steamer grounded heavily on a shoal. She hung there for more than three hours until the incoming tide freed her. Then, after a private conference between Mr. Allaire and Captain Carleton White, the steamer proceeded down the bay.

Drawing abeam of Sandy Hook Light, the *Home* veered to starboard and began her long trip toward distant Charleston. On and on the paddle wheels carried her, until by Sunday morning there was much talk among the passengers and crew of a record passage between Sandy Hook and Charleston.

That evening the wind changed and came strong from the northeast. The waves built up to ten feet in height. After a few violent wrenchings, the steamer began to take in water. The storm grew in force and intensity. By midnight the *Home* was wallowing in the dangerous seas of a mighty gale, a predicament for which she had never been built.

The rolling, pitching and straining of the ship soon weakened the engine bed, slowing down the paddle wheels. Whenever a wave caught the *Home* under her port guardrails, the ship listed sharply to starboard. This threw the port paddles out of water, where they vibrated alarmingly as they turned uselessly in the air. Sometimes it was ten or twelve minutes before the captain could bring the *Home* around and get the ship back on an even keel.

James B. Allaire was much embarrassed by this turn of events. He had made the journey to satisfy his uncle that the *Home* could reach England, and here she was in difficulty on a trip from New York to Charleston. He retired to his stateroom and did not appear for hours.

The crew set emergency sails on the masts, which steadied the ship for several hours. But after sunset Sunday the storm grew more intense. The seams in the hull widened and the water streamed in. It required the entire crew to keep the pumps from losing their battle with the sea. Despite their frantic efforts, around midnight the water in the hold began to climb, slowly but inexorably. Inch by inch it rose, until Captain White was so frightened that he sent out an appeal for help to all able-bodied men. Hand basins, buckets, pails, chamber pots and pans were called into service as bailers. Many of the panic-stricken women volunteered for duty. In spite of everything, the water rose higher and higher.

With the coming of dawn, the bleak, forbidding shores of Cape Hatteras were seen ahead. Soon Cape Hatteras Light was visible twenty-three miles away. Captain White ordered the course changed so that the *Home* would clear the terrible reefs surrounding Hatteras Island, and before long the lighthouse faded from view. By two o'clock in the afternoon it was agreed that the danger of hitting the shoals was over. A new course was chosen to bring the *Home* nearer to land. Captain White decided he would beach her on the nearest shore if there was no other safe alternative.

Hour after hour the *Home* had been weakening and working loose. By this time every successive wave was actually tossing the bow three or four feet from the rest of the vessel's framework! Soon the entire hull began to work up and down, bending and twisting as though it were a deckload of laths that had been swept overboard.

This sickening motion roused terror among the passengers. Many gave up all hope of survival and consigned themselves to their Maker. Others made desperate preparations to save themselves, cutting blankets into long, thin strips with which to secure themselves to spars or timbers when the ship went to pieces. The two life preservers on the boat had been appropriated by two men, and the *Home* carried just three lifeboats —sufficient for only half the number of passengers.

At six o'clock Monday night water reached the engines; they gave a final vibrating quiver and died. In the strangeness of that unexpected silence, every passenger felt that the end could not be far away. Beyond sight of land, the ship was running before the wind with her emergency sails. Without the engines, her speed was more than halved.

Shortly before nine o'clock that night the storm clouds broke, revealing the moon shining eerily. By its pale light the distant shores of Ocracoke Island were visible, and soon afterward it became clear enough to see the welcome flashes of the island's lighthouse.

Captain White decided to beach the *Home* at Ocracoke and gave orders to the helmsman to that effect. Nearer and nearer the straining side-wheeler came toward the beach. Soon the moonlight revealed close at hand the glistening backs of the great waves as they hurled themselves up on the shore. Captain White ordered all hands to prepare for a violent shock when the 220-foot vessel hit the sand. By ten o'clock the *Home* was in the outer breakers. Soon a mighty wave worked itself under the stern, lifted the *Home* high amidships and sent her forefoot crunching to pieces as she struck bottom more than four hundred feet from the island.

There was instant chaos and confusion. Above the noise of the breaking timbers could be heard the desperate shouts of men, the high shrieks of women and the children's piteous cries of terror. The *Home* settled into the sand and began to break up. Mr. Allaire had come out on deck some time before to talk with Captain White. After a hasty conference, they ordered the women and children forward so that they would be nearest the shore. The screaming and wailing continued, with husbands and wives clinging together and children clutching their mothers. The gale-force wind pushed the giant billows through the weakening structure of the *Home* and on toward the shore, where they broke with a thunderous crash.

By now most of the women and children had reached the forecastle. Several waves swung the *Home* around until her bow was at an angle toward the beach. Then a tremendous comber began to rush toward the doomed ship. Catching the women and children on the forecastle, the wave pulled them all into the ocean together. All but two of the women drowned almost at once. Only one of the children, a boy of twelve, was thrown up on the beach alive.

The two women who survived could be seen clinging desperately to fragments of wreckage as they floated toward the island. Mrs. LaCoste of Charleston, an elderly woman who was so heavy she had trouble walking, had lashed herself to a deck settee before the wave washed her off the forecastle with the others.

Shipwreck news always travels rapidly, and as Mrs. LaCoste struggled feebly toward land, the islanders were there waiting for her. Each wave pushed her closer to them, until finally a giant wave caught the frightened woman and carried her along at an alarming speed. As it broke against the sand, it swept Mrs. LaCoste high on the shore. When it started to recede, the undertow began to pull her out to sea again. At that terrifying moment the islanders rushed into the surf and rescued her.

Out on the wreck of the *Home* plans were made to launch a craft into the sea. The jolly boat was put over and three men jumped aboard. Before they could push off, a wave caught the boat and capsized it, drowning all the men. Another wave then snapped the lines and sent the empty jolly boat to crash on shore. The longboat was dropped into the sea and twenty-five passengers scrambled aboard. Another great wave caught and capsized the longboat; every one of the twenty-five persons perished.

A short time later large fragments of the paddle-wheeler began to break away from the hull of the vessel. Many of the braver men attached themselves to the floating timbers; a few reached shore safely. The *Home*'s smokestacks began to totter shortly afterward. The port stack fell just as a woman passed beneath, carrying her baby toward the upper deck. Both mother and child were killed instantly.

A Mrs. Schroeder of Charleston had lashed herself to a deck-rail brace. When a wave swept her overboard, she dangled there, submerged with each passing wave. Mr. Vanderzee of New York noticed her helpless position. Reaching down over the side, he seized her by the clothes and held her up for some time, but was unable to pull her over the rail. Finally the strain proved more than he could stand, and he was forced to release her. As she dropped into the water again, the brace gave way. When a wave caught her and threw her up on the shore, she frantically dug her feet into the sand and clung to the brace. Despite her efforts, the undertow pulled her halfway down the beach. Still tied to the brace, she rolled up again before the next great billow thundered on shore and engulfed her. Time after time she was swept almost above the high-tide mark, only to be dragged out by the next sea. Her strength was rapidly ebbing. Just as Mrs. Schroeder lost consciousness, a summer visitor at Ocracoke, a man named Littlejohn, rushed into the water and saved her.

By this time Mrs. LaCoste and Mrs. Schroeder were practically naked. Gently the islanders carried them up the beach and covered them with sand as protection against the cold. They were later taken to the home of William Howard on the island.

Out on the *Home,* the Reverend Mr. George Cowles of Danvers, Massachusetts, was struggling to help his wife to safety. The well-known minister always had experienced a "strong and invincible dread of the sea" but was persuaded to take the voyage because of the fast passage of the *Home.* While helping his wife reach the ruins of the quarterdeck, he met Steward David Milne, son of a minister. Placing his hand on Milne's shoulder, he comforted him with a verse from the Bible: "He that trusts in Jesus is safe, even amid the perils of the sea." As he finished speaking another great wave swept across the forecastle, and when it was gone both the Reverend Mr. Cowles and his wife had vanished.

The *Home*'s forecastle snapped off a short time later. On it were Captain White and seven men. They floated ashore safely. Of the estimated 150 persons who went aboard the *Home* in New York, twenty passengers and twenty of the crew survived.

By noon they found themselves "among a set of savages" from Ocracoke Village. Several families did everything in their power to help the survivors. These benefactors included the Howards and the Wahabs, leading families on the island. Before the end of the week, the forty survivors had been taken by inland water craft toward their respective destinations.

In all, twenty bodies from the *Home,* including that of Mrs. Cowles, washed ashore and were buried by William Howard in his cemetery.

It is easy to criticize a sea captain after a disaster. Several passengers from the *Home,* led by a Mr. C. C. Cady, claimed that Captain White was intoxicated most of the journey. However, Steward Milne quickly came to the captain's defense and praised him warmly.

"Captain White drank only two glasses of absinth cordial all the time during the trip," said Milne. "It was a passenger, Captain Alfred Hill, who was drunk, and others confused the two. Captain White didn't eat, sleep or lie down in his office until he was entirely worn out by fatigue and watching day and night at the wheel."

At the time of the disaster India rubber life preservers were just coming into use. There were only two aboard the *Home*; both carried a passenger ashore. One of these survivors remarked that had the side-wheeler been supplied with 150 life belts instead of two, there would have been fewer deaths that October day in the violent surf off Ocracoke Island.

CHAPTER 2

In Memory of the *Pamir*

The German sailing ship *Pamir,* which was closely associated with the great commercial house established by Ferdinand Laeisz, has now been at the bottom of the sea for some time. In the last few years of her existence, this steel four-masted bark made headlines whenever she arrived in port or sailed away. She was a commercial, deep-water, wind-propelled vessel, one of the few survivors of her rig afloat.

To many who followed the sea either as a profession or as a hobby, a mention of the *Pamir* would reawaken memories of the days of old, bringing back names such as shipping experts Robert Hilgendorf and Reederei F. Laeisz. The long, glorious history of the Laeisz sailing ships of Hamburg, Germany, is not as well known as it should be. These great German sailing vessels, many of them using the initial letter *P* in their name, set many important records.

It was a dramatic sight when a Laeisz ship sailed into a crowded anchorage. The motto of the "Flying P" was, as Laeisz stated, "My ships can and will make rapid voyages." And indeed they did. Shortening sail as they neared port, seamen would also be rigging cargo gear and opening hatches to get ready for quick handling of the cargo even before the anchor rattled down. The departure of a Laeisz ship also was accomplished with similar speed and economy of motion.

617

Along with such craft as the *Preussen, Potosi, Padua* and *Passat,* the *Pamir* was beloved by millions. The 3150-ton four-master was a solid craft. Built in 1905 at the Bloehm and Voss yards in Hamburg, she seemed destined to live forever. During her half century on the high seas, she had survived World War I without trouble and had weathered many gales.

Obtained by the Italian Government in 1924, the *Pamir* later was sold to Gustav Erickson of Finland, owner of a large fleet of sailing ships. He would not have bought her, together with her sister ship the *Passat,* unless he considered her outstandingly seaworthy. Both these reliable sailing ships plied the Australian run. They brought wheat and other goods to Europe, earning substantial funds during an eight-year period.

When World War II began, the *Pamir* fell into British hands. Impounded and registered in the New Zealand navy, she served for a time as a school ship. During the war the bark made six journeys to the west coast of America. Next, a British grain importer chartered her for four years, putting her in the Australian corn cargo business. Then, although there was an acute shortage of merchant shipping at the time, the British company gave the *Pamir* back to Erickson.

A Belgian salvage company bought the *Pamir* and the *Passat,* outbidding the shipbreakers. Meanwhile, West German groups insisted that the two ships should be acquired for training German marine officers. Their reason was that a first-class German marine officer, in order to qualify for a position, had to have sailed as a boy in one of the big windjammers. People began to ask about a new German mercantile marine, wondering where the future captains and officers would come from if there were no more sailing ships in which they could learn the ropes and get their training.

Shipping regulations in Germany still required that a candidate for a helmsman's papers and even a master's certificate must have done a certain amount of training in sailing ships whose total area of canvas was at least twice the ship's length, considering the beam. The *Pamir* and the *Passat,* each with a minimum area of canvas of about 2800 square meters, met these requirements—and there were no other qualified German craft.

Finally a Hamburg shipowner named Schlieven bought both craft. After having them modernized, he engaged them as cargo sailing ships to train future officers of the merchant navy. Thus the *Pamir* and the *Passat* were brought back to Germany, were refitted and were soon equipped with all the latest devices.

And so it was that the *Pamir,* carrying a 900-horsepower Krupp-Diesel engine as auxiliary, sailed under the German flag again after thirty-eight years. On January 10, 1952, she left Hamburg on her first voyage, bound for Rio de Janeiro.

Almost before she was out to sea she encountered trouble. At the eastern entrance to the English Channel during a storm, the screw of her auxiliary engine fell off and an anchor was lost overboard. The storm developed rapidly, turning into a gale that gave the forty-nine cadets aboard a real taste of excitement and danger. They watched as two British ships came to the *Pamir*'s aid. When she put over her remaining anchor and the flukes caught, the immediate danger was averted.

Better weather soon followed. Nevertheless, the incident reminded the older officers of an earlier disaster that ended in death at sea for many German sailing cadets. On February 8, 1938, the Hapag training ship *Admiral Karpfanger,* a 2853-ton four-masted steel bark of Hamburg, had sailed from Port Germein, South Australia, for Falmouth, England, with forty German sailing cadets aboard. She was never heard from again.

In 1952 the *Pamir* experienced no further incidents of danger en route to South America. After thirty-four days on the ocean she sailed into Rio. Necessary repairs had been made at sea, and as she came up the bay the beautiful German training ship with her smart young cadets received a tumultuous welcome.

When the *Pamir* reached Rotterdam at the end of her second

South American voyage—October 30, 1952—she was impounded by a Dutch ship's chandler, for Schlieven was in financial trouble. Not only had he sunk all his capital into purchasing and refitting the two sailing ships, he had also amassed a considerable number of other debts. Since his vessels were not earning the amount of money he had expected, the inevitable happened: a bank foreclosed. For two years the *Pamir* and *Passat* remained at their moorings.

A *Pamir* and *Passat* fund was set up in 1955 to enable the two craft to sail the high seas again. Sufficient money was raised to buy them, and both were put into service in 1956 as training ships.

On June 1, 1957, the *Pamir* sailed from Hamburg on her sixteenth round trip to the Argentine. At this time she was one of the most stable sailing ships that ever put to sea, with six watertight compartments, new steel masts and sixteen-millimeter iron plates.

Captain Hermann Eggers, who had already made seven trips in the *Pamir,* had planned to command the voyage, but a sudden family crisis made him go on leave. In his place sailed Captain Johannes Diebitsch, a mariner with extensive knowledge and experience. When the *Pamir* started back to Europe from Buenos Aires in September 1957, the ship was supposedly in perfect shape and there was no apparent cause for anxiety.

The good summer sailing weather came to an end abruptly. On September 20 Captain Diebitsch received warning of a hurricane, which the United States Weather Bureau had christened Carrie. It is believed that Diebitsch then attempted to sail around the storm.

Contrary to all expectations, Carrie did not veer to port as normal hurricanes do. Instead, the mighty gale headed for the central Atlantic and caught the *Pamir.* The tall-masted ship, under full press of sail and on a northerly course homeward at the time, was battered to such an extent that she was unable to ride out the blow.

What will always be an unsolved mystery is how Captain Diebitsch and Chief Mate Rolf Dieter Kohler planned to meet the situation when they realized Hurricane Carrie was going to catch them. We shall never know; neither officer survived, and the logbooks went to the bottom with the *Pamir*.

On board the sailing craft was Captain Fred Schmidt, a writer of sea stories. For years he had taught in the navigation school at Lübeck. Schmidt signed on for this particular voyage to take pictures for an illustrated work he was writing about life in oceangoing sailing ships. His last letter, written an hour before leaving Buenos Aires, is full of enthusiasm for the vessel and her crew. He was already looking forward to publishing the photographs and articles at the end of the voyage. The hurricane caught the *Pamir* that Sunday evening, and all Schmidt's plans for the future ended abruptly.

The first the world knew of the trouble was on Sunday, September 21, 1957, at 1500 hours Greenwich time. The *Pamir* sent out an SOS that she was struggling desperately in a heavy gale. Her position was given as 30° 57' North, 40° 20' West. She stated that she had a 45° list, was in danger of sinking and had lost all her sails. The British coast radio station at Portishead rebroadcast the message at once so that all available craft could reach the scene.

Ships within a near radius hurried to the general location after receiving the SOS. The closest of all was the American freighter *President Taylor*. Her radio operator announced to the world that she was making full speed for the *Pamir* and hoped to arrive at the scene at 2300 hours that night.

The Canadian destroyer *Crusader* then radioed that she would arrive at the same general location within twelve hours. The *Manchester Trader*, a British steamer, picked up an SOS and immediately relayed it to all other stations. Shortly after this the *Trader* received a broken message stating in part that the *Pamir* had met trouble and had her ". . . foremast smashed by the heavy sea."

Nothing further was ever heard from the *Pamir*'s radio.

Other craft announced their plans and positions. The British tanker *San Silvester* signaled that the *President Taylor* was due at the scene at 2300; the *Penn Trader* was expected to arrive at the same time. The Norwegian motor tanker *Jaguar* was 160 miles north-northwest, making eight knots. The German motor ship *Nordsee* was making ten knots and the British motor ship *Hauraki* was proceeding at fifteen knots. The *Tacoma Star* and the Dutch oceangoing tug *Swarte Zee* also started for the sinking *Pamir*.

At eight o'clock that Sunday evening the *Pamir*'s captain had received final warning that a hurricane could be expected within two hours. A survivor explained what occurred when the hurricane warning was announced:

We were given orders to secure all rigging. All hands were sent aloft, but before we could start taking in sail, the hurricane overwhelmed us.

Captain Diebitsch's order to trim sails came too late. A mighty squall tore the foresails away, and the mast snapped. From that moment disaster followed disaster. Things went so quickly that no one could say exactly what happened. The power of the storm forced the ship over on her side. We took on a 30° list, which increased to 35° and finally to 40°, the limit of the instrument's recording device. Of course, by this time the decks and holds were awash. The order "All hands on deck" was given. We all put on our lifesaving jackets; the ship heeled over more and more, shivering beneath the weight of mountainous seas. No longer could we get a foothold on the almost vertical deck, and it was impossible to lower a lifeboat with this heavy list. We held on fast to the rail on the starboard, for the port side was already underwater.

When our ship suddenly capsized, we plunged down into the water, one after the other. Many of the boys must have been drowned at this moment. Those with any strength left attempted to swim away, but the suction of the ship drew us after her. Our only thought was to get away from her.

Now it was every man for himself. Small groups reached pieces of wreckage, to which they clung. There were fifteen men in my group. At last we sighted an empty boat drifting ahead of us. It took me an hour to swim to it, and only nine others reached it. We clung fast to the boat while the heavy seas broke over us. After long weary efforts, we managed to climb into the lifeboat, which was full of water, kept floating by its ballast tanks.

Meanwhile, shortly after eleven that evening, the *President Taylor* and the *Penn Trader* arrived at the position the *Pamir* had given. Of course they did not know if it was correct. In the dark, stormy night it was extremely difficult for the two cargo boats to find the damaged vessel. They cruised about the area looking for the sailing craft or survivors of the shipwrecked crew.

The *Tacoma Star,* a Blue Star Liner, now arrived on the scene. A few minutes before midnight, lights were sighted in the distance by the *Penn Trader,* but she was unable to find the *Pamir.* Soon after this lights appeared at another location, then disappeared also. The report of sighting flashing lights traveled around the world, arousing new hopes. Since the *Pamir*'s radio had become silent, it was feared she had gone down with all hands. Throughout the night searchlights from four ships shone constantly, shifting back and forth across the water but revealing nothing of the cadet ship. Hours went by. Shortly before dawn the Canadian destroyer *Crusader* arrived to help in the search.

The world hoped that the *Pamir* might have been driven before the storm with her radio out of action. A broken foremast, which the *Pamir* had announced, was no reason to fear the worst. But the *Pamir* had reported a 45° list as well, the real cause for alarm.

When daylight came, the air-sea rescue squadron on the Azores and the Coast Guard cutter *Astacan* began a systematic search of the sea west and northwest of the Azores. Bad weather and poor visibility finally forced them to abandon their efforts. It appeared that the *Pamir* had disappeared with all hands, leaving not the slightest trace to tell of her fate.

At noon the next day the British Coast Guard station at Portishead in Somerset, England, relayed a message from the tanker *San Silvester* that she had sighted an empty lifeboat and taken it aboard. Badly damaged, it bore the name Lübeck, the *Pamir*'s home port. The rudder of the lifeboat was still lashed inside, and it was apparent that it had been washed overboard. Two more lifeboats were sighted that afternoon, but the stormy Sunday came to an end without a single member of the crew having been found.

Then came good news. Late that night the American freighter *Saxon* sighted a lifeboat. As they drew closer, the watchers counted five sailors aboard, actually the surviving members of the ten who had clambered into the craft some hours earlier. The boat was full of water; it could not be bailed out because of the overwhelmingly rough seas and stormy weather. Details of the rescue of these five fortunate survivors were relayed all over the world. It was now definite from what the cadets told their rescuers that the *Pamir* had foundered in Hurricane Carrie.

The survivors said that only a small number of the crew had been able to take to the boats. Just two lifeboats were available because of the terrible list on the *Pamir*. They explained how their five companions had washed overboard, one by one, unable to retain their hold. The survivors estimated that there had been twenty-five men in the second lifeboat. Her lights had been sighted briefly just before the five men had been rescued, and they guessed the second boat could not be far away.

Strangely enough, twenty-four hours went by without a single report concerning the other craft. Meanwhile, it was erroneously announced by a careless radio operator that forty survivors had been rescued.

The ships kept up their hunt for the remaining sailors and cadets. Finally the United States Coast Guard cutter *Absecon* sighted the missing lifeboat. Sadly, only one man was in her. He was quickly rescued.

The sole survivor told a dramatic story of how the others had panicked into swimming to a waiting vessel whose men did not see the lifeboat. The ship seemed just a short distance away, but when they leaped into the water and started to swim, she steamed off, slowly at first. With all twenty-four men in the sea swimming desperately, the vessel gathered speed and disappeared into the gathering darkness. All twenty-four drowned as the remaining occupant of the lifeboat watched helplessly. He was the last survivor to be saved. Eighty-one men lost their lives.

What was the reason for the disaster? According to Quincy historian John R. Herbert, one theory is that the captain was too slow in shortening the canvas, and the ship went over. Another thought is that the *Pamir* was a very sensitive ship, and although she "could go like the dickens," she did not have a deep keel and could easily tip over.

In his scholarly book *The Set of the Sails*, Alan Villiers

mentions both the *Preussen* and the *Potosi,* stating that they were "magnificent spectacles and great pieces of sailing ship engineering," but "were probably poor things aerodynamically." When Villiers speaks of aerodynamic problems, he is probably referring to the difficulties of shortening sail quickly when a sudden storm comes, as well as the problem of wind pressure on the rigging, masts and spars of a square-rigger even with her sails furled. "Going under bare poles" is a term often used when a ship hits a storm and has her sails secured.

The usual square-rigged hull was not a deep-keel ship resembling a Gloucester fisherman. The square-riggers usually had hulls more like steamships. The problem of wind ships in storms often came when skippers, in an attempt to prove their craft could make fast runs, waited too long to shorten sail and thus suffered disaster.

The tragedy of the *Pamir* shows the problem of handling sail in a storm. The testimony of the few survivors indicates they did not have sufficient time to shorten canvas. Thus the ship rolled over and sank.

The people of Lübeck have preserved the lifeboat of the *Pamir* at St. Jakub's Kirche as a memorial to the lost cadets. The battered sides of the lifeboat, which carried many of the cadets after the *Pamir* sank, still show the jagged and splintered timbers that speak of the violence of the cruel sea. The lifeboat has become a shrine of remembrance, erected by the parents and relatives of the lost crew. Over the sides of the craft are draped scores of triangular black pennants, each bearing the name of a lost cadet. Covering the walls of the alcove are wreaths from many maritime nations offering messages of condolence, together with inscriptions from parents and relatives of those lost, commending their sons to the mercy of God.

CHAPTER 3

Plundering the *Howard* and the *Persia*

The wreck of the *Howard* in 1807 and of the *Persia* in 1829 have at least two common bonds: both were plundered, and neither received the historical notice they deserve. Sidney Perley of Salem, whose volume *Historic Storms* is everywhere cited for its detailed analysis of shipwrecks in general, missed the two vessels completely. Years later Bruce D. Berman ignored both wrecks entirely in his *American Shipwrecks.* Joseph E. Garland in his 1971 book *Eastern Point* was the first author to make an adequate report of the two Cape Ann wrecks, although I had mentioned the *Howard* and briefly recounted the story of the *Persia* in my 1943 volume, *Storms and Shipwrecks of New England.*

A much earlier writer, the Reverend Dr. William Bentley, kept a stupendously effective diary from 1784 until his death in 1819, in many instances far surpassing Samuel Sewall in the fullness of his entries on marine subjects. His first mention to any extent of storms at sea was made in 1786:

22 . . . Capt. Jona. Mason junr being obliged on account of the Ice to anchor in Nantasket Road, was carried upon Point Allerton by the breaking up of the Ice, & in securing the Vessel, the Mate (37) lost both legs & this week died.

627

Although there were countless shipwrecks and other disasters before the turn of the 19th century, the first marine calamity on Eastern Point of which any real details have come down through the years was the loss of the ship *Howard,* at a point less than two hours away from her Salem home.

The storm was mentioned by Bentley as the "loss of an India ship belonging to Mr. W. Gray of this port in sight of our lights & off Cape Ann, worth 100 th. D." The details were included in several newspapers, and the residents of the North Shore soon learned of the tragedy.

A strong northeast storm was sweeping across Cape Ann's rocks and beaches, buffeting the *Howard* as she neared the end of her lengthy voyage from Calcutta. Suddenly the lookout high in the rigging spied breakers ahead, indicating that the *Howard* was in dire trouble. But he had no chance to alert the crew. A moment later, as Grape Vine Cove came into view, the three-masted vessel broke her back almost at once and began to smash to pieces on the rocks of Cape Ann.

No identifying light had warned those aboard the *Howard.* A great wave hurled Marblehead Captain Bray, his mate and two sailors over into the terrifying combers then hitting the rocks. Those still aboard the broken ship tied themselves on the quarterdeck, but they soon yielded to the elements and were pulled off the ship and into the stones and rocks of Grape Vine Cove.

At first no one on shore knew of the wreck of the *Howard,* but soon endless material was belching forth from the sea, piling up on the beach in such confusion as only a terrible shipwreck can produce. Crowds soon lined the shore to salvage what the sea had provided for them.

As great bales from the cargo washed open, the folk along the rocky beach fought for the valuable goods and cloth, often using knives to detach pieces of material from the main bale, with cuts and bruises to show for their efforts. It is easy to criticize poor people for taking goods from a disaster along the coast, but there was little else in the wintertime to produce any sort of revenue. The Reverend Dr. Bentley gives a succinct review of the situation in his diary entry for March 4, 1807:

4. The shipwreck at Cape Ann has not given a higher opinion of Cape Ann than we have been taught to hold of Cape Cod. The disposition to pilfer was not easily restrained even by guards, and if we cannot prevent thefts at fires in our best towns, we cannot preserve our goods scattered on the shore when the storm is over. Much must be allowed for description, but after many deductions, pilfering is a sad vice when it has any excuse for it or any temptation to it. The Law must have a lash to it & the soldier can only execute it. It is said an offer of 5th D. was made for the savings & if they exceeded 7th D. all above that sum was to be returned to the Owner.

It was not too easy for even the minister to be definitely sure that taking goods from a wreck was wrong in all cases. He writes again in his diary on March 17, 1807:

17. Dr. Phelps of Cape Ann Harbour, assures that sufficient evidence had been obtained that the charges respecting the pilfering of the Shipwreck cargo belonging to the Ship Howard were false. That the principal articles of value missing instead of being plundered were concealed in the piles on the shore by the persons employed to collect the remains in hopes that being sold on the spot they might profit from the concealed articles, & that the truckmen had been discovered as privy to such secret villainy. . . . The

most aggravated charges were at first brought against the inhabitants.

Several of the tricks resorted to by the thieves are worthy of mention. One thief filled a bag with loose hay and then was chased over several acres of land by a sentry, who caught the thief, a local rogue named Jack Low. As the guard was emptying the bag, containing merely hay, Jack Low vanished. How much important material Low obtained by running back to the wreck we shall never know, but it probably was substantial.

The remaining wreckage was loaded on carts to be brought from Gloucester back to Salem. The caravan of wagons was stopped by a tree that lay across the road, the drivers getting down to lift the tree out of the way. When the task was completed, the driver of the last team returned to his wagon to find that every parcel of goods had been stolen. The rogues of the area, indeed fast workers, may have felled the tree as part of their scheme.

We do not have the sagacious Dr. William Bentley to record the loss of the brig *Persia* in his diary, for he died in 1819. But the newspapers were reporting in much more detail in 1829, when the *Persia* was lost with all hands on the night of March 5.

Captain Thissell of the *Persia* and his mate Nathaniel B. Seward were both from Beverly. The brig had been loaded with rags at Trieste for Salem. A violent easterly storm caught them in the darkness off Cape Ann, a very short distance from Cape Ann Light.

Although the wreck of the *Howard* had indicated the need for a spindle or lighthouse at Cape Ann, nothing was done until 1828, when the government took action to erect a daytime marker to replace the venerable oaks that had been markers for centuries. No man could touch these natural markers by order of the government, but the trees died one by one, and efforts at replacing them failed. A daytime marker was agreed upon, but before it was constructed the *Persia* was lost with all hands. Five months later the beacon was erected.

It was snowing thickly that night of March 5. The *Gloucester Telegraph* tells us that a watch in the pocket of the steward stopped at about eleven-thirty, indicating that the brig went down about eleven. The *Persia* had cut in too close to the Point in the heavy snow. Whether or not the daytime beacon was in place would not have made the slightest difference. There was actually no visibility, making it impossible to help those aboard. As far as is known, they perished almost at once in the breakers.

Nine bodies were eventually found, including the captain, mate, cook and steward. All were easily recognized. The long-boat came ashore untouched, causing many of the people of Gloucester to believe that the crew had tried to get ashore in the boat, a belief fortified when one smart sailor found that there were marks where the gripes had been cut. The five un-identified bodies were buried from the Reverend Mr. Jones's Meeting House, and a goodly representation of sailors marched with the dead crewmen to the cemetery.

Certain marks on the unknown bodies were recorded, includ-ing the letter "I" inside the left arm of one victim. Another had an "L" on his stockings. A third, who was about five feet four, had a large scar on his right cheek and four doubloons in his pockets. Two more of the crew were later discovered firmly wedged in the rocks, requiring the efforts of no less than six men to extricate them. There were probably thirteen aboard.

The *Salem Courier* reported that the rags from the *Persia* were sold at auction, adding that if they were left at Western Point they would be "certainly stolen." The *Gloucester Tele-graph* did not let the remarks of the Salem paper pass unchal-lenged, stating that if "our inhabitants are more dishonest than our neighbors in cases similar to the above, we doubt."

CHAPTER 4

A Brave Dog to the Rescue

Artist Winslow Homer made a tremendous impression when he presented his first exhibition. To a generation of art lovers and critics who were familiar with importations from the Continent, his efforts must have appeared gross, stark, imposing, even austere. His picture entitled "Saved" depicts the rescue from the *Harpooner,* with the breeches-buoy, the sailor and the pregnant mother.

Prominent in the disasters along the Newfoundland coast is the tragedy of the British transport *Harpooner,* hurled to her doom in 1816. Aboard were 385 men, women and children returning from Quebec to London after the War of 1812. Most of the passengers were attached to the Fourth Veteran Battalion of the British Army, and there was also a canine passenger on board. Before leaving Quebec the *Harpooner*'s master, Captain Joseph Bryant, had purchased a fine Newfoundland dog he named King. By the time they were a week at sea the captain and the dog were close friends.

On Saturday morning, November 9, 1816, the *Harpooner* was proceeding on her course past Newfoundland when a violent gale of snow and rain hit the area. Soon the mighty seas were pushing the transport off her route toward the great cliffs of Saint Shotts. At eight o'clock that night the second mate's watch was called, and an hour later came the cry dreaded by all sailors: "Breakers ahead! Breakers ahead!"

A moment later the *Harpooner* hit heavily and then slid off that reef, only to crash against another. The vessel began to fill and settled over on her larboard beam, half submerged but supported by the rocky ledges surrounding her.

In the midst of these disastrous events the dog King rushed up to his master and seized his coat sleeve, pulling him in the direction of the cabin. The dog was just in time, for the cabin was ablaze from several lighted candles that had overturned on impact. Captain Bryant, with the help of a dozen sailors, soon put out the flames.

A short time later a mighty wave picked up the *Harpooner,* lifted her completely off the ledges and sent her wallowing in the heavy seas closer to shore. All was now hopeless confusion. Many men, women and children rushed up on deck; scores of others drowned in their cabins.

Again the ship hit on a gigantic undersea ledge and lodged there fast on the rocks. This time the masts were toppled by the force of the blow. Several passengers tried to float ashore on them, only to be dashed to death at the foot of the cliffs.

By four o'clock the next morning, when the storm seemed to let up, Captain Bryant had to devise some way of getting his passengers ashore. He knew that the *Harpooner* could not stay afloat much longer. As the first step in his plan he asked his mate, Mr. Hadley, to take four men in the jolly boat and try to reach a rock on shore.

Ten minutes later the men pushed off in the jolly boat. Several giant waves swept in and nearly capsized them, but finally they managed to reach the shelter of a huge rock one hundred yards away from the *Harpooner.* Just as they were about to land, the jolly boat was smashed to pieces under them. The five men scrambled to safety and soon climbed onto the highest point of the rock. There they discovered that the rock was still a good distance from the shore. Nevertheless, it was so high that they would be safe indefinitely.

Mr. Hadley now shouted across to Captain Bryant, "Let your log line float in so we can secure it." The captain signaled to show that he understood. Soon the log line began to drift in toward the rock. It came closer and closer. Then suddenly the current swept it away from the rock. Time and again the log line was rereeled and let over, but always the current proved too strong.

Parts of the ship were now breaking off and drifting toward the rocky shores. Captain Bryant realized that at any moment the *Harpooner* might break up altogether and that all on board would be lost. Then he had an idea born of desperation.

Calling his dog King, he tied the log line to the animal's collar. Then he pointed to Mr. Hadley on the rock. "Go get him!" shouted the captain.

A moment later King sprang from the rail into the sea.

From his perch on the rock, the first mate began whistling and shouting to the dog. Fifty yards from the ship, King encountered a heaving mass of wreckage that swept him under the surface of the sea. When he emerged, he had a small timber caught in the log line. King seemed to be having difficulty breathing, and Captain Bryant ordered the dog pulled back to the ship. The order came just in time, for King was choking because of another fragment of wood twisted between the line and his collar.

"I'll know better now," said the captain. Removing King's collar, he looped the log line around King's shoulders and secured it with a bowline. On the signal to jump, King sprang into the swirling seas again and made for the rock where the mate was waiting with his men. This time King swam much more easily, and the men played out the line rapidly as he neared the rock. Soon he was caught in a giant swell. With a mighty crash he was pushed high up on the rock within a few feet of the waiting men. But before they could reach him, the undertow snatched the dog back into the raging ocean at the foot of the cliffs.

When the next wave broke the men were ready. The mate had locked arms with the others, forming a human chain. As King was again lifted high on the rock, he swept in past Mr. Hadley, who made a frantic try for him and missed. As the undertow began to pull the dog out again, the log line came in near enough for the mate to grasp it. "Hold on," he shouted. The men fought with all their might to prevent the deadly undertow from carrying King back into the ocean.

For a split second it seemed that both men and dog would be dragged out into the boiling sea, but the sailors clung desperately to the rocky crevices on the ledge. A moment later the men were able to pull King to safety.

The mate shouted to the captain that King had made it to the rock with the log line. The captain now tied a heavier line to the end of the log line and signaled ashore for the sailors to pull away. Finally the heavy line reached the rock. The sailors then retrieved from the sea enough timbers to build a makeshift tripod. When the tripod was secured to the rock, several of the *Harpooner*'s crew decided to attempt swinging hand over hand along the hundred yards of line between the ship and the rock.

The *Harpooner* had struck at nine o'clock Saturday night, November 9. It was almost Sunday noon when the first sailor swung out and started for shore. He landed on the rock amid cheers from the other survivors. A short time later a block was rove on and a sling arranged. One by one the survivors were hauled up onto the huge boulder. Only one passenger who attempted the trip failed to gain the rock. This unfortunate man was struck by a gigantic wave as he swung out onto the line, lost his hold and fell to his death in the ocean.

Each trip in the sling took ten minutes. Late Sunday afternoon there were still over 140 people left on the ship. Since the storm seemed to be dying down, several of the men decided to risk throwing themselves into the sea and swimming for shore. Most perished immediately.

Around four o'clock Sunday afternoon it was decided that the women should try to ride the sling. The first woman to make the attempt was a soldier's wife who was expecting a child at any moment. Her husband was placed in the sling first in order to hold her in his arms, and then the trip shoreward began.

All eyes were upon the couple as they moved slowly toward the rock. The survivors watched tensely as a wave swept over the pair. When it had passed, they could see that wreckage had caught in the block. The next wave freed the line, however, and the soldier and his wife neared the great rock where the men waited to help them. Now the most difficult part of the task was at hand: hauling the double load up the face of the boulder.

The men on the rock went down the line hand over hand to reach the couple, now almost submerged by the surf. Finally they succeeded in pulling the husband and wife to safety. Less than two hours later, sheltered from the wind and spray by the other survivors, the soldier's wife gave birth to a baby boy.

By now the situation on the *Harpooner* was desperate. The vessel could not last much longer. The sun had set and there were still more than one hundred survivors waiting to be taken ashore. At seven o'clock Sunday night the heavy rope, frayed by constant working and swinging across the sharp rocks, snapped in two. There was no way of replacing the line, and many gave themselves up to despair. The tide slowly rose again, great waves sweeping over the wreck. The *Harpooner* was going to pieces.

The first break came around midnight at the stern. Then, at four o'clock Monday morning, the *Harpooner* split in two up to the forecastle. In the mad scramble for safety, dozens were swept overboard to their death. Captain Bryant stayed aboard his ship until almost the last, when a gigantic wave caught him and pulled him under. He was never seen again.

The very last person to leave the broken vessel was an old subaltern, Lieutenant Mylrea of the Fourth Veteran Battalion. Over seventy years of age, he remained on the vessel until everyone else had either been rescued or lost. Then he thought of his own life and leaped into the sea. Miraculously, he floated to the rock and was pulled to safety. Of the last one hundred aboard the *Harpooner,* over fifty drowned.

The 177 survivors remained on the rock until dawn. The men were able to start a fire, and they carried the soldier's wife and baby near its warmth.

Low tide at daybreak, November 11, 1816, allowed five men to wade ashore. A mile away they found the home of a fisherman. They were taken to Trepassey, and by Wednesday evening, November 13, all but five of the survivors had reached that town to be billeted in the homes of the good people there. Near the wreck at Saint Shotts, in the fisherman's house, the soldier, his wife and the newborn baby were recovering from their terrible experience. All survivors reached Quebec the following spring.

In the tragedy of the *Harpooner* 208 persons lost their lives. King, the dog, was responsible for saving more than 155 of the 177 survivors.

CHAPTER 5

A Whale Sinks the *Essex*

Several years ago I made a pilgrimage to Pittsfield, Massachusetts, and the surrounding area where Herman Melville lived. His *Moby Dick* is, of course, one of the great literary classics in the English language, and the passing years have enhanced his reputation as a master of literature.

Melville's own career was exciting. Born in New York in 1819, he later sailed aboard a whaler to the Marquesas, where he deserted and was captured by cannibals. An Australian ship rescued him. After returning to America he wrote several books built around his experiences among the man-eating natives. In 1851 he finished writing *Moby Dick*.

At first the book failed to receive acclaim. But literary experts gradually came to appreciate the novel's merits, and when the author died in 1891 it had been accepted as a great work. In the years since his death, *Moby Dick* has established a permanent place in the world's great literature. There are several interesting and little-known facts in the background of events that led Melville to write *Moby Dick*.

In May 1839 Jeremiah N. Reynolds, an author whose name time has obscured, published in *Knickerbocker* magazine a story entitled "White Whale of the Pacific," about a whale named Mocha Dick. A summary of this tale, and excerpts from it, appear in this chapter.

Reynolds's words concerning the American whaler show his deep interest in the profession:

Yet vast as the field is, occupied by this class of resolute seamen, how little can we claim to know of the particulars of a whaleman's existence!

That our whale ships leave port, and usually return, in the course of three years, with full cargoes, to swell the fund of national wealth, is nearly the sum of our knowledge concerning them.

Could we comprehend, at a glance, the mighty surface of the Indian or Pacific Seas, what a picture would open upon us of the unparalleled industry and daring enterprise. ... You are ever upon the whaling ground of the American seaman.

A group of those same American seamen mentioned by Reynolds met on the island of Nantucket one day early in August 1819, the year Melville was born. They were good neighbors and were planning a whaling voyage to the South Pacific. The meeting was called to sign the papers that would launch their journey. Each person who contemplated joining the long expedition of about three years duration put his name to the document.

SHIPPING PAPER

It is agreed between the Owners, Master, Seamen, and Mariners of the Ship *Essex* of Nantucket, George Pollard, Jnr. Master, now bound on a whaling voyage in the Pacific Ocean and elsewhere

That in consideration of the shares affixed to our Names, we the said Seamen and Mariners will perform a Whaling Voyage, from Nantucket, and return to the said port of

Nantucket. Promising hereby to obey the lawful commands of the said Master, or the other Officers of the said Ship *Essex;* and faithfully to do and perform the Duty of Seamen, as required by said Master, by night or by day, on board the said Ship *Essex,* or in her Boats; and on no account or pretence whatever, to go on Shore, without leave first obtained from the Master or Commanding Officer of said Ship *Essex:* Hereby engaging, that forty-eight hours absence, without such leave, shall be deemed a total desertion.

And in case of disobedience, neglect, pillage, embezzlement, or desertion, the said Mariners do forfeit their Shares, together with all their Goods, Chattels, &c, on board the said Ship *Essex:* Hereby for themselves, heirs, executors, and administrators, renouncing all right and title to the same. And the Owners of said Ship *Essex* hereby promiseth, upon the above conditions, to pay the Shares of neat proceeds of all that shall be obtained during said Voyage, agreeable to the Shares set against the names of Seamen and Mariners of the Ship *Essex* as soon after the return of said Ship to Nantucket as the Oil, or whatever else may be obtained, can be sold, and the Voyage made up by the owners of said Ship *Essex* or by their agent.—

In Testimony of Our Free Assent, Consent, and Agreement to the Premises We have hereunto set our Hands, the Day and Date affixed to our Names.

The master of the vessel was the first to affix his signature. His first mate, whose pen was later to give the world a classic account of the dangers of whaling at sea, was the next to sign. Then, one by one, the others planning to make the voyage affixed their signatures.

It was the twelfth of August that year when the *Essex* sailed from Nantucket Island. Known as a three-boater, she was registered at 238 tons and had a relatively small crew. The size of the crew was not important, however, as almost every man aboard was a specialist in his field. Captain Pollard planned to lower his own starboard boat; Owen Chase, mate, would lower the larboard or port boat, while Second Mate Matthew Joy was in charge of the waist boat. It was the men who were thoroughly versed in their occupation who made the great hauls. The crew aboard the *Essex* had carefully studied the habits of whales and discovered their many feeding grounds.

The course of the ship was charted accordingly. She sailed for the Western Island Grounds, after which she cruised for a time in the Saint Helena and Tristan da Cunha areas. She rounded Cape Horn and arrived at Santa Maria Island in Chile the following January.

Santa Maria, mentioned by Reynolds in his tale of Mocha Dick, had been used for many years as a post office for whaling vessels. The *Essex* planned to drop outgoing mail and pick up news from other Nantucket whaling vessels.

Whaling that year was good along the Chilean coast, and by the time the season ended the *Essex* had the equivalent of 1000 barrels of oil. Thus in one-third of her time out, she was half filled. The men were jubilant, expecting a quick trip home with relatively high profits.

After stopping at the port of Tumbes on the South American coast, Captain Pollard aimed his vessel for the Galápagos Islands to pick up turtles for food. Down through the centuries pirates, buccaneers and whalers all had gone ashore here to take aboard large numbers of these edible creatures. After about 300 turtles of varying weights had been brought out to the *Essex*, the ship sailed to Charles Island, where another sixty turtles were caught.

Neither at Galápagos nor Charles had whales been sighted.

Captain Pollard surmised they had not yet reached that point in their annual migration. Arriving at the equatorial grounds, the *Essex* soon began to sight spouts. She reached longitude 119° West, just below the equator and about halfway between the Galápagos and the Marquesas.

A day long to be remembered in whaling annals—November 20, 1820—dawned brilliant and relatively calm. By eight o'clock that morning a number of spouts were noticed on the lee bow. Watching them, the Nantucket whalers saw that there was a school of large whales engaged in blowing and playing on the surface of the sea.

Captain Pollard planned to take the school "head and head," as the saying went. The wheel of the *Essex* was "put up," all hands were called and the command to get the boats ready echoed down from the masthead. Springing to their line tubs, the crew bent on head irons and awaited the next order. Prospects looked better than ever. The reef of spouts was the longest of the voyage, and the giant mammals were enjoying to the utmost the squid they had found in great profusion.

Soon the *Essex* reached a position half a mile ahead of the school. Her main yards were backed so the vessel would remain as motionless as possible. The men were now ready to launch and meet the whales head-on.

"Hoist and swing," came the command, and eighteen out of the crew of twenty leaped into the three boats, leaving aboard only the steward and the cabin boy, Owen Coffin, who was Captain Pollard's nephew. The three boats were in the charge of Captain George Pollard, Mate Owen Chase and Second Mate Matthew Joy, whose boat a few days before had been stove in by an indignant whale. Soon the three craft were headed toward the school, and a short time later each had isolated a separate prey.

Running head-on toward the approaching whale, the whaleboat aimed to come in alongside the monster, heave the har-poon and sheer off fast enough to avoid the terrific death-dealing smash of the flukes.

Mate Chase soon struck his whale. Unfortunately he had chosen a stubborn fighter. The creature turned in its course instead of driving ahead at the feel of the iron. The monster stopped short, reversed course, and with its tail struck the whaleboat, breaking through the sides.

Chase cut the lines at once. The men stuffed their jackets into the openings and started rowing for the *Essex,* which they reached safely. Hoisting the boat aboard, the mate was about to start repairing her for a quick trip back to the line of spouts when he noticed a large sperm whale, probably eighty-five feet long, lying off the bow of the *Essex* with its great head facing the vessel.

Chase watched the giant, which spouted two or three times and then disappeared under the surface of the sea. A short time later it surfaced again and started swimming toward the *Essex.*

"His appearance and attitude gave us at first no alarm," Chase said later. "But while I stood watching his movements, and observing him but a ship's length off, coming down for us with great celerity, I involuntarily ordered the boy at the helm to put it hard up, intending to sheer off and avoid him. The words were scarcely out of my mouth before he came down upon us with full speed and struck the ship with his head, just forward of the forechains; he gave us such an appalling and tremendous jar as nearly threw us on our faces. The ship brought up as suddenly and violently as if she had struck a rock and trembled for a few minutes like a leaf. We looked at each other with perfect amazement, deprived almost of the power of speech."

Chase believed that the whale had been stunned by the tre-mendous concussion when it smashed through the bulkhead, and he was relieved when it started slowly swimming away. A long section of the false keel, loosened by the whale, came floating to the surface. The ship was leaking badly, and Chase soon rigged the pumps and set a signal for the other two boats to return.

Then it was that he saw the monster again. It was about "one hundred rods to leeward" and "apparently in convulsions." Leaping, twisting, thrashing, beating the water with its mighty flukes, crunching and snapping its enormous jaws as though "distracted with rage and fury," the monster terrified those who watched. Then it started swimming across "the bows of the ship to windward."

Owen Chase already had grave fears for the safety of the *Essex,* whether or not the whale attacked again. The vessel was beginning to settle down by the head despite the pumping. Chase decided to clear away the two remaining boats and to make plans for "getting all things ready to embark in them."

Suddenly one of the crew noticed that the giant cachalot was bearing down on the ship again. Petrified with fear, the sailors watched the huge mammal churning the ocean into foam as it tore through the water. Its head was unusually high above the surface, a one-hundred-ton battering ram.

Aiming straight for a point directly under the port cat head, the whale crashed completely through the bows as it hit, slid under the keel and went off to leeward. None of the men ever again saw the monster that delivered this death blow to the *Essex.*

The sailors were overwhelmed. That a whale would have the temerity to sink a whaleship was beyond their comprehension. Slowly they recovered. "The shock to our feelings was such I am sure none can have an adequate conception," said Chase later.

"We were dejected by a sudden, most mysterious, and overwhelming calamity," he went on. "We were more than a thousand miles from the nearest land, and with nothing but a light open boat, as the resource of safety for myself and companions. I ordered the men to cease pumping, ordering everyone to provide for himself. Seizing a hatchet at the same time, I cut away the lashings of the spare boat. . . ."

During the few minutes remaining before the ship rolled over, the men had time to save two navigation books, two quadrants, two trunks and two compasses. Barely ten minutes had elapsed since the first attack by the maddened whale. Pulling away from the plank-sheer, the crew watched with resignation as the vessel fell "over to windward and settled down in the water."

Meanwhile, some distance away, both Captain Pollard and the second mate were attempting to secure the whales they had already harpooned. One of the men in Second Mate Joy's boat, while busily engaged in passing short warp through a dead whale's fluke, happened to glance off toward where the *Essex* had last been seen, but there was no sign of her.

"Master Joy," he exclaimed, "where is the ship?" There was no answer the mate could give, and everyone in the boat became intensely worried. They cut the lines holding them to the whale and started rowing for the approximate location where they had left the *Essex*.

In the other boat, Captain Pollard had also noticed that his ship had disappeared. Bewildered, he ordered his whale cut free, and his boat started rapidly toward where the *Essex* had been.

"The Captain's boat was the first that reached us," Chase explained later. "He stopped about a boat's length off, but had no power to utter a single word.

"I could scarcely recognize his countenance, he appeared so

much altered, awed and overcome with the oppression of his feelings, and the dreadful reality that lay before him.

"He was in a short time, however, enabled to address the inquiry to me, 'My God, Mr. Chase, what is the matter?' I answered, 'We have been stove by a whale.' I then briefly told him the story. After a few minutes of reflection he observed that we must cut away her masts and endeavor to get something out of her to eat."

The three boats then pulled to where the ship lay floating on her beam ends. Using the boat hatchets, the men cut away the shroud lanyards and then were able to chop through the masts, after which the *Essex* righted.

Using a quadrant in Mate Chase's boat, Captain Pollard then observed a meridian altitude of the sun to get his latitude. He estimated that their position was then 0° 40' South and 119° West longitude. This would make the nearest land the Marquesas, 1500 miles to the southwest.

Meanwhile the crew started removing what stores they could. Taking off the booby hatch, they reached down into the after storeroom and discovered a 600-pound hogshead of dry biscuits. They also pulled out 200 gallons of water, which they divided among the three boats. Two turtles, firearms, bullets, powder, percussion caps, files, rasps and boat nails completed the complement of each whaleboat.

That afternoon the wind began to blow and a towline was made fast to the *Essex,* with one boat moored fifty fathoms away, a second eight fathoms beyond, the third eight more fathoms behind the second.

At dawn the wind was still blowing and the sea was rough. When the sun came up the whalers went aboard the water-logged *Essex* and took light spars to use in the small boats for masts and canvas for sails. All three craft were fitted with two masts and a flying jib. Two spritsails were finished, each with double bands. The topside of each boat was raised about half a foot, which gave them additional free board for the expected storms.

For two days and two nights the three boats with the twenty men aboard lay alongside the wreck, hoping another whaler might appear. None came, for in 1820 other vessels in the area were few and far between.

Finally Captain Pollard called a council of his mates to decide what should be done. By this time the deck on the *Essex* was starting to give way and the cargo of oil was beginning to break up, spreading over the sea. It was agreed by the whalers that they should start within a few hours, at noon on November 22, 1820, and sail south-southeast. They decided against heading northwest toward the Sandwich Islands, for they believed that they would encounter bad storms along that course.

Actually, while they had been debating, the *Essex* and the three whaleboats had drifted across the equator. When Captain Pollard took his final sight before starting out, they were in longitude 120° West and latitude 0° 13′ North.

"Taking all things with consideration," wrote Chase, "it would be most advisable to shape our course by the wind to the southward, as far as 25° or 26° South latitude, fall in with the variable winds and then endeavor to get eastward to the coast of Chili or Peru."

Chase's whaleboat had been damaged. It was planned that six men were to make the journey with him, leaving seven men each on the two remaining craft. The men agreed upon daily rations of one biscuit, which weighed nineteen ounces, and half a pint of water.

On November 27, five days later, Chase's boat was struck by an unidentified fish. To repair the boat, provisions had to be jettisoned. All this time schools of dolphins played around them but evaded attempts to catch them.

On the last day of November the crew of each boat killed a turtle and drank the blood. Then they turned the reptiles upside down, made a fire inside the shell and cooked and ate the meat.

On December 3, Second Mate Joy's boat disappeared during the night, but was sighted by the others the next morning. Five days later a gale smashed into the little fleet and the masts were unshipped. The storm was hard enough to endure during the day, but the night was dreadful. Heavy squalls battered the craft. Lightning flashed, illuminating the otherwise complete blackness that shrouded them. Fortunately the gale ended without causing serious damage.

Observations taken December 9 indicated that the boats were in 17° 40' South latitude. Flying fish that smashed against the sails were quickly eaten, bones and all.

Of this period Owen Chase wrote: "The privation of water is justly ranked among the most dreadful of the miseries of our life; the violence of raging thirst has no parallel in the catalogue of human calamities. It was our hard lot to have felt this in its extremest force, when necessity compelled us to seek resource from one of the offices of nature."

It was essential a few days later to cut the rations in half. The men were now so desperate that when barnacles were discovered on the bottom of the boats they scraped them off and ate them.

On December 20 land was sighted. Owen Chase called it "the blessed vision before us," and told of how the seamen "shook off the lethargy of our senses." It appeared at first a "low, white beach and lay like a basking paradise before our longing eyes."

Landing with difficulty on the rocky shore, the men searched for water, but it was several days before a spring was found, which could be used only at low water. A few fish were caught, some birds were trapped and eggs were devoured.

Owen Chase's observation indicated a latitude of 24° 40'

South, longitude 120° 40′ West. He decided that they had landed at Ducie's Island. Actually it was Henderson Island, 2000 miles northwest of Ducie's. Not far away, two to three days sail under fair conditions, lay Pitcairn's Island, a land of relative plenty where they would have been welcomed and fed by the mutineers from the *Bounty* and their families. But the twenty whalers knew nothing of this.

After the discovery of water three of the men expressed a desire to be left on the island. Because food was a vital problem, it was agreed that William Wright and Seth Weeks, both of Barnstable, and an Englishman, Thomas Chapple, would be allowed to remain. This arrangement lightened each boat by one man.

Before the main party sailed away, a gruesome discovery was made of eight human skeletons in a cave hidden by tangled underbrush. Side by side, it was evident that the victims, weakened by lack of food and water, had crawled there to die. Further search revealed the name *Elizabeth* carved into a tree near the site. Possibly a ship by that name had foundered nearby and the survivors had reached the island, only to perish later.

This encounter hurried the departure of the seventeen whalers. First, however, Captain Pollard wrote an account of the *Essex* disaster, enclosed it in a tin box and nailed it to a tree.

On December 27, 1820, the three men who had chosen to stay waved farewell to the others as they pulled off the rocky shore. Captain Pollard now believed that he could reach Easter Island, to the northeast. But contrary winds and currents made him abandon this objective, and he was forced to choose a new goal: Juan Fernández Island, 2000 miles away, off the South American coast.

On January 10, 1820, Second Mate Matthew Joy died. He was sewn into his blanket with a stone tied to his feet. Then the body was consigned to the deep with prayers.

A severe gale began on January 12, and that night Chase's whaleboat lost sight of the other two. The mate marked down the position at the point of separation as latitude 32° 16′ South and longitude 112° 20′ West. He wrote: "For many days after this accident, our progress was attended with dull and melancholy reflections. We had lost the cheering of each other's faces."

Alone now, he had to make further cuts in the bread allowance. One and a half ounces a day was the new apportionment, and shortly afterward one of the five men, Richard Peterson, was caught stealing bread. Chase made him return it, and the unfortunate thief was so penitent that he then refused to eat his tiny ration, thus slowly starving himself.

A large shark began to follow the boat but did no serious damage. Porpoises were sighted on January 16, and two days later many whales were seen spouting. Peterson, refusing food to the end, died of starvation on January 20, and his remains were given a sea burial in latitude 35° 07′ South, longitude 105° 46′ West.

The other sailors were in terrible condition by now. One day the mate tore the leather from the steering oar and began to chew it. Not a man was strong enough to steer, and the boat drifted along by itself during this period.

A terrible day was endured February 8, 1821. Their sufferings were then drawing to a close, and death faced every man. Isaac Cole had become delirious, and about nine o'clock in the morning developed "a most miserable spectacle of madness." All that day he lay in the greatest pain and misery, "groaning piteously until four o'clock, when he died in the most horrible and frightful convulsions."

Preparations for burial were made, but Chase decided to bring up the painful but necessary subject of keeping Cole's body for food. "Our provisions could not last beyond three days," Owen later wrote. "I have no language to paint the anguish of our souls in this frightful dilemma." After a discussion the group agreed that to keep alive they would use the corpse for sustenance.

The food lasted until the morning of February 15. During the interval their strength returned. The very next day a cloud was sighted, which the mate believed was hanging over the island of Más Afuera. Early the next day the boy Thomas Nicholson resigned himself to death and lay down in the boat.

At seven the same morning the man at the steering oar, Ben Lawrence, suddenly shouted, "There's a sail!"

"The earliest of my recollections are that immediately I stood up," Chase explained later, "gazing in a state of abstraction and ecstasy upon the blessed vision of a vessel about seven miles off.

"The boy, too, took a sudden and animated start from his despondency and stood up to witness the probable instrument of his salvation. Our only fear was now that she would not discover us, or that we might not be able to intercept her course, we having put our boat immediately as well as we were able in a direction to cut her off, and found to our great joy that we sailed faster than she did."

Approaching closer to the craft, which now they recognized as a brig, the three survivors were gratified to notice that the vessel was shortening sail, thus allowing them to come alongside. She was the *Indian* of London, and her master was Captain William Crozier.

"I made an effort to assist myself along the side but my strength failed me altogether," Chase later stated. "We must have formed at that moment, in the eyes of the Captain and his crew, a most deplorable and affecting picture. . . .

"Our cadaverous countenances, sunken eyes, and bones just starting through the skin, with the ragged remnants of clothes stuck about our sunburned bodies, must have produced an appearance to him affecting and revolting to the highest degree."

The first food allowed the three survivors was a gruel made from tapioca, given them in tiny doses at first, after which the portions were increased. In a few days the three were able to walk.

They had been picked up in latitude 33° 45′ South, longitude 81° 03′ West. At noon that February 18 when they were rescued, the *Indian* actually sighted Más Afuera, proving Chase right in estimating his position. It was figured that the twenty-seven-foot whaleboat had been at sea for nearly three months. They had drifted, sailed and rowed 3700 miles!

On February 25 the *Indian* sailed into Valparaiso, Chile, where the three whalers were landed.

During this period the boats of Captain Pollard and Second Mate Joy were suffering comparable hardships. When he could no longer see Chase's whaleboat, Captain Pollard thought that his mate's craft had been sunk. Third Mate Obed Hendricks had been transferred to take command of the other boat after Joy's death.

These two craft attempted a course that would allow them to reach the island of Juan Fernández, 2000 miles distant. However, on January 27 heavy seas came sweeping in and the two whaleboats were separated. They were then in latitude 35° South and longitude 100° West. The craft in the charge of Third Mate Obed Hendricks was never seen or heard from again.

Finally, on February 23, 1821, the island of Santa Maria off Chile was sighted. By this time only two men in Captain Pollard's boat were still alive, Pollard himself and Charles Ramsdell. That same day the two survivors were seen by the Nantucket whaleship *Dauphin,* whose master was Captain Zimri Coffin. The men were taken aboard and given the best of care. They finally reached Valparaiso, where they were soon reunited with the three other shipmates who had arrived previously.

Captain Pollard could not forget the trio they had left behind at Henderson Island. Commodore Ridgely, commander of the *Constellation,* was then ashore in Valparaiso. He arranged for Captain Raine of the British ship *Surrey,* on his way to Australia, to stop at Henderson Island and rescue the three men, if they were still alive.

Back at Henderson Island the whalers had been successful in their efforts to get enough food. On April 5, 1821, they were aroused by the sound of a cannon. Rushing to the highest point of land, they saw a welcome sight: the *Surrey* standing in toward the island. The castaways, who had been marooned on Henderson Island for 102 days, were soon taken aboard the British vessel, which headed at once for civilization.

After landing in Australia, they sailed to London, where Britisher Thomas Chapple went to his home and Weeks and Wright took a ship for Boston.

Meanwhile, Captain Pollard, exhausted by worry and responsibility, had a relapse in Valparaiso and was sick in bed for a considerable length of time. Eventually he took passage for home on the *Two Brothers.*

Owen Chase, Ramsdell, Lawrence and Nicholson arrived home on the Nantucket whaler *Eagle* on August 9, 1821. Word of the tragedy had preceded them, and the wharves were packed with Nantucketers as the four survivors slowly made their way from the ship toward their homes.

Captain Raine had taken the tin box with Captain Pollard's letter from Henderson Island. Its contents have been preserved:

Account of the loss of the SHIP *Essex* of Nantucket, in North America, (written at Ducie's Island Dec. 20) 1820, commanded by George Pollard, junior, which shipwreck happened on the 20th day of November 1820, on the equator in long. 119° W., done by a large whale striking her in

the bow, which caused her to fill with water in about ten
minutes. We got what provision and water the boats could
carry and left her on the 22'd of November and arrived
here this day with all hands except one black man who left
the ship at Ticamus. We intend to leave tomorrow, which
will be the 26th of December, 1820, for the continent. I
shall leave with this a letter for my wife, and whoever finds
and have the goodness to forward it, will oblige an unfortunate man, and receive his sincere wishes.

George Pollard, Junior

Captain Pollard was the last of the survivors to reach Nantucket, due to the relapse he had suffered in Valparaiso. Eventually he took passage on the *Two Brothers*. After resting briefly
at home, he commanded the *Two Brothers* when she sailed
again on November 12, 1821. But his hard luck stayed with him.

Almost half a year later, the *Two Brothers* was wrecked on
a reef north of the Sandwich Islands, and again Captain Pollard
faced an open-boat journey. A few days later he and his men
were all rescued by the whaler *Martha*.

Believing himself "utterly ruined," Pollard decided to give
up the sea. "No owner will ever trust me with a whaler again,
for all will say I am an *unlucky* man."

Arriving home April 27, 1825, the captain never went to sea
again, and later became a town watchman.

CHAPTER 6

The Halifax Disaster

On the morning of December 6, 1917, the *Mount Blanc* and the *Imo* collided in Halifax harbor, causing what forever afterward has been called the Halifax Disaster.

In New York the French ammunition craft *Mount Blanc* had put aboard a deadly cargo of picric acid, benzol and trinitrotoluene, and was on her way inbound to Bedford Basin for convoy. The Norwegian ship *Imo,* loaded with goods for Belgian relief, as a huge sign in red letters on a white background stated, was outbound.

For some strange reason, forever to be unknown, the two craft came together, with the *Imo* knifing deep into the vitals of the ammunition ship, spilling the benzol against the rest of the cargo. The benzol poured into the picric acid, setting it afire, and soon the great *Mount Blanc* was ablaze.

Ordering full-speed astern, the captain of the *Imo* slowly backed her toward the Dartmouth shore. Aboard the *Mount Blanc* the forty-two members of the ship's company launched two lifeboats, rowed desperately for the opposite shore, landed on the beach and disappeared almost at once into the dense woods there. They knew what lay ahead!

Alone, but noticed by hundreds along the shore, the blazing *Mount Blanc* drifted down the harbor toward the open sea. All over the city the day was barely beginning for the people of

655

Halifax. Workmen were engaged at their duties in the various factories along the waterfront, while businessmen were journeying to their offices. Housewives had just sent their children off to school and were getting ready to do their shopping.

Then, cutting through the early morning noises, came the sound of the fire alarm, for a watcher had sighted the burning ship and notified the fire department. Many workers looked out into the harbor at the *Mount Blanc.* Frightened but fascinated, they watched the beautiful blue-green flames leaping higher and higher into the air, changing to great billows of grayish smoke far overhead.

Suddenly, as they watched spellbound, there was a terrific, cataclysmic concussion, followed a split-second later by a detonation that overwhelmed everything. The *Mount Blanc* had exploded.

A tidal wave roared toward shore, swept over the entire waterfront, then receded almost as fast as it had formed. Tugs, schooners and ships all thumped on the harbor bottom as the wave rushed back into the bay. The *Imo,* battered ashore by the wave, was pushed high on the beach at Dartmouth. The explosion literally wiped out every home, office building, church, school and factory along the waterfront, leaving only rubble and rubbish in their places.

Stewart Webb, a survivor of the holocaust, was a twenty-five-year-old hatch boss in charge of loading 96-pound bags of flour into the hold of the *Curaca,* a vessel tied up to a dock in Halifax. In 1978 when he talked with me, he remembered very well his experiences during and after the explosion. All around him people had died, but he emerged alive. He told of believing that his craft had sunk when the wave caused by the explosion struck. After regaining his feet, he looked out but could see nothing as the heavy black smoke surrounded him. Something hit him on the head so that he again fell to the deck. Stunned, he took a few minutes to realize that he would have to move. A cable swinging above him caught his eye. Grasping it, he swung out over the side of the ship, landing in the stays of the main rigging.

"I caught hold of the rigging and started climbing." From about twenty feet above the deck he could see that the sun was shining. He looked around. "Everything was burning. Everything was on fire." Entire blocks of buildings were rubble. The *Curaca*, now away from the pier, was still rolling.

As Stewart returned to the deck of the ship, he realized there was no one visible. Then a man appeared on the wharf and took a line Webb threw him from the stern and another from the bow to make the ship fast. Gradually he found two men on the vessel able to move, Jim Shields and a man named Larry, both blackened and practically unrecognizable. The three of them hunted throughout the *Curaca*, finding six men injured but still breathing, as well as other bodies. They transferred the living to a tugboat passing late that afternoon, and all nine men went to Campbell's Wharf.

Stewart Webb did not see anything left of the *Mount Blanc*, but other sources say that a battered hulk, the remains of the ammunition ship, could be seen protruding from the harbor water. The Halifax Narrows will always be associated with this terrible explosion. From 1600 to 2000 people were killed there, and 6000 others were injured. Ten thousand persons were made homeless, and total damage amounted to more than $35 million.

CHAPTER 7

The Wreck of the *Jennie M. Carter*

One of the best-remembered New England wrecks, at least by past generations, was that of the three-masted schooner *Jennie M. Carter,* perhaps because no one ever came away from her alive. The *Carter* had a gross tonnage of 296.22, her length was 130 feet, her breadth 35 feet and her depth 10 feet. She was built at Newton, Maryland, in 1874, and her home port was Providence, Rhode Island. The details of just what happened will always be in doubt, but a fairly reliable series of events can be deduced.

At five o'clock on the morning of Friday, April 13, 1894, the schooner was seen drifting along Salisbury Beach opposite the end of the plank road by a Mr. Fowler, a resident of Hampton, Massachusetts. Evidently even then there was not a soul aboard. An hour later the lifesavers at Plum Island Point sighted her just as she went aground. The crew at the station were at that moment sitting down to breakfast. They all sprang up, donned oilskins and rubber boots, and launched their lifeboat. Crossing the harbor, the surfboat proceeded up Black Rocks Creek to the scene of the wreck.

Meanwhile, Fowler and a companion had followed the *Carter* along the beach. When she grounded they waited a short time, then climbed up into her chains and reached her deck. To their surprise they did not find a single person aboard.

About an hour later the lifesavers boarded the wreck, and Surfman Phillip H. Creasey discovered that a clock in the cabin was still going. When he tossed it ashore the hands registered 10:25.* Also taken ashore were the compass, the ship's papers and the quadrant. By this time the schooner's back was broken by her heavy cargo of paving blocks, and there was no hope of salvaging her.

According to reports the *Carter* was carried directly over the Breaking Rocks Ledge where the *Sir Francis* had hit in 1873, then drifted ashore opposite the present site of the old Ocean Echo, a dancehall of the period.

On April 10 at ten o'clock in the morning the *Carter* had been sighted by the schooner *Smuggler* off Highland Light, her rudder missing and the jibboom, bowsprit and foretopmast gone as well. The *Smuggler* lay by for two hours, but at that time Captain Wesley T. Ober of the *Carter* was confident that he could reach land without assistance, and so the *Smuggler* sailed away.

Later the new yawl of the *Carter* was discovered near Sandy Beach by Patrolman C. M. Noyes of the Plum Island Station. The handle of a gripsack was found tied to the gunwhale of the boat, indicating that perhaps someone had put his belongings in the yawl as an effort was made to reach shore. Keeper Elliot of the Plum Island Lifesaving Station did not concur in this theory, believing instead that all the crew were gathered at the anchor attempting to lower away when a great wave came over the side and took every man into eternity.

For some time on the morning of the disaster there was a

---

*The clock is now in the home of a resident of Quincy, Massachusetts. He obtained it from Herbert E. Hanson of Dorchester, who in turn received it from a relative who had been given it by Surfman Creasey a few years after the disaster. According to the present owner, the clock still runs, although it is so noisy that he winds it up only for visitors.

report that every man in the crew had reached shore safely and had been taken up to the Hampton Beach Hotel. But a visit by interested people disclosed that no one from the wreck had been seen in Hampton, or anywhere else for that matter.

Another point of dispute was the alleged presence of a woman on board. When the lifesavers reached the wreck they discovered several lady's garments in the cabin. Later Captain A. L. Crowley of East Boston, brother of the *Carter*'s steward, stated that the captain's niece had made the trip. Later it was discovered that this was not true. Quite often the captain's wife went with him on sea journeys from port to port, but apparently she did not go on this trip. It is now believed that there were no women on board during the fatal voyage. There had been seven men on the schooner: the captain, the mate, the cook and four seamen, not one of whom was ever seen again alive.

By Friday afternoon the seas were washing off the deckhouses. The mizzenmast fell, and the other masts also went during that night. A large crowd, many of them disorderly, gathered on the beach to watch the craft break up.

The first body to come ashore was that of Sven Sigfred Petersson of Sweden, a twenty-five-year-old seaman who had been in America only a few years. The captain's body washed ashore near Knobb's Station, Plum Island, on April 19; his remains were sent to Sedgwick, Maine, there to be interred with those of his father.

A coat belonging to the mate, J. W. Preble, came ashore on April 23. A letter in it from West Harrington, Maine, was dated December 18, 1893.

The great cargo of paving stones was sold at auction on the morning of April 23. Crowds continued to go down to Salisbury Beach to view the remains of the wreck, which at least until 1956 showed a few blackened fragments of her keel at unusually low tides during times of a full or a new moon. The loss of the *Carter* was one of the most tragic shipwrecks of the area.

I still have one of the cobblestones that formed part of the cargo of the *Jennie M. Carter,* whose wooden ribs stuck up out of the sand the last time I visited her.

PART SEVEN

Supernatural Tales

CHAPTER 1

The Phantom Bark *Isidore*

More than a century ago the story of the bark *Isidore* was told and retold at hundreds of firesides all over Maine. Those who were superstitious said that there were many warnings that should have been heeded before the vessel sailed. Others claim that fate took a hand and that all aboard were predestined to perish. In any event, it was a weird departure the *Isidore* made from the harbor of Kennebunkport that November morning more than one hundred years ago. In place of the usual cheers and final shouts of encouragement, there seemed to be a vague premonition of approaching danger hanging over the wharf. Several of the women became so overwrought that they sobbed aloud.

On November 30, 1842, the bark dropped down the harbor and stood to the eastward on the starboard tack. Early that afternoon snow began to fall, and the wind freshened considerably. The *Isidore* made one or two tacks to work her way out of the bay. When the weather shut in about four o'clock, she was lost to the sight of the watchers ashore. In the morning the snow lay in drifts around town. Soon news came up from Ogunquit that the wreck of a large vessel was strewn along the shore. The *Isidore* had lost her battle with the elements, having hit the Bald Head Cliffs just north of Cape Neddick Nubble.

Then the stories of the strange warnings were remembered.

665

Two nights before the ship was scheduled to sail, a seaman named Thomas King, who had already received a month's pay in advance, had a terrible dream. In his nightmare the *Isidore* was wrecked and all aboard were lost. The dream so affected him that he visited Captain Leander Foss of the *Isidore* and begged to be excused from his contract, but the captain laughed at his uneasiness and told him to be on hand before sailing time. However, King hid in the woods until he could see the masts of the *Isidore* as the bark sailed out of the harbor. Later criticized when he reappeared, he was held in great respect when news of the foundering reached Kennebunkport.

The night before the departure of the bark another seaman had dreamed of seven coffins on the shores of the ocean. One was his own, according to a voice in the dream. He told his friends about it the next morning before the ship sailed. The seaman's body was one of those later recovered from the wreck.

A gravestone was erected in the cemetery at Kennebunkport to Captain Leander Foss of the *Isidore,* whose body was never found.

The *Isidore* has become the phantom ship of the Maine Coast. One day at dusk an Isles of Shoals fisherman saw a bark close-reefed, with shadowy men in dripping clothes who stared straight ahead from their stations on the bark. He and many others say the bark is still sailing the seas with its phantom crew.

~~~~~~~~

CHAPTER 2

Telepathy from the *Minerva*

Captain James Scott, an English mariner, married Mary Richardson on July 14, 1760. Because Captain Scott was at sea a good part of the time, Mary went to live in Marshfield with her brother Jeffrey Richardson II and his wife.

On March 4, 1787, Mary's brother was suddenly awakened about three o'clock in the morning. "Brother Scott has arrived and called to me," he told his wife.

"Go back to sleep," she admonished, "for it is only a dream."

Jeffrey Richardson was strangely troubled, however. "It was more than a dream," he replied, but tried to go back to sleep.

A short time later he heard his brother-in-law call to him again. The terror in his voice prompted Jeffrey to get up. Looking at the clock, he found it was about half-past three. Dressing hurriedly, he went to the door, opened it and was met by a swirling blizzard.

From the appearance of the high drifts around the house it evidently had been snowing for some time, and he noted from the northeasterly direction of the wind that it would be a fearsome night for sailors on the ocean, especially if they were off a lee beach.

Jeffrey went back to his bedroom, very disturbed, and again awakened his wife. "I am sorry, my dear, but I simply cannot get James from my mind. There is a great snowstorm outside

667

from the northeast, and I am afraid that he is in serious trouble."

"What do you think you should do?" asked his wife. "It will not do any good to awaken Mary and get her to worry about it, will it?"

"No, perhaps not, but I am going to go down on the shore as soon as it gets lighter."

Jeffrey lay down without taking off his clothes and fell into a fitful sleep. About six o'clock that March morning such a mighty blast shook his home that he leaped to his feet. Glancing outside, he noticed that it was still snowing, but by now the first gray streaks of dawn were lighting up the sky despite the severe storm.

Jeffrey ate a quick breakfast, said good-bye to his wife, put on every storm-breaking garment he possessed, and left the house. It was a long walk to the Marshfield shore, but by seven o'clock he reached his destination.

A terrifying sight met his gaze. In every direction great masses of wreckage were strewn along the beach. Dead bodies were coming ashore, mixed in with seaweed and fragments of timbers. Other people were already exploring the beach, and Jeffrey approached one of them.

"Not a soul escaped alive," the man told Jeffrey. "And I don't think anyone was on the beach when the ship hit!"

"What was her name?"

"I don't know, but the lighter stuff floated ashore down near Cut River, and the quarterboard might be there. It is a terrible thing, isn't it? Not a single survivor!"

Jeffrey walked down the shore, stumbling through the wreckage and the snowdrifts, until he came upon an area where the timbers and cargo were piled three feet high. Several men were busily salvaging equipment from the surf and stowing it above the reach of the tide. Walking up to one of them, Jeffrey asked about the name of the vessel. One of the workers pointed to the south. "We did come across fragments of the quarterboard," he explained, "but you'll have to piece them together."

Jeffrey went in search of these bits of wreckage, and soon he came across what had once been the last two letters of a word, ending in *V A*. Continuing his hunt, he found a section bearing the letters *I N E* and *R*. The evidence was incontrovertible. Captain Scott's craft was named the *Minerva*.

Sick at heart, Jeffrey walked up and down the shore for the remainder of the morning. His wife and Mary Scott arrived at the scene shortly before noon, and he could postpone no longer telling them the terrible news that Captain Scott had been drowned almost within sight of his own home.

All three were spared the shock of watching the men working on the shore rescue the body of Mary's husband from the waves at low tide, for they had left the beach by then. Just before dark the remains of the master of the *Minerva* were carried to the church, and the family was notified shortly afterward.

Captain Scott's body was so marked by the surf that it was difficult to recognize him, but a large watch that he always carried with him confirmed the identification. This watch was kept by his widow for the remainder of her life. She moved to Essex Street in Boston shortly after the tragedy and is believed to have died there about 1820.

Her children grew and prospered, and one of them inherited the watch. In 1957 the watch was in the possession of Roscoe E. Scott, a resident of Cleveland, Ohio, from whom I was able to receive many particulars about this strange story of mental telepathy and death.

CHAPTER 3

Forget-me-not

About the year 1815 the rocky shores of Nahant attracted many Boston families during the summer months. Swallow Cave, John's Folly, Dorothy's Cove, Pulpit Rock and many other interesting locations became as familiar to Boston families as the Old State House and the Great Elm on Boston Common. Many prominent Bostonians, including social, political and literary figures, came to stay for a time at Little Nahant or Nahant.

Shortly after 1815 a Medford family journeyed to Nahant for the summer. The cottage into which they moved was next door to a summer home occupied by a group of Italians of high birth. One of them was a young man by the name of Faustino, who soon became interested in the young lady of the Medford family named Alice. Before long they were often seen together exploring the cliffs and crags of the rocky Nahant shore. When the first suggestions of fall began to show, the couple declared their engagement. In those days, however, it was customary to obtain parental consent of both families. Faustino's parents were still in Leghorn, Italy, also known as Livorno. Going to Boston, he made final arrangements to sail across the seas for this blessing on his coming wedding.

The last afternoon before the sailing the two lovers were sitting high on the Nahant ledges overlooking Egg Rock. As they sat gazing out over the spacious Atlantic, the thought came into the boy's mind of the legend of the forget-me-not flowers that grew at distant Egg Rock, and of the significance of these tiny blossoms. The story was that a girl who received from the hand of her lover a forget-me-not flower growing on that particular island should remain forever constant.

"Dear Alice," he cried, "give me this final opportunity to show my love. On yonder rock grows the forget-me-not flower. Let me journey out to it and secure for you the blossom taken from its highest pinnacle."

Alice tried to prevent him from making the trip to the rock, but he at once was afraid she doubted his courage. As he stood up, the faintest caress of a breeze caused his hair to blow across his brow, and Alice was seized with a premonition of danger. Again she implored him not to make the journey, but he ran down to Little Nahant Beach where his sailboat was moored.

An old man cautioned him, "Do not go out in your sailboat now, son, for the wind is rising. Wait for the next tide."

"The next tide will take me away from my beloved Alice," said the boy. "So it is now or never."

Waving a fond farewell to the watching Alice, he sailed for distant Egg Rock. But the winds were increasing rapidly, and the waves mounted higher and higher. White water showed all around Egg Rock when the sailboat approached, but the boy jumped lightly out and made the painter fast. Climbing up the sides of the high rock, he reached the sheltered nook where grew the forget-me-nots. High in the air he held them while he waved at his sweetheart a mile away in Nahant. Then he ran down to the sailboat.

By this time the surf and wind had combined to create a terrifying situation. Waves were breaking eight and ten feet high. When he finally pushed off with his sails set for shore, the wind took him far off course. The sailboat was soon in the breakers off the rocks where the couple had sat less than two hours before. Closer and closer the craft came. Alice, high on the cliff, watched with curious fascination this last act of her lover. Then came a mighty wave, larger than the others, which caught the sailboat in its merciless grasp and rushed the helpless lad with the speed of the wind toward the rocky cliffs. The poor boy looked up for a final moment into the eyes of his intended bride. Then the sailboat struck the rocks, broke up and was gone, together with Alice's lover. He had perished beneath the waves in a vain attempt to bring her the *Floure de Souvenance*.

Alice was brought back to her home in a state of collapse. Early the next morning fishermen knocked at her door; the body had been found and was, even then, lying on the great beach between Lynn and Nahant, covered with a blanket. Alice threw a shawl over her shoulders and rushed out of the house. A short time later she reached the beach. As she drew near, her sorrowing friends gathered around the lifeless body. She stood over her dead lover as they slowly withdrew the blanket from his form. His right hand was firmly clenched, and as she leaned over him, she noticed something still clutched in his grasp—a few stems of the flower for which he had given his life.

Taking one of the flower stems, Alice slowly walked away. Despite the terrible shock she was able to reach her home, but there she became desperately ill. Removed to her Medford residence, she never walked again. As the first flowers of spring made their appearance, Alice, mourning her lover to the end, died. She was buried in the family lot at Medford, and was soon forgotten by most of her friends.

But there were those who said that strange moanings— "Faustino! Faustino!"—were always heard near her grave whenever the wind began to rise, as though she were still protesting her lover's departure in that gathering October gale a century and a half ago.

ABOUT THE AUTHOR

EDWARD ROWE SNOW, the author of more than ninety books, is a master storyteller famous for his tales of the sea and New England history. *The New York Times* has called him "just about the best chronicler of the days of sail."